RACE/CLASS CONFLICT AND URBAN FINANCIAL THREAT

RACE/CLASS CONFLICT AND URBAN FINANCIAL THREAT

JENNIFER L. HOCHSCHILD

Russell Sage Foundation · New York

The Russell Sage Foundation

The Russell Sage Foundation, one of the oldest of America's general purpose foundations, was established in 1907 by Mrs. Margaret Olivia Sage for "the improvement of social and living conditions in the United States." The foundation seeks to fulfill this mandate by fostering the development and dissemination of knowledge about the country's political, social, and economic problems. While the foundation endeavors to assure the accuracy and objectivity of each book it publishes, the conclusions and interpretations in Russell Sage Foundation publications are those of the authors and not of the foundation, its trustees, or its staff. Publication by Russell Sage, therefore, does not imply foundation endorsement.

ROR: https://ror.org/02yh9se80
DOI: https://doi.org/10.7758/ptkg1499

Library of Congress Cataloging-in-Publication Data

Names: Hochschild, Jennifer L., 1950- author.
Title: Race/class conflict and urban financial threat / Jennifer L. Hochschild.
Description: New York : Russell Sage Foundation, 2025. | Includes bibliographical references and index. | Summary: "The foundation of racial and class inequality shapes many of American cities' policy disputes and corresponding political alignments—except when it does not. In this book, Jennifer L. Hochschild, begins with three controversial assertions: Particular policy issues in a city are associated with distinct political alignments, often independent of national-level partisan polarization or even political alignments around other policy issues. Race and class inequality underlies and often constructs these policy issues and associated political alignments. But not always: an existential threat, often based in market forces, sometimes supersedes race and class inequality in shaping policy disputes and political activity. The book's examination of those assertions is organized around a central puzzle: When is race and class inequality at the core of a policy issue? If it is at the core, how is it manifested and how does it shape the policy arena and its accompanying politics? If race and class inequality is not at the core of a policy issue, what else is—and why is that alternative force more important? Hochschild engages with that puzzle by examining four policy arenas and their accompanying politics in four large American cities: policing, especially the tactic of Stop-Question-Frisk in New York City; development, especially near the rail-to-trail BeltLine in Atlanta; school reform, especially charter schools in Los Angeles Unified School District; and fiscal policy, especially public sector union pension funding, in Chicago"— Provided by publisher.
Identifiers: LCCN 2024027123 (print) | LCCN 2024027124 (ebook) | ISBN 9780871549068 (paperback) | ISBN 9781610449281 (ebook)
Subjects: LCSH: Urban policy—United States. | City dwellers—United States— Social conditions. | Discrimination—Political aspects—United States. | Equality—Political aspects—United States. | Sociology, Urban—United States.
Classification: LCC HT123 .H625 2025 (print) | LCC HT123 (ebook) | DDC 307.760973— dc23/eng/20240820
LC record available at https://lccn.loc.gov/2024027123
LC ebook record available at https://lccn.loc.gov/2024027124

The paper used in this publication meets the minimum requirements of American National Standard for Information Sciences—Permanence of Paper for Printed Library Materials. ANSI Z39.48-1992.

Text design by Suzanne Nichols. Front matter DOI: https://doi.org/10.7758/ptkg1499.1170

RUSSELL SAGE FOUNDATION
112 East 64th Street, New York, New York 10065
10 9 8 7 6 5 4 3 2 1

For Eleanor, Raphael, and Henry

Policing in the African American community,
and the general public, is to maintain the superior position
of the dominant racial group in terms of control,
not necessarily numbers. . . . Also to protect material
possessions of that particular group.
—Leader of New York City advocacy
organization, 2016

We're rife and rampant with race and class issues.
—Professor in Atlanta, 2016

I think the race conversation, and frankly the class conversation,
has not been a huge part of the reform conversation here. . . .
It's about money. L.A. is a declining enrollment district.
—Professor in Los Angeles, 2017

They're all about the revenue. No, the pension thing
has very little to do with race.
—Chicago alderperson, 2017

Contents

══ Illustrations ══

Figures

Tables

═ About the Author ═

Jennifer L. Hochschild ⓘ is the Henry LaBarre Jayne Professor of Government, professor of African and African American studies, and professor of public policy at Harvard University.

⸗ Acknowledgments ⸗

I begin with gratitude to my friend, coauthor, and co-principal investigator. Although Vesla Weaver cannot be held responsible for anything in this book, it would not exist without her partnership in developing the proposal, designing the survey and choosing cases, and conducting interviews and discussing their implications. Her conviction about the need for more systematic study of class within race motivated our engagement, and her fiercely brilliant writing since then has helped to keep me focused. Vesla and her coauthors' research on race-class–subjugated communities suffuses all of *Race/Class Conflict and Urban Financial Threat*.

I am deeply grateful for support from the Russell Sage Foundation in a 2015–2017 award to Jennifer Hochschild and Vesla Weaver for "'They Treat Us Like a Different Race': A Multi-City Project on Class-in-Race Inequality" (award number 83-15-16). The project would not exist without RSF's confidence and funding. The Wissenschaftszentrum Berlin für Sozialforschung (WZB) honored me with the Karl W. Deutsch Guest Professorship in the fall of 2023, thereby offering a perfect environment for research, writing, and exploring Berlin's wonders. Similarly, Nuffield College at the University of Oxford and the Department of Methodology at the London School of Economics each provided a position as a visiting professor for parts of 2024, offering equally terrific colleagues and ideal locations to make what seemed by that point to be endless revisions. My thanks to Jutta Allmendinger, Daniel Ziblatt, Jane Green, Desmond King, and Patrick Sturgis for making these visits possible, enjoyable, and productive.

Several students—Christopher Chaky, Mara Roth, and Kirsten Walters—made such notable contributions that they stand out as first among equals. Deep thanks also to an amazing list of additional students whose research, analysis, and interviews spread over a decade: Angie Bautista-Chavez, Maya Bharara, Sofia Corona, Libby Dimenstein, Kaela Ellis, Kiara Hernandez, Sarah James, Scott Kall, Gabriel Karger, Cara Kupferman, Gabrielle Malina, C. J. Passarella, Jose Rivera, Bruno Villegas, Michael Zanger-Tischler, and Ryan Zhang.

Particular thanks go to many people. They include Chris Chaky and David Beavers for analyzing the CIG survey; Angelo Dagonel and Juan Carlos Orrego Zamudio for constructing elegant maps, figures, and graphs; Brianne Gilbert of Loyola Marymount University for analyses of the Los Angeles Public Opinion Survey (now the Angeleno Poll); Joshua Lupkin of the Harvard University Library for his enthusiasm in acquiring articles from the *Los Angeles Times*, *Chicago Tribune*, and other newspapers; Samantha Williams for sorting hundreds of Los Angeles schools into their proper categories, and then analyzing them; Christy Storey and especially Terry Sloope of the A.L. Burruss Institute of Public Service and Research, Kennesaw State University, for providing crosstabs of the MAS surveys; Kirsten Walters for analyses of media and organizations; and Mara Roth for pretty much everything.

A conversation, email, or comments on a draft at a crucial moment can have outsize effect. Such was the case for exchanges with Margaret Brower, Jamie Druckman, Sam Weiss Evans, Bruce Fuller, Derek Hyra, Devin Judge-Lord, Kay Merseth, John Mollenkopf, Shauna Shames, Raphael Sonenshein, Patrick Sturgis, and Stephanie Ternullo. Participants in seminars at the Center for American Political Studies at Harvard, in association with the Charles S. Hyneman Distinguished Lecture at Indiana University, at Nuffield College in the University of Oxford, at the WZB Berlin Social Science Center, and at the Department of Methodology of the London School of Economics similarly posed cogent questions and made comments that substantially changed and, I hope, improved the argument and analysis.

The Russell Sage Foundation provided essential intellectual as well as research support. Suzanne Nichols cheerfully and relentlessly kept asking when the manuscript would be completed; I had to keep working on it if only to be able to give her an answer. I am grateful to Sheldon Danziger for hosting in September 2023 a workshop whose participants not so gently persuaded me to completely revise the framing. RSF later provided perceptive and constructive reviews that compelled yet more revisions; I am indebted to fellow scholars for devoting so much valuable time and expertise to my work (especially reviewer number one, with sixteen single-spaced pages of comments!). Jennifer Rappaport, production manager at RSF; copyeditor Cynthia Buck; graphic designer Lili Schwartz, who created the wonderful cover; and the enormously helpful Chris Phillips at Circle Graphics were invaluable in managing the book's production, prose, and presentation respectively. It takes a village. . . .

As I wrote and repeatedly revised, several teachers and colleagues sat figuratively on my shoulders. Robert Dahl and C. Edward Lindblom enabled me to dare to emulate (if never match) their intellectual reach and moral depth. Robert Lane taught me the wisdom available if one listens carefully to others. Douglas Rae showed me that one should not play touch football unless one is really committed to the game; the lesson is broader. William Julius Wilson urged that there is no point in having a wonderful academic job if you don't use it to say something provocative and important. Christopher Jencks modeled how to care deeply about choosing the right questions and then enabling the evidence to answer them. Luis Fraga embodied generosity of spirit. Michael Walzer exemplified how to combine brilliant philosophy and deep devotion to democracy. Lucius Barker taught me the importance of being able to laugh at crucial moments. Ira Katznelson gave me the two touchstones I still use to identify worthwhile social science—"compared to what?" and "under what conditions?" (as well as great walk-and-talks). Theda Skocpol personifies tough-minded integrity. Judy Gruber, Edwin Dorn, and Deborah Baumgold show the ways that deep friendship combined with colleague-ship can enrich one's entire adult life. All of these contributed, directly or indirectly, to this book. I thank them, and others, for demonstrating how to be an admirable person as well as scholar. The remaining errors and choices in *Race/Class Conflict and Urban Financial Threat* are, of course, my own.

Finally, I thank Tony Broh, whose kindness and steadfastness have seen us through some bad patches and deepened the value of our many joyous occasions. The book is dedicated to my children, for whom I am always grateful and of whom I am always in awe. I miss Melissa, always.

= Chapter 1 =

Race, Class, Metaphors, and Cases

The foundation of racial and class inequality shapes American cities' policy disputes and corresponding political alignments—except when it does not. Less aphoristically, I begin with three controversial assertions: Particular policy issues in a city are associated with distinct political alignments, often independent of national-level partisan polarization or even political alignments around other local policy issues. Race/class inequality underlies and often constructs these policy issues and associated political alignments, but not always. A financial threat, often based in market forces, sometimes feels so existential that it supersedes race/class conflict as a driver of policy disputes and political activity.

As the book's title hints, my examination of these assertions is organized around a central puzzle: *When* is race/class conflict at the core of a policy issue? If it is at the core, *how* is it manifested and how does it shape the policy arena and its accompanying politics? If race/class inequality is not at the core of a policy issue, what else is? And *why* is that alternative force more important?

Race/Class Conflict and Urban Financial Threat engages with that puzzle by examining four policy arenas and their accompanying politics in four large American cities. The arenas are policing, especially the tactic of stop-question-frisk (SQF) in New York City; development, especially connected with the rail-to-trail BeltLine in Atlanta; school reform, especially charter schools in the Los Angeles Unified School District (LAUSD); and fiscal policy, especially public-sector union pension funding in Chicago.

Narratives of each case comprise the core of the book. The narratives are organized so that the reader can compare the policy goals, policy implementation, political disputes, advocacy activity, public opinion, and impact on residents across the cases. These comparisons enable, in turn, answers to four questions in each case: (1) Is the policy intended to affect race/class inequality? (2) Is the policy implemented in ways that

1

https://doi.org/10.7758/ptkg1499.1732

affect race/class inequality? (3) Are the people engaged with the policy partly or wholly organized by race and class categories? (4) Are policy recipients or broad outcomes at least partly identifiable by race and class categories? If the answer to one or more of these questions is "yes," that suffices to elevate race/class inequality into the center of a policy arena. If the answer to none of them is "yes," that requires me to address why race/class inequality is not at the center of a policy arena—and what has taken its place.

Thus, answering these four questions provides the clues needed to solve the puzzle of *when, how,* and *why* race/class inequality does or does not lie at the center of an urban policy dispute. For impatient readers, here is the initial solution to the puzzle. First, *when*: race/class conflict largely shapes the policy implementation, political activity, and impact on residents of New York's SQF and Atlanta's BeltLine development. Second, *how*: New York's practice of SQF demonstrates race/class *hierarchy*, in that predominantly White, well-off, more powerful people control predominantly non-White, poor, less powerful people. Atlanta's BeltLine development demonstrates race/class *interaction*, in which actors who have more resources and exercise more power are both Black and White, while disadvantaged actors are mostly but not entirely Black. Third, *why*: LAUSD's charter school dispute and Chicago's public-sector pension funding are not mainly structured by race/class inequality because a severe financial— and therefore political—threat supersedes it as a source of conflict.

In sum, four cases (policing, development, schooling, and budgeting) illuminate a three-layered puzzle (when, how, and why) by answering four questions about race/class conflict (with regard to policy intent, implementation, actors, and outcomes). By the final chapter, once all of the interlocking pieces are fitted into place, we will have a base from which to examine more broadly circumstances that can dislodge the foundation of race/class inequality from its durable role in shaping U.S. history and actions.

The Cases

An introduction can be rather abstract and abbreviated; following such an overview with concrete cases and their results will enable the reader to absorb the central thesis of *Race/Class Conflict and Urban Financial Threat*.

From 2004 through 2012, New York City police made approximately four and a half million stops of pedestrians, questioning and sometimes frisking them; about 12 percent were arrested or received a summons.[1] Blacks comprised fewer than one-quarter of New Yorkers but about 55 percent of those stopped by police in each year; Whites comprised one-third of the city's residents but about one-tenth of those stopped. Almost all the stopped pedestrians were male; 60 percent were aged eighteen to thirty-five (compared with 28 percent of the population). New York's East Side averaged about two hundred stops per thousand residents from 2003 through 2022, while Ocean Hill–Brownsville averaged more than ten times as many. In 2008, under 5 percent of officers with the rank of captain or higher were Black, along with 18 percent of patrol officers; a decade later, about one-tenth of officers were Black but slightly fewer patrol officers were.[2] In the years after 2000, political and civic alliances in New York were increasingly organized around contention over racial disparities in policing in general and SQF in particular.

In short, the answer to three of the four questions determining if race/class conflict shapes the policy issue of SQF in New York is "yes." Arguably the goal of SQF policy is independent of race/class inequality; the tactic is intended to fight crime and maintain social order for all New Yorkers. But the policy's actual implementation, the configuration of supporters and opponents, the characteristics of recipients, and the outcomes can all readily be described in terms of consensually understood race/class groupings.

I give each case an epitomizing metaphor in order to keep its central point in clear view. The metaphor for SQF is a Target with a distinct bull's-eye (see figure 1.1). A Target is a visual manifestation of the assertion that the disproportions in policy implementers, recipients, and outcomes reveal much more than the historical legacy of a police department consolidated a century earlier out of a largely White immigrant workforce, or a citizenry with racially disparate age distributions and poverty levels, or a city in which some categories of residents are more likely to be involved with crime than others. A Target with a bull's-eye visually expresses the argument that an identifiable set of people are distinctively subjected to multiple forces that can be brought to bear by external, powerful institutions. As one moves outward from the bull's-eye through the Target's rings, the likelihood of being the subject of those forces declines; that is, the second ring might comprise older or middle-class Black men or Latinos, while subsequent rings incorporate Black and White women and people of other ethnicities. In the outermost ring of probability we may see well-off White men and women in affluent neighborhoods. As the potentially targetable population becomes less disadvantaged in racial and class terms, the likelihood of being stopped, questioned, and frisked diminishes to insignificance. In short, a policy that can be visualized as a Target is a policy substantially shaped by the power disparities inherent in race/class (and perhaps gender, age, neighborhood, or other) hierarchy.

Atlanta's BeltLine and its surrounding development is a second case showing *when* race/class inequality shapes a policy arena. The BeltLine is a twenty-two-mile rail-to-trail project that encircles the most populous parts of the city of Atlanta. From its start in the mid-2000s to its projected finish in 2030, it will cost about $4.8 billion in a mix of public and private

Figure 1.1   Metaphors of Policy Issues across Four Policies in Four Cities

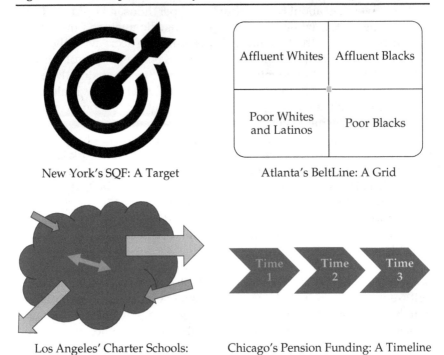

Affluent Whites	Affluent Blacks
Poor Whites and Latinos	Poor Blacks

New York's SQF: A Target   Atlanta's BeltLine: A Grid

Los Angeles' Charter Schools: Chicago's Pension Funding: A Timeline
Open Borders

Sources: Author's images from Microsoft Word.

or philanthropic funding. It will include parks, new housing, commercial development, and (aspirationally so far) a robust public transit system.

The completed BeltLine will not be structured by race or class (or age, neighborhood, gender, or any other population criterion); it follows the nineteenth-century rail beds circling Atlanta's central city. The trails and parks and their elaborations will be open to everyone and mostly free. The planned public transit is aimed at equalizing and expanding access to and from all neighborhoods, and planned affordable housing is intended to keep working-class, disproportionately Black, residents in the city. None-theless, the BeltLine's implementation manifests race/class interaction, in two ways. First, construction has been accompanied by an efflorescence of commercial development, apartment buildings and condominiums, land reclamation projects, and other mostly large corporate enterprises. As one small example, *Atlanta* magazine reported in 2019 that private investment had exceeded $6 billion; a few months later the mayor placed a moratorium on development near one trail segment, "citing overheated gentrification."[3] Intense investment is a feature, not a bug, of the BeltLine; a central goal of its promoters is to give a major economic boost to the struggling city. But its effect falls unevenly, since newcomers generally prosper while many poor residents see their rents and cost of living increase. Better-off newcomers bring a range of racial and ethnic backgrounds; poor residents are disproportionately Black.

Although the amenities of the BeltLine can benefit all Atlantans, it also reinforces a second form of race/class inequality. City elites, both Black and White (with a sprinkling of people of other ethnicities), are gaining an even more disproportionate share of wealth and power. Blacks control most of the political and policymaking power, while Whites own most of the corporate, development, and philanthropic wealth.

In short, with regard to the four questions asking *when* a policy is shaped by race/class conflict, the answer for Atlanta's BeltLine is "yes" to two and possibly to all four. Construction of the BeltLine and its features is intended to reduce race/class inequality. The policy is implemented in ways that both increase and decrease structural inequality. Supporters and opponents, as well as policy recipients, are identifiable in terms of race/class categories, but there is no sharp racial distinction between the powerful and the powerless. The long-term consequences of BeltLine construction will surely affect race/class inequality, but it is not yet clear what the balance will be between increasing and decreasing unequal outcomes.

Regarding *how* race/class inequality shapes Atlanta's BeltLine, the dominant metaphor is a two-by-two Grid, with the two rows representing class fractions and the two columns representing consensually understood racial groups (see figure 1.1). That is, race/class conflict manifests as an interaction, not a hierarchy as in New York's SQF. Some Blacks as well as Whites are advantaged; other Blacks as well as some non-Blacks are disadvantaged. Each cell of the Grid combines a class and a race—well-off Blacks, well-off Whites, and so on. The cells are, in theory, equal and symmetrical with equivalently mingled racial and class forces. Thus, a grid differs not only from a target but also, for example, from a pyramid, in which a small elite dominates a poor and powerless mass of recipients, or a linear continuum, in which only race or class need be taken into account. Even if, as we will see, a perfectly symmetrical Grid does not quite characterize Atlanta, the metaphor presents a distinct answer to how race/class inequality shapes a policy arena.

The presenting puzzle for LAUSD's charter school dispute is *why* the dispute, though so much more vitriolic than in the other three cases considered in *Race/Class Conflict and Urban Financial Threat*, is driven by some other force than race/class conflict. There is no clear race/class hierarchy or interaction shaping the policy arena; all participants share the goal of improving and equalizing students' educational outcomes and life chances.

Roughly four-fifths of students in both traditional public schools and independent charter schools are poor Latinos and Latinas. The teaching staff and administrators in both sectors are racially and ethnically mixed; virtually all identify with the progressive left. The state's basic per pupil funding formula and supplemental support for students with particular characteristics is the same in both sectors. Students move between sectors at different points in their educational progress, and families may have students in both sectors. And yet the union (United Teachers of Los Angeles [UTLA]) and some school board members seek to have independent charter schools drastically curtailed, if not eliminated, while charter school proponents aim to expand them, perhaps at the expense of traditional schools.

For most of the twentieth century, schooling in Los Angeles included a bitter history of racial and ethnic animus and segregation. But since roughly 2000, the core problem has become geographic, economic, and political, not racial. The district boundaries are fixed for the foreseeable future, but families' residence is not. Enrollment has declined from about 740,000 two decades ago to about 420,000 in traditional schools and 115,000 in charter schools as of 2023. State funding has declined commensurately; further declines are anticipated. The superintendent is tiptoeing into discussions of school closures, layoffs, and pension deficits. UTLA wants charter students, and their funding, back in traditional schools. In short, the district faces a severe financial threat that will shape workers' jobs and incomes, and leaders' political futures; charter schools face their own existential financial, and thus political, threat if they cannot stave off the challenges from proponents of traditional schools. In those circumstances, the temptation to combat in what some describe as LAUSD's reincarnation of Europe's Hundred Years' War is apparently too great to resist.

Answers to the four questions about *when* race/class inequality shapes a policy arena show that race/class conflict does not explain LAUSD's charter school war; none has a clear "yes" answer. Actors on both sides share the goal of reducing race/class inequality through public schooling. How to implement that goal is certainly disputed, but implementers are demographically similar and their disagreements focus on financial, administrative, and pedagogical concerns rather than on the nature or extent of inequality. Political actors are not substantially divided by race or ethnicity, or by class. Neither policy recipients, whether defined as district residents or as families and students, nor policy outcomes are clearly distinguishable by race or ethnicity, or class.

Given that race/class conflict does not shape the charter school debate, *how* it might do so is irrelevant; *why* some other force predominates becomes the relevant question. The answer lies in the financial and enrollment constraints edging toward crisis, with their associated political dangers. I capture the combination of fixed boundaries and free movement across them through the metaphor of Open Borders (see figure 1.1). After all, since American public schools are constitutionally required to enroll all school-aged children living in their district, it is no surprise that families with sufficient resources will seek to move into a district with presumably better schools. As the past two decades show, that more often entails moving out of LAUSD rather than into it, at an ever-increasing rate.

Finally, Chicago's struggle over pension debt also supports the argument that a force other than race/class inequality sometimes shapes an urban policy issue and its associated political activity. Public employee defined-benefit pensions were more or less invented for Chicago teachers at the turn of the twentieth century—and the first warning that the pension system was underfunded came in 1917, when a commission warned of "insolvency" and concluded that the system was "moving toward crisis." Similar commissions have issued similar warnings at least once a generation since then, with no greater impact than the first. By the 2010s, Chicago owed at least $35 billion to four public-sector union pension funds (for police, firefighters, municipal employees, and laborers) and, sharing responsibility with the state of Illinois, another $30 billion or so to the teachers' union. The pension debt is at least three times as large as Chicago's annual (non-COVID-related) budget of about $16 billion. Bond ratings agencies have downgraded the city's credit ratings and regularly issue stern warnings about future reviews.

Since roughly 2015, Chicago has raised taxes and fees, tightened its actuarial standards and procedures, and imposed such a stringent regimen on eventual pensions of new workers that it risks violating the federal "Safe Harbor" law. But the pension deficit is still growing; the combination of mathematical imperatives and political incentives to promise future rewards but eschew present payments remains impregnable.

The four questions that enable an explanation of *when* race/class conflict shapes a policy arena are all answered by "no" with regard to Chicago's pension funding. Policy actors concur, at least in principle, on the goal of stably funding the pensions, and they do not perceive race/class considerations to have any relevance. Among policy implementers, political activists, civic and advocacy associations, and policy recipients, none are clearly distinguishable by race or ethnicity; there is some class-based tension, but not a great deal. The policy outcome will be equally distributed among recipients, conditional on their incomes, years of service, and other contractual terms but not by race or ethnicity. Across the five relevant unions, workers are fairly evenly distributed by race or ethnicity (and by gender).

Thus *how* race/class inequality is manifested is irrelevant in this case; the relevant part of the puzzle is *why* Chicago's pension issue is so hard to resolve. After all, unlike in LAUSD's dilemma, there is little dispute about what needs to be done or even how it might be achieved. The puzzle's answer, again, lies in the impact of financial stress and its attendant political threats to public and private city leaders. They need to find many billions of dollars over a few decades in a way that unions, politicians, taxpayers, service recipients, voters, and bond agencies will all accept. The epitomizing metaphor is a Timeline (see figure 1.1). A Timeline extends in two directions. It points backward to the set of choices that, implemented over the past century, generated the city's huge unredeemed promises. A Timeline also points forward, in this case to a fairly new state policy that aims to redeem those promises by reducing pension benefits for future workers—a politically brilliant and deeply unjust solution to a situation dire enough to threaten, some say, the city's stability.

As the next four chapters show, it would be a mistake to argue that financial and political exigencies ever completely supplant race/class conflict in explaining urban policy issues. They do not; the foundations are too deeply embedded, behaviors too patterned, and power and resources too unevenly dispersed for race and class ever to be irrelevant in the United States. Nonetheless, moving from New York's SQF through Atlanta's BeltLine and LAUSD's charter schools to Chicago's pension funding is a move from a policy arena in which race/class hierarchy is the explanatory core to one in which race/class interaction is crucial, and then to two in which race/class inequality is submerged, mostly unrecognized, and largely irrelevant. That evolution traces a long path, and *Race/Class Conflict and Urban Financial Threat* proposes to theorize, describe, explain, and reflect on it.

Race and Class

My starting premise is that colonial America, and the ensuing U.S. nation, was built on a foundation of race/class inequality. Before I justify that premise, we need a clear convention for employing the vexed terms "race" and "class."

What Is Race? What Is Class?

Excellent scholarship has explored the usages of race in the United States and, less centrally, of class.[4] I do not venture into the thickets of those analyses; instead, I offer workable definitions that are too simple for many purposes but that enable us to focus on the core issues of this book.

For "race," I use the socially conventional categories emerging roughly from biogeographic ancestry that accord with what most Americans mean when they use one or another term.[5] Following the U.S. census, the six groups are Black or African American, Asian (or Asian American), American Indian (or Native American) or Alaska Native, Native Hawaiian or other Pacific Islander, non-Hispanic White, and "some other race."[6]

The terms in parentheses do not appear on the census; although terms within each group may have different connotations when deployed by sophisticated users, I use them interchangeably. For reasons of data availability and their relative invisibility in many cities' policy discussions, I mostly set aside American Indian or Alaska Native, Native Hawaiian or other Pacific Islander, and "some other race." That leaves my focus on three "racial" groups.

Distinguishing "race" from "ethnicity" adds a further complexity. Again following the U.S. census, ethnicity in this book refers to the socially conventional category of Hispanic or Latino (or Latino/as or Latinx), regardless of race.[7] However, for purposes of linguistic simplicity, and following academic convention, I analyze Blacks, non-Hispanic Whites, and Latinos in parallel fashion in the survey analyses. For the same reasons, *Race/Class Conflict and Urban Financial Threat* usually uses the term "race" to stand in for "race and/or ethnicity," except where the distinction is relevant.

Defining "class" for my purposes presents a different problem: American scholars offer few rather than many probing discussions of its meanings. Americans overall tend to shy away from defining or parsing class categories and seldom engage with structural or institutional class-inflected frameworks, such as relationships to the means of production or distinctions among capitalists, bourgeoisie, and proletariat. In contrast to almost a full page of groups specifying race, the census offers no class-based categories. Thus, like most sociologists and demographers, I rely on a more Weberian than Marxist understanding of class differences, with distinctions by household income and occasionally level of formal education functioning as possibly inadequate indicators of class variation.

The Race/Class Foundation of American Politics

Ever since as a beginning assistant professor I taught Karl Marx and W. E. B. Du Bois in a public policy school (as a result of which one senior faculty member questioned my chances for tenure), I have argued that the United States was built on a foundation of race/class inequality.[8] Over four centuries, the racial foundation has cracked in some places and been reinforced in others, but it has not been demolished—that is what it means to be foundational.[9] Historian Edmund Morgan shows that without race-based slavery, there would have been no freedom, assertions of equality, or democracy for Whites in the American colonies.[10] Historian Robin Einhorn argues that development and protection of race-based enslavement led to the distinctively American system of strong states, a weak federal government, and unusual tax systems.[11] The Constitution's three-fifths clause for determining slots in the U.S. House of Representatives shaped the first half-century of federal governance; southern denial of Blacks'

voting rights shaped the next century's federal and state actions. According to political scientist Paul Frymer, the nation's continental expansion
was organized around the federal government's commitment to creating a
White settler nation by controlling migration, cabining Native Americans,
and pursuing aggressive foreign policies.[12]

The foundational impact of race involves groups well beyond Whites
and Blacks. Intentionally or not, early European colonists brought dis-
eases that decimated Native populations; the newly vacated spaces with
their bounty of land and resources provided astonishing opportunities
to many European immigrants. Nineteenth- and twentieth-century federal
governments ignored the question of immigration from sub-Saharan
Africa, initially encouraged European immigration, restricted and then
eliminated most Asian immigration, opened the Mexican border, termi-
nated most immigration except from Latin America, and finally opened
immigration for Europeans and Asians while limiting entry from Latin
American countries—all in the service of constructing "a nation by
design."[13] After a century of being disregarded for individuals, the three
post–Civil War constitutional amendments, especially the Fourteenth,
eventually enabled challenges first to racial/ethnic and later to gender,
religious, and other forms of inequality.[14] In short, pretty much everything
in the United States, from the invention of baseball and pizza to the health
consequences of living in "urban 'heat islands,'" is racially inflected, if not
racially caused.[15]

Development of a capitalist economy and its associated class inequality is an equally deep foundation of the American polity. The colonies
developed distinct forms of capitalism—mercantilist, proto-industrial,
agricultural—depending on their location, endowments, and leadership.
More generally, "the capitalist transformation of rural America . . . changed
our entire society—its class structure, gender relations, rural ideologies,
migration patterns, distribution of resources, organization of the state
and of knowledge."[16] Analysts from Alexis de Tocqueville onward have
shown how Americans' voracious appetite for new technology, land, and
raw materials shaped the society into an increasingly corporate economy.[17] The political and economic systems are thoroughly entwined; each
sustains and shapes the other, as publications entitled "The U.S. Political
Economy of XXX" that fill Google Scholar make clear.[18] The impact of
American capitalism spills over the border: to choose only one example,
the U.S. invention of a federal reserve system created "a leviathan that
overshadows the world economy, dominating it, controlling the flow of
money, affecting all our lives."[19]

Racial domination and capitalist imperatives merged over centuries
to consolidate the intertwined race/class inequality that *Race/Class Conflict
and Urban Financial Threat* explores. African enslavement enabled proto-
industrial plantations, whose exports then helped to build the world

economy.[20] Profits from African enslavement contributed essentially to American victory in the Revolutionary War. Postrevolutionary Americans' success in linking political democracy and economic independence, for some, arguably depended on subordination of marginalized groups.[21] Colonization of the "empty" expanse of the North American continent provided untold wealth. European immigrants of supposed lesser races, Asian temporary workers, and Mexican circular migrants supplied essential labor for western expansion and the industrial explosion that economist Angus Deaton labels "the great escape"—again, for some Americans ("inequality" is in his subtitle)—from subsistence living and early death.[22] After World War II, White Americans were disproportionately able to move into the middle class because of economic policies such as bond market maneuvers and affirmative action for White homebuyers.[23]

If we focus on cities and suburbs, as most relevant for this book, race/class conflict remains at the descriptive and explanatory center.[24] Well-off Whites left cities during the era of efforts to desegregate urban public schools, sometimes because of such efforts.[25] Metro-area highways and infrastructure, housing policies, and land use regulations promoted Whites' well-being, retarded Blacks' progress, and isolated racial/ethnic groups from one another.[26] Residential racial segregation was intentional, pervasive, and fierce; access to public services and resources followed segregation patterns.[27] Intertwined barriers of poor public transit, inadequate training, racism, and labor market idiosyncrasies inhibited racial minorities' access to well-paying urban jobs.[28] Despite strenuous and persistent opposition, legal and electoral rules and practices mostly reserved power for White politicians.[29] Even Black mayors could make little headway against the power and resources arrayed against race/class equality; many arguably succumbed to neoliberal temptations.[30] Immigrants were met with "English only" laws and practices. Undocumented immigrants face increasing barriers to incorporation and success that arguably leave them worse off than native-born Black Americans, who can at least claim rights of legal citizenship.[31]

Most verbs in the previous paragraph are in the past tense; many of these institutional barriers have been breached. Nevertheless, the inertia of deep foundations—or in alternative metaphors, path dependency or White supremacy—ensures that, despite genuine change, race/class inequality in large U.S. metropolitan areas is a safe starting presumption.

Forces Other than Race/Class Inequality?

But perhaps that presumption is mistaken; there are, after all, alternative narratives of the race/class history of the United States. On the one hand, America's original sin may partake of Indian genocide, patriarchy, heteronormativity, imperialism, or religious fanaticism or apostasy rather than or

Figure 1.2   Goddess of Democracy in Tiananmen Square, Beijing, 1989

Source: Photo by Forrest Anderson/The Chronicle Collection via Getty Images. Reprinted with permission.

in addition to enslavement and xenophobia. On the other hand, America may have no encompassing original sin; despite its flaws, perhaps the United States comes closer than any other country to John Winthrop's salvific "city upon a hill, [with] the eyes of all people . . . upon us," or Abraham Lincoln's "last best hope of earth." After all, the Declaration of Independence, constitutional democracy, birthright citizenship and easy terms for naturalization, admission of new states on equal terms with older ones, early adoption of White male suffrage, promotion of free public education and land-grant universities, unfettered immigration for almost a century, emancipation and Reconstruction, the Bill of Rights and the Fourteenth Amendment—all were radical, egalitarian innovations upon first appearance. It is not an accident that the revolutionary Ho Chi Minh's 1945 proclamation of the Democratic Republic of Vietnam began by quoting the "immortal statement" of the Declaration of Independence, or that 1989's Chinese student protesters constructed a Goddess of Democracy in the image of the Statue of Liberty in Tiananmen Square (see figure 1.2).

Along the same lines, millions of would-be migrants to the United States presumably know their own interests when they risk their lives to cross the border. Over 160 million adults worldwide told the Gallup Poll in 2021 that they would like to migrate to the United States.[32]

Commitment to this egalitarian, democratic, liberalism may even be gaining ground, or at least holding its own. In recent decades, the United States has been whipsawed between support for sustaining its foundational race/class inequality and a newer dedication to overthrowing it.[33] Electoral majorities across recent elections show the nation's division. Democratic candidates have won a majority of votes in House of Representative elections five times since 2000, while Republican candidates have won seven times.[34] Since 1976 (also twelve elections, for the sake of symmetry), votes for the Democratic presidential candidate have outnumbered votes for the Republican eight times.[35] Given much greater flows of information during a presidential campaign and higher voter turnout—and assuming that Republicans are less committed than Democrats to rejection of race/class inequality (a large assumption, itself contestable)—the presidential votes suggest that a majority of voting Americans endorse at least some moves toward greater equality for all.

More directly relevant to this book, portraying the United States as fixed within an unchanging structure of race/class conflict not only would be empirically simplistic but also would leave little room for *Race/Class Conflict and Urban Financial Threat*'s cases of Los Angeles charter schools and Chicago pension deficits. I cannot convincingly portray policy activity involving millions of people and billions of dollars as driven mainly by forces other than race/class inequality, as I do in chapters 4 and 5, unless those alternative forces sometimes shape American policy and politics. I am, in short, a tentative, cautious, would-be optimist about our country's capacity to jettison its tainted origins.[36]

Contemporary Manifestations of Race/Class Inequality

Any hope for a convincing optimism must first confront daunting evidence. Economic inequality—across all Americans, between racial/ethnic groups, and within groups—has grown over the past half-century. Figure 1.3 shows that fact in three ways.

Panel A shows the substantial rise and partial fall in the Gini coefficient (the most common and efficient measure for comparing individuals' holdings) for all Americans' net worth over the past thirty years.[37] Panel B disaggregates that measure of individuals' holdings *across* race or ethnicity. It shows that the gap between non-Hispanic Whites and "others" (mostly Asian Americans), on the one hand, and Blacks and Hispanics, on the other hand, has always been substantial but has dramatically increased since 1990.

Panel C disaggregates still further, showing Gini ratios for income (not wealth) inequality *within* the four largest conventionally defined

Figure 1.3   Economic Inequality in the United States across and within Groups

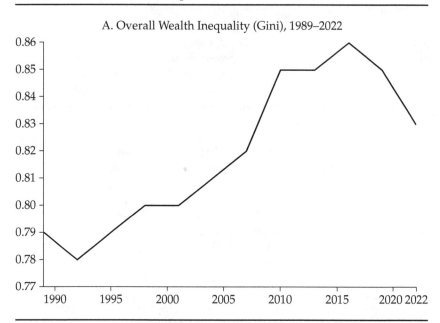

A. Overall Wealth Inequality (Gini), 1989–2022

Source: Author's derivation from Aladangady and Forde 2021 and Aditya Aladangady, email to the author, May 6, 2024.

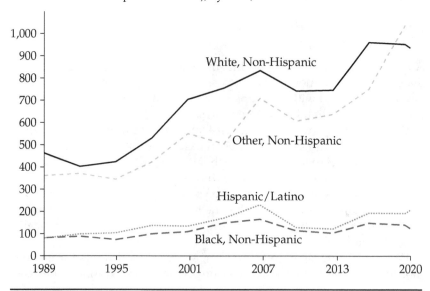

B. Average Household Net Worth (Thousands of Dollars per Household), by Race, 1989–2020

Source: Author's derivation from Aladangady and Forde 2021.

Figure 1.3   *Continued*

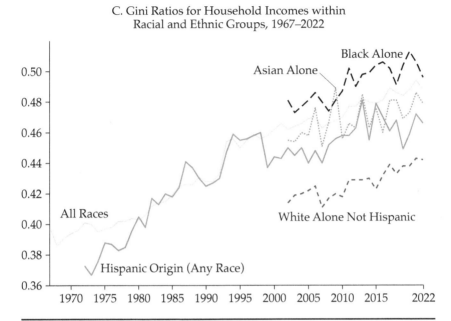

C. Gini Ratios for Household Incomes within
Racial and Ethnic Groups, 1967–2022

Source: Author's derivation from Federal Reserve Bank of St. Louis, n.d.

racial/ethnic groups. The longest line (All Races, light gray) shows the steady rise in Americans' household income inequality since 1967. The second-longest line (Hispanic Origin, dark gray) shows the almost parallel rise in income inequality within the Hispanic population in the two decades after 1975, with a clear decline in the late 1990s resulting from the rise in immigration of low-income Latin Americans, especially Mexicans. Given their predominance in the population, the results for non-Hispanic Whites (White Alone, gray dashed line), not surprisingly parallel the overall Gini ratios, with relatively little variation in internal income inequality over time (owing in large part to sample size). What is surprising is the relative lack of income inequality among Whites; the bulk of Whites reside in the loosely defined middle class. Asians show the most variation across time, partly because of their relatively small share of the American population (Asian Alone, dotted line).

Blacks are distinctive: in all but one of the twenty years with data, they show the highest level of intragroup inequality (Black Alone, black dashed line). That is, class differences as measured by household income are greatest *among* African Americans, despite the fact that disparities *between* Whites' and Blacks' net worth are large and growing. In sum, figure 1.3

shows not only class inequality (panel A) but also race/class hierarchy (panel B) and race/class interaction (panel C)—precisely the patterns that we will see when comparing the cases of New York's SQF and Atlanta's BeltLine.

Differences in income and wealth within and across groups both reflect and contribute to differences in everything else—from family dynamics to schooling attainment and achievement, employment extent and status, involvement in the criminal justice system, health, political activity and power, policy influence, and pretty much any other aspect of experience and life chances. A vast literature on this topic can be summarized by three pieces of evidence. Most broadly, class matters—literally—for life chances. Comparison of 1.4 billion tax records from 1999 through 2014 shows that the gap in life expectancy between the wealthiest and poorest 1 percent of taxpayers was almost fifteen years among men and ten years among women. "Inequality in life expectancy increased over time. Between 2001 and 2014, life expectancy increased by 2.34 years for men and 2.91 years for women in the top 5% of the income distribution, but increased by only 0.32 years for men and 0.04 years for women in the bottom 5%."[38] That gap in life expectancy between wealthy and poor Americans has in fact been growing for almost a century, showing a "huge spreading out" from the twentieth century's early years to its end.[39]

Mobility up and down economic ladders provides a different type of evidence that class matters for life chances. Around the turn of the twenty-first century, more than half of the sons born to fathers in the top income decile in the United States remained in the best-off 30 percent as adults, while fewer than one-fifth fell into the worst-off 30 percent. Conversely, about half of the sons born to fathers in the bottom tenth of income remained in the bottom 30 percent, while fewer than 15 percent made it into the top three-tenths of male income-earners.[40]

Separately from class background, race and ethnicity matter in shaping life chances. Economist Raj Chetty and his colleagues at Opportunity Insights analyzed IRS data on twenty million children and their parents from 1989 through 2015. They found that "white and Hispanic children have fairly similar rates of intergenerational mobility. . . . The income gap between Hispanic and white Americans is shrinking across generations." Despite complexities associated with recency of immigration, "Asians appear likely to converge to income levels comparable to white Americans in the long run." In contrast, "there are large intergenerational gaps between black and American Indian children relative to white children." Those persisting gaps "lead to disparities in earnings for these groups that persist across generations."[41]

As these results suggest, the interaction of race and class matters in shaping life chances. A Black child born into the top fifth of the income distribution is "roughly as likely to fall to the *bottom* family income quintile as he or she is to remain in the top quintile," whereas a White child in the top fifth is almost five times as likely to persist in that status as to fall to the bottom.[42] Finally, gender matters, in surprising ways. In families with similar incomes, "black men grow up to earn substantially less than the white men"—but "black women earn about 1 percentile *more* than white women conditional on parent income."[43]

Why Only Race and Class?

I do not claim that race and class are the two most important dimensions in explaining American inequality. How could one test such a claim, and why would one want to do so? Analysts often add gender to create a triadic intersection; legal scholar Kimberlé Crenshaw and other renowned scholars have developed a rich theoretical, normative, and empirical research literature around that claim.[44]

Nonetheless, gender identity, difference, or inequality does not play a central role in three of the four cases in this book. Only one policy issue is highly gendered; like much of policing, the practice of SQF is overwhelmingly likely to target men (or people perceived as men), arguably because the decision to stop someone depends on a perception of physical threat. Gender differences are only marginally salient in disputes over infrastructure development, school reform, and pension funding. A skeptic might note that the relative unimportance of gender in my cases is partly endogenous to this project; Vesla Weaver and I chose cases in order to examine tensions structured by race and class. Had we included gender as a third foundational explanatory category, we might have chosen to investigate, for example, cities' health care systems or child protective services.[45]

That would be a perfectly appropriate choice—for a different book. In addition to race and class, one could also or instead focus on the perils of undocumented immigration, religious discrimination, inequality on the basis of sexual orientation and gender identity, or mistreatment on the basis of mental or physical disability.[46] The choice to focus on some dimensions of inequality at the inevitable expense of others calls for explication but not necessarily criticism. At any rate, I propose to show when and how race/class inequality is central to policy and political disputes, along with why it sometimes gives way to other forces that are even more compelling to actors, analysts, or both.

Evidence

Investigation of specific political and policy disputes provides depth, revealing new questions, unforeseen complexities, and challenges to old assumptions. Surveys, in contrast, provide breadth; they uncover central tendencies and group variation, surprising juxtapositions of attitudes, and precisely measurable variation. A focused case is always vulnerable to concerns about generalizability, while a survey cannot explain what lies beneath respondents' choice of one among several preordained viewpoints. "Which research method is better?" is a bootless question. "How do cases and surveys illuminate one another?" is a valuable one. *Race/Class Conflict and Urban Financial Threat* examines the latter question.

The Cases

Explaining the choice of locations and cases in *Race/Class Conflict and Urban Financial Threat* elucidates its inductive logic. Regarding location: Vesla Weaver and I chose three of the largest metropolitan areas in the nation, along with one of the largest metro areas in the remaining region, the South. In addition to engaging with the intrinsic importance of policy and political disputes in dominant population centers, we sought variation in historical development, demographic profiles and trajectories, electoral and implementing institutions, and local political culture. We focused on metro areas, particularly their central cities, because metro areas are large enough to reveal complex racial or ethnic and class dynamics, but small enough to be analytically tractable across four distinct arenas. Perhaps most importantly, Rahm Emanuel might be correct in arguing that "pressing questions are being asked today of our national governments by the citizens of the world. The answers to those questions are found in cities."[47]

The choice of a case within each metro area reveals a more complicated pathway toward this book. Inspired by a comment in a neighborhood conflict in Chicago—"In Africa, I suppose they would say different tribes, but here they [the Black middle class] treat us like a different race"—Vesla Weaver and I aimed to examine variation in policy goals and political activity associated with class inequality within races, especially African Americans.[48] We sought, in the more formal words of Cedric Johnson, to move beyond the "prevalence of metanarratives of 'black oppression,' 'the black experience,' and 'the black community' that . . . do not square with the actual interests that animate black political activity in real time and space."[49] To capture those interests, we sought policy issues that were broadly important in urban America, particularly significant in one location as indicated by salience and resources invested, widely different in content, and prima facie entwined with within-group class variation.

Comparison between policing in New York and BeltLine development in Atlanta satisfies our goal of examining differences in policy goals and political activity associated with groups' disparate actual interests. However, repeated analyses of policy choices, politicians' and advocates' positions, survey results, interview transcripts, media reports, scholars' research, and policy documents made clear that intragroup contention was not occurring as we had anticipated with regard to schooling in Los Angeles and public-sector budgeting in Chicago. Some other force was driving those cases; the book therefore needed to explicate not only when and how race/class inequality is a central feature in urban policy-making, but also why it sometimes is not. After several years of contending with the evidence, I concluded that an explanation required deviation from the original research goal. In short, the logic and narrative development of *Race/Class Conflict and Urban Financial Threat* is inductive; the book's findings and conclusion emerge from scrutiny of the cases, rather than being built into them.

Interviews and Documents

In 2016 and 2017, Vesla Weaver, several students, and I interviewed actors knowledgeable about the relevant policy and politics in each location. We focused mostly on the city within a metro area. We spoke with thirty people in New York, fifty-one in Atlanta, forty-four in the Los Angeles Unified School District, and thirty-eight in Chicago. They were selected to include knowledgeable (often directly involved) elected and appointed officials, policy administrators, community activists or advocates, leaders of civic associations, business or economic actors, scholars and other experts, clergy, and, unsystematically, the occasional Uber or cab driver. We sought relatively more members of a category especially important for a given policy issue—that is, many community activists in New York and many civic association leaders in Chicago. We aimed for a racial/ethnic mix of interview subjects in each category, but we did not seek specific distributions. We did not focus on gender or other characteristics. Appendix table A.1 provides basic demographic information about the set of interview subjects in each policy arena; each anonymous quotation in the text identifies the public role and race or ethnicity of the interviewee.

We promised confidentiality to any interviewee who preferred it, and I preserve anonymity for all except where it is clearly impossible and was not requested. Interview subjects were informants who provided judgments, insights, facts, historical context, interpretations, and evaluations; they were not themselves subjects of the research.[50] Discussions were structured conversations that lasted up to ninety minutes; they covered the same topics for a given issue but were modified as appropriate to the interviewee. We described the project in as much detail as the interview subject wanted, then asked something like, "So, tell us what we most need to know." We followed up on the subject's lead with more focused questions and sought also to cover predetermined topics at some point during the conversation. We asked about racial, class, and intersectional dynamics, distributions of power and resources, goals and implementation practices, political strategies, emotional valences, and impacts on policy recipients. Conversations varied in length and depth, and we did not attain access to everyone with whom we aimed to speak. Thus, interviews are broadly but not exactly comparable; any effort at quantitative or precise assessment across people or topics would be a category mistake.

We taped interviews or took detailed notes, after which student assistants transcribed and coded the conversations using Dedoose software. We hand-coded thematic and conceptual observations.[51] We also analyzed print media, including the largest mainstream paper in the city, the business or educational press where relevant, and newspapers targeted at African American and Latinx readers and issues where available. I supplement this material with organization websites and reports, opinion polls, census and other public data sources, election documents and results, scholarly publications, and later, less formal, interviews and conversations.

The Class-in-Group (CIG) Survey

Vesla Weaver and I fielded a survey called Class-in-Group (CIG) in early 2016. It was conducted by the survey firm Ipsos (then called GfK), and drawn from its KnowledgePanel, a recruited, "probability-based on-line panel [with a] statistically valid representation of the U.S. population."[52] Given our focus on metropolitan areas, the CIG sample was unusual, perhaps unique. With a total of 3,307 respondents, it comprised about one hundred randomly chosen non-Hispanic White adults in each of the twelve largest U.S. metropolitan areas and as many Latinos/as (of any race) and non-Hispanic African Americans as were available in that metro area across the firm's respondent panels.[53] That strategy yielded 809 African Americans and 1,285 Hispanics (of any race). The survey was conducted in Spanish and English, with a median completion time of twenty-four minutes. It did not include demographic questions, since Ipsos had previously collected that information. Appendix table B.1 provides more detail about the metropolitan areas included in the CIG sample, and appendix C provides question wording, organized by chapter, for the items analyzed in *Race/Class Conflict and Urban Financial Threat*.

Each narrative also includes results from local area surveys where available. I had access to only one of these datasets, so results in most cases are limited to what was publicly available or what the researcher could provide to me.

Cases, Not Case Studies

The four issues to be interrogated are cases, not case studies, a distinction meant to signal that each narrative in *Race/Class Conflict and Urban Financial Threat* is both broader and narrower than a fully developed case study would be. The narratives are narrower because, unless essential for my analytic purposes, I pay little attention to forces, events, and people that led to and shaped the policy dispute under investigation. For example, I offer little history before roughly 2000, except where needed as in the case of Chicago's pension policy. Similarly, I generally pay little attention to the policies' general contexts, actors' back stories or motivations, or links with other issues; I rely on the rich extant scholarship in each case.

The narratives are broader than a case study, however, since they take aim at the puzzle of *when* race/class conflict is at the core of a policy issue, *how* it is manifested, and *why* some alternative force is in some circumstances more important. That is, taken in sequence, the cases provide the elements of a testable theory about the degree to which the American foundation of race/class inequality explains contemporary policy and political disputes. (In an implicit shorthand, I tend to treat "race/class inequality" and "race/class conflict" as interchangeable.) This sequence leads me to posit that the foundation is firm but not impregnable and to consider features of American society that have escaped their origins, even if into something not much more appealing.

Determining When, How, and Why

My strategy for addressing the theoretical puzzle—*when* race/class inequality is central to a policy or political dispute, *how* it manifests, and *why* some other force sometime supersedes it—is to answer four questions in each case narrative.[54]

First, *is the policy intended to increase or decrease race, class, or race/class inequality, or is it largely unconcerned with that issue?* Policies such as poll taxes or elimination of inheritance taxes arguably are promulgated in order to reinforce racial or class inequality; policies to ensure access to public accommodations or eliminate special tax provisions have the opposite purpose. Less obvious policy goals, however, may require careful interpretation since they can be facially neutral, include several purposes, or be too vague to have much bite until interpreted or implemented.

Implementation may or may not follow clearly from policy goals. It has its own form of complexity: processes to put policy goals into practice may be multifaceted, internally contradictory, insufficiently resourced, exponentially expanded, or simply vague and complicated.[55] But my second task is nonetheless to answer this question: *Is policy implementation intended to, or does it in fact, increase or decrease race, class, or race/class inequality, or is it largely unconcerned with that issue?* A key measure, though not the only one, is whether implementers or their practices treat groups of city residents who are consensually identifiable by race and/or class differently from other groups. If the answer is "yes," the analyst needs to address the next layer of the puzzle: *How* do implementation and race/class inequality shape one another?

Implementation does not take place in a vacuum. Categories of people who have a stake in the policy outcome or are otherwise invested in it vary with the issue. But they usually include some combination of issue or group advocates, civic leaders or associations, experts and members of the media, the broad public, and people with financial or other material interests in policy outcomes. By definition, public actors are involved, ranging from elected officials who have campaigned on the issue through regulators and members of the judiciary who end up ruling on one or another aspect of the goal or its implementation. Thus, the third analytic question is: *Are engaged actors who consistently support or contest the policy consensually identifiable by race and/or class, or do they consistently invoke race/class categories in their engagement with the policy or political arena?* A positive answer might point to actors of one race or ethnicity who are consistently on different sides of the issue from actors of another race or ethnicity, or who are consistently concerned with different aspects of implementation; what matters is whether a complete and accurate depiction of engaged actors necessarily includes their race and/or class. As with the second question, an answer of "yes" implies a further inquiry: *How* do actors shape, or aim to shape, the nature of the race/class inequality involved in that policy arena?

Fourth, policies that matter have a set of recipients and discernible outcomes, which may or may not match the policy's goal. Recipients can range from all of a city's residents through a substantial segment to a precisely targeted subset of the population. Outcomes can similarly range through changes that affect the whole city to those that benefit or harm some or a precisely targeted set of policy recipients. The crucial analytic question is: *Are policy recipients who consistently gain or lose, or a specifiable part of the city's residents who receive the policy outcomes, consensually identifiable by race and/or class?* Gains and losses may be relative or absolute, and what counts as a gain or loss may itself be part of the policy and political dispute. Nonetheless, I must persuasively decide whether a complete depiction of the impact on recipients and the distribution of outcomes among recipients includes their race and/or class. Here too, if the answer is "yes," I must then determine *how* race/class inequality is affected among policy recipients and outcomes—whether it is deepened or reduced, groups are divided in new ways, relative group positions change, beneficial or punitive outcomes align with race and/or class of those affected, and so on.

After answering each question, I must then determine relationships among them. Can answers to each be summed into an index, or is one question much more important than the others in a given circumstance?

Can an answer be precisely determined, or is it a judgment call? Unless it is demonstrably inadequate in a given policy arena, the simplest decision rule is that if the analyst gives a "yes" answer to any one question—that is, if race/class inequality manifests in goals, implementation, actors, or outcomes—then the policy is plausibly understood to be connected with foundational race/class inequality. At that point, the analysis moves to the question of *how*. There is, however, no formula here; narrative details will contribute to determining how a "yes" answer to one or more questions iterates with the others.

Finally, if the answers to the questions are "no"—if race/class inequality is not central to goals, implementation, actors, or outcomes—I move on to the third layer of the puzzle: determining *why* some other force is determinative. Here I have few guidelines; as an inductive project, *Race/Class Conflict and Urban Financial Threat* develops answers out of the cases. My starting assumption is that some combination of social, economic, and political imperatives is strong enough to shift policy engagement away from the standard race/class foundation or even to render it irrelevant. As the book's title suggests, I find, at least in the cases of the L.A. charter school dispute and Chicago's pension funding saga, that what important actors perceive to be an existential threat to financial stability and its associated political success suffices to shift their attention away from race/class inequality and onto the threat itself.

Thus, although short of a full theory that can be operationalized to test hypotheses, the exercise of answering the four questions suggests a solution to the puzzle at the core of this book: *when* race/class inequality is central to a policy and political dispute, *how* it manifests, and *why* some other force sometimes supersedes it. We can build on that.

Table 1.1 summarizes the logic of *Race/Class Conflict and Urban Financial Threat* as laid out in this chapter.

Preview of Coming Attractions

Each of the next four chapters addresses a case, in the order presented by the metaphors of figure 1.1. In each chapter, I first present the beginning and end of the case by describing the policy's institutional setting, main recipients, and core goals. The narrative then shifts from description to dynamics, explaining how the policy's core goals are implemented, the politics surrounding goals and implementation, the activity of people and organizations invested in the issue, and the broader public's perceptions and opinions. The narrative then addresses the impact on policy recipients and overall outcomes. Finally, I use the preceding narrative to answer the four questions about the role of race/class inequality in explaining the policy's goal, implementation, actors, and outcomes. Doing so enables me to link the particular case to the book's overarching puzzle

Table 1.1   The Logic of *Race/Class Conflict and Urban Financial Threat*

Puzzle

When is race/class inequality at the core of a policy issue?

If inequality is at the core of a policy issue, *how* is it manifested and how does it shape the policy arena and its accompanying politics?

If race/class inequality is not at the core of a policy issue, *why* is some alternative force more important?

Cases

Policing: New York Police Department's Stop-Question-Frisk

Development: Atlanta's BeltLine and associated development

Schooling: Los Angeles Unified School District's charter schools

Fiscal policy: Chicago's public-sector pension funding

Questions

Goal: Is the policy intended to affect race, class, or race/class inequality?

Implementation: Is implementation intended to, or does it in fact, affect race, class, or race/class inequality? If "yes," how does it do so?

Actors and onlookers: Are actors consensually identifiable by race and/or class, or do they consistently invoke race/class categories in their engagement with the policy or political arena? If "yes," how are actors arrayed?

Recipients and outcomes: Are policy recipients who consistently gain or lose, or policy outcomes that consistently affect the city's residents, consensually identifiable by race and/or class? If "yes," how are recipients and outcomes arrayed?

Source: Author's analysis.

of *when* and *how* race/class inequality is central to a given policy dispute or *why* it is not.

The final chapter returns to the theory development that is a chief purpose of *Race/Class Conflict and Urban Financial Threat*. It evaluates the extent to which each case epitomizes its issue and points to connections with similar issues in other metro areas in ways that could enable generalization. I suggest necessary steps to construct a testable theory and conclude with observations about the surprising links between claims of race/class foundations in the United States and practices of pluralist policymaking and politics.

═ Chapter 2 ═

Race, Class, and Policing:
Stop-Question-Frisk
in New York

*I now believe that, for the most part, police officers in
my community do not care about the citizens; they treat
the area like a war zone, and brutalize people who challenge
them or get in their way.*
— Black New Yorker, quoted in Office
of the Attorney General 1999, 82

*We are the first people who want threats off the street,
we don't want to live near a rapist or murderer — but we want
constitutional rights, privacy, respect.*
— Black leader of a New York City
advocacy organization, 2016

The New York Police Department (NYPD) employed over 26,000 uniformed officers in 1990; the number reached 40,000 in 2000, after which it declined slightly to 35,000 in 2010. By no coincidence, crime was following the same trajectory: after crime had been rising steadily for almost two decades, the city with 7.3 million inhabitants suffered 32,500 felony assaults and 2,263 murders in 1990.[1] That is a murder record that no city had matched before (or has matched since), and the number of police and intensity of policing rose accordingly over the next decade. Crime eventually started to fall: NYPD reported about 185,000 major felony offenses in 2000, 105,000 in 2010, and 97,000 in 2020.[2]

Crime victimization, suspicion of criminal activity, and perceptions of crime were all heavily racialized in New York. The detailed NYPD "Crime and Enforcement Activity Reports" begin only in 2008, when 34 percent

https://doi.org/10.7758/ptkg1499.5870

of victims of misdemeanors were Black and 50 percent of suspects were. On the other end of the crime scale, 62 percent of murder victims and 61 percent of suspects were Black.[3] It is therefore neither surprising nor intrinsically problematic that policing was also racially disparate.[4] But the Stop-Question-Frisk (SQF) policy, which arguably started as a legitimate and appropriate element of a new crime control strategy in the late 1990s, had grown into something of a monster roughly a decade later. The number of stops rose from hundreds a year to thousands to tens or even hundreds of thousands a year, and stops were very disproportionately aimed at poor young Black men and at poor non-White communities. The measurable impact on crime was slight and the level of harassment extraordinary.

The stark evidence of its minimal effectiveness, its impact on elections from the city's mayoralty to the nation's presidency, its unintended capacity to unify fractious civic and advocacy organizations, the extended damage to the reputation of police and to social control in the city, and its constitutional importance—all make the trajectory of SQF significant well beyond even its direct impact on millions of people. More particularly, SQF's reinforcement of race/class conflict establishes the model against which the other cases in *Race/Class Conflict and Urban Financial Threat*, and by extension cases beyond the boundaries of this book, can be gauged. SQF's explanatory metaphor is a Target, given that the power of government was used to target the least powerful among the governed.

Setting

In the context of an apparently inexorable rise in crime over the previous two decades, former federal prosecutor Rudolph Giuliani was elected mayor in 1993 on a "tough on crime" platform. He appointed William Bratton to be commissioner of police. "People wanted a clamp-down and Giuliani and Bratton gave it to them," in the succinct summary of one former insider whom we interviewed. Sociologist Michael Jacobson provides more details. New York's strategy for crime control "underwent an incontrovertible and massive shift" in the 1990s from the more traditional practice of punishment after conviction to a new practice of policing at "its 'front end,'" that is, instituting "sanctions at the pre-trial stages of the criminal justice process." With the introduction of COMPSTAT, a data mapping system aimed at immediately identifying locations where crime was spiking, and the high profiles and strong promises of Giuliani and Bratton, "the pressure on precinct commanders to reduce crime was palpable."[5]

Along with politicians and the police department, public sentiment focused on rising crime from the 1970s through the 1990s. In August 1997, the earliest date for which its results are publicly reported, a Quinnipiac University poll of New York City's registered voters found that crime and violence were the most important problem facing the city, a view shared by 19 percent of Whites, 18 percent of Blacks, and 15 percent of Hispanics.[6] The police restructuring was widely popular: 87 percent of White New York voters, 85 percent of Hispanics, and 69 percent of Blacks approved of Giuliani's handling of crime.[7]

Soon, however, views of crime control became racialized. By 1999, seven-tenths of Whites and almost as many Hispanics, but only two-fifths of Blacks, still approved of Giuliani's crime control measures. That poll came soon after the police killing of Amadou Diallo, but Black respondents also reported additional reasons for disapproval. Just 5 percent endorsed Giuliani's "handling [of] relations between blacks and whites," and a long array of questions showed sharp racial differences in New Yorkers' perceptions of discrimination, fear of police brutality, expectation of being unfairly harassed, and agreement that some responses to crime violate rights.[8] The combination of high crime, intense policing, a tough-on-crime mayor, and increasing racial divergence in perceptions set the context for SQF's rise a few years later.

Policy Recipients in the Target's Bull's-eye

Since the SQF program's development in the 1990s, NYPD officers have temporarily detained, questioned, and sometimes patted down civilians on the street on millions of occasions. At its peak in 2011, NYPD recorded 685,724 stops, searching for weapons and other contraband. SQF was, according to the authors of the most thorough book on the topic, "the dominant crime control strategy for twenty years."[9] Figure 2.1 shows the pattern of SQF's rise and fall.

In 2011, "the number of stops of young black men . . . actually exceeded the total number of young black men in the city."[10] Although exaggerated, 2011 was not an aberration. Observers repeatedly noted how much more

Figure 2.1   Reported SQF Stops and Their Outcomes, New York City, 2002–2023

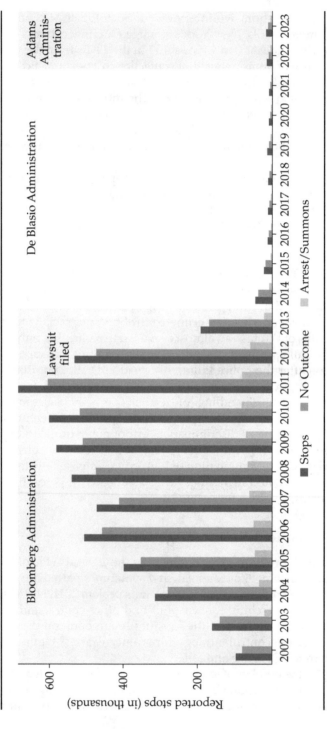

Source: Author's derivation from data, New York Civil Liberties Union 2023.

Figure 2.2   Race and Ethnicity in SQF Stops, New York City, 2003–2023

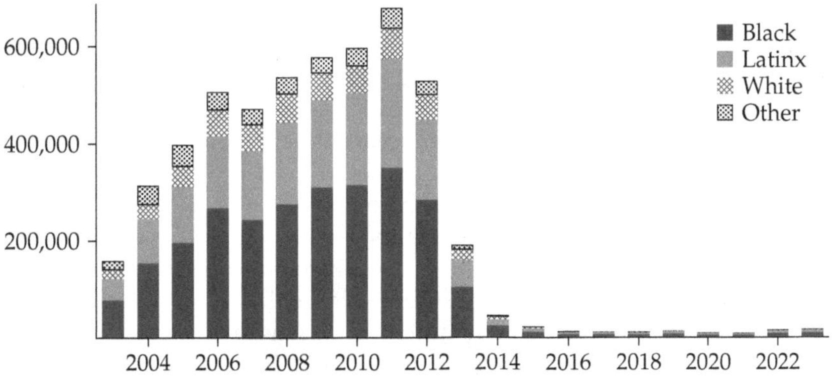

Source: Author's derivation from data, New York Civil Liberties Union 2023.

likely African Americans—and how much less likely Whites—were to be policy recipients. That observation required no special insight or evidence; figure 2.2 shows the pattern. According to the New York Civil Liberties Union (NYCLU), using data from NYPD, over half of stops from 2003 through 2023 were of African Americans (under one-quarter of the city's population), while about one-tenth of stops were of Whites, who comprised one-third of the city's population. Latinos were involved in three-tenths of stops, slightly over their share of the population.[11]

Most references, including my own thus far, to Blacks, Whites, or any other racial or ethnic category assume that the persons being stopped are men. That is a reasonable assumption, but worth explicit attention given the importance of gender, along with race and class, in most intersectional theories. The New York Civil Liberties Union's publications do not bother to report the gender of SQF's recipients, but one piece of research does. Based on a small New York sample from 2014 through 2019, epidemiologist Maria Khan and her colleagues report that 93 percent of those stopped identified as male, and 4 percent as female.[12]

Age mattered also; young men of color were especially likely to be stopped. In the two decades after 2003, Black men ages fifteen to twenty-four were stopped at a rate of close to 4,000 per 1,000 residents. Black men a few years older (ages twenty-five to thirty-four) were the next most likely group to be stopped. Then young Latinos, among whom fifteen- to twenty-four-year-olds were stopped close to 2,000 times per 1,000 residents. Whites aged fifteen to seventeen, in contrast, were stopped only 876 times per 1,000 residents.[13] Lest the blizzard of numbers obscure the main point, they add up to the fact that each Black teen and young adult in New York was stopped on average almost four times, comparable Latinos almost twice, and comparable Whites less than once.

Along with individuals' characteristics, community characteristics contributed to SQF's precision targeting. As early as 2003, NYPD identified twenty-four (eventually thirty) impact zones, that is, areas with high crime rates, to which it deployed additional officers. These zones had higher rates of stops per block—and crucially, more stops per reported crime—than other places in the city.[14] Most were in precincts with few Whites; "nine of the ten precincts with the highest stop rates have been in predominantly Black and Brown neighborhoods (defined as over 80 percent residents of color). Six of the ten precincts have been home almost exclusively to Black and Brown residents (defined as over 90 percent residents of color)."[15] Like race and ethnicity, class was distinctive in communities with a high number of stops. By the mid-2000s, the proportion of owner-occupied housing in a given precinct was significantly related to the stop rates of Blacks and Hispanics, but not of Whites. The results held up even with controls for racial composition and proportion foreign-born in the precinct.[16]

In fact, differences in SQF involvement across communities were even greater than differences across individual recipients. Cumulative stop rates since 2003 per 1,000 precinct residents range from 36 in New Springville and Elm Park (precinct 121) to 4,490 in Midtown South, Times Square, and the Garment District (precinct 14).[17] Those two precincts are outliers. But the pattern is clear: regardless of the goal of crime control and maintenance of public order, SQF concentrated unwanted authoritative attention on poor, young Black men and Latinos in low-income, minority neighborhoods. The people in the Target's bull's-eye were indeed, as Weaver and her colleagues phrase it, race-class subjugated residents of subjugated communities.[18]

Policy Goals

New York State's criminal procedure law section 140.50 established the rules for SQF policy, based on the U.S. Supreme Court decision in *Terry v. Ohio*.[19] The *Terry* ruling held that Fourth Amendment rights are not violated when police stop and briefly pat down a person's exterior clothing if the officer has reason to suspect that a crime was, is being, or will be committed, and a reasonable belief that the person is armed. The suspicion must rest on "specific and articulable facts . . . taken together with rational inferences"; an officer cannot act on merely a hunch. The practice of stop-question-frisk had been established but not strictly regulated before *Terry*; after the decision, most cities, including Chicago, Milwaukee, Boston, Philadelphia, Los Angeles, and Toronto, invigorated their implementation of SQF.[20]

SQF also had a second origin story, the theory of "broken windows" policing. As first laid out by criminologist George Kelling and political scientist James Q. Wilson, the theory holds that "at the community level, disorder and crime are usually inextricably linked, in a kind of developmental sequence. . . . Serious street crime flourishes in areas in which disorderly conduct goes unchecked." Because "the police exist to help regulate behavior," stops aimed at not only suspicious behavior but also violations of norms of social order could create a flexible, scalable practice that would improve quality of life while reducing the likelihood of crime.[21]

Many find the policy to be of great value. Even after New York's implementation had been declared unconstitutional, NYPD commissioner Bratton vigorously defended SQF as "a basic tool of policing. . . . You cannot police without it. . . . If you did not have it, then you'd have anarchy."[22] Interview subjects committed to challenging SQF's use implicitly concurred by distinguishing the policy from its practice. As one of the most authoritative among them, a White attorney, put it, "We want the police to . . . help address crime, but that's a very different thing than just stopping and searching every young person that you see. . . . Our goal was not to end stop-and-frisk or to end effective, proactive policing. It was to stop illegal stop-and-frisks, stop racially discriminatory stop-and-frisks." The Police Foundation agreed with the distinction. Its document on "5 Things You Need to Know about Stop, Question, and Frisk" warns police officers that "SQF has previously been implemented in a manner found to be unconstitutional" and "use of SQF can create disparate and seriously harmful impacts." But it also informs them that "stop, question, and frisk has deterrence value."[23]

The practice may be returning. "Mayor Eric Adams, who made crime fighting the centerpiece of his first year in office, says he believes the practice can be effective if officers are trained properly. In the first nine months of his administration, police reported 11,232 pedestrian stops— a 22% increase over the entire year of 2021, according to the NYCLU."[24] A year later, a *New York Times* headline observed that the mayor was being "Accused of Breaking His Promise for a New Kind of Policing."[25]

Implementation

> *It is not policy. It's the practice of some officers who*
> *do not uphold that slogan that's printed on the side of*
> *those cars that say "Courtesy, Professionalism, Respect."*
> —Black clergyperson

The gap between explicitly race- and class-neutral intent and race- and class-saturated practice took some years to reach its full extent. New York's

Office of the Attorney General was carefully neutral in its 1999 evaluation of this burgeoning policy:

> Although rarely referenced in publicly-disseminated Departmental strategy documents, the role of "stop & frisk" in furthering the Department's goals of order maintenance, deterrence, crime prevention, and a direct attack on gun violence is clear. Given the Department's focus on apprehending violent criminals and preventing more serious crimes by aggressively enforcing laws aimed at low-level criminality, "stop & frisk" serves as an important wedge into the criminal element. . . . Thus, a model which values both proactive police interventions short of arrest and an aggressive approach to low-level disorder is well served by aggressive use of "stop & frisk."[26]

By the early 2000s, NYPD had developed explicit rules for this new policy and practice. The rules specified when, why, and how an officer could make a stop, procedures for what to do during the stop, and detailed templates for reporting the incident.[27] Those rules were probably not faithfully adhered to.[28] But at least formally, SQF's implementation had a widely praised theoretical rationale, clearly defined boundaries, an articulated structure, and a process innocent of race and class bias.

Even while NYPD was developing standard operating procedures for the use of SQF, however, advocacy groups challenged the practice. In 1999, in the aftermath of Amadou Diallo's killing, the Center for Constitutional Rights (CCR) brought a class action lawsuit, *Daniels et al. v. The City of New York et al.* It alleged that NYPD's Street Crime Unit conducted stops without reasonable suspicion or equal protection of the law, thus violating the Fourth and Fourteenth Amendments to the Constitution. NYPD disbanded the Street Crime Unit and settled with CCR in 2003. The settlement required the department to develop a written policy prohibiting racial profiling, train its officers on SQF's legal bases, and conduct community workshops to educate residents about their rights when stopped. NYPD also agreed to audit and report officer stops. The settlement did not assign a monitor.[29]

The *Daniels* settlement was by all accounts ineffective. Monitoring and training seldom occurred; SQF stops shot up in number and in race/class targeting (there was no room to increase gendered targeting), and police violence persisted. Many perceived that in predominantly minority neighborhoods, the stops had changed character for the worse. As one interview subject, a Black attorney, put it, with surprising tact, "The policing is done in the majority of New York City neighborhoods for safety, but in some particular New York neighborhoods, policing is done to capture the criminals"—that is, police focused on adversarial control rather than on coproduction of social order. Her conclusion dispensed with the tact: "It's like reverse. It turns on its head. So if you're in that neighborhood, there's a presumption that you're criminal." As soon as the *Daniels* settlement expired in 2008, the Center for Constitutional Rights filed a new federal class action suit, *Floyd v. City of New York*.[30] It alleged that unconstitutional profiling and stops had continued and worsened since the *Daniels* settlement.

NYPD revised its procedures in 2012 to include precinct leaders' regular inspection of all officers' reports and periodic reports focused on "reasonable suspicion stops" in order to compare the demographics of people stopped to those of violent crime suspects. Whether these new rules were a genuine attempt to return to the policy's original neutral goals or a "public relations strategy," as one informant put it, they generated findings that were explicit, specific, measurable, articulable, and focused on disparate treatment. Its own extensive data collection, in fact, became NYPD's Achilles' heel.

A trial ensued in the *Floyd* litigation. As the Center for Constitutional Rights summarizes the multiyear legal and political process, in 2013 Federal District Judge Shira Scheindlin found the NYPD "liable for a pattern and practice of racial profiling and unconstitutional stops." The ruling appointed a monitor to oversee reforms to NYPD, expanded body camera use, and mandated reforms in police training and discipline procedures. The ruling also began a joint remedial process for deliberation over further reforms, involving a long list of stakeholders that included the communities most affected by SQF.[31] The city planned to appeal, but after a new mayor took office in 2014, it agreed to implement the court-ordered reforms.[32]

The number of SQF stops declined from almost 700,000 in 2011 to below 20,000 per year from 2014 into the early 2020s. Mayor Bill de Blasio, who had campaigned in 2013 on a promise to reform SQF, appointed Bratton police commissioner; Bratton promised that SQF, which "has to be done," would be "done respectfully" and "consistently."[33]

Politics

The Target metaphor epitomizes the results of the transition from goal to implementation. SQF's stated intention was to prevent crime and promote public order and community safety; its most prominent effect was to harass poor young Black men and Latinos, especially in poor minority neighborhoods. Political incentives and maneuvering tracked and interpreted, as well as helped to create, the gap between policy intent and practice.[34] As the number of stops rose rapidly in the 2000s, political contention deepened—but not, as is often the case, around what facts were relevant or what the data showed. Pretty much every disputant used the same NYPD data (sometimes supplemented with other evidence) and agreed on the patterns shown. They disagreed instead on two crucial questions: Was SQF's implementation evidence of race/class-targeted police harassment, whether intentional or not? And was the magnitude of the stops justified by the program's impact on crime and public order? More simply, was the practice of SQF biased, and even if so, did the end justify the means?

Some argued that, unfortunate as it was, the *Floyd* data showed that police were in fact stopping individuals whose characteristics fit the *Terry* guidelines. Journalist Richard Cohen wrote that Blacks in New York "make up a quarter of the population, yet they represent 78 percent of all shooting suspects—almost all of them young men. . . . Those statistics represent the justification for New York City's controversial stop-and-frisk program, which amounts to racial profiling writ large."[35] As late as 2015, de Blasio's predecessor as mayor, Michael Bloomberg, similarly defended SQF's tight intersectional focus on the grounds that it was "controversial, but . . . 95 percent of your murders and murderers and murder victims fit one M.O. . . . They are male minorities 15 to 25. That's true in New York, that's true in virtually every city in America. . . . The first thing you can do for people is to stop them getting killed."[36] Economists Decio Coviello and Nicola Persico found "evidence that the officers making the stops are on average not biased against African Americans relative to whites."[37] It is perhaps relevant that by 2012, fewer than half of NYPD police officers were White; almost one-fifth were Black and three-tenths were Latino.[38]

Others claimed racism or at least racial bias in practice. As early as 2007, statistician Andrew Gelman and his colleagues found that Blacks and Latinos "encountered more stops" even, crucially, after controlling for race-specific estimates of crime participation and precinct variation.[39] "The stops of whites are more 'efficient.'"[40] Evidence on police use of force—24 percent of stops for Hispanics and almost as many for Blacks, but only 16 percent for Whites—was another ground for claiming racial disparity.[41] Still other scholars found that "blacks and Hispanics were disproportionately stopped in these low hit rate contexts," in part owing to "lower thresholds for stopping minorities relative to similarly situated whites."[42] Even if a slight majority of street-level police were not White by 2012, those in charge mostly were: only 8 and 13 percent of "all other ranks" above sergeant were Black or Hispanic, respectively.[43] Political actors could, in short, find research support for both arguments that race/class/age discrimination was a central feature of implementing SQF and arguments that it was not.

The deeper question was whether the program's impact on crime and public order was politically and morally sufficient to justify the stops, even if they were biased. Again, both sides brandished data. On the one hand, the proportion of public high school students reporting that they recently carried a weapon dropped from 18 to 9 percent from 1997 to 2011, with a drop among African American students from 6.6 to 2.6 percent.[44]

As one young man put it, in an article otherwise castigating the policy, people now "keep their guns at home. They don't want to be arrested."[45]

Supporters further pointed out that from 2004 through 2013, on average 12 percent of NYPD stops resulted in a summons or arrest, implying that about 482,000 crimes were prevented or punished.[46] Furthermore, some argued, since frequent SQF stops were intended to deter the carrying of weapons or drugs, the very fact that only a small proportion of stops prevented or punished crimes could be seen as evidence that the policy was successfully inhibiting unlawful behavior.[47] Though not supporters of SQF, John MacDonald, Jeffrey Fagan, and Amanda Geller found that in neighborhoods designated by the New York Police Department as impact zones an "increase in stops made based on probable cause indicators of criminal behaviors [but not more general investigative stops] were associated with crime reductions."[48] Criminologists David Weisburd and his colleagues found impacts that were "modest but suggest meaningful declines on average in crime"—enough for them to conclude that "SQFs focused on microgeographic hot spots are likely to reduce crime."[49]

But to both sets of analysts, the results are too weak for the ends to justify the means. The Weisburd group concluded that other policing strategies were probably more effective than the modest deterrent effect of SQF, and that "the level of SQFs needed to produce meaningful crime reductions are costly in terms of police time and are potentially harmful to police legitimacy." Furthermore, SQF as a primary tactic to reduce crime "is not consistent with legal norms in the United States."[50] MacDonald concluded flatly that "the additional use of stop, question, and frisk [beyond other policing strategies] made almost no difference" in crime reduction.[51]

At its simplest, the arithmetic was daunting. Even if, as a commonly cited figure held, 12 percent of SQF stops were successful, their huge increase by 2012 implied millions of *unsuccessful* stops (some of which included frisking). And a darker argument eventually prevailed: as Weisburd and his colleagues hinted with their concerns about police legitimacy, most scholars came to concur with Fagan and his coauthors that "order-maintenance policing strategies ostensibly targeted at 'disorderly' neighborhoods were in fact focused on minority neighborhoods, characterized by social and economic disadvantage." And worse: "this racial bait and switch" was becoming institutionally solidified regardless of its impact on crime; the "most interesting and important" pattern was the "persistence of these policies even as the objective indicia of poverty and disorder fade in . . . a steadily improving and safe City."[52]

Beyond these arcane disputes, the general public's attention was focused on whether SQF contributed to New York's almost miraculous rebirth after the turn of the century. The previous few decades' devastating rise in violent and property crime, along with public disorder, had been reversed.

Figure 2.3   Did SQF Cause the Decline in New York City's Crime?

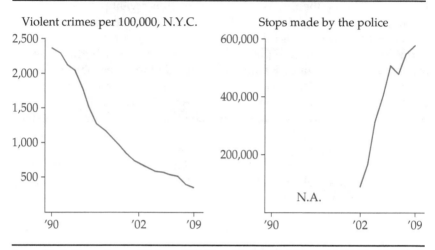

Property values rose, immigrants were reducing high vacancy rates by moving into poor communities, gentrification commenced, and street life become vibrant.[53] Broadway once again became known for theater. SQF, argued proponents, was an essential element in keeping New Yorkers safe and out in public. An illustration in the *New York Times* provided apparent support for this view. Figure 2.3 shows a graph with a dramatically steep decline in New York's violent crimes, beside a graph with an equally dramatic rise in police stops.[54]

Examination of the graphs shows that virtually all the decline in crime occurred *before* 2002—that is, almost before SQF was initiated. But the dominant impression is of crime going down and police stops going up. Regardless of its intent, the visual impression of causation is powerful.

As the section on public opinion will show, these startling inverse correlations were politically salient and powerful, making opposition to SQF difficult for many years. Individual testimony was one tactic for cutting through the data. As early as 1999, a middle-aged Black woman described being grabbed from behind, hustled to a waiting car, and physically searched. The effect was profound: "'I don't trust police officers. Following the incident, I couldn't sleep well for months. Eventually, I went to the doctor who prescribed sleeping pills.' Rather than walk the five blocks to her job site, now she takes a taxi."[55] Some years later, a man who had been stopped five times "incorporated into my daily life the sense that I might find myself up against a wall or on the ground with an officer's gun at my head. For a black man in his 20s like me, it's just a fact of life in New York." Another aimed more broadly: "The temperature in the city at the time was that the police were at war with Black and brown people on the streets."[56]

Even many residents in saturated neighborhoods who would benefit the most from protection against crime and social disorder described SQF as more harmful than helpful. As one interviewee, a Black consultant, put it, "It's a community trauma, right? So even if it didn't directly happen to, like, my mother wasn't stopped and frisked, right? My father, I don't think, has ever been stopped and frisked. But they are in this community. So it doesn't have to happen directly, but it envelops the spirit in the air in the neighborhoods where you live." A White professor described, in pained detail, intraracial disputes about other issues, but had seen no "evidence of that kind of schism within black New York," that is, between well-off and poor Blacks around police tactics. "Black New York was outraged by the way it was being policed and the rest of New York didn't care. . . . And [in] all my contacts with the city—professional, personal, resident, nonresident—during that time [roughly 2004–2014], Black folks have been furious the entire time."

Residents of Latino communities added concern about being challenged on their immigration status to fear of and anger about excessive *Terry* stops. As Vesla Weaver and Gwen Prowse summarize, "One segment of the population effectively lives under a different set of rules and, as a result, experiences differential power and citizenship."[57]

As public opinion surveys will show, the claim of Black (or White) unanimity is not quite correct. A Black public official spoke for

a moderate voice in the middle that understands that young people should not be shot for doing something that's normal. But at the same time . . . we need to deal with that crime in our communities. . . . I don't want to walk down the block and see someone pissing in public or playing music at four in the morning, or smoking pot on my steps, so I'm a believer in public safety and ensuring we don't create an environment where we have lack of, you know, civility.

Less sympathetically, another interlocutor, a Black consultant, concurred about the existence of the moderate middle: "I get pushback on the community level because . . . we as a community have been conditioned to see police as like the panacea for all of our problems. . . . And so that's where, if there's a division, that's where the division comes. Because the first question that usually pops up, 'Well, what about the murderers? Well, what about the rapists?' Right? People always go to the extreme, right?" The Reverend Floyd Flake, a former member of Congress and leader of the twenty-thousand-member Greater Allen AME Church in Queens, shows no hesitation in going to that extreme:

> I'm one of the people who has to bury these young kids. . . . You have people going into birthday parties, graduation parties, bringing guns in because they were not invited, they're killing people. So my thesis is that there's just too many guns in the community. . . . And so I think it's a voice, my voice is a voice that says, "Look, I'm not against [SQF] particularly, I am against the deaths and funerals that I have to preside over."[58]

Given these mixed views and perceptions, many elected officials initially tiptoed around such a dangerous controversy. A 2010 City Council hearing on NYPD's SQF policy in public housing was something of a non-event, since neither police nor public housing officials were willing (or legally able, in their view) to testify. It did prod City Council speaker Christine Quinn, until then an SQF supporter, to say that NYPD's failure to engage "reinforces some of the worst suspicions."[59] But when city comptroller and mayoral hopeful Bill Thompson stated that NYPD commissioner Kelly "has done an excellent job. I haven't said 'stop Stop and Frisk. It's a useful tool,'" Quinn backtracked: "Any of us would be lucky with Ray Kelly as commissioner."[60] Similarly, then-state senator Eric Adams modulated between describing SQF as "a good policy. I've used it," and a statement that "the abuse of it" as "some form of quota" was problematic.[61]

Mayor Bloomberg continued to defend SQF's role in reducing crime and saving lives. But as the number of stops and Blacks' anger both grew, public actors paid more attention and politicians' divide around SQF sharpened.[62] Council members introduced bills to control aspects of policing, confronted Kelly, met with federal officials, and marched in protests. In 2012 the Manhattan borough president specified SQF's failures, noting the racial-ethnic disproportion among those stopped and the "distrust of law enforcement in communities of color."[63]

By the 2013 mayoral contest, City Council member Bill de Blasio was campaigning on a platform of police reform, promising to appoint an independent inspector general with subpoena power and to withdraw the city's appeal of the *Floyd* ruling of unconstitutional bias. In exit polls, three-fifths of New York's primary voters agreed that "stop and frisk" was "excessive, and results in innocent people being harassed"; a majority of them voted for de Blasio.[64] Columnist Michael Greenberg declared that "the issue that most contributed to de Blasio's victory was stop and frisk. He unequivocally denounced the practice at a time when Kelly's approval rating topped 70 percent and Bloomberg's popularity still rode high. (De Blasio himself at the time was polling at around 10 percent)."[65]

In sum, as SQF expanded in magnitude and public visibility, as targeting by race, class, age, and location sharpened, as racial tension around

Figure 2.4   Newspaper Articles about SQF, New York City, 2000–2020

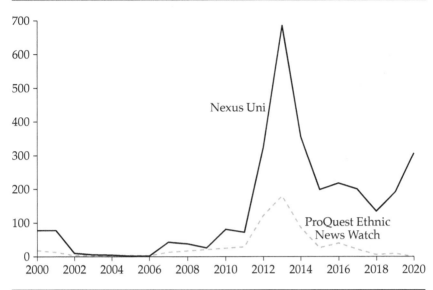

Nexus Uni

ProQuest Ethnic
News Watch

Source: Author's analysis; see note 66.

the policy deepened, and as public actors were pushed to take stands, the underlying structure of race/class hierarchy both strengthened and became more apparent. Many New Yorkers came to believe that not only individuals but institutions and practices were racially and economically biased and coercive, and were targeting the most disadvantaged. Concern about control and even oppression by public authorities, along with demands for redress, moved into the media, organizations, and general public opinion.

The Media

Reporting on SQF in New York's newspapers increased in both the Black-oriented press and the generally oriented media as incidence and attention rose.[66] New York's mainstream press published almost eighty articles in 2000 and 2001 that included something about SQF, mostly in connection with the NYPD's 1999 killing of Amadou Diallo. New York's much less voluminous Black-oriented newspapers published eighteen and thirteen articles in 2000 and 2001, respectively.

As figure 2.4 shows, after declining almost to nothing in the 2000s, attention to SQF in both mainstream and Black newspapers skyrocketed from 2012 to 2014. Half of all relevant articles in the mainstream press, and three-fifths of those in the Black-oriented press, were published in those three years. Press attention peaked in 2013—the pivotal year for organizational activity, the *Floyd* decision, and the mayoral contest—with 686 generally oriented press and 180 Black press articles. From 2015 on, as the use of SQF declined dramatically, so did newspapers' attention. Mainstream articles shifted from a local to a more national frame, such as descriptions of Bloomberg's defense, then repudiation, of SQF when he was running in presidential primaries, or Giuliani's role in the policy's development for the Trump administration. The Black-oriented media mostly ceased referring to SQF.

Of most relevance here, both types of newspaper, especially the Black press, at least hinted at SQF's pattern of race/class targeting. Using word lists ranging from eleven to thirty-four terms, Kirsten Walters examined six themes likely to appear in articles: politics or elected officials, litigation or other legal activity, data, geography or neighborhoods, crime and safety, and racial or other demographic terms.[67] Since the denominator is all words from all articles that include "SQF" or its synonyms (excluding stop words such as "a" or "the"), the proportion of thematic words is very small. But their relative shares are telling. From 2000 through 2019, 2.8 percent of all words in relevant Black newspaper articles refer to characteristics such as race, class, or gender, or to discrimination. That compares with about 1.8 percent of Black press articles referring to legal proceedings, 1.8 percent referring to politics, and 1.5 percent referring to crime and safety. Only 1.7 percent of mainstream SQF articles refer to demographic characteristics or discrimination; a slightly higher proportion refer to politics and a slightly lower proportion to law or to crime and safety. In short, the media noted and engaged with SQF's targeting— more, in fact, than with any other theme in the Black press. Nonetheless, it was left to advocacy organizations to bring race/class targeting to high public visibility.

Organizations

Kirsten Walters and two research assistants read and categorized the most relevant 350 SQF-inflected articles from the mainstream press and 425 from the Black-oriented press.[68] We focused on references to organizations or their spokespeople, with organizations defined broadly as entities with some structure (and usually a formal name) in the private sector. We searched for organizations in online sources, scholarly publications, social media, and documents linked to the *Floyd* litigation. We also sought references and information in interviews, many of which were with organization activists.

Organizations ranged from tiny affinity or neighborhood groups to citywide collectives to branches of national nonprofits, religious entities, and civic or good government associations. Since our purpose was to examine organizations' collective role in shaping and responding to the racial and class dimensions of New York's SQF, not to study them per se, we did not count or otherwise classify the groups. I cannot claim that *Race/Class Conflict and Urban Financial Threat* engages with all such entities, but I am confident that it analyzes the most active, visible, and focused among them.

By the mid-2000s, although NYPD's rising reliance on targeted SQF was only beginning to attract political and media attention, it was rousing organizations. Demand for police reform is, after all, an old story in New York's activist community. As one informant, a White criminal justice expert, put it, "Every fifteen years we have another commission that's focused on rooting out corruption and abuse in the police department. This has been happening literally since Theodore Roosevelt was the police commissioner [in the 1890s]." Although initially "it was difficult to really build a movement outside of the [*Floyd*] courtroom," eventually something new occurred; in the words of a Black community activist, "Since 2010 or 2011, I've seen the most impactful community organizing that I've ever seen."

It was not easy. Organizations differed in their scale and stability, strategies and tactics, resources, issue priorities, and levels of radicalism. Conversations in 2008 and 2009 focused on "Can we agree on a set of shared priorities?" as a White attorney put it. "For pretty much the next two or three years, things were still very . . . stuck. We weren't really able to build the vibrant coalition." Building the coalition, according to an Asian community organizer, entailed "lots of conversations and back and forth and working out of . . . 'What are we unifying on in terms of how we understand the problem, what we think the solutions will be?'"

Focus sharpened and a sense of urgency grew by the end of the decade. With almost seven hundred thousand stops in 2011, "it was starting to resonate in the public and the polling," a White attorney recounted, "and then we got this important court ruling" (the denial, in 2011, of the city's motion to dismiss the *Floyd* litigation).

> And meanwhile, of course, the Police Department just steadfastly continues to say, "Not only have we not done anything wrong, but we're saving lives." The community supports us. [After 2011's tsunami of *Terry* stops], the momentum is very strong. The wind is kind of at our back on this issue just in terms of the public's views of it and the politics of it. I mean, 2012 is when it was like, "Oh, this is really a political issue in the city."[69]

While many advocates focused on the direct harm in encounters between the powerful and the powerless, some were developing a more structural analysis of race/class hierarchy. The Asian community organizer observed that

> NYPD treats specific communities, whether it's geographic or based on who people are, as criminal or as potentially criminal, and engages in heavy-handed, discriminatory abuse of policing and overpolicing of low-level offenses in certain neighborhoods, low-income communities of color. . . . So yeah, we're dealing with a police force that perhaps serves and protects the interests of the system and of the elite, but is engaged in widespread discriminatory practice against everybody else.

Some advocates also began to see encounters as a zero-sum contest between the people in the Target's inner and outer rings. It was becoming "really clear," this interview subject continued, "that this [SQF] was about race and class—*whose* 'quality of life' are police trying to protect?"

Most pointedly, as another Asian community organizer put it, "Safety is relative. Your safety can mean the unsafety of another person, which is primarily black and Latino young people."

SQF's race/class concentration, most advocates came to agree with varying degrees of intensity, was intentional targeting rather than an inadvertent consequence of combating crime or social disorder. A Black attorney phrased it coolly: "Historically there has been a go-after-them-and-arrest-them history within the Black and Brown communities of New York City." A Black community organizer was more vehement: "You just cannot stereotype and stigmatize a community or individuals inside a community and think it's okay to run down on them and frisk them, and they haven't committed any crime. . . . They live already within a troubled community. They're victims of that. And then to have the police, who we charge and hire to be ones who are supposed to provide safety, victimize us, it's an additional victimization." And putting it most starkly, the Black attorney, mimicking a hulking sergeant, growled, "You're to follow orders and, orders that are quite explicit, to go out, you know, '*Get these kids.* Presume that they are criminal. Presume that they're up to no good.'"

With early and continuing philanthropic support, organizations that covered the range of New York's political left joined in a coalition, Communities United for Police Reform (CPR). Some coalition members promote specific disadvantaged groups (Picture the Homeless, the Audre Lorde Project); others focus on particular substantive issues (Center for Popular Democracy, Churches United for Fair Housing). Some are "grassroots [groups] . . . that are actually doing organizing," an Asian community organizer remarked. Others, a White attorney noted, bring ties to "politically powerful allies, like the big unions. . . . They make political donations, and they're huge." To persuade "the whole spectrum—the more lefty people to the very central people—to take a stand on this [ending SQF] was, 'Okay, well, that's a game-changer.'"

Four strategies evolved, mostly with division of labor among groups. Some focused on mainstream politics—promoting legislation to combat discriminatory policing and placing SQF at the center of the 2013 mayoral election. Some success ensued: over Kelly's objections and Bloomberg's veto, the 2013 City Council passed two of the four bills in the Community Safety Act, a legislative package to combat discriminatory policing and improve police accountability.[70] The partial defeat disappointed advocates, but debate over the Community Safety Act made it "impossible to run for citywide office in New York City without taking a position on stop-and-frisk."[71] More generally, anger at SQF was coalescing. Previously seen as the "heir to his [Bloomberg's] throne," Speaker Quinn's failure to vote for the Community Safety Act helped to defeat her candidacy. Soon thereafter, "we were stunned how quickly Bill de Blasio rose to power," said a White attorney, not only in the 2013 Democratic mayoral primary but also in the subsequent general election. "And it was all on stop-and-frisk. That was the seminal issue of that election."

Nonetheless, some in the CPR coalition were unimpressed. "We don't see police abuse and discrimination being curtailed by legislation," said a White community organizer. "Police right now violate the law really regularly." This interviewee thought mainstream efforts might even be harmful: "The problem with promoting legislation that we think will have next to no effect is it diverts attention and diverts resources." Litigation was one alternative. Like other efforts, opposing police targeting through the courts has a long New York history, with demonstrable success in the *Floyd* decision.

A third strategy promoted citizen and expert monitoring of governance institutions, mainly through analyzing data and disseminating results. The New York Civil Liberties Union remained the lead actor here, having initially submitted a public records request in 2007 for NYPD's full database of SQF worksheets. After successfully suing the police department for the information, the NYCLU released the first analysis of SQF data in 2012. Continued releases, noting race or ethnicity and the economic status of neighborhoods as well as of individuals, demonstrably affected media narratives, scholarship, and advocacy.[72] "Data actually played a major, major, huge role in stop-and-frisk. It wasn't till the numbers started coming out," said a Latina community organizer, "that people started paying attention and wanting change." Others concurred: "An important and essential total story was *data*," said a Latino community organizer. "You can't look at the data without seeing huge discrimination. [When you] see the racial demographic breakdown: 'This is happening to one set of people and not another.' Data gave advocates facts and truth. We don't have to convince you with anecdotal stories."

Activists' fourth strategy was to intensify public pressure on political actors. Reverend Al Sharpton's National Action Network (NAN) mostly

Figure 2.5   Fifth Avenue Silent March, Father's Day, 2012

Source: New York Daily News via Getty Images. Reprinted with permission.

worked independently from the other major groups as it mobilized
New York's Black community for marches and protests. The highlight
of the network's activity was the Fifth Avenue Silent March in 2012 (see
figure 2.5). It involved about three hundred entities, ranging from police
reform groups to the National Association for the Advancement of Colored
People (NAACP), the Service Employees International Union (SEIU),
and gay rights organizations.[73] Participants included elected officials and
mayoral aspirants such as Christine Quinn, Bill de Blasio, and William
Thompson. The media reported the "silent march to end stop and frisk"
much more extensively than any other grassroots action, before or after.[74]
Organizers, said a Latinx community organizer, saw the march as "a big
turning point."

The National Action Network also held weekly open meetings, worked
with clergy to identify SQF victims, and advocated for remediation on
their behalf.[75] Most generally, it provided the essential link between the
often White-dominated advocacy and legal groups and the communities most affected by SQF. As a White attorney put it, "When NAN gets
involved, you sort of are operating on a different scale. They just have so
much reach, and they're such a trusted entity in the Black community. . . .
It's particularly, [in a] legacy Black community like Harlem, older people
who vote and are really engaged and know the elected officials—if the
Reverend says, 'Do this,' then, that's enormous." The Black-oriented press

wrote about Sharpton's NAN in 10.2 percent of articles that referred to SQF, compared to 2.4 percent of comparable articles in the generally oriented press.

Not surprisingly, advocates tend to skate over critiques or failures when portraying activities and accomplishments, but we did learn of a few cracks. One tension was over choices for action; a Black community organizer recalled telling Sharpton, "'Dude. Nothing has changed. We've marched. We've marched all (*pause*)—how many more marches?' I don't even go to marches no more, 'cause how many more marches are we going to have when there's no change in legislation?" But protesters countered that "*your* strategy has not effectively gotten at the heart of the beast," in the words of a White community organizer. "That legislative strategy leaves the beast intact." (This person proposed a new tack: "You have got to reduce the budget. You have got to reduce the personnel.")

Another tension is generational: "With the advent of Black Lives Matter . . . folks my age have sighed a sigh of relief and said, 'Okay, good, let the young people do it. Okay? I'm tired.'" Then this Black attorney added, "But the truth of it is, they don't have it." She named some groups and said, "*Those* are traditional organizations . . . [that have] been getting these bills done." Younger activists retort that "that's the very reason that Black Lives Matter came into focus," as one Black community activist put it. Older people, this person continued, "superficially always try to address these issues, not really looking deep into it or to . . . find out the root cause of it." Racial, ethnic, and gender-inflected differences also surfaced. Even while lauding "a great deal of solidarity and camaraderie with folks of different ethnicities," one experienced activist, a Black business leader, observed that "when there are issues of police violence against women or police violence against people who have queer identities, different gender identities, I think that there is a lot of apathy toward them. There's an indifference to it."

An advocate's work is never done. But crucially for my purposes, despite pulls toward other pressing problems and disagreements about strategy and tactics, most organizational actors remained focused on what they all agreed was SQF's targeted reinforcement of race/class hierarchy. Sent through many channels, this sustained message largely succeeded, for a while anyway, in overcoming narratives about crime control and public safety, as evidence on public opinion shows.

Public Opinion

The *Floyd* ruling on SQF's unconstitutional bias did not depend on public opinion. Nor do development or implementation of policing policy respond in any clear or overt way to people's views. Despite its uncertain role in judges', bureaucrats', and politicians' behavior, however, public opinion matters in *Race/Class Conflict and Urban Financial Threat*, especially because it provides evidence for answering the third question about the centrality of race/class conflict in characterizing and explaining a policy issue. That is, patterns in public views help us determine whether actors are consensually identifiable by race and/or class, or whether they consistently invoke race/class categories when engaging with the policy or political arena.

In the early 2010s, when data about SQF were first available, New Yorkers' mixed views mirrored politicians' ambivalence. When city residents were told in a 2011 CBS News/*New York Times* poll about reports that "sometimes law enforcement officers stop people of certain racial or ethnic groups because they believe that these groups are more likely than others to commit certain types of crime," four out of ten men and three out of ten women deemed the practice justified.[76] A year later, even in response to a question that was arguably biased against SQF, views were *more* favorable: over half of male and 40 percent of female New Yorkers agreed that SQF was "acceptable."[77] A longer series of SQF items in Quinnipiac University polls shows that about half of New York's registered voters supported the policy through its height in 2012 and precipitous fall in 2013 (see the "total" line in figure 2.6).[78]

However, the racial divide apparent in figure 2.6 (along with a gender divide, not shown) was stable. The 2011 CBS News/*New York Times* poll found that fewer than half as many Blacks as Whites (22 to 49 percent), along with only 27 percent of Hispanics, agreed that SQF as practiced was justified.[79] Similarly, in 2012, even though each race's support was higher than in 2011, just over one-quarter of Blacks compared with just over half of Whites found the practice of SQF to be acceptable. (Hispanics now resembled Whites, with 49 percent support.)[80] Consistently, among both voters and general population, about seven in ten Blacks, around half of Hispanics, and not quite four in ten Whites disapproved of SQF policy, at least as practiced.[81]

Additional poll questions help to explain Blacks' rejection of SQF. First, most did not perceive it to be effective; barely one in seven agreed that stop-and-frisk had reduced the number of guns or the amount of violent crime in the city. (Whites were more sanguine about its impact.)[82] In four Quinnipiac poll items, with varied wording, about two-thirds of Blacks, compared with only two-fifths of Whites, and Hispanics in between, agreed that crime would not rise if SQF were reduced.[83]

Second, people of color perceived a systematic pattern of police racism in which SQF was embedded. Blacks and Hispanics were much more likely to say that police favored Whites over either group, that the police were sometimes "insulting," and—especially relevant here—that they had been stopped "just because of your race or ethnic background."[84] Five times in the New York City Quinnipiac polls conducted from 2014

Figure 2.6   Disapproval of SQF among New York City Registered Voters, by Race or Ethnicity, 2012–2013

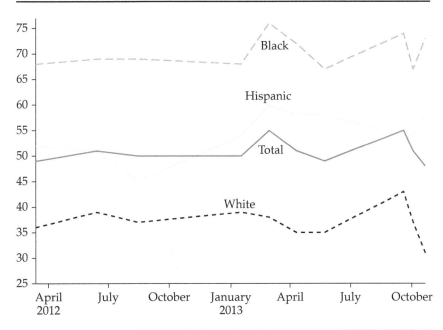

Source: Quinnipiac University 2012a, 2012b, 2012c, 2013a, 2013b, 2013c, 2013d, 2013e, 2013f, 2013g.

through 2017, in a wide range of questions, voters of color pointed to police discrimination ranging from rudeness and unwarranted stops to "excessive force" and "brutality." (Some Whites perceived the same racial discrepancies, but in smaller proportions.) People of color expressed a fear of being stopped by the police.[85]

Strikingly, even after all this experience with SQF's implementation, half or more New Yorkers of color endorsed the policy goal it was intended to foster. The Quinnipiac poll asked five times between 2008 and 2015, with varied wording and sometimes including examples, if police should "crack down on quality of life offenses" in the city. On average, half of Blacks and up to two-thirds of Whites and Hispanics approved; an even higher proportion of Blacks endorsed quality-of-life policing in their own neighborhood.[86] In a sad irony, that arithmetic implies that, like Bratton and Kelling by that point in the policy's history, at least one-quarter of Blacks endorsed quality-of-life policing while opposing SQF.[87]

The *Times* and Quinnipiac polls show less clarity on class differences (as measured by income) in SQF views. Respondents with family incomes below $30,000 did not differ from those with higher incomes with regard to justifying racial profiling and accepting SQF.[88] However, poor respondents were less sanguine than the well-off on questions about SQF's impact on guns on the street or violent crime.[89] Quinnipiac polls show the same mixed results as the CBS News/*New York Times* polls: low-income respondents disapproved of SQF more than did more affluent respondents on three occasions, while results were inconsistent on three other occasions. In sum, variation by class in New Yorkers' views of SQF is less systematic, and arguably weaker, than is variation by race. The Target was partly, but not fully, visible to the public at large.

The Class-in-Group Survey

Policy and political actors are most interested in the content, not the underpinnings, of New Yorkers' views. The information they need about public opinion comes from top-line percentages and crosstabs that sort supporters and opponents by race, class, and race/class intersection (and probably precinct). Scholars, in contrast, often seek explanations that enable them to distinguish race or class from other potential influences on views, such as age, gender, political ideology, or partisan commitments. For them, the crucial measures are regression analyses that enable tests of hypotheses by revealing the relative importance of potential explanatory factors when others are held constant.

Our Class-in-Group (CIG) survey has a large enough sample to permit both kinds of analysis. As a reminder, CIG includes 3,307 respondents across the twelve largest metropolitan areas in the United States, among whom are all Blacks and Latinos in those metro areas enrolled in 2016 in GfK's representative respondent pool, and at least 100 Whites in each area (randomly chosen from the respondent pool). Subsamples include 1,213 non-Hispanic Whites, 809 non-Hispanic Blacks, and 1,285 Latinos and Latinas of any race. Each respondent is weighted to be representative of his or her racial or ethnic group in the U.S. population as of 2016.

CIG includes three items measuring trust in police: Do police promote community stability and good relations? Do they testify correctly about suspects in court? And do police maintain public safety? (A reminder that question wording is in appendix C.) David Beavers combined them into an index by adding responses to each item, from zero (no trust) to two (complete trust), then converting the sum to a scale of zero to one. Overall, respondents are more trusting of the police than not, averaging a score of 0.62 on the scale. Race and class inequality each matters: Whites are more trusting than are Blacks and Latinos, and high-income respondents are more trusting than middle- or low-income respondents. Race or ethnicity and income intersect: Blacks, Latinos/as, and Whites with low incomes score 0.49, 0.55 and 0.66, respectively, on the scale; high-income

Blacks, Latinos/as, and Whites score 0.55, 0.65, and 0.73, respectively. (Respondents with moderate incomes are in between, in each race or ethnic group.)

Panel A of figure 2.7 presents a standardized coefficient plot showing the relative importance of plausible explanatory variables when controlling for the others. Panel B shows a marginal effects plot of the three-way interaction between race or ethnicity, income, and gender—that is, the interaction between race and class separately for men and for women. (Details of CIG analyses and the regression tables underlying the CIG figures are in appendix tables D.1 through D.4.)

As panel A shows, the independent variables (in this and the rest of the CIG analyses in the book) comprise four clusters: (1) the basic demographics of race or ethnicity, household income, and gender; (2) other individual characteristics plausibly associated with attitudes—education, age, political ideology, partisanship, and metro-area residence; (3) three core beliefs about American society—perceptions of equality of opportunity, a sense of being a rights-bearing citizen, and perceptions of racial discrimination; and (4) four sets of interaction terms—race/class, race/gender, class/gender, and race/class/gender.[90]

As is the case for other CIG analyses in this book, horizontal bars in panel A of figure 2.7 that do not cross the "0" line are statistically significant and probably of substantive interest. Panel A shows that middle-aged and older respondents are more likely to trust the police than are younger respondents (the excluded category). Liberals trust the police less than do conservatives, and those who believe that Americans have an equal opportunity to succeed or who perceive themselves to be rights-bearing citizens trust the police more than those who disagree. Most interestingly for my purposes, although crosstabs show classic patterns of race/class intersection in levels of police trust, none of the twelve interaction terms are close to being statistically significant when other variables are controlled. Instead, racial difference—between Blacks and Whites, or between Latinos/as and Whites—is both statistically and substantively significant. Race and ethnicity matter in views of police behavior; when all else is held equal, class, gender, education, partisanship, and residence do not. (See appendix D.1 for full regression analyses.)

Panel B of figure 2.7 addresses three-way interactions—that is, how race/class categories when analyzed separately by gender are associated with trust in police. Even discounting wide confidence intervals due to small subsample sizes, results show that when all other potential explanatory variables are held constant, canonical intersections do not matter much. In only two of the six clusters do we see clear differences in views across household incomes within racial or ethnic groups—between high- and low-income White women, and between high- and low-income Latinas.[91] Again I conclude that race and ethnicity matter in views of

Figure 2.7   Trust in Police: Class-in-Group Survey, 2016

A. Standardized Coefficient Plot

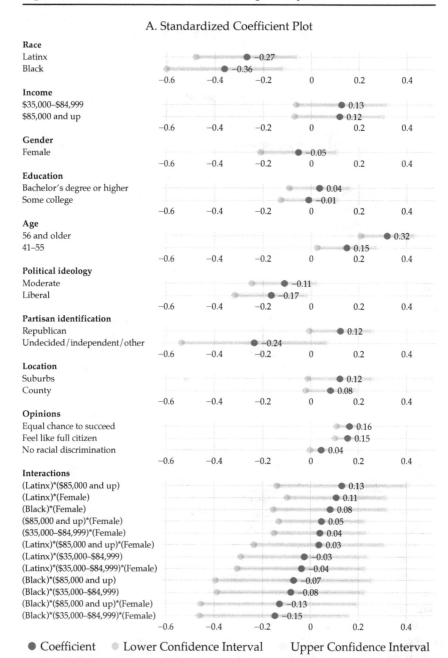

● Coefficient   ● Lower Confidence Interval   Upper Confidence Interval

Source: Author's analysis of 2016 CIG survey.
Note: Excluded variables are: for race, White; for income, $0 to $34,999; for gender, male; for education, high school or less; for age, eighteen to forty; for political ideology, Republican; for partisan identification, Democrat; for location, central city. Results for each variable in Opinions are independent measures of agreement.

Figure 2.7   *Continued*

B. Marginal Effects Plot of the Interactions of Race, Class, and Gender

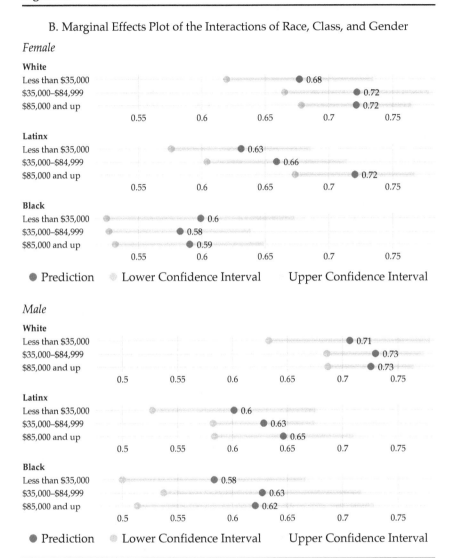

Source: Author's analysis of 2016 CIG survey.

police behavior even when other factors are controlled for, but adding in income and gender reveals little.[92]

The CIG survey also examines an issue even more directly linked to SQF—whether police are "looking for any reason to give" a man of the respondent's race or ethnicity ("young men" for Whites) "a hard time."[93] Crosstabs show that more than half of Blacks (53 percent, compared with 29 percent of Latino/as and only 14 percent of Whites) perceive police bias against their group (or, for Whites, against young men). Intersectionally lower-status respondents (poor and middle-income Blacks) are *five times* more likely to perceive unfair treatment than are intersectionally high-status respondents (affluent Whites)—57 to 11 percent. Affluent Blacks, at 43 percent concurrence on biased police treatment, resemble poor Blacks more than they resemble affluent Whites. In this hierarchical context, class matters, but race matters more.[94]

Panel A of figure 2.8 probes possible explanations at the individual level for views about police bias, and panel B focuses on the interaction of race or ethnicity and class, separately for men and women. These can be read in the same way as the graphs in figure 2.7, and results are broadly similar.

Respondents who believe that the United States offers equal chances to succeed, and (marginally) those who see themselves as rights-bearing citizens, are significantly less likely than their counterparts to perceive police bias. Conversely, liberal, Latinx (marginally), and especially Black respondents perceive police bias more than do conservatives and Whites, respectively. High-income Black women are more likely than all others, including Black men,[95] to perceive police bias (panel B); they are the only intersectional group with an unambiguous position, statistically speaking. More broadly, African Americans (especially women) and Latinas are most likely to agree that the police target men in their group.

In light of perceptions among people of color of police targeting, it is no surprise that more than three times as many CIG Blacks as Whites (42 to 13 percent, along with 30 percent of Latinos/as) agree that group members have an obligation to poorer members (or to "Americans" in the case of Whites) to join protests against unfair police treatment.[96] Nonetheless, metro-area African Americans do not distinctively oppose policing per se.[97] When asked to choose between prison terms or "probation and treatment" for drug sellers, African Americans' responses are virtually identical to those of Whites.[98] All three groups endorse in similar proportions the prescription that "violent criminals are [to be] punished to the full extent of the law," and they would devote a similar share of their town's budget—over one-fifth, second only to public schools among six proffered options—to "police and public safety." As one anxious mother put it, "'I need help, and if the cops are the ones giving it, that's fine by me.'"[99]

Figure 2.8 Do Police Harass Young Men in Your Group? Class-in-Group Survey, 2016

A. Standardized Coefficient Plot

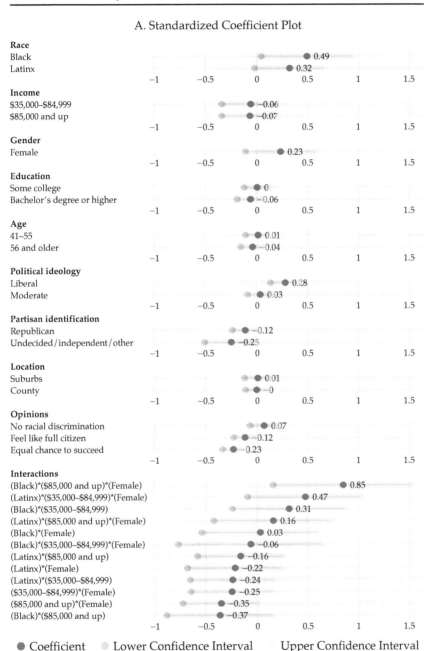

● Coefficient   ● Lower Confidence Interval   Upper Confidence Interval

Source: Author's analysis of 2016 CIG survey.
Note: Excluded variables are: for race, White; for income, $0 to $34,999; for gender, male; for education, high school or less; for age, eighteen to forty; for political ideology, Republican; for partisan identification, Democrat; for location, central city. Results for each variable in Opinions are independent measures of agreement.

(*Figure continues on page 54.*)

Figure 2.8   *Continued*

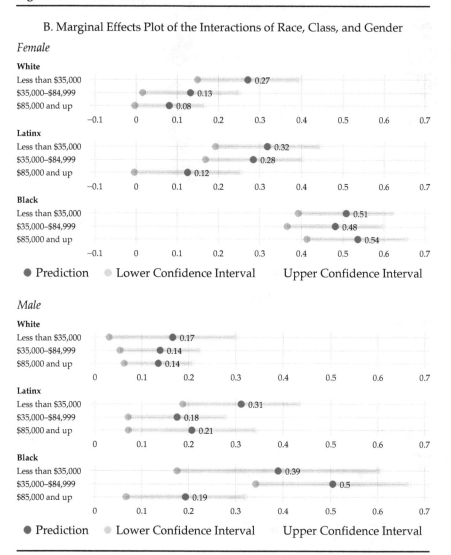

B. Marginal Effects Plot of the Interactions of Race, Class, and Gender

Female

White

Less than $35,000	0.27
$35,000–$84,999	0.13
$85,000 and up	0.08

-0.1   0   0.1   0.2   0.3   0.4   0.5   0.6   0.7

Latinx

Less than $35,000	0.32
$35,000–$84,999	0.28
$85,000 and up	0.12

-0.1   0   0.1   0.2   0.3   0.4   0.5   0.6   0.7

Black

Less than $35,000	0.51
$35,000–$84,999	0.48
$85,000 and up	0.54

-0.1   0   0.1   0.2   0.3   0.4   0.5   0.6   0.7

● Prediction   ● Lower Confidence Interval   Upper Confidence Interval

Male

White

Less than $35,000	0.17
$35,000–$84,999	0.14
$85,000 and up	0.14

0   0.1   0.2   0.3   0.4   0.5   0.6   0.7

Latinx

Less than $35,000	0.31
$35,000–$84,999	0.18
$85,000 and up	0.21

0   0.1   0.2   0.3   0.4   0.5   0.6   0.7

Black

Less than $35,000	0.39
$35,000–$84,999	0.5
$85,000 and up	0.19

0   0.1   0.2   0.3   0.4   0.5   0.6   0.7

● Prediction   ● Lower Confidence Interval   Upper Confidence Interval

Source: Author's analysis of 2016 CIG survey.

Denouement: The Four Questions
and the Puzzle of *Race/Class Conflict*
and Urban Financial Threat

In apparent refutation of supporters' claim that SQF preserves public safety, crime rates in New York remained steady through the end of the 2010s, with misdemeanor and felony rates declining and violation offenses increasing slightly, after its use was drastically reduced.[100] Public, politician, and media attention to SQF largely disappeared when most concluded that its dramatic reduction was having no harmful effects; as one informant, a White attorney, summarized, "The New York City political class is not really—I would say they're a little bit checked out on policing issues."[101]

Organizations' attention to SQF correspondingly declined, and they redirected their efforts to other policing issues such as police violence and the abysmal state of the Rikers Island jail. Some advocates perceive the victory over SQF as having only dented race/class hierarchy. One Black informant who worked for an advocacy organization, for example, noted that the fight against "stop-and-frisk was very, it was very narrow. It wasn't broad enough. It doesn't really address the issues of police brutality." Some even see the victory as insignificant: "As long as you have an institution that's founded in racism and white supremacy," said a Black businessperson, "and now you have people within that institution who have internal biases or implicit biases, and now they have the perfect tool, which is a gun—as long as you have these interactions with folks, it's just going to keep happening, right?" The groups targeted by SQF remain in the bull's-eye: "Ninety percent of marijuana arrests are black, Latino, not white. Tells you who is being searched. The number has dropped, but racial disproportionality hasn't changed," pointed out a Latina informant from an advocacy organization. Looking back to the euphoria of the *Floyd* decision, one interview subject concluded simply that "right now, we are a little weary."

But others saw genuine change, such as the White professor who observed that

> what's going largely unnoticed is the extent to which there has been what we ordinarily think of as transformative change. . . . People were saying "the NYPD is being put in a position where they would not be able to do their jobs," and "the streets are going to run red with blood," everything, all that has been gained in the city would be lost, and it's going to be 1990 again. And two years on from that . . . stops are down 96 or [9]7 percent. It gets another percent every time I look. . . . Jail's down. Prison's down. All the other markers of enforcement are down, and not only are the streets not running red with blood, but crime is at recorded historic lows. And kids are getting diverted straight into support pre-arrest, and lots, and lots,

and lots of marijuana arrests are not being made, and they're not making, for all practical purposes, misdemeanor arrests in Manhattan at all. . . . And the city's fine. So there's been huge change . . . tremendous change, in a short period.

One analyst even concluded that *Floyd v. New York* was "one of the greatest victories in the struggle to end police abuse of people of color" in the city's history.[102] At least for a while, the bull's-eye had defeated the targeters.

The comment about "tremendous change in a short period" was made in 2017. It was followed, of course, by COVID and a small but notable rise in crime in New York—and also in SQF. Stops rose in the city to fifteen thousand in 2022, the highest number since 2015. NYPD data show that African Americans comprised 59 percent of the people who were stopped, an increase from about 55 percent in the early 2000s. Conversely, 7 percent of the people stopped in 2022 were White, compared with 10 percent or slightly higher in the early 2000s.[103]

Most relevant for *Race/Class Conflict and Urban Financial Threat*, the independent monitor of the New York City Police Department reported that the city's Neighborhood Safety Teams, newly deployed to address gun violence in high-crime neighborhoods, sometimes use SQF unconstitutionally. Around 2020, roughly 70 percent of those stopped by the safety teams were Black; the majority of people stopped were under age thirty, and almost all were men. The monitor concluded dryly that "the demographic data reported here, when put in context with the high percentage of unlawful stops, should be examined carefully by the Department."[104]

It is too soon at this writing to tell if SQF might reemerge as a core New York policing strategy with the same target. But a blog post on, ironically, Bloomberg News is not reassuring:

Mayor Eric Adams has . . . expressed support for the tactic [of SQF], arguing repeatedly during his campaign and in his first year in office that the practice could be used equitably. An NYPD spokesperson echoed that sentiment in a statement saying, "The NYPD uses this tool with increasing levels of precision, stopping individuals based on organic, specific observations." City Hall representatives didn't immediately respond to requests for comment.[105]

SQF was important on its own terms, especially for those caught up in the policy and political dispute. But from the perspective of building a theory of when and how race/class conflict shapes American urban policies and politics, and why it sometimes does not, SQF is invaluable.

Consider the clarity of the responses that this case enables to the four questions deployed to resolve that puzzle:

Is the policy intended to affect race, class, or race/class inequality? Yes. SQF was intended to promote and maintain social order and to prevent crime. Given that poor communities of color were disproportionately the scenes of disorder and crime, a well-implemented policy of SQF was anticipated to reduce the impact of underlying race/class inequality.

Is implementation intended to, or does it in fact, affect race, class, or race/class inequality? Yes. Despite what were surely many efforts to apply the policy fairly and with due regard for the risks of bias, SQF as implemented at least through 2012 worsened race/class inequality—along with inequalities of gender, age, and community. After 2013, implementation of any sort declined precipitously.

Are engaged actors consensually identifiable by race or class, or do they consistently invoke race/class categories in their engagement with the policy and the political arena? Yes. Many community organizations and civic groups responding to SQF were primarily composed of people of color, and most had as a core mission the reduction of race/class inequality. As the general public became more attentive to SQF, racial divides grew to the point where the primary distinction in opinions was between Blacks (and Latinos, to a lesser degree) of all classes and Whites.

Are policy recipients who consistently gain or lose, or policy outcomes that consistently affect the city's residents, consensually identifiable by race or class? Yes. Ironically, and sadly, SQF started as a challenge to the existential threat of unprecedentedly high levels of crime; Mayor Bloomberg continued to point to that threat long after it receded, to his political cost. Instead, as the Target metaphor indicates, over time poor young Black men and Latinos in New York's disadvantaged communities of color lost status and security even if some gained through a reduction in crime. This eventual set of policy recipients and outcomes was so expansive and identifiable that a court decision determined SQF's disparate treatment to be unconstitutionally biased.

The answers to these four questions solve the first two layers of the book's theoretical puzzle: *when* is race/class conflict at the core of a policy issue, and *how* is it manifested? With regard to *when*: race/class inequality is at the core when at least one of the four questions is answered positively; in this case all four are. Race/class inequality appears in the policy goal (as a problem to be solved); race/class conflict appears in implementation (as exacerbation of the initial problem), in the political and organizational actors (as an organizing and motivating principle), and in the outcomes (as a measurable result).

The Target metaphor shows *how* race/class conflict is manifested in this case. Poor young Black men and Latinos in disadvantaged communities of color were in the bull's-eye; they had few resources, even less power, and no institution from which to operate. Nonpoor, non-young, often non-Black or Latino actors with more resources and power, operating within an institution that epitomizes state control, could and did dominate the bull's-eye. Race/class inequality in the implementation of SQF was a hierarchy—and as such provides the template to which the other cases in *Race/Class Conflict and Urban Financial Threat* are compared.

═ Chapter 3 ═

Race, Class, and Development:
The Atlanta BeltLine

*The BeltLine . . . is the greatest idea you've heard since the
Atlanta airport. I'm a huge believer.*
—White nonprofit developer, 2017

What we've got is a sidewalk to gentrification.
—BeltLine Rail Now protester,
quoted in Deere 2019

*You have a significant contingent in the metro Atlanta area
of middle- to upper-middle to upper-class African Americans,
and you have this growing underclass of Blacks, and I think
the separation, the division between the two, is stark.*
—Black civic association leader, 2017

*There's no story about race in America that can afford to ignore
the realities of class interest.*
—Jesse McCarthy, *The Nation*, 2015

Atlanta's metaphorical counterpart to New York's Target is a two-by-two Grid, with four formally symmetrical manifestations of race/class interaction. That is, race and class shape the behaviors in and trajectory of both cases, but the nature of their intersection differs. Unlike with New York's stop-question-frisk (SQF) policy, analysis of Atlanta's BeltLine must attend as much to advantaged Blacks as to advantaged Whites or poor Blacks. African Americans' power in Atlanta lies largely in the realm of politics and policy, while that of Whites is predominantly

59

https://doi.org/10.7758/ptkg1499.6196

economic—but deployment of resources, power, and institutional control moves across the color line. Hence the "legend of the Black Mecca," in which Atlantans are "too busy to hate" and in which economic and political incentives enable cross-racial alliances, even if not appreciation.[1]

Beyond their metaphors, the BeltLine and SQF differ in analytically important ways. To begin with, the nature of the politics differs: engagement around SQF sought to end an activity that those in authority endorsed but half of New Yorkers opposed, while engagement around the BeltLine seeks to promote an activity that almost all Atlantans endorse. Second, the dynamics of change differ: after decades of effort characterized by alternating successes and setbacks, opponents of New York's SQF attained their objective through one dispositive act—the *Floyd* ruling of unconstitutional bias in implementation. BeltLine construction has also seen decades of effort characterized by successes and setbacks, but attaining supporters' objective is literally as well as fancifully a matter of moving forward by inches through many small steps. Third, the characteristics of the policy outputs are almost opposites. SQF involves transitory verbal and sometimes physical encounters among a few people that are repeated with little variation thousands of times and leave no visible trace. Policy recipients are precisely definable. The BeltLine is a solid, immovable, highly visible object that, once constructed, will exist regardless of transitory and varying human encounters. Policy recipients are fluctuating, unpredictable, and at most loosely defined.

These differences compel us to be careful in making comparisons, but they also reinforce the premise of *Race/Class Conflict and Urban Financial Threat*—that race/class inequality is the foundation of a wide array of American urban policies and their associated politics. It operates differently in different contexts; in Atlanta, race/class inequality manifests as an interaction and the ruling metaphor is a Grid:

Affluent Whites	Affluent Blacks
Poor Whites and Hispanics	Poor Blacks

Setting

The Atlanta BeltLine is basically a long pedestrian walkway. Atlanta BeltLine Inc., which "oversees all aspects of planning, developing, and execution," describes it as "one of the largest, most wide-ranging urban

Figure 3.1   The BeltLine in the Boundaries of Atlanta

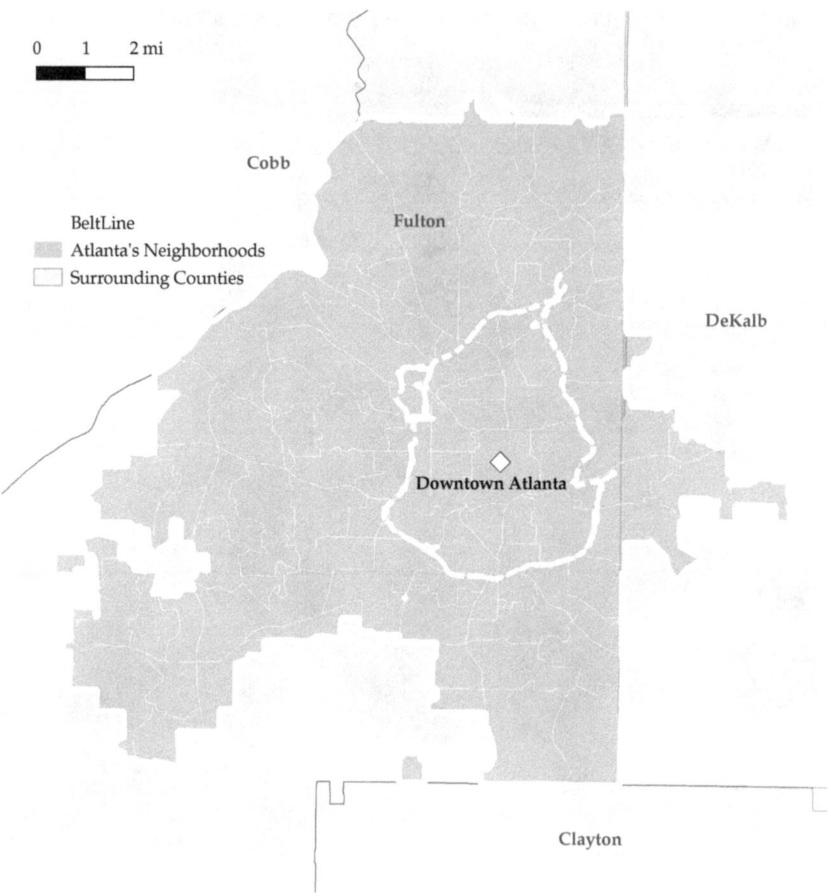

Sources: Author's analysis. Data are from the U.S. Census TIGER/LINE shapefile repository.

redevelopment programs in the United States. This network of public parks, multi-use trails, transit, and affordable housing along a historic 22-mile railroad corridor is enhancing mobility, connecting intown neighborhoods, and improving economic opportunity and sustainability."[2] The plan includes an additional ten miles of trail to connect the BeltLine to downtown Atlanta, housing and commerce, and other curated spaces and amenities. The full project may cost more than $5 billion. Figure 3.1 schematically shows the project's shape and locates it in the Atlanta metro area.

The forty-five neighborhoods abutting the BeltLine range from elegant suburban spreads to dense urban neighborhoods, sparsely populated residential areas, commercial hubs, and uninhabited brownfields. Even

Figure 3.2   Distribution of Class and Race in Metro Atlanta, 2020

A. Proportion of Residents with a B.A. Degree or Higher

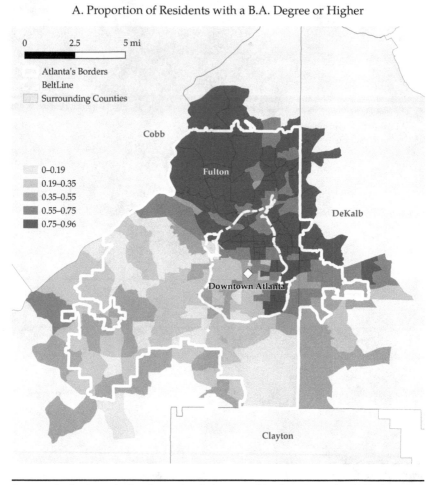

Sources: Author's analysis of tract-level demographic data from the 2020 American Community Survey (Five-Year Estimates).

contiguous communities may have distinct racial and class compositions, as figure 3.2 displays. Panel A shows the residential patterns of Atlantans with a college degree or higher; panel B shows the shares of African Americans in various neighborhoods.[3]

Comparison of the two panels shows the almost complete overlap of advantaged or disadvantaged race and class in many parts of Atlanta. Most residents in northern communities and the indented section in the southeast, for example, are highly educated Whites, while the sectors due

Figure 3.2   *Continued*

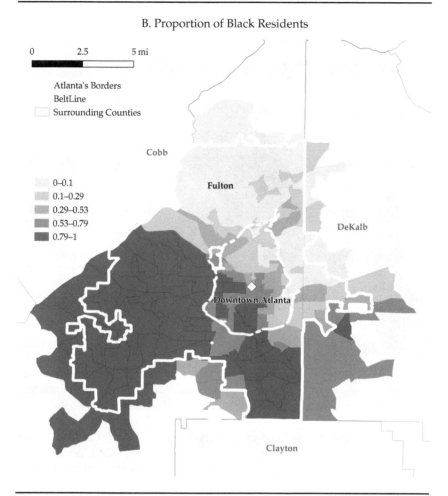

B. Proportion of Black Residents

Sources: Author's analysis of tract-level demographic data from the 2020 American Community Survey (Five-Year Estimates).

south of downtown Atlanta are home mostly to Blacks with low levels of formal education. Figure 3.3 makes the same point in a more abstract way, by consolidating the maps into a scatterplot of intersections between race and income across Atlanta's neighborhoods. With a few notable exceptions, it shows, once again, a tight relationship between economic status and racial composition.

Overall, Atlanta is the second most economically unequal city in the United States, with a 2020 Gini index of 0.579, compared with an index for

Figure 3.3   Intersection of Income and Race in Atlanta's Neighborhoods, 2020

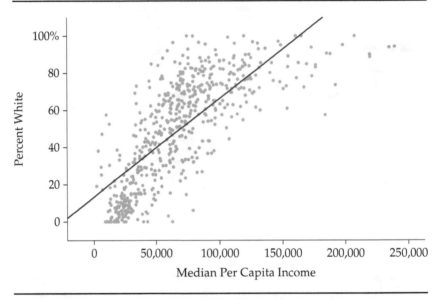

Source: Adapted with permission from Best Neighborhood, n.d.

the United States of 0.482.[4] And as we can infer from the maps, economic inequality is highly racialized: the median Black and White family incomes in Atlanta are, respectively, $28,000 and almost $84,000.[5] Constructed on top of the nineteenth-century railroad beds, BeltLine trails cut through the high-status northeast part of the city, the low-status southwest, and the mixed and changing neighborhoods literally and metaphorically in between; the elongated sidewalk is a visual, physical manifestation of intersections and inequality. A BeltLine aiming to "connect neighborhoods" has its work cut out for it.

Policy Recipients

As that description suggests, Atlanta's neighborhoods are social and even emotional realities. Longtime residents attach particular histories, resonant facts, influential encounters, and cherished relationships to their sense of neighborhood; newcomers, in turn, may try to redefine neighborhoods as part of creating their own sense of legitimacy and standing.[6] Place names can be shorthand for worldviews: "Pittsburgh neighborhood looks different from Cabbagetown, or from Peoplestown, you can see the difference," said a White leader of a civic association. "In the suburban [neighborhoods] . . . the houses all look the same, so I may have a home-owner's [status], but you don't have the same . . ." Interview subjects often defined their work goals, even their values and career choices, by neighborhood boundaries; unlike New York's advocacy organizations, which are mostly named for a target population or an ideological commitment, Atlanta's organizations are mostly named by location. Interview subjects included their neighborhood when introducing themselves. The White civic organization leader spoke for many as he sought to explain that sense of rootedness:

> [I] worked in Washington for four years. I decided I wanted to go back to Atlanta because I realized I was not going to make any personal contribution. . . . [At this point,] I'm not trying to solve Atlanta's problems, I'm not trying to solve the region's problems, I damn well aren't trying to solve the country's problems. So the reason I wanted to do this job was, I want to focus on these four neighborhoods. If we can address historic conditions in these four neighborhoods, and I can contribute to that . . . (*voice trailing off, the interviewee shifts to a different topic*)

These intense particularistic attachments imply that the BeltLine's costs and benefits affect policy recipients differently. Some Atlantans prize the new amenities it brings to their community. Some, perhaps the same people, are eager to unify the city across neighborhood lines, physically through trails, public transit, and access to unfamiliar locations and emotionally through shared pride in the city's history, innovations, and transformative energy. As Atlanta BeltLine Inc. pledges, "All legacy residents, new residents, and business owners—regardless of age, gender, gender identity or expression, sexual orientation, race/ethnicity, ability, income, or political ideology—benefit and prosper from the economic growth and activity associated with the Atlanta BeltLine."[7]

But the BeltLine simultaneously reinforces the geographic nature of the city's race/class inequality: instead of revitalizing the whole metro area, development risks re-creating the "raw and painful history of racist land use practices and their effect on vulnerable people and places."[8] The history is indeed deep; as historian Karen Ferguson has written, "members of the city's so-called underclass can trace their continued exclusion from the public life of the city back to the enormous social, economic, and political barriers to African American progress during the Jim Crow era, which black reformers were most often unable and sometimes unwilling to lift for the poorest members of the black community."[9] So outcomes are more visibly and explicitly double-edged for the BeltLine than for SQF; the goal of this narrative is to explore the policy process and accompanying political developments that generate that set of mixed results. In so doing, I add an additional answer to *Race/Class Conflict and Urban Financial Threat*'s puzzle by examining not only *when* race/class inequality shapes a policy arena but also *how* it does so. The key to the puzzle's solution in this case is that some winners are Black and some losers are not Black; this is a case of race/class interaction, not SQF-style hierarchy.

Policy Goals

Whatever their many disagreements, almost all actors in New York agree on SQF's stated intention—to reduce crime and enhance community order and safety. Actors in Atlanta, in contrast, do not agree on the list of or priorities among policy goals for the BeltLine.

No one publicly disputes the first and most essential goal—completion. The Atlanta BeltLine Inc.'s mission only begins with the thirty-three miles of urban trails. It also promises a twenty-two-mile rail transit system, $10 billion in economic development, 50,000 permanent and 48,000 construction jobs, 5,600 units of affordable workforce housing and 28,000 new housing units, 1,100 acres of environmental cleanup, 1,300 acres of new or restored green space, 46 miles of improved streetscapes, and public art.[10] Enthusiasm is high; the Eastside Trail saw about two million visits during 2022, and many concur with its chronicler that the BeltLine is "the most promising symbol of the city's potential for rebirth."[11]

By 2022, virtually all the land needed for trails and parks had been acquired, and funding was secured for the rest. As of 2023, about half of the trails were completed or usable; others are under construction and all segments are in at least "early design." Although even the optimistic Atlanta BeltLine Inc. depicts only a small stretch of streetcar line or light rail as being underway, it aims to work with MARTA (metropolitan Atlanta's transit agency) to add a public transit system throughout the city and into the suburbs.[12]

Even more expansively, this huge construction project aspires to remake Atlanta. Urban designer Ryan Gravel's famous 1999 master's thesis at Georgia Institute of Technology, which first gave concrete form to the vague idea of transforming the railroad beds, grew out of New Urbanist principles of city development and management.[13] Toward the end of the twentieth century, planners and activists promoted urbanist Jane Jacobs's vision of walkable mixed-use city neighborhoods that organically mingle residences and businesses. These unplanned uses of urban space would promote community as well as diversity of class, background, purpose, and activity.[14] The New Urbanist movement coalesced around a charter that advocated these "principles": "Neighborhoods should be diverse in use and population; communities should be designed for the pedestrian and transit as well as the car; cities and towns should be shaped by physically defined and universally accessible public spaces and community institutions; urban places should be framed by architecture and land-scape design that celebrate local history, climate, ecology, and building practice." One charter principle could have been written for the BeltLine: "Conservation areas and open lands should be used to define and connect different neighborhoods and districts."[15]

As the vision of a BeltLine reinvigorating and connecting neighbor-hoods gained traction in the early 2000s, goals proliferated. As Gravel put it, the idea of a BeltLine "quickly . . . [became] integrated as part of the solution for leading issues at that time—mobility, density, crime, and the scarcity of city parkland, to name a few."[16] In the rough sequence presented in Gravel's book, project aims expanded from transit to neighborhood conservation and protection of family homes, economic development of "underutilized urban land," and eventually "catalyst infrastructure." Later goals included a pedestrian greenway trail, thousands of acres of connected parks, thousands of units of affordable housing, a new public realm of streets and buildings on old industrial land, public art and cultural facilities, an arboretum, a parade (and protest) site, environmental cleanup, wastewater management, and half a dozen more.[17] Atlantans have energetically taken up Gravel's invitation to "feel fully entitled to add more" goals, which now encompass bocce ball courts, bicycle paths, farmers' markets, yoga classes, art shows, nature walks for people with disabilities, job training programs, and a "solar-powered bar."[18] Goal proliferation is a feature of the BeltLine, not a bug; as Gravel boasts, "We created this massive grassroots movement of people in support of this vision for their future, without any official plan."[19]

Interview subjects concurred about the diffusion of BeltLine goals. Some proffered a long list themselves. For instance, a Black professor observed that "it has the ability to address transit concerns. It has the ability to address economic development concerns. It has the ability to address racial and class and equity concerns. It has the ability to address the environment." But as this speaker hinted ("Look, *as an idea*, the BeltLine's fantastic, right?"), that long list embodies ambiguities as well as aspirations.

A few interviewees were cynical about the whole enterprise: "It's just a chi-chi plan to help new gentrifying populations avoid riding MARTA," said a Black community organizer. Or as a Black civic association member put it, the BeltLine and its surrounding development is "driven by our love for big, new, shiny things." But they were a small minority.

Some proponents focus on the BeltLine's potential transportation benefits for the disadvantaged: "There's an opportunity with the BeltLine," said another Black civic association member, to "look at it as a multi-modal transportation corridor that can help connect people to jobs and school and businesses and things like that." After all, in the words of a Black public official, "transit was supposed to be the big piece . . . where it was originally to connect, to be that ring . . . to be able to connect neighbor-hoods that we might be missing out."

Or perhaps housing is an even higher priority: "The BeltLine came through, which was supposed to be for affordable housing," noted a Black clergyperson. "There were people who cared about housing and real housing advocates," said a White civic association member. "They defined that vision around those themes. . . . The value of the BeltLine is pretty high, even without the transit. . . . We're building in funding for affordable housing, which Atlanta did not have."

A different set of proponents give priority to goals more likely to appeal to affluent residents of well-off neighborhoods. "We need to increase green space," said a Black public official. "We [the official and a colleague] don't care whether transit is ever built . . . because we are building a network of trails that Atlanta did not have." Another interview subject, a Black public official, "like[s] the fact that it's connectivity for all the communities . . . and also all communities being able to be walkable, being able to get out and exercise, see nature, more family time. It was encouraging people to get out of their homes."

Business leaders and political elites enthuse about population growth and economic development. Population trend lines had been worrisome for decades. The number of Atlantans fell by almost one-fifth from 1970 (497,000) to 2000 (416,000), even as population in the inner suburbs doubled. The city's population remained low through the next decade, but by 2020 the number of residents had rebounded to 499,000. BeltLine construction and development of adjacent neighborhoods are consensually understood to be part of that turnaround, which many with commercial or political interests are eager to keep going. JLL, a Chicago-based real estate and investment services firm, reported in 2021 that, in the Atlanta metro area, "the pace of growth is the third highest in the nation," and that the BeltLine "has spurred a cultural and economic revitalization of Atlanta's urban core—retail, office, and multifamily developers are inject-ing unprecedented amounts of capital into BeltLine-adjacent projects while Atlantans continue to pack the trails for leisure, commuting, and living."[20] Even though JLL has a "vested interest in companies doing business here," most BeltLine observers would concur with the facts if not the tone of JLL's promotional material.[21]

Two forms of goal diffusion are occurring here: many goals held by one actor, such as Gravel, and many actors and organizations with different priorities. One explanation for the diffusion is structural. New York's SQF was implemented by one hierarchical agency, NYPD, in a fairly stable policy environment and under the direction of one statutorily authoritative actor, the mayor. In contrast, the contours of the BeltLine have changed many times over three decades of planning and construction as old situ-ations and authoritative actors give way to new. At particular points, it has needed authorization from dozens of governing institutions, from the Georgia legislature and Atlanta mayor to banks and Neighborhood Planning Units (NPUs). It requires constantly renegotiated coordination among public, private, and nonprofit sectors. It must raise $5 billion, which implies responsiveness to everyone from philanthropists with targeted interests to residents with neighborhood-specific demands, developers seeking profit, and politicians attuned to the next election. To succeed, BeltLine policy must offer some form of success to virtually all comers. "This is a project that will only happen if the community at large believes it is theirs," was the first lesson learned by Atlanta BeltLine Inc.'s CEO in 2014.[22] Multiplication of goals is inevitable.

The second explanation for diffuse goals is conceptual. SQF emerged mostly from strictures derived from one Supreme Court ruling, prescriptions from one theory of urban policing, and policing strategies from one commissioner. The BeltLine's underlying principles, in contrast, are expansion, participation, and innovation. As one enthusiast, a White civic association member, put it, the BeltLine "is changing the way we think about the city and changing our expectations for living here." "DIY [do-it-yourself] Urbanism" celebrates the fact that "public space is inherently anarchic. Residents use this communal resource in countless ways at their own whims and often for their own ends."[23] That is a good description of the BeltLine's goals, to the dismay of a few and delight of many.

The BeltLine's proliferation illustrates the horizontal dimension of the Grid model of race/class interaction. Mostly regardless of race, powerful entities in the top row seek increased population, housing construction, environmental enhancement, cultural amenities, and commercial development, both for their own sakes and to attract young, moderate-income workers, voters, and taxpayers to the city.[24] Mostly regardless of race, entities in the bottom row seek public transit, affordable housing, jobs, and neighborhood preservation and betterment—all to improve the lives of legacy residents and workers and to persuade the next generation to remain in the city. This characterization is a bit too simple, mainly because Whites are not symmetrically distributed between the Grid's top and bottom rows. But its explanation of the multiple goals is plausible enough that one interview subject's summary of the BeltLine's impetus is persuasive. "It's less about race and more about class. . . . It all boils down to class," concluded this Black civic association member. "Now, it could be with a hit of race . . . but I think it's more class. It's more not wanting to be with poor people."

Implementation

A project as complex, sprawling, and long-term as the BeltLine is inevitably implemented in ever-proliferating ways by multiple actors.[25] Five analytic threads organize the relevant features of this complexity.

First, unlike NYPD's centralized process for implementing SQF, the BeltLine's many operations are decentralized, with little capacity or apparent desire for coordination. Supervised by the mayor and the sixteen-member City Council, all with their own power bases and pressures, Atlanta BeltLine Inc. is responsible for trail development and some affordable housing. MARTA, the public transit operator with a fifteen-member board of directors from four counties and the city of Atlanta, sites transit lines, builds terminals and stations, and sets fares. Developers, corporations, and property owners make most decisions about constructing, selling, and managing land and buildings, subject to city ordinances about, among other things, affordable housing. City, school district, county, regional, state, and federal governments provide mandates, regulations, demands, constraints, and funds for one or another aspect of the project. Courts set terms. With no formal authority or external accountability, philanthropists and foundations may exert considerable influence by wielding generous contributions. Advocacy organizations struggle with mixed agendas, seeking both to bring new energy and resources into sparsely settled poor neighborhoods and to prevent better-off newcomers from displacing current residents. Neighborhood Planning Units and residents of the forty-five adjacent neighborhoods exercise moral or political suasion and provide votes but have no authority or control.

This "great implementation monster that we've created," in the words of a Black public official, is a mechanism for fragmentation, even among actors committed to fostering the multiple policy goals. It is also a context in which those with long-term "'power to' (moving from an incapacity to act toward enjoying such a capacity)" are most likely to prevail. They are the people or institutions that "enjoy systemic advantages because they embody or command useful resources"—that is, they instantiate the Grid's top row.[26]

Second, and again unlike the case of NYPD's official rules and procedures, many BeltLine goals lack precise objectives, rules for making trade-offs, or measures of success. As a Black public official summarized, "Because it's unclear what the goals of the policy are, it's also unclear whether implementation is meeting these goals." Everyone gives at least lip service to protecting neighborhoods, increasing affordable housing, improving job opportunities, solving the transportation fiasco, and enhancing the quality of life in poor neighborhoods; indeed, many are fully committed to Atlanta BeltLine Inc.'s vision of "making Atlanta a global beacon for equitable, inclusive, and sustainable life." But implementing other goals—developing new housing, increasing the taxpaying population, and fostering new commerce—can conflict with promoting equity and stability. Absent authoritative, monitored, and enforced rules, along with clear criteria for setting priorities and measuring success, some goals are almost inevitably pursued at the expense of others, some measures of success are softened in response to exigencies of the moment, and some interpretations of success will clash with others.

The most significant version of this tension again points to the horizontal dimension of the Grid: what control can and should the bottom row—those with relatively little power and few resources—exercise over the apparently inexorable imperatives of the booming real estate market that the BeltLine is creating and intensifying? As one Black developer sighs, "It's just, the math is not making sense." New York's SQF shows that precise objectives, criteria for trade-offs, and measures of success do not suffice to overcome race/class inequality, but they at least offer tools under the right conditions for reducing ambiguity about its level and trajectory. The very expansiveness and fluidity of the BeltLine's goals make it hard to determine when and how market-driven development is benefiting the city as a whole, the well-off at the expense of the poor, the poor whose communities were previously ignored or exploited, or some combination thereof.

Third, and relatedly, fragmented and uncertain financing for the BeltLine and associated activities has determined choices, timing, and leverage. Donors support the goals they cherish—planting trees, improving trails near promising parcels of land, subsidizing housing costs for a low-income neighborhood. Government funding, intended to be the bedrock of the BeltLine's finances, has turned out to be disconcertingly unstable. The Atlanta Public Schools, Fulton County, and the City of Atlanta agreed in 2005 to create a twenty-five-year Tax Allocation District (TAD), within which most property tax increases would fund BeltLine construction.[27] But the state supreme court found the TAD's rules to be unconstitutional, so a state constitutional amendment became necessary—after which the Atlanta Public Schools and Fulton County demanded and received some of this revenue.[28] That diversion, combined with the 2008 recession, cut the projected $3 billion in tax revenues to a 2012 estimate of $1.4 billion.[29] Looking back, a White civic organization member conveyed the prevailing sense of existential crisis: "you can look at our numbers. We were right there with Detroit. People don't like to say that we were, but we were." Even a decade later, a 2022 Atlanta BeltLine Inc. update to its FAQs was not sanguine: "The TAD, Atlanta BeltLine Inc.'s funding source for affordable housing, was expected to yield $240 million through 2025. It has only yielded $25 million, or 10% of the original projection."[30]

Unsurprisingly, fragmented, uncertain, and reduced financing harmed low-income, disproportionately Black Atlantans more than high-income Atlantans. In the words of one sympathetic observer, a Black state official, "When the BeltLine started, they had a grand plan, and then '08 came, and sort of the bottom fell out of the money that they were going to get. So they went where the developers were willing to do it [construct the first trails and amenities], which was where it was easy and they knew it would work." Development distortions followed, to the point where Ryan Gravel, the "father of the BeltLine," and Nathaniel Smith, another board member who had founded the Partnership for Southern Equity, resigned from the BeltLine Partnership board in 2016 in protest. They explained that "our coalition's progress has not been commensurate with the scale of the challenges at hand. The recent announcement of $7.5 million from TAD bonds, for example, will likely support fewer than 200 affordable units out of Atlanta BeltLine Inc.'s obligation to 5,600—it is a drop in the bucket when compared to the need. . . . This work is increasingly urgent." Gravel and Smith reminded hearers that the BeltLine's "advantages must accrue to everyone, especially those who are otherwise most vulnerable to the changes it brings," and they exhorted BeltLine leaders to "become more intentional about who they will benefit."[31]

Not much happened. A year later, the *Atlanta Journal-Constitution* published the results of an extensive investigation of "how the Atlanta BeltLine broke its promise on affordable housing"[32] (see figure 3.4). Its journalists reported that the BeltLine's "mission of keeping black families and middle and low-income residents from being pushed from their neighborhoods became an afterthought to building parks and trails." The affordable housing units that did get built "were along the [poor, predominantly Black] southern half instead of near jobs and top schools" in the wealthy, predominantly White northern half of Atlanta.[33] According to the *Journal-Constitution* investigation, Atlanta BeltLine Inc. even passed up millions of dollars of potential funding during the first decade of construction.[34] Its soon-to-be-ex-CEO conceded that "with that qualifier [of the almost-disastrous impact of the Great Recession], I would say in terms of effort, I'd give us a C. In terms of total units for where we need to be by the end of the program, we're probably at a D."[35] It was arguably no one's fault that BeltLine funding was inadequate, unstable, and late, but its impact on race/class inequality is also unarguable.

The persistence of an uncontested failure to build housing for poor and working-class Atlantans points to a fourth implementation issue: when practice falls short of the BeltLine's promises, there are few clear lines of accountability or compensation. One pair of interview subjects, both of them White members of an advocacy organization, volleyed this point back and forth:

A: In 2007, [a prominent expert] was like, "You are not going to reach your goal [with regard to affordable housing]." And everybody was very much aware and just, nobody had the political will to do anything about it.

B: Well, and the Great Recession had a lot to do with it.

A: Well, that too, but even after that.

Figure 3.4   *Atlanta Journal-Constitution,* on BeltLine Developers' Failure to Build Affordable Housing

Source: Photo by Willoughby Mariano, 2017. Reprinted with permission.

B: Nobody was building anything for five years, and so . . .
A: Yeah, but even after that.
B: Right.

A Black public official was more explicit about the BeltLine leadership: "The more that we work with them, the more we realize that it really is kind of a show. . . . They pay lip service, and then the way they show up is like, 'You guys aren't serious about this.'"

Accountability is not completely absent. The BeltLine CEO resigned within a month of the *Journal-Constitution*'s article, and the City Council began the first serious discussion of its long-expressed commitment to affordable housing. New ordinances passed in 2017 and 2021 requiring large new rental developments near the BeltLine to include affordable housing or to pay a fine, which would itself be used to fund affordable housing. Atlanta BeltLine Inc.'s 2022 annual report boasted that "Atlanta BeltLine is now 56% of the way to reaching its goal of creating or preserving 5600 affordable housing units by 2030," and that, "to date, 96 homeowners have been accepted to the tax relief program."[36] *Atlanta* magazine concluded in the same year that "when it comes to creating mixed-income communities, [the new ordinance is] working. Sort of. . . . In a city where rent hikes are outpacing wage increases and hundreds of affordable units vanish annually, at least it's something."[37]

Despite more attention to affordable housing, the fifth implementation issue is the seemingly inexorable rise in the cost of living, due partly to the BeltLine's success. Also in 2022, Bloomberg News declared metro Atlanta to be "The Poster Child for the U.S. Housing Crisis."[38] Even the city reported that *"new housing construction has focused on higher-cost demand. . . .* Between 2000 and 2017, Atlanta's median rent increased by over 70%, but Atlanta's median income only increased by 48%."[39] By yet another measure, "the median price for housing in Atlanta has doubled over the last 10 years, and according to one study it is considered one of the most overinflated housing markets in the U.S."[40] Housing prices have risen and the supply of affordable housing has declined in many cities, but it nonetheless seems appropriate to attribute these changes in Atlanta partly to the BeltLine's popularity. As Daniel Immergluck and his colleagues have repeatedly shown, since its inception, the closer a property is to the BeltLine, the steeper the rise in rental costs or purchase price.[41]

Overall, BeltLine implementation is a stunning success. Atlanta BeltLine Inc. has largely recovered from the crises of earlier decades. All of the land for a complete circuit of the city is in hand, and every segment is complete, underway, or being planned. Parks, malls, apartments, and trails are replacing polluted, derelict, and sometimes dangerous patches of land. A Black developer enthused, "It's incredible. . . . The mileage of the BeltLine is increasing dramatically every year. It's just full of activity and vibrancy, and it's just fabulous." That speaker is far from the only Black supporter. "I can walk to the BeltLine . . . do my exercise if I want to there, ride my bicycle along with everybody else, eat and shop. . . . So living in town [now] affords me access to all of that, that I remember growing up," said a Black civic association member. A Black public official reported telling skeptics, "'How do you not see that the BeltLine benefits Black people?' . . . Black people live everywhere in the city. . . . It's touching our community . . . you gotta use it to make it, you see that it's a benefit." Atlantans' chief complaint has evolved into worry that too many people besides themselves are walking or biking on the trails; etiquette notices are now ubiquitous.[42]

But along with this undoubted success comes persistent concern about underlying structures of advantage and disadvantage. Some interview subjects, like this Black community advocate, described the dubious pleasure of having earlier suspicions proven correct:

> So the BeltLine, when it first started . . . claimed . . . "We're going to treat each one [section] equally, we're going to have affordable housing in each of the areas, we're going to have this, this and that, and, you know, there's not going to be any difference." Of course, there was great skepticism on this side that that would occur and I think that that skepticism has been borne out.

Developers balk at major investments in less profitable affordable units, well-off neighborhoods resist low-income housing, and legacy neighborhoods seek protection against too many new buildings and residents. Former mayor Shirley Franklin was and remains one of the BeltLine's foremost boosters, but even she points out that the commitment to affordable housing got "stuck. . . . The market forces are moving faster than the public policy and public infrastructure."

Politics

Entrepreneurial elected officials were essential for turning Gravel's 1999 rail-to-trail-and-transit master's thesis into a feasible project, and for sustaining it through difficult decades. Early proponents fostered community support and recruited City Council member Cathy Woolard, who chaired Atlanta's Transportation Committee. She in turn persuaded Mayor Franklin to give her support. The mayor's initial reaction was, "Oh, hell no. Absolutely not. I got things to do—I've got potholes, and I've got budget shortfalls, and I have sewage problems." But she came to realize that "we can take all this community interest—it was kind of a glitzy project—and this is a way for us to ensure a plan for development as opposed to this helter-skelter approach that has happened all over the region where you build it and then figure out how people are going to move around."

Enthusiasm spread. Experts and foundation leaders developed increasingly detailed plans for green space and other amenities. Eventually, "there was active civil engagement, I mean dozens and dozens and dozens of meetings." The most important demand in these meetings, according to Franklin, "was to build in an affordable housing concomitant." Her focus shifted from persuading people to consider the idea to "get[ting] the other governments to agree" and setting up advisory and management structures to accommodate the proliferating goals, interests, and participants.

Over the next decade, the mayor's office under Franklin and then Kasim Reed negotiated with the school board, MARTA, surrounding counties, the state legislature, federal regulatory and funding agencies, state and federal courts, and Georgia's voters. The city government established multiple, sometimes overlapping, advisory or decision-making groups to finance, plan, construct, and oversee the project. Philanthropists and organizations brought influence and funds. Mayor Reed was reported as wanting to "fast-track the BeltLine"; like Mayor Franklin, he contributed attendance at ribbon-cutting ceremonies and efforts to obtain funding. To my knowledge, no public official, member of the city's social or economic elite, civic group, journalist or editorial writer, or neighborhood association ever publicly opposed the project; in Franklin's summary, "No one wanted to be seen as undermining the BeltLine because the BeltLine was so popular, especially in gentrifying neighborhoods."

As that clause suggests and as we have already seen, "the lantern parades became more important, and BeltLine yoga became more important, than the affordable housing crisis."[43] Political explanations add a spin to the powerful economic incentives. One element is electoral competition. Political scientist Tammy Greer suggested that former mayor Kasim Reed might win his new bid for election in 2021 because "those who may be unhappy with the former mayor and his economic policies—that included those folks that were involuntarily displaced because of those expansions—are no longer in the city and, therefore, are not eligible to vote in the upcoming election. . . . He will receive more points than some may think because of the new groups of voters that are current residents of the city of Atlanta."[44] Another close observer made a similar electoral calculation with regard to a different group: elected officials can afford to let neighborhood associations "rail against the system" because "they had no ability to do anything about the railing. And so the City Council members sit there and listen to you rail, and know you're going to go back home." As a result, this Black civic association member said, "the political sector didn't know, and didn't really give a damn. Black or White. They enjoyed occupying their seats. . . . The neighborhoods that they, quote, 'represented' [are] in such distress" she concluded, because "there was no attention. . . . They sort of blew it off. They were focusing more on jobs and development, commercial development."[45] The *Christian Science Monitor*, hardly a radical medium, spelled out the implication: "That feeling of being disposable is not necessarily attached to race. In this majority-Black city, those displaced and those with the authority to help them tend to be the same race."[46]

Politicians need financial support as well as votes. "That goes back to the classist issue in the Black community," explained a Black public official. "Because you do have African Americans who are interested in being developers around the BeltLine. . . . And I think they [developers] have committed, because of their class connections, to try to maximize the development of the system." Some developers agree. The newly elected Black president of the Atlanta Commercial Board of Realtors, T. Dallas Smith, told his colleagues in 2022 that "the economic driver for this state is in this room," and he exhorted them "to leverage it."[47] He encouraged his audience to promote development in the predominantly Black and poor neighborhoods in Atlanta's west and south rather than permit "racism and stigma" to stand in the way.[48] "Let's look at some other areas [beyond the northeast and midtown]. . . . As brokers, we're leaving a lot of money on the table by having that narrow view of what we think the wrong side of the tracks are."[49]

A final political calculation involves Blacks' incentive not to be too critical of the city's leadership out of concern about disrupting Atlanta's carefully balanced racial order.[50] Atlanta has had a Black mayor since Maynard Jackson's first victory in 1974. The City Council is disproportionately African American, and Blacks arguably hold more genuine political power in Atlanta than in any other American city.[51] Although the fabulously rich are mostly White, some Blacks hold great personal and corporate wealth.[52] But as a Black developer put it, "There is a fear in the Black community . . . that we're going to lose Black leadership in the city. And it is reasonably likely that that's going to occur. And there's a little panic going on in the Black community." (For himself, he added, "my view of it is, all I want is good leadership.")

Electoral, financial, and racial incentives are inevitably intertwined, with clear implications for both politicians' support of the BeltLine and their delicate handling of affordable housing policy. As a White developer and civic association member who has built affordable housing put it, "People feel a lot of pressure to say that they are affordable housing advocates. I don't think that anyone has a clear vision of what that means or looks like, and they are really nervous about getting too far out on that limb and alienating the business community, which has historically been who drives decisions in Atlanta, while still having sort of their affordable housing chops. So my perception is that most political leaders are really trying to navigate that." Another interview subject, a Black civic association member, was less tactful:

> Atlanta's development is shaped by the political elites and institutional elites [who] tend mostly to be Black professionals, what you might call Black bourgeoisie. And then the economic elites or those who fund their campaigns tend to be White elites, you know, the capitalists who control Atlanta's financial sectors and communication sectors, banking, etc. So basically they teamed up to, I won't say they had some cabal where they

came up with this diabolical plan, right, like, "Push all the Black people out." But in effect, that's what's happened. So the BeltLine was a useful tool because when you look at the scheme of the BeltLine, it in many ways encircles the city around areas that were once key nodes and points where you might find public housing.

Immergluck's explanation is the simplest: "Black electoral power and white economic strength continued to perpetuate a system that favored the interests of capital over the city's less affluent residents."[53]

A few observers go further, depicting politicians as simply corrupt. The Black share of the city's population declined from 57 to 47 percent between 2000 and 2020, while the proportion of non-Hispanic Whites increased to 39 percent. So perhaps there is a "plan to depopulate black Atlanta" in which Black elected officials are complicit; after all, "the black exodus happened in an era of black mayors and majority black city councils." The plan includes, in this view, "heightened class war between black elites and the black underclass," "gentrification and displacement in urban core neighborhoods," "shortage of affordable housing," and "discrimination in both housing rental and sales."[54] Most generally, "'*Atlanta Way' neo-liberalism [is] intended to advantage corporate interests and affluent white people. Black people have been pushed out and those that remain live under a Black political class which is beholden to white capital.*"[55]

A pattern of race/class inequality can encompass political corruption as well as more ordinary ways in which politicians' activity can harm the worst-off. But it points, more interestingly, beyond individual incentives toward obdurate structural imperatives, or at least what seem to be imperatives. On the one hand, the 2008 economic crisis made attention to affordable housing feel like a low priority. As one White civic association member put it, when the BeltLine leadership realized that "'we're a third of what we thought we were going to be, fighting to get our heads back above water,' they got so focused on getting back on funding that focusing on affordable housing, I think, may have seemed like a luxury they could not afford." But on the other hand, Atlanta's recent success makes attention to affordable housing seem to many almost like a waste of economic opportunity. As Gravel put it, "Accountability to that vision ["the Atlanta BeltLine is for everyone"] has been one of our biggest challenges. . . . The rapidly recovering economy and incredible new growth in the urban core of Atlanta has made those challenges more urgent. While many of the needed investments and policies are known, actually implementing them is often very difficult."[56] More directly, "the economic driver for this state is in this room [full of realtors], and we're going to leverage it."[57] If stabilizing the situation of low-income residents near the BeltLine is a low priority both when the city faces economic failure *and* when the city faces economic success, race/class inequality is indeed deeply embedded.

Organizations

Atlanta has no equivalent of the Communities United for Police Reform's mostly coordinated front that challenged New York's SQF. Instead, as one Black city official put it, "each community has their own characteristic and their own set of issues that they're concerned about. . . . So it just really depends." This is a common view: "That's where the disconnect is," said a Black civic association member. "It's no one individual community in these neighborhoods. There's various communities of interest, of competing interests, competing needs, competing visions of what redevelopment could or should be." Given the geographic specificity of housing developments and BeltLine walkways, the "competing interests" of particular beloved neighborhoods are at the core of the disunity. An Asian public official sketched a rough map of this dynamic: "If here's the BeltLine, the folks that are here (*pointing to one spot*) are like, 'I'm excited. It's really cool.' . . . The folks down here (*points four inches along the line*) are probably like, 'Ooh, it's going to cause problems.' As you move closer to here (*points to an area a further few inches away*), it starts to blend. . . . Who supports it, who doesn't—it just intensifies as you get closer to the BeltLine. So, if you did a heat map, strong support, strong opposition, and mild."

Two main types of BeltLine advocacy fill the vacuum left by the absence of a New York–style united front: top-down organizations, many of which are independent of a geographic location, and bottom-up organizations, which are almost always connected to a specific neighborhood. Once again, the explanatory logic corresponds largely to the rows of a race/class Grid—that is, race differences may affect the intensity and focus of engagement with the BeltLine, but class differences typically shape the nature of that engagement. Top-down groups include public-private partnerships, national and local nonprofits, philanthropists, developers, corporations, politicians, and some churches. Bottom-up groups are mainly neighborhood advocacy associations, often linked with churches or nonprofits; members or clients are disproportionately middle- or low-income Black residents and middle-income in-migrants of various races or ethnicities.

Top-down organizations, the Grid's top row, have the most impact on BeltLine implementation. The core actors have evolved from Gravel's informal Friends of the BeltLine to the mayor's 2004 Atlanta Development Authority to 2006's Atlanta BeltLine Inc. and the Atlanta BeltLine Partnership.[58] Other early influential actors included the PATH Foundation, focused on multi-use trails and green space, and the Trust for Public Land, a national land conservation group.[59] Along with Atlanta-based nonprofits, these foundations bought land, drew up strategic and construction plans, and worked to secure public and private funding. Much of this early work occurred behind the scenes, involving a dedicated and public-spirited alliance but excluding nonparticipants and implicitly promoting some goals at the expense of others.[60]

The BeltLine Partnership simultaneously began a $60 million capital campaign, to which prominent Atlanta philanthropists and business leaders contributed funds and leadership.[61] After the 2008 recession and legal setbacks reduced TAD income, the coalition became even more dependent on these sources, as well as on developers.[62] Despite multiple task forces and other participatory efforts, public engagement in BeltLine hearings and meetings diminished. In the eyes of some, residents at large began to receive only perfunctory attention.[63]

By the time the BeltLine emerged from these formative years and its financial crisis, philanthropic donors, according to a 2008 BeltLine Partnership survey, saw funding for housing and transit as matters best left to government.[64] But the city's financing strategy created, as a Black public official explained, "somewhat of a disincentive that I think some of the leadership around the BeltLine have bought into." In the logic of a tax allocation district, the more property values and thus property taxes rise, the more BeltLine funds increase. The consequence is predictable:

> If I'm the agency charged with building the project, I want that digest to be as big as possible, because it's what gives me the budget to hire people and hire contractors and do everything that I need to. When you talk about carving out this section of [housing] affordability, it by definition means you're slowing the growth in that digest. . . . I think unfortunately, an individual or individuals who chooses to focus on collecting as much increment as possible so that it goes directly into the budget of the implementing agency so they can go and implement. . . . that is a hindrance [to funding affordable housing], that is a conflict.

As so many of our interlocutors did, he concluded with the inexorable arithmetic: "Where you're going to get that delta [the largest increase from current to new housing value, and thus property tax receipts] is on the South Side and on the West Side, [where] poor African Americans [live]. And so, to a large extent, [that is] what's driving the increment to build these [luxury] projects in these poor neighborhoods."

This combination—the BeltLine Partnership's reliance on resource-rich entities, donors' commitments to parks and trails, donors' perception of the government's responsibility for transit and housing, the government's acceptance of that responsibility, politicians' incentives to go where the votes and resources are, and the city's fiscal and tax policies that create incentives for luxury housing and commerce—generated a development momentum that neighborhood organizations could not combat. Atlanta has no *deus ex machina* like a federal district court that can halt the momentum of policy implementation in its tracks, as *Floyd v. New York* did to SQF.

Neighborhood associations, economic development corporations, non-profits, and Neighborhood Planning Units[65] began with at least cautious enthusiasm about the BeltLine's promise.[66] Many retain some support. But as housing prices rose near newly-opened sections of trail, groups representing predominantly Black, lower-income neighborhoods began expressing concern about displacement and submersion of their rich history: "There are people moving in . . . who don't want to engage the community as it is but who want to make it in their own image."[67]

As frustration grew about inaction on affordable housing and public transit, new organizations arose and older ones shifted their focus. But unlike New York advocacy groups' eventual convergence on a cluster of strategies to stop SQF, Atlanta's groups seem unable to coordinate goals and activities. As a White professor ruefully summarized, "There's community groups in the Turner Field neighborhood, there's community groups in Vine City, but I don't think anybody is really working together. It's fragmented. It's not a huge social movement. And they don't have very much power." A Black public official concurred: "It's fragmented. So there is a lack of any sort of coalition or broad organized advocacy movement along housing issues. . . . Maybe because of the lack of that broad-based coalition, you have yet to see a comprehensive, sort of sweeping affordable housing strategy from the city level." Yet another, a White interviewee who worked for an advocacy group, said, "Grassroots people are concerned, they've got ideas, they've got potential solutions, but nobody's sort of championed and said, '*This* is what we're going to do to tackle the problem.'" Even the determinedly optimistic Gravel concedes that "I sometimes see where the role of organized community advocacy is missing in our progress."[68]

In addition to the many reasons why advocacy groups typically find it hard to coordinate, the Grid metaphor suggests two more.[69] First, in contrast to most African American New Yorkers' agreement that SQF harmed their whole group, Black Atlantans have different economic and personal relationships to gentrification. Some discover that they can sell their houses for a profit. "It's an opportunity for both," noted a Black community organizer. "It's an opportunity for a person who never had that much money to say, 'I want to get it.' Is it the right decision for them? Probably not. Is it taking advantage of them? Probably not." Some long-term residents find themselves pleased to be living in a newly denser, less disadvantaged, more vibrant and commercially active environment.[70] But financial exigency impels others to move despite a preference to remain in place. Displacement or its threat can be traumatizing; as one Black community organizer put it, "You don't want to lose what your essence is, and your essence is your culture and your character."

It is not simply a racial divide; as a White professor put it, "This is middle-class African Americans and poorer African Americans. . . .

Figure 3.5   Neighborhood Protest against Rising Housing Prices, Atlanta, 2020

Source: Photo by Lynsey Weatherspoon/Redux. Reprinted with permission.

Middle-class [newcomers] will say, 'We're cleaning up the neighborhood,' and the poorer, long-term residents will say, 'You're pushing us out.'"[71] The Grid formation makes the problem especially complicated for advocacy organizations; as the person just quoted ruefully observed, "There's serious tension between the two [Black] groups, there's all sorts of insults that go back and forth." The protesters whose signs are portrayed in figure 3.5 were not swayed by the fact that the object of their protest, Mayor Keisha Lance Bottoms, is Black.

A structural and therefore deeper reason for the difficulty of coordinating across Atlanta's advocacy groups is that they have an almost impossible task. Stopping SQF was certainly difficult, but not expensive, whereas any serious strategy for stabilizing poor neighborhoods and providing affordable housing is. Neighborhood associations cannot possibly pay the costs. As a White corporate leader, observed, "There's something the mayor did recently, and it's a start, but it's very paltry. . . . It's $5 million that would go into [subsidizing poor residents in response to] the tax increases. I think it should be maybe $100 million for that. Five million doesn't do that." A sympathetic White developer explained more fully: "This stuff being built, very expensive, the numbers are such that it takes a lot of subsidy for a low-income person who is already in the neighborhood. . . . You [a developer] could do very few units of a high-rise that cost $200,000 [per unit] for someone that could pay near zero in rent." Regardless of race, community groups on the bottom row of Atlanta's Grid have no access to hundreds of millions of dollars over many decades.

Activists proffer a rich array of policies to overcome this financial gap. They include, among others, an affordable housing trust fund, additional tax allocation districts, the Westside Fund's anti-displacement property tax refund, the Westside Future Fund, an urban enterprise zone, support for rent and jobs in legacy neighborhoods, mandates or incentives to developers, public housing on city-owned land, and freezing property tax assessments for low-income homeowners. Many of these proposals have been implemented to some degree or in a few locations. But even the most committed advocates are not optimistic for the long term. Gravel observes, "There are lots of tools available—affordable housing, zoning, other strategies—we know what we should do, but we're not doing it. There is a lot of support for affordable housing in this city but politics means it is not happening."[72] If he includes foundational race/class inequality in "politics," Gravel is right.

Media and Public Opinion

The BeltLine does not play the contentious role in Atlanta's politics that SQF did in New York's. At least in public, all candidates and officeholders praise it and its many amenities; all concur on the urgent need for affordable, stable housing and robust public transit.[73] Neighborhood change is an irregular and continuing process, not a defined event; neighborhood residents do not speak with one voice or at one time. Persistent low-level controversy and multiple, sometimes small, changes seldom emerge as action-forcing drama.

In such a context, rich media attention is sparse. The general press frequently describes a developer's purchase, a philanthropist's contribution, completion of a segment, or a particular BeltLine activity, and it enables guest columnists to express views. But except for the *Journal-Constitution*'s 2017 investigation of Atlanta BeltLine Inc.'s affordable housing failure, the press seldom provides broad analysis, commentary, or contextual framing and gives only occasional attention to its political or community tensions. Unlike in New York, Atlanta is too small to support an energetic tabloid press or public media aimed primarily at the Black community, so multiple sources of public engagement do not exist.[74]

Maya Bharara and I sought precision for this conclusion by examining the BeltLine's salience in the five mayoral elections from 2003 through 2021. We considered newspaper articles and, where available, Vote Smart records, campaign websites, and videos of mayoral debates and forums.[75] The BeltLine was noted in passing in each early campaign, mainly to illustrate a candidate's commitment to economic enterprise. (For example, an article in November 2009 quoted Lisa Borders as "continu[ing] to support projects that will create jobs, improve transportation and spur sustainable economic development, such as championing the BeltLine, continuing funding for MARTA, maximizing TADs, and identifying regional transportation solutions."[76]) By 2017, the focus shifted slightly to candidates' concurrence on the need for affordable housing or desire to preserve communities.[77] A 2021 article noted harmony on the need for BeltLine accessibility. When queried in 2021, all candidates agreed on the goal of expanding public transit and expressed support for a light rail on the BeltLine.[78]

As of 2022, candidate websites remained available only for 2021. Three of the five leading candidates said nothing about the BeltLine, and the fourth remarked on it in passing. One change is notable, however: the winner, Andre Dickens, listed among his legislative highlights the establishment of BeltLine inclusionary zoning for affordable housing and a BeltLine senior housing rehabilitation program. In short, although the BeltLine gradually came into public view over two decades, it remained uncontroversial and minimally salient, and was linked only indirectly to problems of race/class inequality. I see no reason to expect attention or content to change.

There are no survey questions, to my knowledge, about the BeltLine. Since its inception in 2013, however, the Atlanta Regional Commission's annual "Metro Atlanta Speaks" survey has included relevant items.[79] As with New Yorkers' views of SQF, top-line results and crosstabs provide the contours of public views. Unsurprisingly, respondents have consistently expressed concern about economic pressures on housing and neighborhoods. From 2016 through 2019 (the first and last years in which this item was asked), at least three-fifths of city residents rated the metro area's affordability as only "fair" or "poor."[80] In 2019, almost half agreed that if they had to leave their home imminently, "I could not afford to move to another house or apartment in the area where I currently live."

Metro Atlanta Speaks surveys enable indirect views of affordable housing. An item in 2019 and 2021 offered five possible ways to "attract and retain a skilled workforce to the metro Atlanta area," including "more affordable housing options." Almost three-tenths of Atlantans chose that response in both years, more than any other alternative, including job training. Across the metro area, Blacks focused on affordable housing a little more than did Whites and Latinos (25 percent compared with

19 percent for each of the other two groups). Class differences were greater; in 2019, 30 percent of low-income metro-area residents focused on affordable housing as a way to recruit workers, compared with 12 percent of high-income respondents, with other income groups lined up in between.

Metro Atlanta Speaks surveys do not ask respondents if they link affordability with neighborhood transition and do not ask for evaluations of that process. But they do show respondents' awareness of what is typically called gentrification. In 2019, for example, 48 percent of Atlantans agreed that "long-established businesses are being replaced by new businesses" in their neighborhoods. Almost three-quarters agreed that older homes in their neighborhoods were being replaced with "new, more expensive housing alternatives," and 84 percent agreed that many properties were being flipped. One-fifth of Atlantans perceived that these changes generated tension among neighbors—perhaps an indirect measure of their own anxiety.

While not directly contradictory, two more explicitly evaluative Metro Atlanta Speaks questions point in different directions. From 2016 through 2019, respondents were asked if "living conditions in the metro Atlanta area will be better, worse, or about the same as today" in three or four years. Twice as many Atlantans were optimistic as pessimistic (roughly 40 to 20 percent) in all four years. Young metro-area adults were always the most sanguine; the number of optimists declined from roughly two-fifths to one-fifth as respondents' age categories rose. Other answers reveal an interesting mismatch between optimism and concerns about housing costs. Although both Blacks and newcomers across the metro area worried the most about affordability, the same set of Black respondents was consistently much more optimistic than were corresponding Whites (the small sample of Latinos varied across the years), and the same set of newcomers was much more sanguine than were long-term metro residents. In fact, long-term metro-area Atlantans were the only set of respondents whose pessimism matched or exceeded their optimism in each year—even though they were relatively *un*concerned about affordability. Worry about housing prices, in short, was not in these surveys driving evaluations of the city's future; length of residence and race were more closely related.

That apparent contradiction is embedded in a larger one. Despite the preponderance of optimism over pessimism regarding the region's future, most Atlantans were deeply critical of their government. Again from 2016 through 2019, respondents were asked to "rate the responsiveness of local governments to the needs of their citizens in metro Atlanta." In 2016, 53 percent of respondents living in the city itself rated their government as "fair" or "poor." That was the high point—from 2017 through 2019, 70 percent or more did so. "Excellent" ratings managed to reach only 6 percent, and only in 2019.

Although there is a certain macabre charm in the depth of Atlantans' shared scorn for their government, we do see some variation within the overall dissatisfaction. Figure 3.6 arrays the 2019 responses of "poor" from metro residents, ordered from most to least dissatisfied by various characteristics.

Differences between contiguous responses are small. They were similar, however, in the previous three years, and the overall pattern reveals the impact of various dimensions of inequality. Poor metro Atlantans were twice as dissatisfied as the well-off; Blacks were one and a half times as dissatisfied as Whites; and women and the young were slightly more dissatisfied than men and older respondents, respectively. Despite scholars' attention to gentrification, long-term residents do not differ from newcomers in dissatisfaction with local government. Overall, the results reinforce the Grid logic, albeit one dimension at a time: income matters most, but poor young Black women who live south of the interstate see their government as much less responsive than do older, affluent White men and Latinos who live in the metro area's north.

This analysis remains incomplete for the purposes of *Race/Class Conflict and Urban Financial Threat* because it examines one axis at a time. However, Metro Atlanta Speaks data can be arrayed through the lens of the interactive race/class Grid metaphor; it survives, though with some limitations, in the items I was able to have analyzed.

Assuming that Whites will always be slightly advantaged compared with non-Whites, even if they are in roughly the same class position, a perfect Grid would show the distribution of opinions seen in the lefthand panels of figures 3.7 and 3.8 (each labeled Model Grid). With the model grid in mind, consider first the Metro Atlanta Speaks request for predictions about metro-area living conditions over the next few years. The right-hand panel of figure 3.7 shows grids of expectations in 2017 of both "better" and "worse" conditions (I exclude responses of "about the same"; all results in this section are for residents of the city of Atlanta only).

In a perfect Grid, affluent Whites would be the most positive about the region's future, and affluent Blacks would be close behind, followed at some distance by poor Whites and Latinos, then, most distantly, by poor Blacks. The opposite order would obtain for pessimism: the cell with poor Blacks would show the highest proportion of pessimists, followed by poor Whites and Latinos, then affluent Blacks, and finally affluent Whites. Figure 3.7 comes close to both patterns. Poor Blacks are the least optimistic and almost the most pessimistic. Well-off Blacks are the most optimistic and tied with affluent Whites for least pessimistic. Overall, class matters as much as race ("better future") or more than race ("worse future") in Atlantans' predictions for their region.

These results do not hold for 2018; in fact, they are almost reversed. For optimism, the Grid returns in 2019, with affluent Blacks most likely

**Figure 3.6   Local Government Responsiveness Is "Poor,"
Metro Atlanta Speaks, 2019**

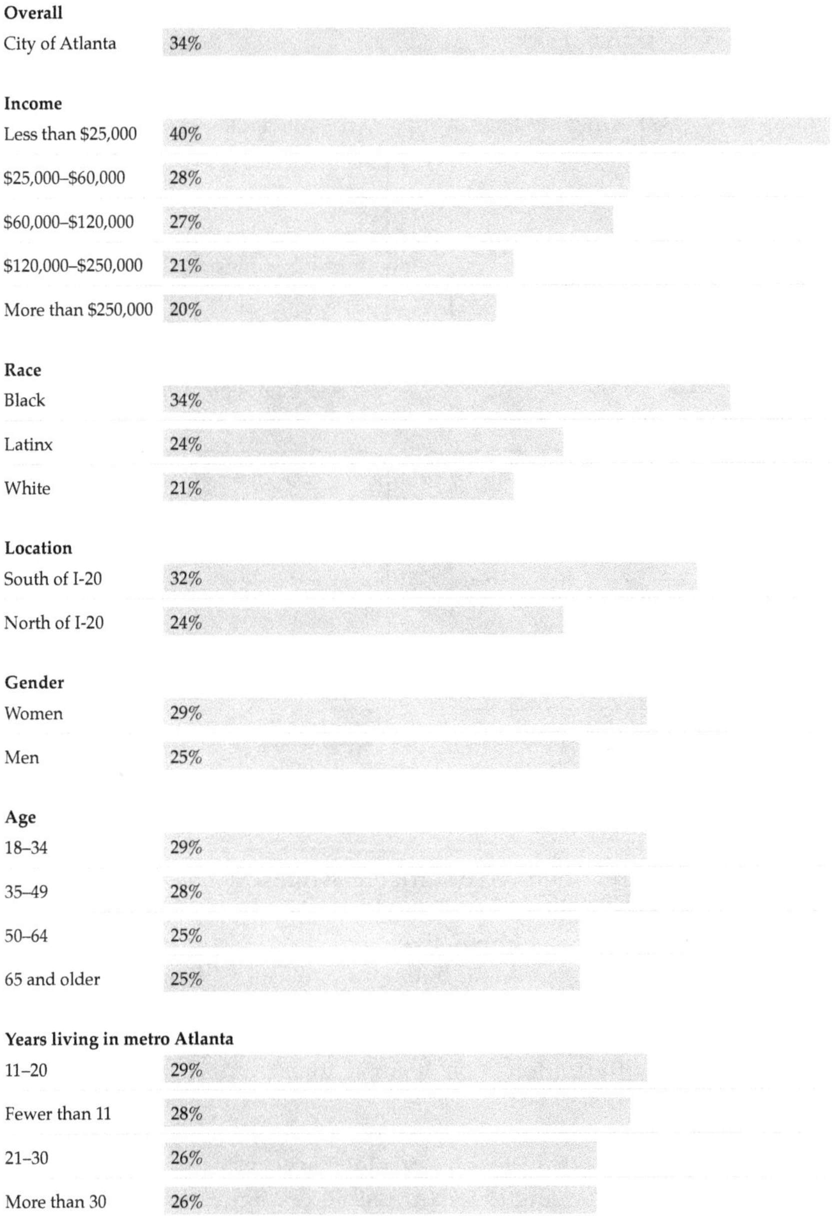

Overall
City of Atlanta   34%

Income
Less than $25,000   40%

$25,000–$60,000   28%

$60,000–$120,000   27%

$120,000–$250,000   21%

More than $250,000   20%

Race
Black   34%

Latinx   24%

White   21%

Location
South of I-20   32%

North of I-20   24%

Gender
Women   29%

Men   25%

Age
18–34   29%

35–49   28%

50–64   25%

65 and older   25%

Years living in metro Atlanta
11–20   29%

Fewer than 11   28%

21–30   26%

More than 30   26%

Source: Author's derivation from Ghimire 2019.
Note: Within each category, results are ordered from most to least agreement that government responsiveness is "poor."

Figure 3.7   Grid of Expectations for Metro Atlanta's Future, Metro Atlanta Speaks, 2017

Model Grid:
high values = optimism or approval

Affluent Whites 60%	Affluent Blacks 50%
Poor Whites and Hispanics 30%	Poor Blacks 20%

Expectations for Atlanta's Future:
"Better"

Affluent Whites 38%	Affluent Blacks 41%
Poor Whites and Hispanics 36%	Poor Blacks 33%

Model Grid:
high values = pessimism or disapproval

Affluent Whites 20%	Affluent Blacks 30%
Poor Whites and Hispanics 50%	Poor Blacks 60%

Expectations for Atlanta's Future:
"Worse"

Affluent Whites 18%	Affluent Blacks 18%
Poor Whites and Hispanics 34%	Poor Blacks 30%

Source: Author's calculations from Atlanta Regional Commission 2017.

to say "better future," followed by affluent Whites, then poor Blacks, and finally poor Whites and Latinos. There is no clear pattern for pessimism in 2019. In short, we see an interactive race/class Grid of public opinion in three of six configurations ("better future" and "worse future" in 2017, and "better future" in 2019), with no consistent rival pattern for the other three.[81] Given the small sample sizes and the need for a four-part array for each configuration to be deemed correct, this is a fairly strong set of results.

The other evaluative item in Metro Atlanta Speaks regards local government responsiveness to citizens' needs. The survey results also reveal three Grid patterns among the six possible configurations. Figure 3.8 shows the two most compelling—in this case, respondents' choice of "poor responsiveness" in both 2017 and 2018.

Figure 3.8   Grid of Judgments That Local Government Responsiveness Is "Poor," Metro Atlanta Speaks, 2017 and 2018

Local Government Responsiveness: "Poor," 2017

Affluent Whites 33%	Affluent Blacks 21%
Poor Whites and Hispanics 42%	Poor Blacks 37%

Model Grid: high values = pessimism or disapproval

Affluent Whites 20%	Affluent Blacks 30%
Poor Whites and Hispanics 50%	Poor Blacks 60%

Local Government Responsiveness: "Poor," 2018

Affluent Whites 23%	Affluent Blacks 16%
Poor Whites and Hispanics 32%	Poor Blacks 39%

Source: Author's calculations from Atlanta Regional Commission 2017, 2018.

A model Grid for criticism of Atlanta's governance has some ambiguity. Within a given class, Whites *or* Blacks might be most critical, depending on whether Blacks are disillusioned by inadequate Black political leaders more than Whites are disparaging of them. For the sake of simplicity, I offer the same Model Grid in figure 3.8 as in figure 3.7—that is, I assume that affluent Whites are marginally more gratified than are affluent Blacks, and that poor Blacks are marginally *less* gratified than are poor Whites and Latinos. But the opposite configuration across each row of the Grid seems plausible.

Figure 3.8 fits within that slightly ambiguous framing. Lower-income residents are always more critical than higher-income residents, regardless of race. The class disparity in disapproval is greater among Blacks than among Whites; well-off Blacks are relatively protective of local public officials. In fact, in three of the four horizontal comparisons, Blacks are less critical than are same-class Whites. Overall, class matters in same-race comparisons, and race matters in (most) same-class comparisons.

A Grid pattern does not hold for "poor" government responsiveness in 2019 or favorable views of government responsiveness in 2017 and 2018.[82] However, it clearly obtains for positive views in 2019. The three results without a Grid pattern are inconsistent with each other. I again conclude that a Grid better characterizes Atlantans' views of government responsiveness than does any other configuration, though ambiguity remains in judging whether we should expect affluent Blacks or Whites to be more disaffected.

Class-in-Group

Subsample sizes in the Metro Atlanta Speaks surveys are too small for the pattern of results from the city to be more than provisional. Our Class-in-Group (CIG) survey, however, includes enough respondents that its evidence on metro-area Americans' views are reliable. The relevant CIG items focus on gentrification, though the term itself never appears in the survey. It asks respondents how housing redevelopment affects the community as a whole, people like themselves, well-off residents, and poor residents. Figure 3.9 provides crosstab results for each item.[83]

Although the same proportions of Whites and Blacks or Latinos anticipated benefits from housing redevelopment for people like themselves, a higher proportion of Whites expected the community, well-off residents, and poor residents all to benefit. That shows differences by race.[84] Next, in ten out of twelve instances, better-off members of each race or ethnicity are more sanguine about the benefits of redevelopment than are their worse-off counterparts. (In the remaining two instances, high- and low-income members of a given group were tied.) That shows differences by class within race. Finally, almost three-fourths of well-off Blacks and Whites agreed that a community as a whole benefits from gentrification; in contrast, barely one-quarter of poor Blacks and Whites, and even fewer poor Latinos, believed that people like themselves would benefit. That contrast between optimism for the community among both affluent Blacks and Whites and pessimism for themselves and their peers among both poor Blacks and Whites shows race/class interaction around the issue of gentrification.

CIG also enables determination of how race, class, and race/class interactions stand up to other potential explanations for evaluations of housing redevelopment. Using the same logic as for views on policing in the previous chapter, figure 3.10, panels A and B, show coefficient plots and marginal effects plots, respectively, with regard to gentrification's benefits for the community as a whole.

Figure 3.9   Housing Redevelopment Benefits Various Sets of Recipients, Class-in-Group Survey, 2016 (Percent of Metro-Area Respondents Agreeing)

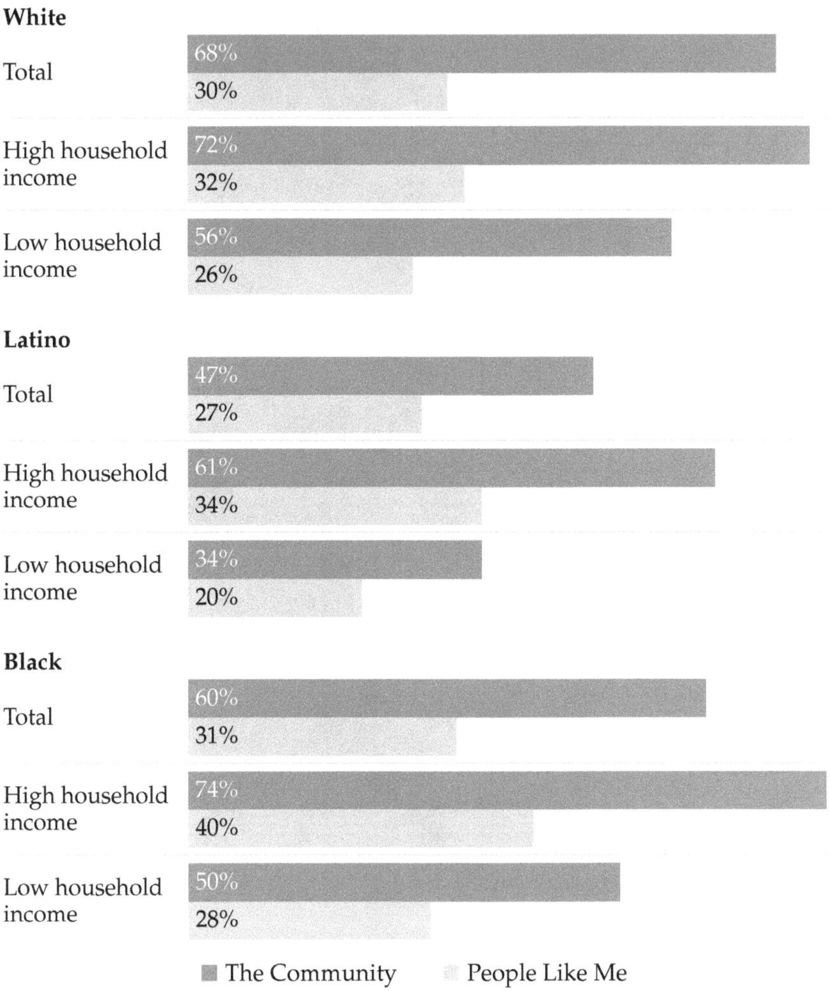

White

Total
68%
30%

High household income
72%
32%

Low household income
56%
26%

Latino

Total
47%
27%

High household income
61%
34%

Low household income
34%
20%

Black

Total
60%
31%

High household income
74%
40%

Low household income
50%
28%

■ The Community   People Like Me

(*Figure continues on page 92.*)

Figure 3.9   *Continued*

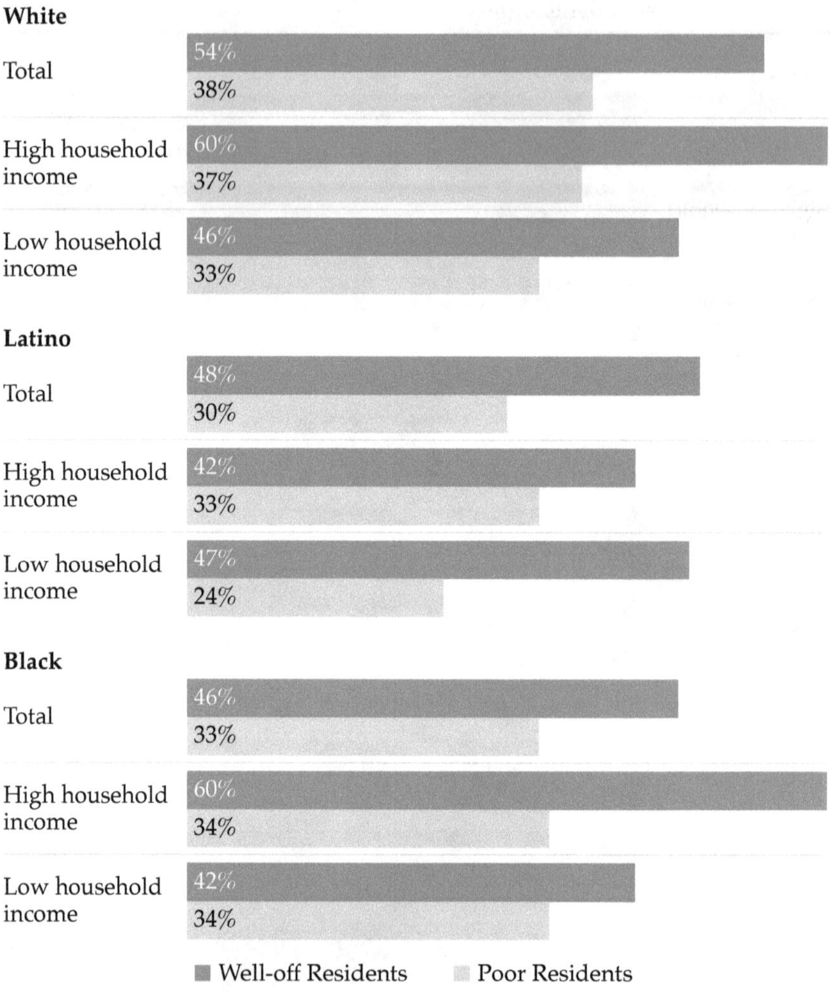

White

Total
54%
38%

High household income
60%
37%

Low household income
46%
33%

Latino

Total
48%
30%

High household income
42%
33%

Low household income
47%
24%

Black

Total
46%
33%

High household income
60%
34%

Low household income
42%
34%

■ Well-off Residents   ■ Poor Residents

Source: Author's calculations from 2016 CIG survey.

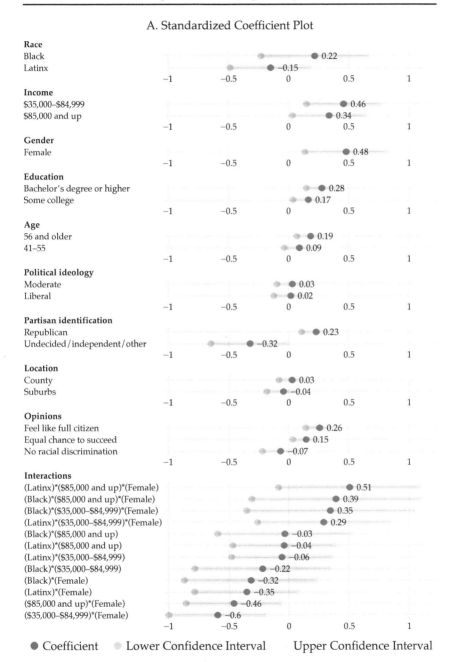

A. Standardized Coefficient Plot

Race
Black — 0.22
Latinx — −0.15

Income
$35,000–$84,999 — 0.46
$85,000 and up — 0.34

Gender
Female — 0.48

Education
Bachelor's degree or higher — 0.28
Some college — 0.17

Age
56 and older — 0.19
41–55 — 0.09

Political ideology
Moderate — 0.03
Liberal — 0.02

Partisan identification
Republican — 0.23
Undecided/independent/other — −0.32

Location
County — 0.03
Suburbs — −0.04

Opinions
Feel like full citizen — 0.26
Equal chance to succeed — 0.15
No racial discrimination — −0.07

Interactions
(Latinx)*($85,000 and up)*(Female) — 0.51
(Black)*($85,000 and up)*(Female) — 0.39
(Black)*($35,000–$84,999)*(Female) — 0.35
(Latinx)*($35,000–$84,999)*(Female) — 0.29
(Black)*($85,000 and up) — −0.03
(Latinx)*($85,000 and up) — −0.04
(Latinx)*($35,000–$84,999) — −0.06
(Black)*($35,000–$84,999) — −0.22
(Black)*(Female) — −0.32
(Latinx)*(Female) — −0.35
($85,000 and up)*(Female) — −0.46
($35,000–$84,999)*(Female) — −0.6

● Coefficient   ● Lower Confidence Interval   Upper Confidence Interval

Source: Author's analysis of 2016 CIG survey.
Notes: Excluded variables: for race, White; for income, $0 to $34,999; for gender, male; for
education, high school or less; for age, eighteen to thirty; for political ideology, Republican;
for partisan identification, Democrat; for location, center city. Results for each variable in
Opinions are independent measures of agreement.

(*Figure continues on page 94.*)

Figure 3.10   *Continued*

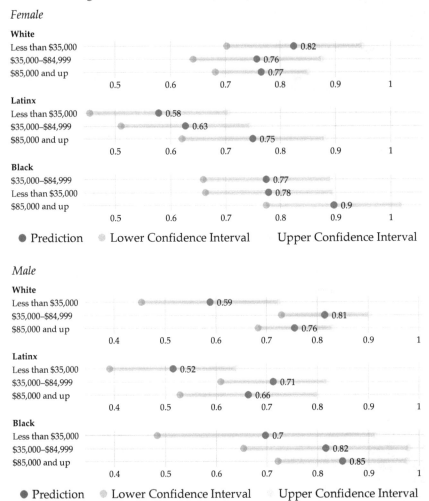

B. Marginal Effects Plot of Race, Class, and Gender Interactions

Source: Author's calculations from 2016 CIG survey.

As panel A shows, women, well-educated or older respondents, and Republicans were significantly more likely to see collective benefits from housing redevelopment than were men, less-educated or younger respondents, and Democrats, when other characteristics are controlled. Respondents who saw themselves as rights-bearing citizens and those who perceived equal chances to succeed were also more likely to perceive community benefits from gentrification. The views of Latinos and Blacks were not significantly different in a statistical sense from the views of Whites; surprisingly, the evidence suggests that, if we control for other characteristics, Blacks are the group *most* sanguine about gentrification. The results in both panels A and B suggest that high-income Latinas and Black women were especially likely to see community benefits, while panel B shows that poor White, Latino, and possibly Black men were less likely to see such benefits than were higher-income members of their respective groups.

The other three CIG items on housing development—benefits to "people like me," well-off residents, or poor residents—show broadly similar results (for details, see appendix table D.2). Respondents with higher levels of formal education, Republicans and independents, or those who lived outside the metro area's central city were significantly more likely to see gentrification as beneficial in at least one of these measures; so were those, in one item each, who saw themselves as rights-bearing citizens or who perceived equality of opportunity. Once controls are included, there are no statistically significant differences by race, ethnicity, income, or gender alone, and almost no significant differences across the twelve interaction variables in each item. In nonstatistical terms, we can conclude from this exercise that race or ethnicity, income, and their interactions are thoroughly entwined with education, perceptions and attitudes, and political views. The Grid's race/class interaction is more a structural feature of BeltLine policy and politics than a portrayal of public views about it.

Denouement: The Four Questions, and the Puzzle of *Race/Class Conflict and Urban Financial Threat*

The BeltLine invites superlatives. "No redevelopment project . . . arguably in the country has been more transformative than the Atlanta BeltLine."[85] The BeltLine is an "'emerald necklace' . . . [that] could rejuvenate the heart and soul of the city. . . . The battle over the BeltLine is a matter of life and death: Atlanta could emerge as a truly great city—or it could fall back into congested mediocrity."[86] Whether the BeltLine will live up to that promise or disintegrate into "rampant, racialized gentrification and displacement" is not yet clear, since completion is years away, many choices remain to be made, and its long-term impact will not solidify for decades.[87]

Housing policy is the most politically salient issue arising from BeltLine construction—and also, not coincidentally, one of the outcomes that could do the most to change, or reinforce, Atlanta's race/class inequality. Although a sympathetic White developer assured us in 2017 that "there is more attention to the issue of affordable housing, in like logarithmic difference, than we have ever seen before," *Realtor* magazine reported five years later that "Atlanta looks to be the housing market in the U.S. with the most potential for growth in the new year."[88] The article was not, one can reasonably infer, referring to affordable or low-income housing.

Booming construction is not intrinsically antithetical to fair treatment of people displaced by rising housing costs. It can even benefit struggling neighborhoods. Greer, for example, is developing a model of "cooperative growth" aimed at creating shared gains between neighborhoods to which newcomers are moving and those to which displaced Atlantans are moving. But even she is not notably optimistic: in the face of substantial indifference, "it is unclear if there is a lack of concern for those displaced residents, or lack of concern to address the underlying effects of gentrification on a community."[89]

Since *Race/Class Conflict and Urban Financial Threat* uses the BeltLine and its impacts as a case to develop a broader set of theoretical concerns, I refrain from following up on that uncertainty or on gentrification itself. What matters here is that the BeltLine epitomizes a different form of race/class conflict from that of New York's SQF. The four questions for judging the impact of race and class on a policy issue and its associated politics again enable us to address the book's central puzzle: *When* does race/class inequality sit at the core of a policy issue? *How* is it manifested? And *why*—if it is not at the core—is some alternative force more important?

Is the policy intended to affect the city's structure of race, class, or race/class inequality? Yes, in part. Among the goals that first motivated BeltLine leaders were providing affordable housing and expanding public transit. Other goals, from environmental cleanup to bicycle paths, tend to be associated mainly with the desires of middle- and upper-income Atlantans, but they need not contradict the equality-seeking goals.

Is implementation intended to, or does it in fact, affect race, class, or race/class inequality? Yes, in both directions. Affordable housing is mandated, some has been built, and more is planned. Significant levels of public transit may, at last, move beyond aspiration and planning. The BeltLine promotes inclusion and accessibility; poor people of color can enjoy bicycle trails or use them to commute to work, and everyone benefits from environmental cleanup and green space. But implementation also enables dramatic rises in housing costs and facilitates displacement of legacy residents by better-off newcomers who are less likely than current Atlantans to be Black.

Are engaged actors consensually identifiable by race and/or class, or do they consistently invoke race/class categories? Yes. All parties involved are acutely attentive to race/class inequality; it is hard to get a few people to focus on anything else. Public-facing organizations and public agencies are carefully constructed to be racially balanced and sometimes to include people of different economic statuses. Most actors are sophisticated in considering how even facially neutral actions can affect racial balance or the trajectory of inequality. Class inequality is often recognized and deplored but less consistently curated.

Are policy recipients who consistently gain or lose, or policy outcomes that consistently affect city residents, consensually identifiable by race and/or class? It depends on what we measure. Newcomers, developers, political entrepreneurs, and commercial interests, who are disproportionately nonpoor Whites, are the clearest gainers; displaced residents, who are disproportionately poor Blacks, are the clearest losers. But even many of the disadvantaged benefit from the influx of jobs, tax revenues, neighbors, and commerce, as well as from the BeltLine itself. That is, newcomers both threaten displacement and demand improved schools, better health care, environmental amenities, and crime control.[90]

Thus, answers to the four questions for Atlanta's BeltLine are more complex than for New York's SQF. In that case, my response to each question was "yes"; in this case, each "yes" requires a caveat or qualification. The "yes" answers are clear enough to resolve the puzzle's first layer: race/class inequality does indeed sit at the core of the BeltLine's construction and impact. But the shadings of the "yes" answers show that the resolution to the puzzle's second layer is not a simple, straightforward Target of race/class hierarchy; it is instead a more complicated Grid of race/class interaction. Answers to the four diagnostic questions for the BeltLine entail recognition that what improves the status of some people of color can worsen it for others. Put metaphorically, policy and political actions can increase the size of one or more cells of the Grid, but only by decreasing the size of others if the Grid is to retain its structural integrity. In short, *how* race/class inequality is manifested differs in important ways between New York's SQF and Atlanta's BeltLine.

Of course, I am far from the first to focus on the interaction of race and class in Atlanta; Clarence Stone's canonical *Regime Politics* set the terms for my own and many other scholars' research.[91] This chapter in part just updates his work, which emerges from a deceptively simple statement: "The concept of systemic power highlights how and why public officials are attracted to a partnership with business, and by extension it shows why other groups—Atlanta's black middle class, for example—might also seek political partnership with business."[92] "Systemic power" is closely related to the starting point of "a foundation of race/class inequality" from which *Race/Class Conflict and Urban Financial Threat* grew. In Atlanta, that inequality takes a distinct form: "If you're a minority," observed a Black clergyperson, "you can sit in the room if your class is high enough."

= Chapter 4 =

Race, Class, and Schooling: Charter Schools in Los Angeles

*If half the effort that has gone into the Charter School War had been
directed toward building the system's learning capacity, we would
have created real winners, both adults and students.*
—Charles Kerchner, 2017

*I think the race conversation, and frankly the class conversation,
has not been a huge part of the reform conversation here. . . .
It's about money.*
—White professor, 2017

Places that shrink are screwed.
—Christopher Berry, quoted in
The Economist 2024b, 17

"There's a larger question at hand here. It's like, 'Well, why aren't we working in partnership? Like, we really should be working based on a unified vision for all kids.' So I do see and hear of some of that happening. (*pauses*) I don't think I see it in my face all the time, so I can't elaborate on it too much." In an otherwise rather unmemorable interview, this Asian charter school teacher put her finger on exactly the issue that shapes race/class dynamics in the Los Angeles Unified School District (LAUSD). All participants in the district's battle over charter schools share this teacher's desire to work based on a unified vision for all kids, and most give at least lip service to working in partnership. Most policy recipients in almost all schools are similarly disadvantaged children of color living in similarly disadvantaged neighborhoods; they and their parents are largely indifferent to

https://doi.org/10.7758/ptkg1499.5767

the conflict. Almost all political and policy actors are committed to using public institutions to promote racial and social justice, economic equality, and societal transformation. Almost by definition, virtually everyone involved in the debate over charter schools believes that public schooling is a crucial route toward those goals. Almost all are left-of-center Democrats and public employees.

Nonetheless, this interviewee's halting admission that "I can't elaborate on it too much" because she so seldom saw teachers and schools working in partnership points to the conundrum of this narrative: why do people who share so many values, characteristics, contexts, clients, and jobs expend so much more of their energy in bitter contention than in efforts to work together to help the students they cherish? New York's SQF and even Atlanta's BeltLine development have seen their share of conflict, but neither case consistently manifests the equivalent of the "astonishing lack of civility in the war over our schools," as historian Jonathan Zimmerman puts it.[1]

As with New York's SQF and Atlanta's BeltLine, I first describe the policy's setting, recipients, and core goals. I then move to the more dynamic themes of implementation, political activity, the roles of media and organizations, and public opinion. I conclude by seeking to resolve the conundrum of bitter enmity among essentially similar protagonists. All of this contributes to resolving the puzzle of *Race/Class Conflict and Urban Financial Threat* by focusing attention on (spoiler alert) its third layer: *why* race/class inequality sometimes does not explain a policy issue and its politics. In this case, that inequality is superseded by an even more powerful force: "It's about money."

The explanatory metaphor is a political entity with Open Borders. L.A. Unified is a huge school district whose boundaries are both fixed in place and open to families' movement across them in search of a better life and preferred schools. The combination of constraint and choice certainly involves race and class; how could it be otherwise for public schools in a large American city? But neither race/class inequality nor dynastic feuds are responsible for what several interlocutors described as the modern version of Europe's endless and pointless Hundred Years' War. The driving force is the financial, and therefore political and institutional, threats entailed in border crossing.

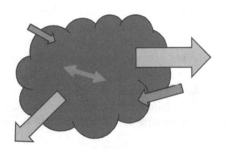

Figure 4.1   Geography of the Los Angeles Unified School District

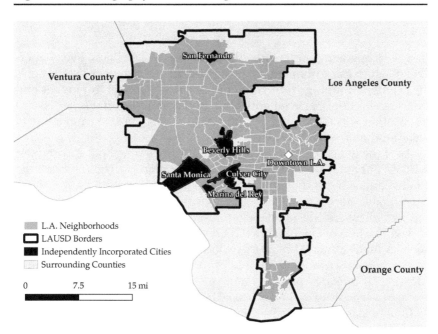

Source: Author's analysis. Shapefiles and geographic boundaries are from the U.S. Census TIGER/LINE shapefile repository.

Setting

The District

LAUSD is the second-largest American school district, encompassing almost all of the city of Los Angeles and all or part of twenty-five adjoining municipalities and unincorporated areas.[2] It encompasses 710 square miles, within which reside about 4.8 million people. The parts of Los Angeles County that are not included in LAUSD have seventy-five (or more, depending on how one counts) separate school systems. Figure 4.1 shows the boundaries of LAUSD in relation to the city of Los Angeles, independently incorporated cities, and surrounding counties.

This map makes a crucial point clear: the boundaries of the district, city, and district in relation to the city all make no systematic sense. Each entity and boundary line is idiosyncratic, established by a series of self-contained decisions starting midway through the 1800s. Later in this chapter, I examine the demographic characteristics of schools in these various entities; what matters now is to note both the entwinement of towns and cities, school district, and surrounding counties, and their mutual incoherence.

Policy Recipients

Schools

LAUSD's operating budget for 2022–2023 was $12.6 billion, over 70 percent of which came from the state.[3] The district operates over 1,400 schools and centers, ranging from conventional K-12 schools to magnet and multilevel schools, special education and home/hospital schools, and a few other specialized programs.[4] Schools range in size from a few to 2,500 students.

As of the winter of 2024, charter organizations run about 275 of those schools. Fifty-one are affiliated or dependent charters. Those schools are funded and run mostly like other LAUSD schools except that they have considerable autonomy in determining curricula and schedules and choosing staff members. Most of their employees belong to the teachers' union, United Teachers of Los Angeles (UTLA). Unlike most independent charter schools, many affiliated charters are located in relatively well-off sections of Los Angeles with relatively high proportions of Whites and Asians.[5] Most are far from downtown.[6] Figure 4.2 shows locations of the two types of charter schools in and near LAUSD.

In accordance with California law, the roughly 220 independent or autonomous charters are nonprofit organizations, approved and loosely overseen by LAUSD (or occasionally another agency) but run by their own volunteer boards. Some are stand-alone, while others are part of an organization, such as Green Dot Public Schools, which operates roughly twenty schools in greater Los Angeles. As figure 4.2 shows, they are mostly located in and around the city's urban core. Most funding comes from the state; independent charter schools also raise funds and receive donations from nonschool actors such as foundations. A 2018 California law forbade charter schools from operating as, or being operated by, a for-profit entity. So long as they conform to their chartered commitments, independent charters manage their own administrative expenses and control their educational choices and staff. Few teachers are UTLA members, although some belong to the California Teachers Association, of which UTLA is a member.

L.A. charter schools operate in a dense policy context. In 1992, California became the second state to authorize their creation and management. They have flourished, with over 1,300 schools enrolling about 12 percent of California's public school students as of 2022.[7] Los Angeles enrolls the largest number of charter school students in the United States (the National Alliance for Public Charter Schools counts about 160,000 by combining autonomous and affiliated charters) and is one of the top large districts in the proportion of students in charter schools—27 percent, according to the National Alliance.[8]

Figure 4.2   Location of District-Affiliated and Independent Charter Schools in Los Angeles County, 2019

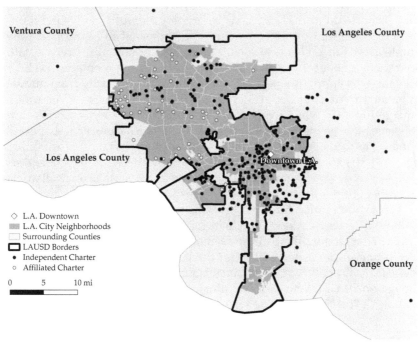

○ L.A. Downtown
▨ L.A. City Neighborhoods
☐ Surrounding Counties
▢ LAUSD Borders
● Independent Charter
○ Affiliated Charter

0   5   10 mi

Source: Author's replication from Stokes 2019, and Kyle Stokes's email to the author, May 6, 2024.

As LAUSD's website describes the legal status of charter schools, upon application, the Board of Education may approve a charter for up to five years. Any California resident may attend a charter school. Although most charters and some LAUSD schools engage in informational campaigns and direct outreach to recruit students, if the number of applicants is greater than the school can admit, admission is based on a public lottery. Charter schools may not be sectarian or a conversion of a private school; they may not discriminate or charge tuition; and they are expected to achieve a racial/ethnic balance that reflects the district's population.

As of 2021, the National Alliance for Public Charter Schools ranks California's charter law twentieth in the nation in incorporating the twenty-one elements of its model law for best practices. The most relevant of the elements here is the judgment that the state has "made notable strides in recent years to provide more equitable funding to public charter schools—although some work remains to be done."[9]

Teachers

The most prominent actor in LAUSD's activity around charter schools is the teachers' union, UTLA. LAUSD employs about twenty-five thousand teachers (out of about seventy-four thousand full- and part-time employees), but UTLA also includes certified non-administrative staff, so it reports about thirty-five thousand dues-paying members. UTLA's revenue was approximately $47 million in 2020, primarily from annual membership dues of about $1,100 for full-time members.[10] The union emerged in 1970 when over a dozen representative organizations consolidated; after an initial unsettled period, the union took its final shape and widened its focus. As UTLA summarizes its history, "With Prop[osition] 13 [in 1978], the source of school funding rapidly shifted to the state; thus UTLA became much more politically active at the state level as districts and other entities routinely vie for a slice of the budget pie."[11]

As this observation hints, UTLA is the most powerful actor within the California Teachers' Association, which is itself one of the most powerful actors in the predominantly intra-Democratic politics of state governance. One observer describes UTLA as "the largest, most complicated, and, these days, most divisive educational labor machine in the state—possibly the nation."[12] UTLA not only dominates the educational arena but also occupies a "privileged position in the pantheon of California's labor organizations." By the 1990s, "its rising power and financial strength since the 1970s had come to eclipse the interests of other worker associations."[13] And UTLA's influence is not confined to labor politics. One interview subject, a Latina civic association member, spelled out to us East Coast naïfs how California politics works. "I want to be clear with you," she said. The California and Los Angeles teachers' unions "are the biggest player in politics in California. The biggest. Just to give you an idea of the dynamics around this, the Democratic Party and L.A. County Dems . . . host all of their Democratic Party meetings at the UTLA building. Every single one. So every endorsement meeting happens there, every single vote on propositions and city elections, every single meeting happens at that UTLA building."[14]

UTLA's resources and power fell, then rose, over the past decade. Membership declined from forty-five thousand in 2008 to thirty-three thousand in 2018, after the Supreme Court invalidated the right of public-sector unions to charge fees to nonmembers.[15] Revenues nonetheless increased because of a 33 percent increase in dues in 2016. Members accepted the large increase so that, as the UTLA secretary explained, "we could invest in organizing to become a fighting union."[16] It attained that goal, as I discuss later in this chapter.

As figure 4.3 shows, teachers in independent charter schools and traditional district schools have similar racial-ethnic profiles. Both differ from teachers in affiliated charter schools, in which smaller proportions

Figure 4.3   LAUSD Teachers' Race or Ethnicity, 2018–2019

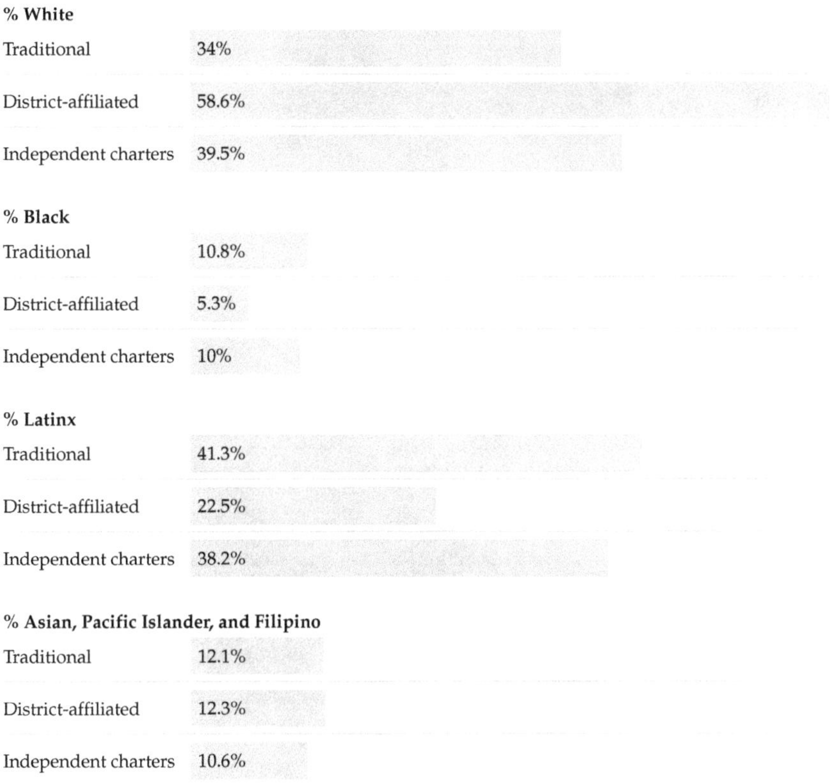

% White

Traditional	34%
District-affiliated	58.6%
Independent charters	39.5%

% Black

Traditional	10.8%
District-affiliated	5.3%
Independent charters	10%

% Latinx

Traditional	41.3%
District-affiliated	22.5%
Independent charters	38.2%

% Asian, Pacific Islander, and Filipino

Traditional	12.1%
District-affiliated	12.3%
Independent charters	10.6%

Source: Author's derivation from California Department of Education 2018–2019.
Note: I report data from 2018–2019 so as not to rely on incomplete data collected during the COVID-19 pandemic. The figure standardizes results by using the proportion of substantive responses for each group as the denominator.

of teachers are Hispanic or Black, and a larger proportion are White. In all three types of schools, a greater share of teachers are White and a smaller share are Latino compared to the shares of White and Latino students (compare figures 4.3 and 4.6).

Students

LAUSD traditional schools enrolled about 422,000 K-12 students in 2022–2023.[17] That represents a steady enrollment decline resulting from a combination of slowing birth rates, rising charter enrollment, the city's population loss due mainly to housing costs, and "student melt" during the COVID-19 shutdown. Enrollment in independent charter schools,

Figure 4.4   LAUSD Enrollment in Independent Charter and Noncharter Schools, 2001–2022 (in Thousands)

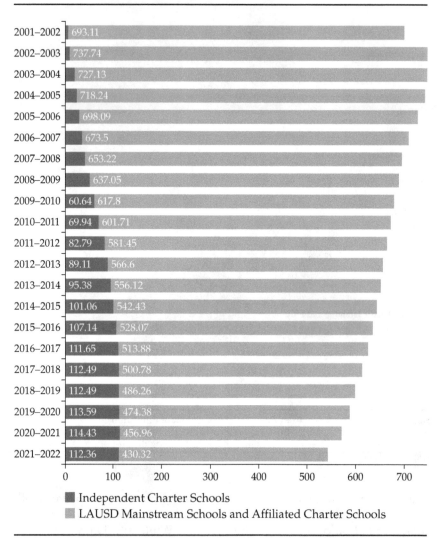

Source: Author's adaptation of Stokes 2020; Kyle Stokes's emails to the author, May 6, 2024.

however, is holding its own. Figure 4.4 displays the symmetrical independent charter school increase and traditional school decrease in enrollment over the past two decades—what might be understood as internal migration across within-district borders.[18] Enrollment in 2022–2023, according to investigative journalist Kyle Stokes's most recent figures, continues that trend.[19]

Figure 4.5   Protesting Proposed School Closure in LAUSD, 2022

Figure 4.4 makes apparent the three trajectories that largely define the financial—and therefore political, individual, and institutional—threat posed by LAUSD's Open Borders. First, enrollment in traditional public schools has declined from its 2002–2003 peak of 738,000 students and is projected to decline by tens of thousands more students over the next decade. Second, after rapid initial growth, the proportion of LAUSD students in independent charter schools is steady or slightly rising. Third, the proportion of LAUSD students in district schools has therefore dropped to just over half of its 2002–2003 high point.

The district is beginning to hint to parents that schools with drastic enrollment declines are in line to be considered for possible closure. The multiple qualifiers in that sentence are intentional: the then-new superintendent, Alberto Carvalho, broached the subject with great delicacy in March 2022: "Two years from now, we need to consider the capacity of schools, enrollment, and make decisions in the way we staff schools."[20] That was enough to generate anger and fear, as figure 4.5 suggests.

In this fraught context, observers as well as participants disagree on whether there are too few or too many charter schools. By one analysis of several years ago, "40,000 students are on charter school waiting lists."[21] But others see charter schools as wastefully competing with each other and with district schools for increasingly scarce students; thus, a school board member concludes that "if you want to put another charter school around a high school that's already surrounded by too many charter schools and is underperforming, . . . that is not in the best interest of serving the community. It isn't even in the best interest of other charter schools, much less LAUSD."[22]

Among many other points, disputants disagree on the characteristics of students in the different sectors. Supporters of mainstream schools charge that charter schools unfairly recruit students with the most motivated and organized parents, thus depriving traditional schools of the participants most likely to help improve education for all students. Demographic data do not address that claim. But they can address the related charge that independent charter schools recruit less disadvantaged students, thereby leaving the more disadvantaged to district schools that must take all comers. Figure 4.6 shows student characteristics separately for traditional district schools, affiliated charter schools, and independent charter schools. Panel A shows racial-ethnic characteristics, panel B shows indicators suggesting a need for intensive school resources, and panel C shows educational attainment and achievement.

Students in traditional schools and independent charter schools have very similar profiles: both are more likely to be Black or Latino/a, and to be more disadvantaged, than are students in affiliated charters. As panel A shows, three-quarters of students in both independent charters and traditional schools are Latino. Fewer than one-tenth in both sets of schools identify as Black, White, or Asian/Pacific Islander/Filipino. Conversely, fewer than two-fifths of students in affiliated charters are Latino; affiliated charter schools have at least four times as many White students, at least three times as many Asian students, and half as many Latino students as the other two types of schools have.

Panel B shows students' educational complexities. Eighty percent of independent charter school students, and a slightly higher share of district school students, are poor by state standards.[23] Affiliated charters teach roughly half as many poor students.[24] Just over one-fifth of both district and independent charter students are English language learners; in what is now a familiar pattern, half as many students in affiliated charters know English as a second language. There are no substantial differences across school categories in the proportions of students with a disability, although these data do not distinguish with regard to the degree or kind of disability.

Panel C shows that students in both types of charters are more likely to graduate from high school than are students in traditional schools. Surprisingly, independent charter students are much more likely than affiliated charter students (as well as those in district schools) to meet the University of California and California State University standards

**Figure 4.6   Comparing Students in Traditional LAUSD Schools, Affiliated
Charter Schools, and Independent Charter Schools, 2021–2022**

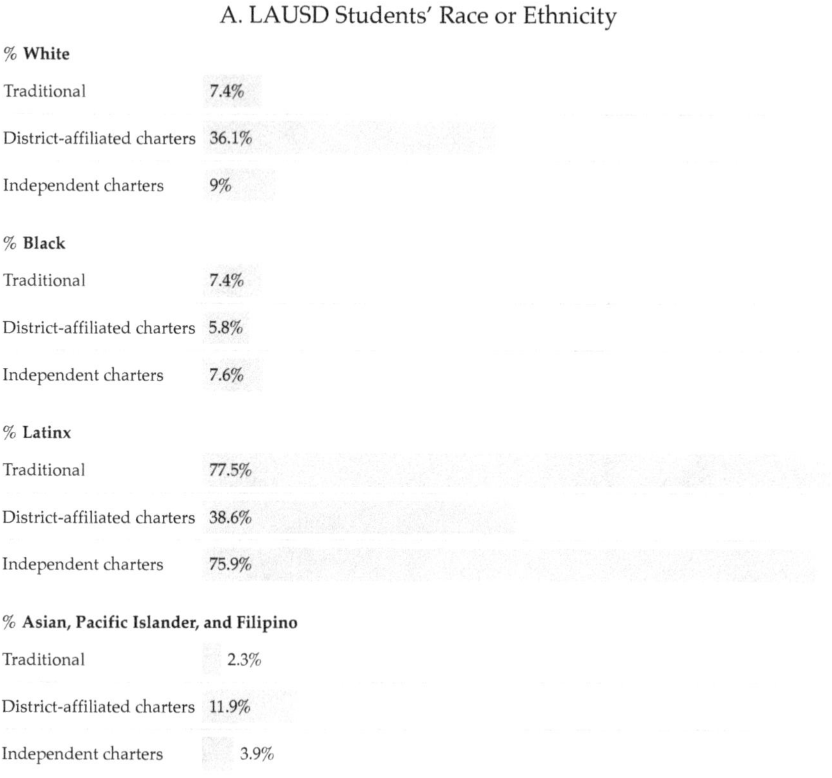

A. LAUSD Students' Race or Ethnicity

% White

Traditional   7.4%

District-affiliated charters   36.1%

Independent charters   9%

% Black

Traditional   7.4%

District-affiliated charters   5.8%

Independent charters   7.6%

% Latinx

Traditional   77.5%

District-affiliated charters   38.6%

Independent charters   75.9%

% Asian, Pacific Islander, and Filipino

Traditional   2.3%

District-affiliated charters   11.9%

Independent charters   3.9%

Sources: Author's derivation from California Department of Education 2023a; LAUSD
Unified 2023.
Notes: In 2021–2022, about 8 percent of students in affiliated charters, 3 percent in
independent charters, and 2 percent in traditional schools were reported as American
Indian or Alaska Native, reported as two or more races, or were not reported. I report
results for 2021–2022 rather than 2022–2023 because affiliated charters did not report about
40 percent of students' race or ethnicity in 2022–2023.

(*Figure continues on page 110.*)

of achievement that make them eligible to enroll in California's systems
of higher education. I have no good explanation for the relatively weak
achievement of the more advantaged affiliated charter students.[25]

Although reams of research seek to measure and explain differences
between mainstream and charter school students' outcomes, that is not my
issue in *Race/Class Conflict and Urban Financial Threat*.[26] Instead, figure 4.6
yields two points more important for my purposes. First, most LAUSD
students in both independent charter and traditional public schools are

Figure 4.6   *Continued*

B. LAUSD Students, Characterized by Special Circumstances or Needs

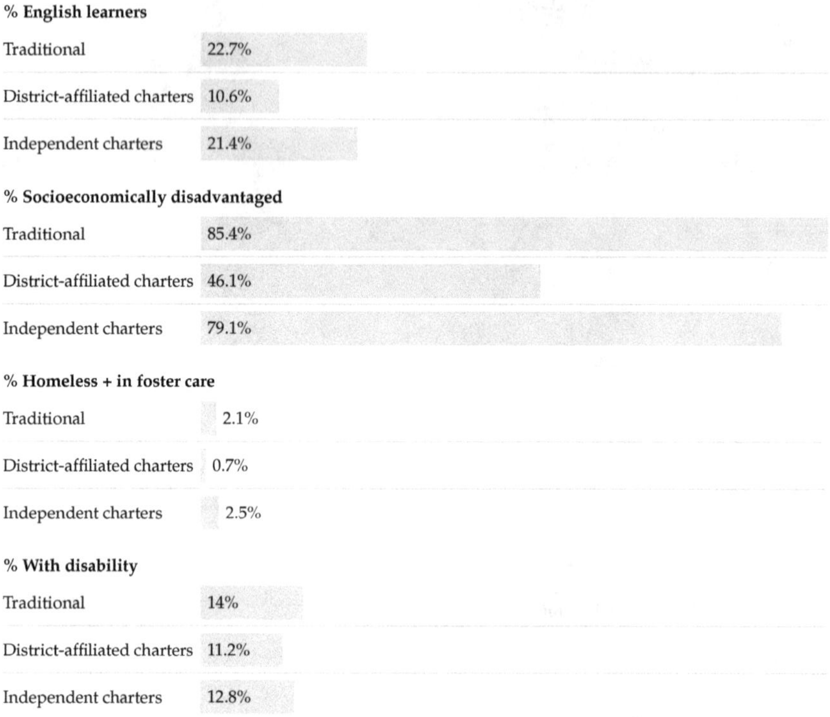

% English learners

Traditional	22.7%
District-affiliated charters	10.6%
Independent charters	21.4%

% Socioeconomically disadvantaged

Traditional	85.4%
District-affiliated charters	46.1%
Independent charters	79.1%

% Homeless + in foster care

Traditional	2.1%
District-affiliated charters	0.7%
Independent charters	2.5%

% With disability

Traditional	14%
District-affiliated charters	11.2%
Independent charters	12.8%

Sources: Author's derivation from California Department of Education 2023b; LAUSD 2023.

C. LAUSD Student Attainment and Achievement

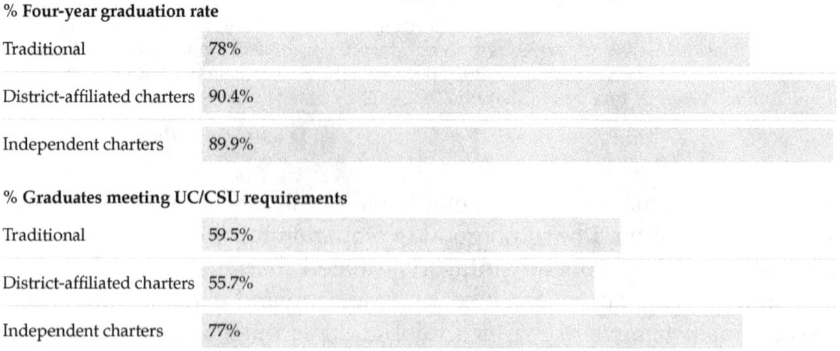

% Four-year graduation rate

Traditional	78%
District-affiliated charters	90.4%
Independent charters	89.9%

% Graduates meeting UC/CSU requirements

Traditional	59.5%
District-affiliated charters	55.7%
Independent charters	77%

Source: Author's derivation from California Department of Education 2022; LAUSD 2023.
Note: I use 2018–2019 for outcome measures because, in response to COVID-19, both California law and district regulations eased criteria for graduation and University of California/California State University (UC/CSU) requirements from 2020 through 2022.

multiply disadvantaged; to a first approximation, independent charter and traditional schools teach the same type of students. In contrast, affiliated Los Angeles charter schools must be understood as distinct from independent charters; though bearing the same category label, they are very different enterprises. Second, these data give no indication that independent charter school students are easier or less expensive to teach than are traditional school students, although we lack systematic qualitative evidence that could test that assertion.

The only indicator shown so far that could explain the astonishing lack of civility in the war over our schools lies in the enrollment changes resulting from the district's internal and external Open Borders. But perhaps there are other causes as well, such as differing ideological commitments embedded in the goals of public schooling.

Policy Goals

Broadly speaking, Los Angeles charter schools and mainstream schools are aiming at the same outcome, ostensibly shared by all other public schools: enabling all students to learn as much as possible and to attain the credentials needed to move toward successful adulthood. Beyond that aim, both traditional and charter schools cherish deep societal ambitions. UTLA is committed to a set of social changes that it sees as essential for successful teaching and learning; as UTLA's then-president Alex Caputo-Pearl put it in 2014, "We didn't want to be just a narrowly focused trade union."[27] His successor, Cecily Myart-Cruz, has developed his vision in considerable detail. UTLA released a seventeen-page statement in July 2020 that endorsed not reopening schools after the COVID-19 pandemic until the school district addressed "the deep equity and justice challenges arising from our profoundly racist, intensely unequal society." Because "the United States has chosen to prioritize profits over people, . . . this document outlines the equity lens that we must use to view both today's emergency and tomorrow's recovery."[28]

The equity lens includes elements of conventionally defined schooling: "no standardized testing infringing on instructional time," curriculum reform, and full federal funding of Title I of the Elementary and Secondary Education Act (financial assistance to local districts for low-income students) and of the Individuals with Disabilities Education Act. The statement's scope then widens in a call for local polities to "set the precedent for more progressive moves at the state and national level." Such moves include paid leave to enable parents to care for sick children, defunding the police, housing security for all low-income residents, paid sick leave for all business employees, and financial support for undocumented families. State policymakers should reassess corporate property taxes and institute both a wealth tax and a millionaire tax. Essential federal policies include, but are not limited to, Medicare for All. Most relevant here is the demand for a charter moratorium, since "privately operated, publicly funded charter schools drain resources from district schools."[29]

The UTLA statement closes by observing that "when 'normal' means deep race and class fissures . . . going back to normal is not an option."[30] In an interview, Myart-Cruz made the implied message explicit: "Are there broader issues at play? Yes, there are. Education is political."[31] Myart-Cruz won a second three-year term as UTLA president in 2023, with three-quarters of the votes from union members who participated in the election.

Myart-Cruz is looking for an argument, but she will not find one among many proponents of independent charter schools in Los Angeles. They frequently express the same view that overthrowing societal hierarchy is necessary for student success. As one Latina activist we interviewed phrased it, "Our entrance into educational justice issues was, 'How do we transform our community and help in, not only poverty, but the criminalization of young people, and the pipeline of jail to prison?' . . . We come at the question of how you improve education in terms of racial justice and 'How do you improve the quality of education to open up access, to ensure equity?'" An advocacy group that runs two charter schools similarly describes its purpose as "break[ing] century-old cycles of oppression, violence and poverty for students, their families, and communities. We believe education can chisel away at racism by teaching diverse histories and perspectives and by disrupting a predominantly white male perspective that has excluded and actively erased the voices and contributions of people of color."[32]

Like the goals of teachers' unions, charter proponents' goals have evolved. Charter schools were first envisioned as "test kitchens of the public education system. . . . The original notion was that charters would launch small-scale experiments—and that larger, less-nimble districts could learn from charters and take their experiments to scale."[33] But antipathy to mainstream schooling increased to the point where "we grew the charter school movement as a conscious movement of dismemberment."[34] Ambition expanded from pedagogical reform to the view that "our students are going to commit to uplift our communities, now and forever," in the words of an Asian charter school teacher. By now, as one Latina charter founder concluded, "We call ourselves a movement"—with the slogans and rallies associated with such a framing. After an LAUSD board member reportedly compared California's policy of co-locating independent charter schools in district schools with extra space to a "Cancer that metastasizes," for example, charter parents and supporters printed posters and T-shirts stating, "Our kids are not a cancer." As figure 4.7 shows, protests at board meetings or district headquarters also use signs to insist that "Charter schools are helping our children."[35]

Despite these and many similar statements, actors on both sides of the charter divide mistrust their counterparts' supposed commitment to

Figure 4.7   Rally of Independent Charter School Supporters, 2023

Source: Photo by Christina House/*Los Angeles Times* via Getty Images. Reprinted with permission.

social justice or even education. A White charter school leader described a recent conversation with an "LAUSD official" who said, "'You know a 'kids first' agenda does not mean 'kids only.' . . . It's an employment, it's jobs for the union, it is dollars to keep the bureaucracy moving, . . . it's OPEB [other post-employment benefits], it's post-employment retirement benefits." Another interview subject echoed this remark; referring to UTLA, this Latino charter school leader said, "They're an institution. They're a business. They need to stay in business, and what keeps them in business are teachers, and the less students that LAUSD has, the less students they [the teachers' union] have, and that has fiscal implications in their business model." Cynics might point to UTLA's recruitment website, which lists "the issues educators care about." Three of the five items are teacher benefits (pay, health care, and retirement; increased staffing; and working conditions and professional rights).[36] Contract and strike demands also mingle educational reforms with benefits for union members (see figure 4.8).[37]

UTLA returns the favor: it is the independent charter school that is a soulless, self-interested business. Union officials always couple "charter

Figure 4.8   LAUSD Staff Strike, with Support from United Teachers Los Angeles, 2023

Source: Photo by Mario Tama/Getty Images News via Getty Images. Reprinted with permission.

school" with "privatization," "commodification," or "corporate." A Latino community activist concluded about charter schools, "It's become a numbers game. . . . You're really looking at them [students] almost as a commodity. 'We need to have warm seats, warm bodies to our seats.' . . . It's a business. . . . They need money." Independent charter schools "have been the wild west in the sense that . . . [they are] seeing a greater and greater market share and seeing their role as really to destabilize the existing institutions," said a White professor. "They haven't been as community-based. They've been market-oriented in the sense of their community outreach has been to individual consumer families and students."

In short, district and independent charter school leaders concur that the core goal is improving education, which requires that schooling be situated in a robust social and racial justice framework. But each side denies the other's sincerity in pursuing the envisioned outcome; each sees the other's ostensible goals as thinly disguised self-interest and financial greed.

Implementation

Among the many tactics aimed at improving education through racial and social justice, I focus on three themes that shape the charter school wars.

Chartering an Independent School

The first implementation issue is creation of an actual charter school. Doing so in California is simple in principle, though full of vexing detail in practice. The 1992 founding law enabled "parents, teachers, or community members" to request a charter, typically from the local school district's board of education.[38] The charter petition specifies the organizer's goals and operating procedures; once approved, the school is freed from the district structure and many state statutes and regulations. Despite some limiting conditions, the California Department of Education's regulations emphasize the law's call for "different and innovative teaching methods" to "stimulate continual improvements in all public schools."[39]

As contention over charter schools rose across the state, a 2019 "comprehensive rewrite" of the 1992 law "expand[ed] the authority of local school boards to reject new charter schools while requiring that they more clearly justify their reasons for doing so."[40] Charter authorizers such as LAUSD may now consider "the potential financial impact of charter schools as a factor in turning down a proposal. That's a huge win for districts and the CTA." However, this analysis continues, even with an unsupportive governor, the new law preserved the right of appeal, limited the authorizer's right to consider financial impact, and, most importantly, "will continue to say that districts shall approve charter petitions that satisfy the requirements of the law. Approval will be the default position."[41]

After describing the package of proposed changes to the charter school law as "certainly represent[ing] an existential threat to charter schools," the California Charter Schools Association (CCSA) gritted its teeth and praised the (somewhat revised) new legislation at the signing ceremony.[42] But initial implementation implied conflict ahead. Within a year, the CCSA protested to LAUSD that "the District is acting well beyond its legal authority, and the Policy contravenes the intent of the Legislature by actively discouraging the establishment of charter schools and dramatically curtailing their ability to remain independent from school districts." The CCSA promised to "consider all legal options available to us if the District proceeds to implement the New Charter Policy without amendments aligning its terms to the law."[43] But the California Teachers Association reportedly praised the draft policy, school board members defended it, and the board narrowly approved the new policy in August 2020.[44]

Little changed immediately. Citing a lack of new information and the need for stability during the COVID-19 pandemic, LAUSD recommended in 2020 at least conditional approval for all charter schools up for renewal in that year; the number of charter schools and their broad regulatory structure thus remained fairly stable.[45] In 2024, however, the school board narrowly passed a measure to restrict co-location of charter schools in buildings housing schools particularly aimed at helping Black and low-income communities. The California Charter Schools Association described the new policy as "a blatant violation of the law" because it threatened harm to one set of public school students in order to benefit a different set.[46] Charter proponents characterized the new measure more vividly as a wedge designed to create conflict between advocates for low-income Black and low-income Latino families. UTLA used its well-seasoned tropes to describe the new policy as "parents and educators . . . fighting back against billionaire privatizers and the destructive tactic of co-location."[47] CCSA, in its turn, sued LAUSD in April 2024, challenging the co-location policy as discriminatory.[48]

Financing

As we heard often, "money is the big thing." At issue is LAUSD's financial stability, about which there are repeated expressions of concern.[49] The district regularly warns, as it did, for example, in 2017, that its "current financial situation is simply not sustainable. Unless something changes, Los Angeles Unified will be insolvent by 2021 when it will have depleted the $1.8 billion reserve."[50]

The district was not insolvent in 2021, perhaps owing to a huge influx of pandemic funds, but arguments over how much independent charters are responsible for LAUSD's precarity are perennial. The state of California provides most school funding, with the level of support depending primarily on enrollment and specified needs such as low income or disability. Thus, other things being equal, students who move from traditional schools to independent charter schools reduce the district's resources without reducing its fixed costs. In rather an understatement, a longtime observer points out that "this funding loss is central to what makes charter schools so controversial."[51]

I underscore, once again, the crucial difference between affiliated and independent charter schools. Affiliated charters' per-pupil state funding remains within the district's budget, and their teachers are members of UTLA, so neither the district nor the union suffers loss if they expand. In fact, affiliated charter schools may keep some students in the public system who would otherwise attend private schools, so they are arguably a net gain to the district and union. In contrast, every student who moves from a traditional school to an independent charter represents a direct budgetary loss. Immigrants to the district who choose an independent charter school correspondingly represent a relative loss to traditional schools.

However, the financing wrangle includes an important twist. Although the journalist Kyle Stokes indeed observed that "this funding loss is central to what makes charter schools so controversial," he began that sentence with a crucial caveat: "Though adding up how much money districts lose when students enroll in charters is not a straightforward exercise."[52] That is, what counts as fixed costs, and how fixed they really are, is debatable. A 2016 study commissioned by UTLA calculates that 56 percent of the district's costs are fixed, so that every student who moves away from "schools run democratically by LAUSD" (as a policy brief puts it) to an independent charter school leaves behind considerable expenses uncompensated by a reduced teaching load.[53] Thus, one headline reads, "LAUSD Loses More than Half a Billion Dollars to Charter School Growth."[54]

But others retort that the claim of a half-billion dollar loss through fixed costs is unrealistically high and that, in any case, fixed costs can be reduced. A spokesperson for the California Charter Schools Association noted that "their response to declining enrollment has been to do nothing. Other districts have looked at a whole range of things including closing schools, including reducing staffing levels, including right-sizing administration."[55] In fact, as of 2016 when this report was written, the number of LAUSD teachers was rising and the district had committed to no layoffs for the coming year. There had been no discussion of closing schools, reducing administrative staff, or consolidating resources despite the decline by that point of over two hundred thousand students in little more than a decade.[56] Furthermore, as one study observes, "LA Unified, which offers one of the most generous healthcare benefits packages in the state for its retirees, has opted to not set money aside to pay for this [current and future health care costs]. It is estimated L.A. Unified has an unfunded liability of $13.6 billion."[57] Most sharply, in one view, the district's focus on charters is merely "a strategic attempt to distract public attention from its own financial mismanagement."[58]

The district's fiscal problems worsened after 2016 and may continue to do so. Buildings are underused or unused, but closing schools is so contentious in all districts that LAUSD so far has eschewed that choice.[59] Pension costs are steadily rising, from under 6 percent of the district's operating expenditures in the early 2000s to predictions of up to half of LAUSD's funds by 2030.[60] The Pew Charitable Trusts finds that, like those of the twelve other largest school districts, L.A. Unified's funded ratio for school employee pension systems declined from 2001 to 2018, in this case from almost 100 to about 60 percent.[61] The district responded to the 2019 UTLA strike with employee raises of about 6 percent over three years and slightly smaller class sizes; it responded to a 2023 strike of nonteaching members of SEIU (supported by UTLA) with a 21 percent increase in teachers' salaries over the next few years, comparable salary increases for nonteaching staff, and a small reduction in class size.[62]

The precise calculations are complex, but the underlying arithmetic is simple: "Where students go, jobs and funding follow."[63] Setting aside actuarial complexities, the crucial point is the quarrel over whether independent charter schools are an almost intolerable drain on urgently needed resources, or whether the union and district are clinging to resources they have no right to and are, in fact, increasing staff costs as student enrollment declines. The battle is engrossing emotionally and politically as well as financially and institutionally. Each side believes that it must win to survive in anything like its current form, so neither perceives any incentive to consider the broader landscape or pursue an accommodation.

Creating Educational Reform

So far, I have had no need to say much about teaching and learning. But actual education does play a role, even if secondary, in efforts to implement the district's goal of preparing students for a successful adulthood. Unsurprisingly, pedagogy is swept up in the charter school wars.

One issue is enrollment itself: opponents charge charter schools with creating "meritocracy"—a pejorative term in the L.A. school environment—by "creaming" off the best students. For example, a Latino school district official maintains that, for "many special needs children, their only option is the district, because charters are not equipped to address, support special needs [students] who are on the more moderate or severe spectrum. And that's a real issue." Critics also assert that both affiliated and independent charters' recruitment efforts are more effective for students whose parents are home in the evening, have use of a phone, and can engage with complex application forms and arrange transportation. As a White civic association member put it, "I have to be a very functional individual . . . in order to navigate the educational system, to research it, to go do site visits, to understand my child's educational needs. . . . That's a very sophisticated level of parent engagement and knowledge. Our low-income families haven't been able to do that for a number of different reasons."

Of course, proponents of both types of charter schools push back. They deny the accusation of meritocracy or creaming, pointing to the many ways they engage in broad community outreach, accommodate parents' work schedules and family constraints, and provide services to help students enroll and stay in school. "You have to work around when parents are available. That's the commitment," said one Latina civic association member. "If you really want parents there, you eliminate barriers to participation." More generally, a Black charter school leader claimed, the core of their appeal is to "figure out how to empower parents . . . with a voice that says, 'I want something better here, we deserve it, this is a great community, and we want something better.' And *they*," she emphasized, "get to define what better looks like." Defenders of independent charters turn the district's accusation of meritocracy upside down, insisting that they are the real egalitarians, since traditional schools devalue struggling students. "For us," said a Latina community activist, "the threat is not charters. The threat is a culture of failure and a lack of urgency."

Charter schools' strongest riposte to the charge of creaming is insistence that at least they are doing *something* to improve L.A.'s dismal educational record for low-income students of color. Comments are heartfelt and frequent: "I don't think most public schools have really done a great job of digging in on that piece," said a White charter school leader. "Because it's really hard and takes an incredibly long time to develop the talent that you need to run a highly effective school." A Latina charter school leader noted that charter schools

> have the opportunity to start completely new. . . . A charter school is created around a purpose and a mission, and so they're anchored in that, versus a district school that . . . was built as an institution where certain kids that are defined by or identified by their attendance boundaries are going to go. . . . That's what charter schools bring, models of creating cultures that result in high student achievement.

A less tactful version of this observation is generational, with young reformers challenging old bureaucrats: "Establishment folks are sort of old guard Democrats, like, 'We're for labor, we're for institutions, we're for this,' and some of the younger folks are like, 'Not necessarily,'" observed a (young) White charter leader.

Everyone agrees that "turning around schools is really hard," as a White civic association member admitted.[64] From district supporters' vantage point, that implies the need to fight back against the "Establishment folks" charge: "there is a real tension between people wanting quick changes for students, and the knowledge that true reform takes time," said another White civic association member. "We need some stability around strategies and then people to recognize what progress should look like—and instead there's this constant drain of students because new charters are opening. And so that landscape creates additional tension that makes it really hard for those reforms to actually succeed and work."

In sum, to the district and especially UTLA, the core implementation problem is the very existence of independent charter schools. Even the 2019 revised law still enables charters to drain resources, implicitly threaten teachers' jobs and compensation, and use subtly racist and elitist tactics to lure students out of a democratic public system into a privatized, corporatized interloper. To charters, the core implementation problem is district stasis, which itself has a racist and elitist tinge. Now that White flight has run its course and advantaged Angelenos have been accommodated with affiliated charters, LAUSD needs a new scapegoat to explain away its mediocre performance and bloated budget. It has settled on independent charter schools.

To no one's surprise, these clashing diagnoses and prescriptions generate political discord, to which I now turn.

Politics

I remind readers that LAUSD's politics do not reflect the larger American political scene. Virtually all actors in the school system are ideologically left of center. "It's kind of like shades of Democrat," a White journalist explained. "There are the Democrats who are supported by the unions, and oftentimes the reformers will find another Democrat who they can support."[65] So far as I can tell, no interview subject, and no publicly influential actors in the school debates, identified as Republican or conservative. The result, said a White charter school official, is

> an interesting sort of division within liberals. . . . If we are looking at class, race, ethnicity, it's kind of the same thing. I mean, when everybody talks to families—Latino families, English learners, immigrant families, Black families—everybody basically wants a really great education in their neighborhood that's free. Obviously charters and district schools are both trying to provide that. We know parents who have some kids at charter schools, some kids at district schools.

This respondent echoes the findings in figure 4.6: "Certainly the demographics of kids at charters in L.A. are pretty identical to the demographics of kids at district schools. So it's like on the actual issue, there's no division, I would say, that we can find or that we see among the actual most important constituents. Which is the families and the students."

Political contests are nonetheless fierce, with school board candidates and elected officials filing lawsuits and accusing each other of dishonorable behavior. In the ostensibly nonpartisan school board election of 2017, for example, one candidate furiously contradicted UTLA mailings portraying him as a supporter of President Donald Trump and Secretary of Education Betsy DeVos.[66] Similarly, "'millions of dollars were used to bully me,' [school board candidate Imelda] Padilla wrote. 'I was called a career politician despite never serving in office before, and I was called a conservative lobbyist even though there is no record of me ever being registered as a lobbyist with the state or the county (much less as a conservative/Republican). They told blatant lies about my actions . . . because they figured no one would verify their alternative facts.'"[67] Even jaundiced journalists agree that school board elections can be characterized by "vile, smarmy personal attacks, distortions and outright lies."[68]

School board elections have also been breathtakingly expensive. Candidates and their supporters spent over $15 million in 2017 in a battle over two seats (out of a total of seven); three years later, board campaigns spent at least $17.5 million.[69] Regardless, barely one-tenth of eligible voters participated in each election[70]—the political battles are deep but not very wide.

Grounds of Disagreement

On occasion, the actual practice of teaching and learning enters a campaign. As we have seen, UTLA calls for smaller class sizes, more support and specialized staff, and better compensation for teachers and staff. Independent charter proponents promote small, individualized schools with links to communities and employers, engagement with group identities or distinctiveness, and sometimes particular substantive foci or pedagogy. Debates over curriculum can occur, as in repeated disputes over fulfilling a mandate that all high school students take the courses required for admission to the University of California or California State University.[71] Most of the time, however, candidates expend little effort in challenging each other's curricular or pedagogical preferences.

Financial tensions cut deeper in board elections. As described earlier, depending on which consultants' report one attends to, alarm over LAUSD expenditures attributes them either to increased salaries, protection of purportedly fixed costs, and rising pension and health care costs—or to the drain of students into independent charter schools. Charter expenditures beyond state support are covered either by lower salaries and benefits, parent volunteers, and donations or fund raising—or by subsidies from corporatist, even Republican, plutocrats seeking to turn public schools into private fiefdoms.

However, financial concerns are often too arcane for effective electioneering, so alternative interpretations of the shared progressive ideology are more prominent in campaign rhetoric. Then-UTLA president Alex Caputo-Pearl described Superintendent Austin Beutner as a multimillionaire with expertise in "corporate downsizing but none in education." He was bringing in Wall Street firms, said Caputo-Pearl, "that have led public school closures and charter expansion . . . [resulting in] a negative effect on student equity and parent inclusion."[72] Union campaigners depict charter funders as billionaires who are "politically supported by Betsy DeVos and Donald Trump"; their "agenda is to drain our schools of resources, say they are failing, and then privatize them." They are an "invasion," a "threat to our children's right to free and quality public education."[73] In a galvanizing moment, a document was leaked in 2015 in which billionaire Eli Broad proposed an almost $500 million initiative to ensure that half of LAUSD's students could eventually enroll in charter schools—thereby lending color to the claim by a Latina school board official in the subsequent election that charter school leaders would "be in the history books someday as having participated in the demise of public education."[74]

Of course, charter-backed campaigns offer their own charges of corruption of progressive ideals. The agenda of the board and its allies is to protect their privileged status through single-minded self-dealing: "It's all about the money. So LAUSD is on the brink of financial disaster . . . because of their unmet obligations [that] are going to destroy public education. And CTA and UTLA have been masterful about talking about how the billionaires are out to destroy public education when the truth is that the ones who are destroying it in fact . . . are their unions and their pensions specifically." In this dance of mutual accommodation, "because they [UTLA] control the elected officials who both approve their contracts and then approve the memos and the agendas that are discussed in public, they're able to determine what gets talked about in public. And so . . . 'What could we do in terms of policy?' . . . —we are not talking about it." The Latina civic association member making these comments established her bona fides in a quintessentially Los Angeles way: "And I will be clear. I am a pro-Democrat, pro-union, pro-benefits person. . . . My mom and dad were both union members." After describing in detail their jobs and histories of union membership, she concluded, "So I'm a union family girl."

Treatment of the public is equally corrupt in this narrative. The board "does not represent the interests of parents and kids who are failing on campuses that are protected by these sweetheart contracts that they just themselves have negotiated in exchange for campaign cash," said a White charter school leader. Everything boils down to power: "You don't have to have a mother and a father, but you have to go to school," said a Black district school leader. "So that's how powerful we are. We say, 'You must send your children to us, and we get paid. Whether your child learns or not, we still get paid.'"

Caputo-Pearl described the upcoming 2017 school board election as "about whether the civic institution of public education is going to continue to survive."[75] The widely circulated slogan, "We can't grow, so charter must GO!!" captures the sentiment (see figure 4.9).[76] But the president of the California Charter Schools Association matched Caputo-Pearl's rhetoric: "Do you hate us that much that you would bargain away the future of poor children and Latino children for this?"[77] No wonder that one longtime observer, a White professor of education, described L.A.'s school politics to me as a "shit show."

Figure 4.9   "We Can't Grow, so Charter Must Go!"

The Nonpolitics of Race and Class

Education scholar Charles Kerchner's lament that "if half the effort that has gone into the Charter School War had been directed toward building the system's learning capacity, we would have created real winners, both adults and students" seems correct.[78] What is most relevant for this book in the war is the contrast with the contention over New York's SQF and Atlanta's BeltLine development—that is, the scarcity of references to race, ethnicity, or class. One campaign mailer accused charter school supporters of antisemitism (its use was halted); they responded that UTLA was itself trafficking in antisemitism by portraying charter backers as scheming billionaires. Beyond that, our extensive search in the media for articles about racism or bias in LAUSD board elections yielded exactly one prominent story.[79] It offered the difficult-to-interpret observation that although 90 percent of District 5's students were Latino/a, both top vote-getters in the 2019 school board primary election were White, having defeated seven Latinx competitors. A reporter reflected that although "charter schools are part of the racial dynamics here, there are members of the community, including some Latino members of the Board District 5 community, who have looked at the candidate field and say that they don't really care as much about the race of the person who is running, rather they are much more concerned about whether that candidate supports or opposes charter schools."[80]

Political actors do sometimes refer to racism, as in this statement by Kelly Gonez when she won election as board president in 2020:

> The Black and brown students we serve cannot thrive in a system built to undermine their promise. As a board we must lead with equity in mind and confront the racist vestiges in our public schools, from discipline practices . . . to resource allocation to staff development, selection, and placement. That means in every board decision prioritizing our most historically under-served students.[81]

For what it is worth, Gonez's election signaled "potentially a shift toward more influence for backers of charter schools," not for UTLA.[82]

It would be foolish to argue that racial and class tensions or hostility are irrelevant in Los Angeles' school politics, both because these dynamics are always relevant in the politics of American education and because there are doubtless undercurrents not made explicit in the media or public discourse. After all, every public official knows of or had direct experience with the decades-long convulsions in Los Angeles over school desegregation and its consequences.[83] Nonetheless, race/class conflict and its local history seem curiously distant from contemporary electoral contests beyond frequent, almost generic, references to "Black and Brown students" or "underserved students." Either participants find the issue of group-based conflict in LAUSD schooling so explosive that no one dares to allude to it publicly or they perceive no leverage to be gained from racially inflected expressions of concern about schooling that everyone adheres to, at least in principle. To my surprise, the latter explanation seems more compelling than the former.[84]

Organizations

As a huge, resource-rich, and politically engaged city, Los Angeles might be expected to have a robust advocacy community focused on schooling. After all, L.A. has a notable history of strong labor unions engaging in reformist activism.[85] Sociologist Manuel Pastor, for example, analyzes movements "across racial lines for community benefits agreements, job training programs, and transit justice" as well as "a progressive labor movement with electoral ambitions and skills" and "an immigrant voice that has gained both the confidence and the capacity to effect change."[86]

Community groups have facilitated a mostly successful transformation of South Central Los Angeles from a predominantly Black to a predominantly Latino community.[87]

Some of that reformist energy has indeed focused on schools. For more than two decades, the Youth Policy Institute was a nonprofit agency that sought to reduce poverty through programs focusing simultaneously on education, health, safety, and job training. Until a leadership scandal and implosion in 2019, the institute worked with dozens of schools and managed several charter schools. Inner City Struggle protested failing schools in the 1990s and now encourages new charter schools for ethnically distinctive or disadvantaged children.[88] Parent Revolution has sought to ensure that residents of underserved communities have the information they need to choose among the full array of schools that their children are eligible to attend. Advocacy organizations have promoted pilot and magnet schools and sought to reallocate funds to schools with poor children of color.

Nonetheless, "the most important thing about education reform is that there is not a popular movement for education reform in L.A.," said a Latina civic association member. "There's not a north star, and I think that's just a very unfortunate situation." What advocacy does occur resembles Atlanta's neighborhood-based diffusion more than New York's concentration through a few umbrella organizations. Groups "approach education reform from a slightly different perspective," which inhibits coordinated pressure, said a White district official. Sociologist Julia Wrigley is less circumspect: LAUSD's organizational environment is "a cacophony of competing groups."[89] A Black charter school leader described the district's reformist activity as "this political sort of football that gets thrown back and forth, and at times it gets stuck in the arena of kind of adult politics. . . . I'm just like, you know, when does it end?"

Like coordination, resources are always an issue for community or advocacy groups. So is officials' unwillingness to relinquish control. These common problems were overcome in the case of New York's SQF through a particular set of circumstances: a groupwide sense of oppression supported by compelling data, identified oppressors, a few clear strategies for exerting pressure on them, a powerful lever for change, and a governance system that can be changed by deploying the right levers. As with housing development in Atlanta, the charter school dispute in Los Angeles lacks all of those features. Advocacy and community groups disagree on who is being oppressed and by whom, they disagree on whether enabling more independent charter schools or raising teacher salaries is the problem or the solution, and they lack clear tactics with demonstrated efficacy in improving student outcomes. The system of public education is the quintessential loosely coupled organization, lacking the hierarchical order of a police department or the enforcement power of a court. Open

Borders, both internal and external, create a much more complex policy system than do Targets.[90]

Given this fragmented context, school employees largely shape civic involvement; as a Latino journalist put it, "it didn't seem to be like there were a lot of preexisting groups—groups independent of this [or that] tangential reform slate or independent of the teachers' union." Such sponsored groups tend to shy away from large, controversial issues: "Our biggest beef," a White civic organization member said, "is that the conversations are rarely about 'What do we value as the important definition of what a quality school is?' versus these other [narrow] battles of 'Should we be using test scores?' . . . It's hard to build alliances on those kind of things. . . . It's very political."

Blame for community inertia falls into the well-worn tracks of the LAUSD charter wars. On the one hand, a White attorney described UTLA's leaders as "very insulated. They don't like any kind of input from outside organizations, and I think it hurts them. . . . Schools in Los Angeles have this really core committed group of activists, but they haven't grown in all the years that I've known them, and there's a reason for that. So, they [UTLA] need to be working to engage more people." On the other hand, district supporters describe charter schools as engaging in bait-and-switch: "huge" numbers of immigrants who "have seen the ravages of neoliberalism" are "advocates of the social justice side" and therefore initially send their children to charter schools. But charters' "veneer that has been provided to these very reactionary policies gets stripped off immediately"; immigrant parents "see right through it" and disengage.

The main result of organizational weakness is inaction. About a decade earlier, according to a Latino journalist, parents "were aware of the low quality of their kids' public schools. They were very aware. [But] the extent to which they moved forward and organized was (*pause*), they often didn't because they were (*pause*), for them to do so as individuals was very difficult. . . . It is very daunting for parents, especially Spanish speakers, immigrant parents." The years since then have seen much spinning but little movement in any direction.

Public Opinion

Surveys and referenda consistently show that African Americans and Latino/as, especially in cities, support charter schools more strongly than do Whites, Asians, and non-urban residents.[91] The pattern holds even more strongly for enrollment. As of 2021–2022, 7 percent of total student enrollment in the United States was in charter schools, up from 4 percent in 2011. In that year, 24 percent of charter school students were Black, 36 percent were Hispanic, 4 percent were Asian, and only 29 percent were White. In contrast, traditional public school enrollment was comprised of 14 percent Blacks, 28 percent Hispanics, 6 percent Asians, and 47 percent Whites.[92] Charter students were more likely to be poor as well as non-Anglo. Sixty percent of students in charters were eligible for free or reduced-price lunches (a standard measure of poverty) compared with 53 percent in district schools.[93] Almost three-fifths of charter schools are in cities, compared with three-tenths of traditional public schools.[94] Black and Hispanic students disproportionately attend urban charters, while White students disproportionately attend non-urban charters.[95]

Despite this portrayal of core constituencies, however, spokespeople for the Democratic party show ambivalence and, in recent years, considerable opposition to charter schools. Former president Barack Obama was an enthusiast; current president Joe Biden is hesitant. Senator Cory Booker (D-NJ) and Democrat John King Jr., a former secretary of education, are supporters; Senators Elizabeth Warren (D-MA) and Bernie Sanders (I-VT) are not. California's Democratic governor Gavin Newsom presided over the 2019 tightening of that state's charter school law. Political activists who identify as progressives show similarly mixed views. After internal controversy, in 2016 the NAACP called for a moratorium on new charter schools.[96] Three local California branches opposed the statement—and were themselves then opposed by NAACP state leaders.[97] The main reason for this tangle is not mysterious; as *The Economist* notes, "The problem is that teachers' unions are at their strongest in precisely the places where charters are best, making the politics of school reform treacherous for Democrats."[98]

Californians partake of these mixed views. In 2019, the Public Policy Institute of California described charter schools to a statewide sample (one-third of whom had not heard of them) and then asked their views. Respondents split evenly—49 percent endorsed while 46 percent opposed them—although parents of children in public schools were a good deal more enthusiastic than were respondents without public school children (59 to 46 percent). Forty-nine percent of residents of Los Angeles County supported charters, putting the region in the middle among the five geographic regions into which the Public Policy Institute divides most of the state. Latinos and Whites expressed more approval than did Asian Americans or Blacks; middle-income respondents were more enthusiastic than both those with higher and lower incomes.[99] A year later, 54 percent of Californians favored charters, with similar distributions by region and race but no variation by income.[100]

The Public Policy Institute surveys offer hints of reasons for Angelenos' mixed views. Across the two years, two-fifths of respondents in the county—more than in all other regions—thought it was "very important" for students in low-income areas to have access to charters. But Los Angeles' residents were also more concerned than residents of most other regions about diverting state funds away from traditional public schools. In addition, the issue had a partisan caste; in both 2019 and 2020, more than two-thirds of California's Republicans, but only two-fifths of Democrats, endorsed charter schools.[101]

Within this broad context, and thanks to colleagues at Loyola Marymount University, we have evidence that focuses more tightly on LAUSD. In 2019, the Los Angeles Public Opinion Survey (now the Angeleno Poll) asked roughly two thousand Los Angeles County residents if school districts should focus on "improving the existing public schools" or on "giving families more alternatives such as additional charter school options."[102] Three-quarters chose the former, with no difference between respondents inside and outside LAUSD.[103] Union households across the county were a little more likely than non-union households (79 to 74 percent) to prefer improvement to innovation.

Nonetheless, LAUSD residents were more dissatisfied with their school district than were those living elsewhere. Asked from 2015 through 2019 to rate the "quality of K-12 education," on average, only 29 percent of LAUSD residents, compared with 44 percent of other county residents, rated K-12 schooling as "good." As many LAUSD residents (27 percent) rated K-12 schooling "poor" as rated it "good," whereas just over one-third as many L.A. County residents (16 percent) deemed their schools "poor" as deemed them "good." (Union and non-union households did not differ in their ratings.)

The Angeleno Poll also asked respondents from 2017 through 2020 how much they "trust" their school district to "do what is right." Here LAUSD disaffection was even greater; fully 53 percent of L.A. Unified residents, compared with 37 percent of L.A. County residents, trusted their district "only some" or "none" of the time. On this item also, union and non-union households did not differ.

In sum, residents of Los Angeles County taken as a whole resemble other Californians in their overall level of approbation of charter schools. But when survey respondents were disaggregated in accord with LAUSD boundaries, district residents were disproportionately dissatisfied with and had little confidence in their schools. That provides them with a motivation to move, if possible, across the Open Border, away from LAUSD schools.

The Class-in-Group Survey

Once again, the CIG survey enables a more fine-grained analysis of how attitudes are associated with race/class inequality. Based on their address when they joined GfK's KnowledgePanel, respondents were slotted into a metropolitan statistical area's (MSA) central city (39 percent of the sample), connected county (44 percent), or suburban county (17 percent). I can thus determine whether urban residents, who are disproportionately people of color, evaluate schooling differently from non-urban residents, who in many locations live in communities with higher proportions of non-Hispanic Whites.

Unlike with New York's SQF and Atlanta's BeltLine, the Los Angeles charter school case does not lead us to expect strong patterns associated with race and/or class; as we have seen, no aspect of this case, possibly excepting the student and teacher compositions of district-affiliated charter schools, shows clear racial or class differentiation in behavior or in attitudes about schooling. As a White journalist summarized, "I really think that parents really don't care what a charter school is, because I've talked to parents who will have one kid in a charter school and another kid in a magnet school and [another] in a traditional school, or like, as their kid moves from elementary to middle to high, . . . they move around." Even protagonists agree; as one White charter school official put it, "The allegiance that parents will have to any school, whether it's a traditional or charter, is purely based on 'Is it going to help my kid?'"[104]

As all of this would lead us to expect, CIG crosstabs regarding school reform are mostly similar, or inconsistently different, across race, ethnicity, class, or their interactions. Perhaps more surprisingly, residential location is also not associated with attitudes. Asked to allocate their local government's budget among six options, with a built-in constraint of 100 percent, CIG respondents assigned 27 percent to public schooling—slightly more than to policing and about twice as much as to any other proffered purpose. There is no notable difference by race or ethnicity, community type, or the intersection of race or ethnicity and community type. Class matters a little more: 23 percent of low-income respondents in all three groups gave the highest budgetary priority to public schooling, while 29 or 30 percent did so in all three high-income groups. Men and women did not differ consistently across or within racial and ethnic, or class, groups.

Regression analyses show a few associations between race or class and views of school budgets (for detailed results, see appendix table D.3.) If we control for other characteristics, affluent or well-educated respondents supported significantly more local school funding than did those with lower income or less schooling. Latinas overall showed slightly less support for school funding than did White women ($p < .01$), but moderate- and high-income Latinas showed statistically significantly *more* support than did all other race/class or race/class/gender interactions. Racial or ethnic differences per se, other interactions, and location in a metro area all showed no statistical or substantive impact. These results do not support a claim that race/class conflict shapes views of public schooling.

One set of CIG items explicitly addresses support for charter schools. Asked their priority among six possible policy reforms to improve education, only 14 percent chose "charter and magnet schools"—the sample's fourth-ranked choice, after higher teacher salaries, teacher and student accountability through testing, and shifting property taxes to poorly funded districts. Moderates and liberals were significantly less likely than conservatives to give priority to charter schools. Consistent with most other evidence, a larger share of Latinx gave charters and magnets high priority; for example, 21 percent of poor Hispanics, compared with 9 percent of poor Whites and poor Blacks, did so.[105] Latinos in all three community types were the strongest charter proponents. Blacks and Whites showed no gender differences, but Latinas gave priority to charters more than did Latinos (22 to 15 percent). In sum, Latinx respondents showed a distinctive profile, but otherwise, separating respondents by race, class, gender, community type, or any interactions yields no broad insight into enthusiasm for charter schools.

Public opinion, in short, contributes to understanding the Los Angeles charter school war mainly in a negative sense: unlike with New York's SQF, public opinion does not point clearly to race, ethnicity, class, or race/class interactions, as an explanation for the bitter divide. We must seek insight elsewhere, starting perhaps from the Angeleno Poll's evidence of LAUSD residents' strong dissatisfaction with and mistrust of their own school district, and the steady loss of students.

LAUSD's Open Borders

Not Race and Class, Really?

Despite all of the evidence so far, it is difficult to accept that conflict over L.A.'s charter schools has little to do with race, ethnicity, class, or their intersections. After all, the history, structure, and practices of American urban schools have been imbued with foundational race/class inequality.[106] So as a final check to my conclusion that LAUSD's charter school war is not driven by race/class conflict, I turn to experts' responses to our direct questions about its role.

Political scientist Gary Orfield, the dean of scholarship on racial segregation in schools, summed up these responses in our conversation with him: "There are African Americans and Latinos on both sides of those divisions." A Latino civic association member insisted that the "prevalent divide" is between public schools and "the private school sector that serves the elite." A White professor ruminated, "I think the race conversation, and frankly the class conversation, has not been a huge part of the reform conversation here, which is very unusual. . . . Trends in L.A. that have led to some animosity with charter schools [are] not so much about race. It's about money." A long-term White leader of a community organization pointed to all types of rifts—there's social and class rifts, there's racial rifts, there's geography rifts because of L.A. and how far apart L.A. is. There are many communities within the city. There's, I think, rifts that are political. . . . There's different rifts when it comes to what school sites versus district agendas are and what they try to achieve. There are financial rifts that happen across all of these things—learning how dollars are spent. There are rifts of different efforts. And I think that the biggest rift from an education program perspective is really around "Are you a charter or are you noncharter?"

The Perception of Existential Threat

Unless all of these experts are wrong, we need another explanation for Zimmerman's "astonishing lack of civility in the war over our schools." The key lies in the implications of the trends shown in figure 4.4 and their extrapolation. LAUSD's enrollment decreased by 32 percent from 2000 to 2019, and it has continued to drop, going from almost 740,000 at the peak to perhaps fewer than 400,000 over the next few years.[107] All projections are for further enrollment decline.

As a political entity with Open Borders, the school district cannot move its boundary, but students can cross it. Additional reasons for enrollment decline reinforce the porous border: immigration into former gateway cities is decreasing; families who remain in the district have fewer school-age children now on average than did previous generations; housing costs are dauntingly high. More generally, Americans are disproportionately moving into the South and Southwest from other states, including California.

Whatever their causes, fewer students imply shrinking budgets, which imply building closures, job loss for teachers and staff, pressure on pensions and other post-employment benefits, declining classroom resources, and overall constraint. As Christopher Berry observed, "places that shrink are screwed." Superintendent Carvalho started warning in 2019 that "we will have to navigate through difficult but important conversations and decisions in order not only to plan for the future, but also to ensure that, during a very unstable and unsustainable set of practices and processes, we come out the other end on solid footing without compromising the viability of our school district."[108] He was blunter a few years later: "[The district lost] 9,000 kindergartners when the pandemic hit. That's a huge, a huge number."[109] The director of the American Association of School Administrators spelled out what Carvalho was still reluctant to say: "You're going to have to sell buildings when they become empty. You're going to have to exit staff because you won't need the number of teachers that you have."[110] Under these conditions, and with no levers to increase the number of students or even to stem outward migration, too many educators yield to the temptation of striving to maintain their share by taking from the only available source—each other.[111]

Bringing Inequality Back In

The charter school war is mostly explained by continuing enrollment losses and the expectation of more, resting on top of a decade of mutual denigration and political vitriol. But race/class inequality remains in the causal mix. Movement out of the district is not random; as Orfield and his colleagues summarize, "When racial change goes neighborhood by neighborhood, community by community, first the white middle class exits, and then middle-class families of any race often stop moving in."[112] Education scholar Bruce Fuller similarly found that

> as class aspirations and educational attainment climbed in the late twentieth century—now shared among white, Latino, and Black families [as well as Asians and Pacific Islanders]—those who could, departed from L.A. Unified. When my team isolated higher-achieving students . . . we found the share of students with a parent who had completed some college fell from 62 percent in 2002 to 48 percent in 2012. . . . [Population loss] stemmed from the exit of better-educated white and Latino families.[113]

The pattern continues. Samantha Williams compared the demographic composition of LAUSD with that of all other Los Angeles County school districts combined, for the first and last years with reliable data (2014–2015 and 2021–2022).[114] Although the demographic characteristics of each student body changed only a little over those seven years, LAUSD students consistently differed from L.A. County students in important ways. As of 2022, L.A. County districts included almost twice as many Whites (9.7 percent in LAUSD to 15.3 percent in the county), about the same percentage of Blacks (7.3 to 6.6 percent), considerably fewer Hispanics (74.5 to 59.9 percent), and a much higher proportion of Asians (3.5 to 10.8 percent). Perhaps more importantly, student characteristics that typically call for greater resources differed. Just over 23 percent of LAUSD students were English learners, compared with 16.6 percent of L.A. County students, and fully 81.4 percent of L.A. Unified students were socio-economically disadvantaged, compared with 59.8 percent of L.A. County students.

Figure 4.10 shows graphically how residents differ on the two sides of the LAUSD border. L.A. Unified residents in densely populated sectors of the district are less likely to have attained higher education than residents outside LAUSD (panel A), and they have lower median household incomes (panel B). The northeastern and southwestern segments of Los Angeles County outside LAUSD, for example, show higher household incomes and higher levels of educational attainment than do close

Figure 4.10   **Education and Income in LAUSD and Surrounding Communities**

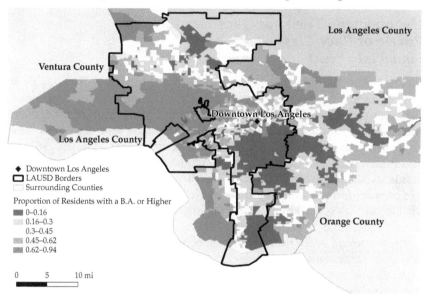

A. Proportion of Residents with a B.A. Degree or Higher

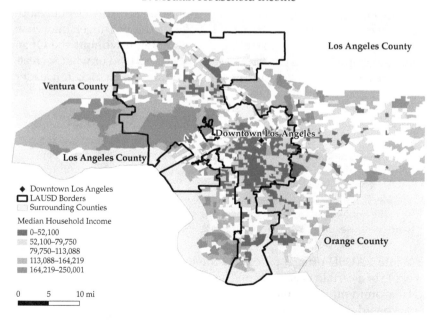

B. Median Household Income

Source: Author's analysis of tract-level demographics on race, education, income, and poverty levels from the 2020 American Community Survey (Five-Year Estimates).

portions of L.A. Unified just inside its borders. Those differences, and their possible implications for the quality of schooling and status of classmates, are not lost on parents of LAUSD students.

Denouement: The Four Questions and the Puzzle of *Race/Class Conflict and Urban Financial Threat*

Los Angeles' school dispute has a different logic from disputes over policing and housing. The Target and Grid metaphors point to issues in which groups differentially located on the continuum of race/class inequality contend against one another for power and resources. The contests we see—between police who are stopping one set of pedestrians and pedestrians themselves, or between developers seeking profits and residents seeking affordable housing—are real conflicts, integral parts of a broader foundational injustice. But in L.A.'s Hundred Years' War, the visible conflict is mostly a destructive distraction from the actual structural problems driving the policy issue. Race/class inequality is part of the context; LAUSD schooling has been shaped by decades of racial and class strife, and Los Angeles County school districts have better-off families and more resources than do most schools in L.A. Unified. But the central explanation for the charter school war is declining enrollment, and therefore resources, within a structure of immovable and porous boundaries.

Just as my depictions of New York's policing and Atlanta's development are not new, so my portrayal of L.A. Unified is not novel. Interview subjects pointed to the underlying problem, albeit without the Open Borders metaphor or its particular role here. Asked who or what is creating the perception of a zero-sum game, one White civic association leader answered:

> The media, the union, the parents, the charters, everybody is. Because the competition for students is fierce, because it drives your budget. It's a huge, huge, huge problem. . . . Their budget—it's not a question of it being mismanaged, they've got huge pension issues, they have a lot of bureaucracy. What, "They should fire everybody"? You can't. It's not like it's that simple. If the answers were simple, people would have done it a long time ago. It's not like you're going to put a huge number of people in L.A. out of work because. . . . And so the wrong conversations are happening.

A White LAUSD official perceived the importance of border-crossing: "People of a certain class, in terms of what their earnings are, don't want to be around other people in schools and their children, who are what they consider lower-class. So they'll move." A Latino LAUSD official agreed: "We weren't paying attention to middle-class families, who moved to private schools. The middle class is the target now—bring them back into the district. . . . [Only] 8 percent of the district is Black—they're gone. . . . The Brown community are next to be moving out."

In a more systematic fashion, a robust scholarly literature examines White flight and middle-class flight from desegregating schools or a city increasingly comprised of poor people of color.[115] Some analyses include a focus on Los Angeles.[116] What makes this book distinctive is my use of LAUSD's travails to address the puzzle of when, how, and why foundational race/class inequality in the United States does or does not shape urban policy and political disputes. Once again, I solve the puzzle by turning to the four questions outlined in chapter 1:

Does the policy's goal include an intent to affect race, class, or race/class inequality? Yes. As judged by their public statements, all participants aim at equality of educational opportunity, teach in ways intended to enhance the schooling outcomes of disadvantaged students, and are motivated by the goal of using education to promote social and racial justice.

Is implementation intended to, or does it in fact, affect race, class, or race/class inequality? How to answer this question is the crux of L.A. Unified's dispute. State laws and regulations are facially neutral regarding implementation of school charters. Each set of actors insists that *their* implementation strategy and practices are best able to reduce race/class inequality, and each denies that their antagonists have the same goal or could achieve it if they did. So, for each set of actors, the answer to the question of implementation's intent to reduce race/class inequality is "yes." But collectively, for the district as a whole, the answer is, "It depends on what evidence you find convincing."

Are actors consensually identifiable by race and/or class, or do they consistently invoke race/class categories in their engagement with the policy and the political arena? Mostly no. This is the biggest surprise to emerge from the narrative. The students on the two sides of the charter dispute (always excepting affiliated charter schools) are essentially the same. Teachers in both sets of schools are racially and ethnically mixed and, almost definitionally, in the middle class. Parents and voters appear not to choose schools or candidates, respectively, along lines of race or ethnicity. Race, ethnicity, and class are probably in many actors' peripheral vision, but they seldom appear in battles over charter schools.

Are policy recipients who consistently gain or lose, or policy outcomes that consistently affect the city's residents, consensually identifiable by race and/or class? The answer is "yes" for a few students and "no" for most. The creation of distinctive affiliated charter schools provided a pathway for well-off, disproportionately White and Asian students to remain in the public school system and be somewhat isolated from poorer students. But the creation of independent charter schools does not generate distinctions among policy recipients by race or class.

Overall, I judge that the answers to the second, third, and fourth questions are closer to "no" than to "yes," and that they outweigh the "yes" answer to the first question. Thus, the first two pieces of the central puzzle must be set aside, since race/class inequality is not at the core of the policy issue. We are left with the third layer of the puzzle: *why* is some alternative force more important?

The answer is that a financial threat that seems existential pushes even foundational race/class conflict to the periphery of a dispute. Only a few interview subjects referred to Detroit's 2013 Chapter 9 bankruptcy—and all but one quickly shied away from the subject. But a Latino LAUSD official admitted, "Detroit—everybody got to move out who was affluent, and left the poor. And that's who we are thinking about here. . . . Detroit is really our model."[117]

In 2023, FitchRatings gave LAUSD a grade "below Fitch's median rating for the local government sector, reflecting the strong likelihood of future structural budgetary imbalances that will require ongoing policy adjustments while the district's enrollment trends remain negative. . . . Fitch expects LAUSD's revenue performance to remain weak over the medium to long term, reflecting declining student enrollments." FitchRatings made the same point several more times, concluding its report with a final reminder of "the district's underlying structural budgetary imbalance given its declining enrollment and spending trends."[118] That message is an unsubtle call for a long-term solution, for which there are few options. Perhaps the central actors will find a way of working in partnership based on a unified vision for all kids. But I see little reason for optimism in the foreseeable future. Realistic fear, reinforced by ideology, political incentives, and personal animosity, underscores the conclusion of a White community advocate: "you can't do anything in this space. . . . What you get is tiresome."

═ Chapter 5 ═

Race, Class, and Budgets: Public-Sector Pensions in Chicago

The city is like family—if parents work all their life, their children should take care of them in old age. [They should be able to] get money from the new generation—but [in Chicago] there is no money because it wasted money on unnecessary projects.
—Chicago cab driver, 2017

There is no clear path to solvency for the city of Chicago. There is no clear path to meeting pension obligations.
—White civic association member, 2017

Our pension obligation continues to grow year after year. So, if we do nothing, be sure, taxpayers, they're coming back for you later.
—Mayor Lori Lightfoot, quoted in *Sun-Times* Media Wire 2022

I am committed to protecting both the retirement security of working people, as well as the financial stability of our government so we can achieve our goal of investing in people and strengthening communities in every corner of the city.
—Mayor Brandon Johnson, quoted in Singh 2023b

https://doi.org/10.7758/ptkg1499.8621

It reminds me of Altgeld in his 1890s' The Cost of Something
for Nothing: *"I'm not going to be here when the chickens
come home to roost."*
—White civic association member, 2017

These five comments summarize the history and politics of public-sector union pension funding in Chicago: (1) commitments were made and must be honored; (2) commitments cannot be honored even though efforts are undertaken; (3) political leaders warn that the problem is getting worse and must be solved; (4) new commitments are made that must be honored; and (5) political leaders bequeath the problem to their successors. That last move may in fact be a sensible strategy—despite more than a century of this recurring cycle, the public pension system has never failed to pay out, Chicago has not gone bankrupt, no mayor has lost his or her job owing to pension mismanagement, and neither pensioners nor citizens are aroused. Perhaps this cycle of "must, can't, try, must, won't" can continue indefinitely.

Chicago's failure to adequately fund its public-sector pensions persists despite surprising consensus around the need to do so. There is no furious contest between two groups, each seeing itself as the locus of racial and social justice but existentially threatened by the other, as in L.A.'s charter school debate. There are no community advocates organizing political activism around race/class inequality and demanding action from city leaders, as in Atlanta's BeltLine development. There is no challenge to powerful state actors from almost powerless city residents regarding constitutional limits to a policy manifesting race/class hierarchy, as in New York's SQF. All there is in Chicago, virtually every relevant partici-pant agrees, is a $35 billion (or perhaps $60 billion) hole in pension funds that the city must, at least in principle, fill by raising taxes, reducing ser-vices, entreating more support from the state (despite its own massive pension hole), squeezing future union members, or all four.

It is hard to imagine any other hugely consequential urban problem in which race/class conflict plays such a small role. It is especially surprising in Chicago, where race and class are at the center of arguably every other public issue. What fills the place of race/class inequality as the foundation of this issue is *time*, which is manifested in ways ranging from the miracle of compound interest to contractual choices ramifying over a century that now require Chicago's next generation to pay for the free ride of past generations. The ruling metaphor is a Timeline.[1]

Table 5.1   **Seven of the Ten Local Pension Plans with the Lowest-Funded Ratio Are in Chicago, 2023**

Rank	Plan	Funded Ratio
#63	Chicago Transit	54.8%
#64	Chicago Water	51.9%
#65	Jacksonville Employees	51.5%
#66	Chicago Teachers	43.4%
#67	Jacksonville Police and Firefighters	43.1%
#68	Dallas Police and Firefighters	40.6%
#69	Chicago Laborers	38.5%
#70	Chicago Police	31.1%
#71	Chicago Municipal	22.2%
#72	Chicago Firefighters	21.6%

Source: Data from Randazzo and Moody 2024, 49.

Setting

The Pension Debt

Like the Los Angeles Unified School District's enrollment, it is surprisingly difficult to settle on a single figure, or even a plausible range, for Chicago's pension debt. The lowest publicly promulgated figure for the four city pension funds (police officers, firefighters, municipal employees, and laborers) is somewhere around $35 billion; that does not include the enormous teachers' union debt, which is partly owed by the state.[2] The highest publicly promulgated figure is Moody's Investors Service's $60 billion estimate as of late 2021 (along with another $31 billion for the teachers' pension fund).[3] Like most published figures of this magnitude, one's choice of a low or high estimate has a political spin as well as a substantive basis, but regardless of which is chosen, it is a lot of money. The pension debt is at least three times as large as Chicago's annual budget of $16.4 billion for 2023.[4] If the city's entire operating budget were devoted to paying down its pension debt for each of the subsequent three years, in other words, that action would just about eliminate a conservative estimate of the debt—except that interest payments and compounded interest on recipients' cost-of-living increases would have kept the debt figure rising even if no other actuarial calculation changed and investments remained robust.

Experts offer various images to enable people to absorb what one White economic actor referred to as "the Detroit situation."[5] The libertarian-leaning Illinois Policy Institute headlined an article "Chicago Has More Pension Debt than 44 States."[6] The Equable Institute, which provides the Policy Institute's data, publishes an annual table (replicated in table 5.1)

Figure 5.1   Chicago Has Increased Pension Contributions in Recent Years, 2004–2025

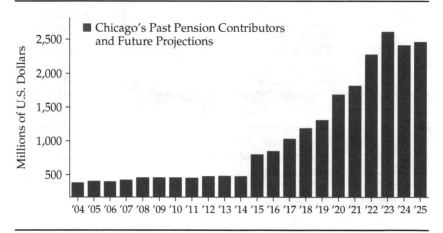

revealing the depth of Chicago's indebtedness. Bloomberg CityLab offers its readers a dramatic bar chart of Chicago's efforts to fill its pension hole (replicated in figure 5.1).[7] The group Truth in Accounting relies on colorful language: in 2019, it identified five "sinkhole cities" in which pension debt controlling for population size is the greatest. Chicago is second on the list, with debt per taxpayer of $36,000.[8] And Standard & Poor's graphically demonstrates Chicago's outlier status with regard to pension costs and unfunded liability (replicated in figure 5.2).[9]

In the face of all of this, newly elected mayor Brandon Johnson confirmed in July 2023 that his predecessors had left him "several long-term structural challenges." But, echoing them, he promised "a better path forward for the city's finances that will protect working families and develop actionable solutions to meet the city's obligations to workers, retirees and taxpayers."[10]

The Pension Funds

How did Chicago get into this situation? About half of our thirty-eight interview subjects in Chicago (not including cab drivers) began their answer to that question with a detailed history of Chicago's public-sector retirement systems. In some cases, the history comprised most of an hour-long interview. That was not the case for any of the other three issues in this book; interview subjects elsewhere would note that their policy had roots far back in the twentieth century, fill in essential trajectories, and then turn to the recent past and the present. But history, as the metaphor of a

Figure 5.2   Chicago Is an Outlier Among U.S. Cities for Pension Burden, 2022

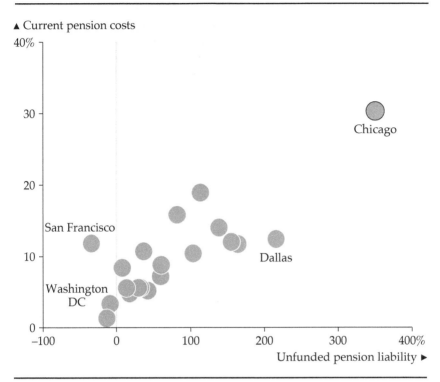

▲ Current pension costs

Note: Data are as of 2022, from Standard & Poor's Financial Services LLC. Current pension cost and unfunded liability figures are a percentage of government expenditures.

Timeline implies, is uniquely important in this case; as political scientist Sarah Anzia reminds us, local pension officials "are heavily constrained by . . . choices made in the past by policy makers at the state and local levels."[11] Thus, I begin with a selective history of Chicago's engagement with public-sector pension funding, highlighting only elements of the case that are important for analyzing race/class inequality.

Five pension funds are relevant to *Race/Class Conflict and Urban Financial Threat*. Illinois created the largest and most venerable, the Chicago Teachers' Pension Fund (CTPF), in 1895, making it one of the oldest defined benefit funds in the United States. It is a mostly independent part of the Illinois State Teachers Retirement System; unlike with the other four relevant pension funds, structural and funding decisions about the Chicago Teachers' Pension Fund are made by the state in conjunction with the Chicago Public Schools system rather than by the city of Chicago.[12] Funding for a given year is set by state law, but the funds themselves come from several sources in proportions that vary over time. In fiscal year 2023, for example, Chicago Public Schools' proposed budget for pension funding included $552 million in a dedicated property tax levy from district (that is, city) residents, $308 million from the state of Illinois, and the rest from mandated contributions from employees' salaries, of which the school system paid almost all for employees hired in 2016 or earlier.[13]

Early twentieth-century policy actors lauded the new system of employee protection and Jane Addams's securing of public funds for it while serving as president of the Teachers' Pension Fund from 1905 to 1907. As early as 1917, however, the General Assembly's appointed Illinois Pension Laws Commission "described the condition of the State and municipal pension systems as 'one of insolvency' and 'moving toward crisis' because the 'financial provisions [were] entirely inadequate for paying the stipulated pensions when due.'" The Commission "reiterated this conclusion" in a report two years later, after the Assembly had ignored their proposal for a "reserve plan."[14]

This is the first instance of a recurring chorus. After more such reports at regular intervals over the next five decades, a state commission warned in 1969, for example, that Illinois stood "foremost in the United States in the maintenance and perpetuation of an inherently unsound and unworkable policy of administration for its public employees."[15] Partly in response, the new state constitution of 1970 mandated payment of contracted pensions, with consequences discussed later in this chapter. Regardless, state oversight commissions continued to warn that pension funding was being kept deliberately insufficient and the debt was rising. By 1979, in yet another report, the governor's office announced that "financing Illinois' pension obligations had 'reached crisis proportions.'"[16] After that, state pension contributions declined further. Another commission found in 2013 that almost half ($41 billion) of the alarmingly rising state pension fund deficits were due to persistent state underfunding. "Effectively, the State used the pension systems as a credit card to fund ongoing service operations."[17] The *Chicago Tribune* was even less tactful: "Take another barrel of cash and toss it into the fire pit. The Illinois Senate rejected a pension fix on Wednesday, another day taxpayers' liability for pension funds climbed by $17 million."[18] In the decade since then, the state's pension deficit has continued to rise.

A combination of external economic disasters, political pressures and incentives, and repeated bad policy choices created this endless do-loop. Consider, for example, the largest relevant pension system, that of public school teachers. In 1995, a financial and educational crisis in Chicago Public Schools impelled first the formation of a state oversight board and then the grant of control to Chicago's mayor, through direct appointment of the school board. Even the power-seeking but politically savvy Mayor

Richard M. Daley did not relish this new authority; "Mayor Daley and the state representatives [from Chicago] were like, 'It's such a mess we don't really want to regain political control.' So there was a bit of a negotiation there," according to a White economic policy expert. That negotiation resulted in a levy formerly earmarked for pensions being provided instead to Chicago Public Schools for other uses. In subsequent years, the school system also enjoyed "pension holidays"; "effectively, this meant that Chicago Public Schools did not make more than a minimal employer contribution between 1995 and 2004."[19] The state also made only token payments, based on the law's language invoking a "goal and intention," but no requirement to pay any stipulated amount or proportion into the Chicago Teachers' Pension Fund.

Further losses ensued. The dot-com bubble of the early 2000s, the 2001 recession, and the national financial crash of 2008 all led to lower returns on pension investments than were projected by the CTPF's over-optimistic budget estimates. "And then," continued the policy expert, "all of a sudden [in 2013] they were like, 'Oh wow, there's this $700 million [annual] bill that we just didn't have to pay before.' So now there's a structural deficit," given the increasing costs of debt service.[20] Chicago's primary good-government organization, the Civic Federation, details the subsequent maneuvers, laws, backtracking, and in-filling; as of fiscal year 2021, the CTPF was funded at roughly 50 percent of a fully funded pension system, with total unfunded liabilities calculated by the state to be $13.2 billion, and by Moody's to be $30 billion. That figure had grown from about $8 billion in 2012, when experts first specified a structural deficit.[21]

Although the history differs in crucial details for the four smaller pension funds over which the city has direct control, the overall trajectory is similar.[22] These funds cover municipal employees, laborers, police, and firefighters. They share several defining characteristics.

First, like most public-sector but few private-sector pension plans, all four funds (as well as the teachers' fund) are defined-benefit plans. Unlike defined-contribution plans, defined-benefit plans create binding constraints on the entity paying out the benefits regardless of its condition or the state of the economy. Such funds provide stability and certainty to recipients, but with a trade-off of being "unpredictable and unmanageable" for budgeters, in the words of a White civic association member. "Funding a traditional pension plan," law professor Amy Monahan writes, "involves relying on assumptions about life expectancy, wage growth, inflation, employee tenure, rates of disability, and investment returns. It becomes even more complicated in the public sector, where funding relies on politicians agreeing to the necessary annual appropriations."[23]

Second, the four municipal plans were each financed for almost a century by a "goofy multiplier," as a White civic association member put it. That is, "it differed between the four systems. One, it was like a 1-to-1; one, it was like a 1.5-to-1. So it's basically like, 'Okay, the city employees put in 100 dollars, so the city put in 150.' But that wasn't tied to any type of actuarial calculation." A White economic actor disagreed only in characterizing the multipliers as "crazy" rather than "goofy": "The city for all four of these pension funds used this crazy formula which is unrelated to benefits at all. . . . And the multiplier has kind of changed in an ad hoc [year by] year way over the course of the past forty or fifty years—and 'That's how much we're going to pay into the system.'" The multiplier strategy grew increasingly insufficient as employees retired earlier and lived longer, as pensions were more frequently determined by the final few years of an employee's salary (or even the final few days in a few highly publicized cases), and as cost-of-living allowances rose.

Third, until recently, all pensioners drawing on funds for municipal employees and laborers, as well as retired teachers, have received annually compounded increases of 3 percent, regardless of inflation and with no cap on the total increase or total annual pension. A White civic association member described changing this feature as "the only benefit that moves the needle."[24] Then-mayor Rahm Emanuel proposed a state constitutional amendment that would, among other things, "provide flexibility to move cost-of-living increases more in line with the economy."[25] For good reason, from a White economic policymaker's vantage point: "I had done a lot of work on pensions before I came to Chicago and when I saw that that was how they did it I could not believe it. I was like, 'This could not be how we're funding our pensions system because it is so far removed from what anyone would think is a good idea.'" The amendment failed.

The Current Situation

"Eventually the math doesn't work. . . . All of a sudden you have a huge deficit," concluded a White civic association member. Even after a century of repeated warnings, political leaders professed to be shocked in 2015 that the city owed its four funds about $30 billion (or more); that the state of Illinois owed some amount well over $100 billion more to its funds, including the sort-of-promised contributions to the Chicago Teachers' Pension Fund; and that the forces driving the expanding debt were continuing, with magnifying impact. Those totals have grown since the city and state began trying to get the debt under control in the mid-2010s. In 2022, the pension funds for municipal employees, firefighters, and police officers were all funded at 22 percent or less of promised benefits, earning a grade of F from Truth in Accounting. (The grade of the relatively small laborers' fund rose to D– because it was 40 percent funded.)[26] Nineteen percent of the city's budget went to pension funds in 2021, and the Civic

Federation projected that pension funds would account for 22 percent in the following year.[27] Figure 5.3 shows the city's own estimate of the daunting rise in its payments into the four smaller funds.

State laws required Chicago to switch from the goofy multiplier to actuarially approved estimation procedures by 2022, but the compounded annual increase persists for workers in some funds who were hired before 2011—as of course does their increased longevity. Other features of the pension plans remain continual subjects for debate and renegotiation, including the timing and steepness of the "ramp" for the amortization period, projections of investment returns and bond markets' response to the city's debt, current and future workers' mandated contributions, demographic projections, conditions for retirement such as age or years of service, the definition of a salary and its length used for calculations, how closely the city or state should actually adhere to its stated laws and regulations, and more.

Policy Recipients

Public-Sector Workers

Although I emphasize structural similarities in describing their history, and in policy implementation later in this chapter, Chicago's pension funds differ in size and therefore in expenditures and share of all recipients. The Chicago Teachers' Pension Fund (CTPF) claims about 92,000 members (once again, the numbers differ across different purportedly authoritative documents). That compares with the Municipal Employees' Annuity and Benefit Fund (MEABF) with 31,000, the Policemen's Annuity and Benefit Fund (PABF) with 13,000, the Firemen's Annuity and Benefit Fund (FABF) with 4,700, and the Laborers' and Retirement Board Employees' Annuity and Benefit Fund (LABF) with 2,500 members.[28]

Although I was not able to find demographic information for pension fund recipients, data on Chicago's union members suggest variation that is crucial to the way the pension issue is playing out. Of the 22,000 City of Chicago teachers included in the 2022–2023 Illinois Report, 75 percent were female. Half were White, one-fifth were Black, and another one-fifth were Hispanic. Four percent were Asian. Over the past decade, the proportions of Black and white teachers have both declined slightly and the proportion of Hispanic teachers has risen.[29] In contrast, only 26 percent of the 12,300 members of Chicago's police department were female. Forty-four percent of police were White, 22 percent Black, and 30 percent Hispanic. In even sharper contrast, only 9 percent of the 4,800 members of the fire department were female. Fire department members were also more likely to be White, at 64 percent; 15 percent were Black, and 18 percent were Hispanic.[30]

Figure 5.3 "Pension Contributions, Historic and Projected," in City of Chicago Budget, 2004–2026

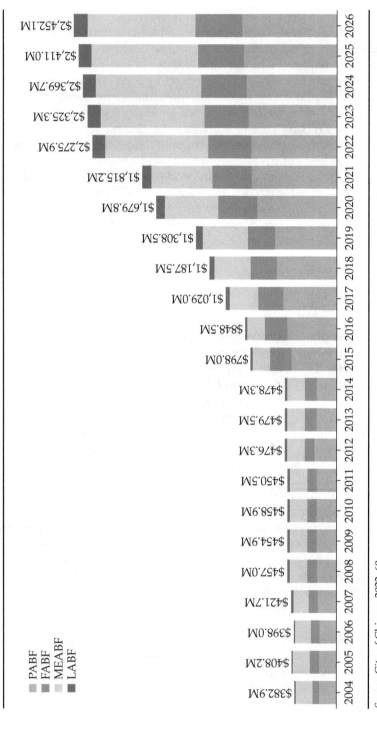

PABF
FABF
MEABF
LABF

2004 $382.9M
2005 $408.2M
2006 $398.0M
2007 $421.7M
2008 $457.0M
2009 $454.9M
2010 $458.9M
2011 $450.5M
2012 $476.3M
2013 $479.5M
2014 $478.3M
2015 $798.0M
2016 $848.5M
2017 $1,029.0M
2018 $1,187.5M
2019 $1,308.5M
2020 $1,679.8M
2021 $1,815.2M
2022 $2,275.9M
2023 $2,325.3M
2024 $2,369.7M
2025 $2,411.0M
2026 $2,452.1M

Source: City of Chicago 2022, 60.
Note: PABF: Policemen's Annuity and Benefit Fund; FABF: Firemen's Annuity and Benefit Fund; MEABF: Municipal Employees' Annuity and Benefit Fund; LABF: Laborers' and Retirement Board Employees' Annuity and Benefit Fund.

Evidence about membership in the other two Chicago unions is more impressionistic. SEIU Local 73 includes 35,000 workers in Illinois and Indiana, most of them in jobs in public schools and municipalities—that is, it represents Chicago's municipal employees. SEIU's resolutions include "end[ing] anti-black racism, structural racism, and all forms of racial oppression" for workers "no matter where they come from." It "values the role of aspiring citizens and recognizes the integral role that new Americans play."[31] As those resolutions perhaps suggest, its members are widely understood to be substantially African American. SEIU Local 1 includes 30,000 "property service workers" in Illinois—that is, laborers. It too is committed to "standing at the forefront of the fight for immigrant, racial, and environmental justice."[32] Its members are widely understood to be substantially Latino/as. In short, membership across the five unions varies by gender and race or ethnicity; collectively, they probably include significant representation of Chicago's largest communities of color.

Taxpayers

We can also define policy recipients as Chicago's taxpayers, who have been required since the mid-2010s to pay higher property taxes and new fees for garbage collection and other services. Property taxes are the city's main revenue source; about 80 percent is now allocated to pensions. Property taxes held steady at about $700 million annually from 1999 through 2007, rose to $860 million by 2014, and to more than $1.7 billion by fiscal year 2023. That is a huge increase over a short period of time. However, according to the Civic Federation, from which these data come, "compared to suburban communities, the City of Chicago composite tax rate, which means the combined rate for all of the taxing bodies that overlap City borders, is relatively low due to the large commercial and industrial property base. The tax year 2021 composite tax rate in the City of Chicago was 6.7%," compared with the lowest suburban rate of 7.2 percent.[33]

Chicagoans' average tax burden may be relatively low on average, but that says nothing about its distribution across classes. Policymakers are aware of that point; in keeping with a 2017 state law, Cook County has established property tax exemptions for senior citizens and eligible middle- and working-class homeowners.[34] Scholars have reported evidence of property tax regressivity in Chicago, and Mayor Johnson pledged in June 2023 not to raise "painfully high" property taxes.[35] But so far at least, Chicagoans reluctantly accept them.[36]

Residents

Perhaps we should understand the recipients of Chicago's pension funding policy to be all of the city's residents, rather than union members and annuitants or taxpayers. All residents, after all, are collectively facing the need to find an additional $30 billion or more over the next few decades and might be collectively facing a diminished quantity or quality of city services as a consequence.[37] It is difficult to explain to residents what they are receiving in return for their new contributions to the city's coffers. One Black alderperson explained his dilemma:

> The most impactful thing on my residents was actually the garbage fee, because that basically guaranteed an extra $220 [annually], give or take, coming out of everybody, many of whom felt "My taxes were enough to cover garbage, so why do we have to pay for it?" You could understand their confusion, and it causes problems for us because the garbage fee doesn't actually pay for garbage. The garbage fee goes towards shoring up police and fire pensions. So the correlation between being able to tell people that "this is to help balance what we spend" doesn't necessarily flow as well when they are able to go online or read or are told, "Well, we did this to shore up pensions." "Well, what does our garbage have to do with police pensions?"

The Teachers' Pension Fund, perhaps speaking for other unions, seeks to blunt this plausibly justified irritation by arguing that even if most Chicago residents do not directly gain from teachers' pensions, they nonetheless benefit. "Retired CTPF members make an immeasurable impact as consumers, taxpayers, and contributors to the local communities. About 91% of all CTPF members, including 83% of annuitants, live in Illinois. CTPF members spend their pension payments close to home, supporting their communities and continuing to shape Illinois and Chicago long after ending their service with the Chicago Public Schools."[38] How persuasive that is might be measured by how reluctant elected officials have been for decades to ask voters to make those payments (especially given the geographic ambiguity of "live in Illinois").

But the Teachers' Pension Fund is broadly correct, in the sense that all of Chicago's residents would be harmed if the pension funds were to fail. As Monahan warns her readers, "Once insolvency occurs, pension benefits due to retirees will either have to be paid out of the government's cash on hand, or simply not be paid at all. Based on their current financial positions, most jurisdictions appear unable to fund pension benefits while maintaining essential governmental services, unless taxes are raised significantly."[39] Illinois's constitution mandates payment of promised pensions, so "not be[ing] paid at all" is an unlikely option. As in LAUSD, few interview subjects touched on the specter of Detroit's bankruptcy, but it clearly hovered in the minds of at least a few.

In short, actors and analysts may define recipients of Chicago's public-sector pension policies narrowly as present or future annuitants, more broadly as taxpayers, or even as all city residents. However they are defined, recipients' class can be salient: annuitants receive payments analogous to working- or middle-class incomes; property taxes largely depend on the assessed value of homes, which are of course the main component of most taxpayers' wealth; and the most stringent insistence on paying down arrears tends to come from the well-off with an eye on bond ratings. What almost no actors or analysts do is evaluate recipients or their preferences in terms of their race or ethnicity.

Policy Goals

Unlike the BeltLine, for example, the policy goal in this case is straight-forward: pay down deficits and ensure that pension funds are financially stable without harming the city, taxpayers, or public services. Almost everyone concurs, with greater or lesser enthusiasm. Public officials seem largely resigned:

> In other states, the court took a more generous reading of the constitutional provisions [about pension promises]. But that's what we are required to pay, that's what we are paying (White public official).

> We don't have a choice, given the state constitution and the Court's ruling [in *Jones v. MEABF*, described later in this chapter]. Plus, I would not change the court's decision; it is not the workers' fault that the government didn't fulfill its obligations. Going forward, this has to be dealt with; it's not fair to change in the middle of the game on people (Black alderperson).

Union representatives and their advocates, not surprisingly, are a good deal more enthusiastic about a robust pension-funding policy:

> Sometimes we try to remind people of the moral responsibilities. . . . "What are you teaching your children? If you want to teach them that it's okay to walk away from a commitment . . . whenever the going gets tough, you go instead of sticking it out?" If those are the lessons you want to teach people, that promises are only kept if they are convenient, well then, you're doing a great job. But if you want to teach children that "Promises—you need to work hard, and if things get tough you need to work harder. You need to make your commitments and honor your pledges"—then you raise taxes, you [find the] money in order to achieve that (White union official).

In perhaps an unusual alliance, civic association leaders agree with union leaders: "So someone has to be grown up enough to say to people, 'This is math. This is what's happened.' . . . Do what they got to do: pay down the pensions as fast as they can. And then raise taxes on an incre-mental basis over time so that . . . we get enough money to pay off the deficit and not harm any one group of citizens at any one particular point in time," in the words of one White civic association leader.

These quotes could be multiplied; as a knowledgeable White consultant summarized the consensual policy goal:

> I haven't seen anyone make the claim that "The city shouldn't be paying," that "They should pay less into the pension fund." It's more about getting more money to pay for both schools and [other services]. . . . Pensions are, like, so complicated, and it's hard to understand, like, "I have to pay a lot more money for this thing and there's nothing we can do about it," and it's for services that were provided twenty years ago. So politically it's obviously not a great thing, and it's difficult to understand, but it's something that we have to do.

Implementation

Ideas for Funding Pensions

With regard to simplicity, clarity, and agreement on the goal, Chicago's pension funding is unique among the cases in *Race/Class Conflict and Urban Financial Threat*. Implementation is, as so often, the sticking point. In a city and state with what appear to be bottomless needs and demands, rising property taxes, and continual flirtation with budget crises, finding millions of dollars per year, hundreds of millions per decade, and billions over several decades is not easy. Experts, advocates, political actors, the media, and civic organizations all offer proposals for squaring this circle.

A few actors are indifferent about means. After all, given constitutional guarantees, retiring union members will receive their pensions regardless of how funds are raised unless the city or state goes bankrupt—and perhaps even then. So one White union representative merely shrugged when asked about implementation: "Our specific position is that 'You have to fund it.' That's it. No specific solutions, positions on solutions." Another claims to have told the mayor:

> "Frankly, you're the one whose job is on the line as far as getting elected next time. So you're committing to us these funds; as long as it isn't something that directly hurts our members . . . that's not something that we're going to fight much about." Our main objective was to make sure our members' retirements were funded, and so we didn't really get very involved in where that was coming from, other than to make sure there was regular funding. . . . We've told our members, and we continue to, "You know, you're getting collectively $4 billion over the next forty years, so we shouldn't be nitpicky about where exactly it comes from."

Other interviewees came a bit closer to grappling with implementation choices, but remained aspirational and vague. A Black alderperson admitted to being "reluctant to mention new taxes. I don't specifically know what to suggest," other than that "revenue must be fair, consistent, and sustaining." A Latino community activist sought "a solution that respects workers' rights while allowing us to create a healthy budget and healthy communities. We cannot be one against the other. That's not a fair decision to have to make, right?" A White union representative insisted that "the tax base is there. We have to have the will in order to raise the revenue we need to both pay our bills and to provide the policing and the schools and health care and all the other services that people rightly expect." Even experts could be vague. "Where we're at right now, all my visionary ideas would be better if they could be started before you got to the point where we are," said a White civic association member. "Now they're hard to deal with. So really, where we are at right now is that we're going to be chipping away. We're looking for balance as best we can." And politicians resorted to a perennial favorite: "[Get] rid of all the waste," proposed a Black alderperson. "Then we can catch up on the pension that's behind. . . . The money that's being wasted alone, we could probably pay it out in a very short window." There is little to work with here.

Some actors, however, were willing to grasp the nettle framed by one Black alderperson as "everyone is good with 'We got to tax someone else'—but we need to realize that we are the only ones left." Some, like this White civic association member, looked for union concessions: "There needs to be room, in fairness, to do what you can to pay every pension you have to pay, but there's got to be some room on the union side to say, 'We're able and willing to work for some adjustment because things aren't as bright as they used to be.'" Some even proposed concrete union adjustments. "Maybe if [pensioners] get to a certain point [of income], no more automatic increase if they have enough for a comfortable life," suggested a Black alderperson, or "all new hires should be on a 401(k)-style plan," as one White economic actor proposed.

Chicago's taxpayers are the obvious source of revenue—obvious at least to people who needn't face the next election. Suggestions included "new taxes on sugary beverages" (a Latino public official); "a dedicated revenue source such as gaming, special tax or fee" (a Black alderperson); and "a financial transaction tax, potentially a commuter tax" (a White union representative). Class politics played a role: "The downtown is booming with million-dollar condos, right?" noted a White professor. "Those people, it seems obvious to me that you can jack up their property taxes." A White union representative proposed closing "a menu of corporate tax loopholes. . . . And what we really need is a constitutional amendment to permit a fair tax, an income tax that is graduated." Still others turn to political scientist E. E. Schattschneider's advice to expand the scope of the conflict; one widely shared demand was that the state "start giving the city of Chicago the aid that we deserve," in the words of a White alderperson.[40] The state should "expand the sales tax base to include consumer services," suggested one White civic association member, or "lengthen the ramp" to the date for pensions to be mostly funded, said another. A White professor noted that "Illinois does not tax any retirement income."

A few initiatives, finally, have the flavor of a policy entrepreneur hitching his or her long-favored proposal to a salient and available vehicle.[41] An Asian alderperson said, "I've been trying to tell the mayor, 'Focus on neighborhood high schools because that will solve the leaking [of well-educated workers out of Chicago]. And if you can do that, you can still raise the tax rate up.'" To a White economic actor, "the solution has to be thousands of middle-income jobs. . . . I'd like the city to get $20 per hour manufacturing jobs into the South and West Sides. . . . With enough tax rebates, and government financing, Chicago would get those jobs. . . . We need trade schools."

The Practice of Funding Pensions

The problem is not, as this impressive array of suggestions shows, a lack of ideas about how to raise the needed money. The Civic Federation, in fact, combined proposals into a list of sixteen "revenue options," presented to Mayor Johnson for his consideration soon after he took office.[42] Nor, as it turns out, has it been difficult since the late 2010s to collect the funds once they are authorized. The implementation problem lies in the difficulty of sustaining fiscal discipline over decades when faced with proximate, urgent pressures on voters and taxpayers.

For example, in 2016 property taxes were raised substantially to comply with what seemed to be newly stern legislative mandates for pension funding. The steep increases generated some controversy, but not a lot; the City Council easily passed the ordinance, low-income residents received tax relief, and the few interview subjects who discussed the matter agreed that, as a White union representative put it, "it's a non-issue. . . . [There's] little public outcry on that." By 2022, over 80 percent of property tax revenue was dedicated to the four city union pensions—"an unusually high share that has doubled since 2013 and makes Chicago 'unique' among U.S. cities," according to a public finance expert quoted by Bloomberg News.[43] Greater contributions from the same source seemed to be in the offing; the Illinois Policy Institute headlined a 2022 article, "[Mayor] Lightfoot Policy Change Could Quadruple Chicago Property Tax in 2023."[44] Four months later, however, came the news that "City Council Passes $16.4 billion 2023 Budget That Avoids Property Tax Increase."[45] Mayor Lightfoot highlighted that feat in her reelection campaign. She lost, but both candidates in the 2023 mayoral runoff election pledged no additional property taxes.[46]

The Illinois legislature and the governor have been even less willing to accept sustained revenue discipline. In 2021, for example, a new state law removed a birth-date restriction for Chicago firefighters so that they would be eligible at age fifty-five for a 3 percent increase in retirement annuity. Mayor Lightfoot opposed the bill on the grounds that it would increase Chicago's pension costs by hundreds of millions of dollars; "when that pension fund collapses, I will be talking a lot about this vote," Lightfoot wrote to the Senate president.[47] The legislature passed the law anyway, on the grounds that it merely made explicit what was already practiced. A later bill repeated the proposal for Chicago police.

Generation and Age as Implementation Strategies

The Timeline metaphor invokes a variety of temporal dimensions, such as decades of goofy multipliers and years of pension holidays, the impact of compounded interest and uncapped annual cost-of-living adjustments (COLA), increasing annuitant longevity underestimated by pension calculations, and increasing interest payments in response to lowered bond ratings. All of these resulted from choices at some point in time that ramified, without full awareness or intent, into an ever-increasing structural deficit. The Timeline also points forward, to a new temporal strategy designed to help reverse the impact of path-dependent deficits: generationally based disparity of payments to annuitants.[48]

At least one elected official, an Asian alderperson, claimed to tell constituents that "you get the government that you pay for, and today you're getting the government that you didn't pay for all these years."[49] But voters remain reluctant. So unions and politicians have joined forces to pass on much of the burden of pension fund payments to Chicagoans who did not yet know, at the time of passage, that they would be assigned that role—that is, *future* public-sector union members. Two 2010 state laws created a second tier of all pension-eligible Illinois public employees hired in 2011 or later.[50] A subsequent law created a third tier for some employee categories hired in 2017 and after.[51]

This change happened in the classic fashion of Illinois lawmaking. A bill that had been under detailed consideration was entirely replaced one morning by an amendment to add a new tier of pensions for all future Illinois public employees. Legislators expressed concern about the plan to vote on the unforeseen new amendment that day: "Throw out a Bill, take it or leave it . . . no time to go home and talk about [it with] the . . . teachers and state workers" who would be affected. Given that circumstance, one representative suggested, "we should postpone this vote until after we've had time to know what's in the Bill."[52] Asked about its financial implications for the coming year, Speaker Michael Madigan replied, "We don't have actuarial numbers relative to this Amendment.

We would say that we would expect that the savings would be over a hundred billion dollars," over an unspecified length of time.[53] With little further discussion, the amendment passed the House, 92–17, and the Senate that evening.

Whether or not the savings will be over $100 billion, give or take a few billion, the new law will indeed have impact. Compared with tier 1 pension recipients, recipients in tiers 2 and 3 must work more years before being vested, must reach a higher retirement age to be eligible for a full annuity, will receive payments calculated from more years of service (and thus lower average salary), may be required to make larger contributions, will receive a lower and uncompounded COLA, and will have a cap on the salary used to calculate pension amounts. The Laborers' and Retirement Board Employees' Annuity and Benefit Fund of Chicago (LABF) explains the three tiers clearly and explicitly; table 5.2 offers a slightly simplified version of the comparison.

Tiered workers may also be treated differently through agreements rather than formal contracts. As of 2020, for example, Chicago Public Schools no longer pays 7 percent of teachers' required 9 percent contribution of their salary to the pension fund—that is, for teachers hired in 2017 or later. The 7 percent payment had been in place since 1981, and it continues for tier 1 teachers.[54]

As of spring 2023, on average, half of the fifty-two thousand employees in Chicago's four pension funds, and almost half of Chicago teachers, are in tier 1.[55] As time passes, of course, more workers will be hired into tiers 2 and 3 while more retirees exit tier 1 through death. Other things being equal, these changes in pension payments will slow deficit growth. The Manhattan Institute estimates that pensions for tier 2 teachers will reduce annual payouts by about 12 percent compared with pensions for tier 1 teachers.[56] Compared with tier 1 teachers, those in tier 2 will work several years longer before their benefits outweigh the costs, and the benefit-to-cost ratio will be considerably lower for them. Figure 5.4 shows this timeline.[57]

Although the Civic Federation is eager to reduce pension deficits, its characterization of the new system is stark: "Tier 2 members [of the Teachers' Retirement System of the State of Illinois] paid about 1.75% of their salary to subsidize Tier 1 benefits."[58] Even the teachers' pension fund managers calculate that tier 2 recipients will receive a net *negative* of 0.01 percent of their pension contributions, compared with a positive rate for tier 1 recipients.[59]

By definition, these inequalities in pension recipiency were negotiated for people who could have no voice in the outcome, since they were not yet hired and in most cases were not old enough to be in the labor force when the law was enacted. This is a fascinating category of policy recipients: a set of people who are structurally nonexistent *before* a law that will

Table 5.2   Employee Tiers and Their Benefits, Laborers' and Retirement Board Employees' Annuity and Benefit Fund of Chicago (LABF)

	Tier 1	Tier 2	Tier 3
Definition	Participation in LABF before January 1, 2011	Participation in LABF on or after January 1, 2011	Participation in LABF on or after July 6, 2017
Eligibility for unreduced minimum formula	Age 50 with 30 years of service, or Age 55 with 25 years of service, or Age 60 with 10 years of service	Age 67 with 10 years of service	Age 65 with 10 years of service
Annuity amount	2.4% for each year of service × highest final average salary Maximum of 80% of highest final average salary for any 4 consecutive years within last 10 years of service	Same as tier 1 Maximum of 80% of highest final average salary for any 8 consecutive years within last 10 years of service Final average salary subject to a cap of ~$123,500, as of January 2023	All same as tier 2
COLA	3% annually, compounded	Applied to original employee annuity amount: lesser of 3%, or 50% of percentage change in CPI-U for 12 months Not compounded	Same as tier 2 Same as tier 2

(Table continues on page 156.)

Table 5.2 *Continued*

	Tier 1	Tier 2	Tier 3
Eligibility for annual increase	Age 53 or third anniversary of annuity start date, or Age 60 or first anniversary of annuity start date	Age 67, or first anniversary of annuity start date	Age 65, or Same as tier 2
Spouse annuity	50% of participant's annuity at date of death, or $800 minimum	66.7% of participant's annuity at date of death COLA, applied to original spouse annuity amount: lesser of 3% or 50% of percentage change in CPI-U for 12 months Not compounded	Same as tier 2 Same as tier 2 Same as tier 2
Child annuity	$220 or $250 per month, depending on whether spouse survives, to age 18	Same as tier 1	Same as tier 1
Employee contribution	8.5%	8.5%	11.5% as of July 2017 11.5% or normal cost, whichever is less, as of January 2019

Source: Author's compilation of information in Laborers' and Retirement Board Employees' Annuity and Benefit Fund of Chicago, n.d.
Note: COLA: cost-of-living adjustment; CPI-U: consumer price index for all urban consumers.

Figure 5.4   Chicago Public Schools Tier 1 versus Tier 2 Pensions

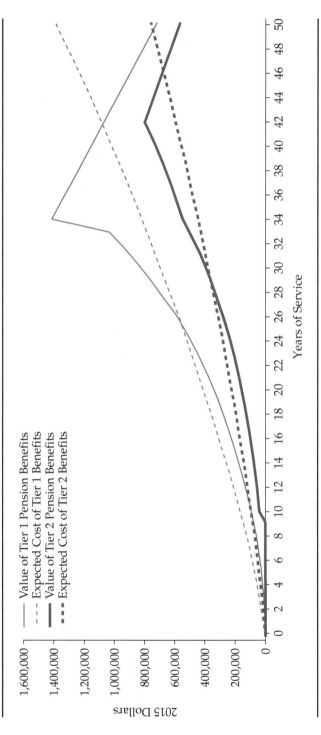

Source: McGee 2016, figure 10. Replicated with permission.
Notes from McGee: "Author's calculations using data from the Comprehensive Annual Financial Reports and Actuarial Valuation Reports of the Chicago Teachers' Pension Fund and the Chicago Public Schools. Solid lines correspond to the present value of retirement compensation and are compared with a cost-equivalent system featuring a smooth-accrual pattern across the teacher's career (i.e, the benefits earned are a constant percentage equal to the normal cost of benefits)."

affect only them comes into being on a particular date, and who become precisely identifiable but remain unable to effect change *after* the law is implemented.

A few of our 2016 interview subjects noted the nascent generational inequality: "Especially for teachers," said a White civic association member, the tier 2 law is "horrible. I mean, it's not a good benefit and they're going to have to do something about it at some point." Even a White union official described tier 2 rules, with some chagrin, as "a big concern for us," noting that the retirement age is "too high . . . for people in the jobs that most of our members do, in addition to not being a great benefit. . . . The pension funds are run to make money by most of the tier 2 people." And a White economic actor noted that "some of my friends, they're part of that generation, they're looking at some of their superiors with a little bit of anger. 'I'm funding your much more generous pension and right now I'm not sure what's happening to me.'" Nonetheless, the dominant reaction to the implementation of tiers was "generally bipartisan ignoring it," in the words of a White policy expert.

A few people even offered at least tepid praise for this maneuver.[60] One sanguine White union representative ("Another five years or so when tier 2 kicks in, if it's deemed to be legal, it'll have positive benefit") insisted that recently hired workers were not protesting. "No, nobody's saying anything about it. Even our employees, I have a lot of people, they understand that's their benefit, it's not a good benefit, but that's their benefit. There's not outrage here." He concludes, with visible relief, "I think in reality, pensions are off the table pretty much with this last action." A Black alderperson agreed: "I have no problem with two tiers, if [recipients] get the benefit of their bargain." The new structure did not apply to either of these interviewees.[61]

For a decade after their promulgation, Chicago's news media barely mentioned tiers 2 and 3. But the generational tier system has become more salient to unions and policy analysts as its impact becomes clearer.[62] The indefatigable Civic Federation puts the crucial point most clearly: "The lower benefit structure coupled with the lack of a reduction to the amount employees pay into their pensions may not be sustainable due to legal and equity issues."[63] This is a reference to the Internal Revenue Service's "safe harbor" rule, which requires that government workers receive pensions with a value at least equal to the benefit they would get if they received Social Security. Tier 2 pension recipients plausibly will not reach that threshold, a concern that had become clearer by 2023 than it was in 2010 (perhaps because the bill had received no actuarial analysis). State legislators have proposed new legislation to increase tier 2 benefits so that they reach safe harbor levels; as I write, those bills remain before the legislature—again unencumbered by actuarial evaluation.[64]

As *Washington Post* editorial writer Charles Lane writes regarding the Chicago Teachers' Pension Fund, "Absent reforms that reduce school systems' legacy costs, intergenerational injustice will deepen."[65] The tiered system is "devastating for retirement planning. No rational young person should sign up for that," in the words of another commentator.[66] But for elected officials and pre-2011 union members—that is, the people who negotiated and agreed to the tier system for their successors—the tiered system is, so far, cause for a great sigh of relief.

Politics

The Chicago teachers' union is possibly the most influential organization in the city. And they've become increasingly so.
—White economic expert[67]

Why should I care about posterity? What's posterity ever done for me?
—Groucho Marx[68]

When narratives of public-sector pension funds repeat the theme of dangerous deterioration over and over for a century, we can infer strong forces shaping their plotlines. Political incentives are one of those forces. It is not an accident that the 2023 mayoral candidates echoed each other and their predecessors. Pension commitments must be honored: "As Mayor, I will immediately put all of the tools available to the City to work for the benefit of retired and active city employees." The problem will be solved "without further burden on taxpayers." Those are the words of the losing candidate, Paul Vallas, but they are interchangeable with the pre-election words of the winner, Brandon Johnson.[69] He too promised to pay the city's pension bill without raising property taxes, by "auditing waste in government, prioritizing payments on our high-interest debts, and spending smarter."[70] In case voters wanted more information, he pledged to create, any day now, "a detailed plan to pay down our debts while ramping up needed investments."[71]

It is easy to mock vote-seeking politicians who eschew a clear stance on an issue that is "inherently political, opaque, and void of accountability."[72] But their rhetorical shuffle points to a genuine question: What impels candidates, all in the same political party, to evade solutions to a worsening problem that everyone agrees must be solved, especially given that the pension-reliant teachers' union (for which Mayor Johnson was formerly an organizer) is "the most influential organization in the city"?[73]

Much of the answer lies, once again, in a Timeline—understood here as the incentive structure that pushes politicians to focus on short time horizons at the expense of seeking to balance longer-term costs and benefits. As an experienced White political actor summarized, "How did we get into this mess? Read [former Illinois governor Peter] Altgeld's *The Cost of Something for Nothing*. 'I'm not going to be here when the chickens come home to roost.'"[74]

Consider the position of a mayor who aims for reelection. Promising workers a big pension in the future *resolves* a political dilemma. Elected officials want neither a tax raise nor a disgruntled or striking workforce; gains promised for the future, to be paid in the future, can gratify workers while averting pressure on the current budget. The eventual cost of the promised benefits is easily obscured; as one White financial expert at an advocacy organization lamented about the legal insufficiency of tier 2 pension benefits, "There's various lawmakers basically saying, 'Yeah, that's an issue, but that's ten years down the road, like we're not going to deal with it now.' And you're like, 'Okay, but it's going to cost that much more in ten years.'" (He then mimed a shrug and a turn away from the interlocutor.) Furthermore, future annuitants generate sympathy now: "So you [an alderperson] will make those votes," explained a White economic actor, "because you know that your challenger next time is going to try to unseat you based on your vote perceived as against the children, against the teachers." Unions can add to the pressure through publicity, funds, organization, and capacity to mobilize voters.[75]

In contrast to a promise to pay later, actually paying into pension funds now *creates* a political dilemma. It is among the least appealing ways to use always scarce resources. By definition, pensions will be paid to people who no longer contribute labor to the city and do not even contribute votes if they move to the suburbs or another state. A conservative politician will note the drain on private-sector growth from tax dollars being diverted into pension funds; a liberal politician will note the drain on expenditures for schools, police, health care, or road maintenance.[76] Crises always seem to warrant priority, perhaps appropriately. Thus, it is sensible to expect constituents to reward politicians for promising pension enhancements and to punish them for trying to fulfill their predecessors' promises.

In the unlikely event that constituents do try to understand the issue, it is very difficult for them to learn about what economists Edward Glaeser and Giacomo Ponzetto define as "shrouded" benefits.[77] Intangible costs are indeed veiled; in more colloquial terms, unlike piles of unplowed snow, "you can't touch it, right?" said a White alderperson.[78] City Council members routinely aver their lack of actuarial expertise; their main job, after all, is to "focus on constituent issues in their own ward," as a White professor pointed out. The very length and depth of the multi-decade narrative of crisis is itself an impediment to taking it seriously; as an Asian alderperson put it, "What we have been told [for many years] is that 'the sky is falling.'. . . . And then, you know, magically we find more money. . . . So the day of reckoning has always been pushed out. And I don't know that people necessarily believe that it's real." Magic is a recurring trope. One interview subject characterized public awareness as "'Someone else will figure it out' or 'There's TIF money' or 'There's some magic fairy that's going to drop money into the pension funds and we don't need to do it.'" This White union representative concluded, "There's a lot to fight through."[79]

The political incentives to postpone and the citizens' lack of incentive to investigate converge. As Alan Jacobs observes, "To the extent that electorates operate with poorer and less salient information about tomorrow's outcomes than today's, incumbents face incentives to make intertemporal policy choices biased toward the present and to avoid long-run investments with pre-election costs. Critically, *this problem presents itself even if both voters and their representatives place substantial value on long-term outcomes.*"[80]

Even if a mayor fights through disincentives and opacity, perhaps in response to worrisome activity in bond markets or concern about default, she faces yet another impediment. The politics of concentrating costs on union members by curtailing pension promises, or on taxpayers by raising fees for unchanging services, all for the sake of shrouded benefits to unknown persons in the vague future, are unpalatable.[81] As politicians know well, "organized groups are both highly attentive to policy consequences that affect them and well positioned to mobilize against policies that cut against their interests," continues Jacobs.[82] The unorganized public is not well positioned to mobilize.

Observers recognize what can seem like a "corrupt process" of pension politics: "There has been a very close connection between the unions and the people that they elect," noted a White civic association member. "And between the elected people taking care of the people who get them elected."[83] Breaking that connection yields swift punishment: Chicago Teachers Union president Karen Lewis called Mayor Emanuel's proposal to restrain pensions "criminal. . . . They just want us all working until we die." Mayor Lightfoot's description of new pension COLAs as "unsustainable" generated "a firestorm of criticism from organized labor."[84] Constituents whose taxes will fund rising interest payments to bond markets do not have a voice in this rhetorical dispute.

What are mayors—perhaps noting the impact of huge public debt on credit ratings or worrying about his long-term reputation—to do?[85] They will receive no help by expanding the scope of the conflict to the state. Illinois is one of nine states with a flat-rate income tax; voters in a 2020 referendum defeated a proposed constitutional amendment that would have permitted a graduated income tax despite, or perhaps because of, the likelihood that new revenues would contribute to filling the state's then-$140 billion pension deficit.[86]

Illinois is also one of eight states with a constitutional provision stipulating that membership in a pension plan "shall be an enforceable contractual relationship, the benefits of which shall not be diminished or impaired."[87] Illinois courts have been among the strictest interpreters of such a provision, and in 2016 the Illinois Supreme Court declared unconstitutional a law that reduced benefits for tier 1 recipients of Chicago's municipal (MEABF) and laborers (LABF) funds.[88]

A final political impediment to reducing pension debt is idiosyncratic. Richard M. Daley, mayor from 1989 to 2011, had the deserved reputation of holding complete sway over City Council members (partly, some claimed, through his treatment of their own pensions).[89] Deficits deepened during his tenure; Daley "was hoping to get the [2016 Summer] Olympics," a White journalist told us, "so he gave decade-long contracts with whatever unions wanted" in order to keep the peace. The mayor's staff "knew it was risky not to do actuarial funding," the interviewee added. "They do have people who know what they are doing. They said [to the mayor,] 'That could be insufficient.'" But as a White civic association member put it, "He went to Springfield and got them [his promises to the unions] passed. Without ever talking to us. Never came to us once and said: 'What's the cost?'" Instead, concluded a White economic actor, faced with a financial crisis instead of the Olympics, Daley "dipped into, like, all the funds and almost drained them."

Daley and many supporters defended this tactic of scoop-and-toss. "He thinks he's doing the city a favor because he's not having to lay off workers, he's not going to cut services or raise property taxes during a tough time," said this interviewee. "But then two years later, we come out of the financial crisis, and you have, like, nothing to show for this mess of a deal. And then we were downgraded to junk," referring to a credit rating by Moody's Investment Service.[90] Daley's solution to the problem? "Leaving office," said a White public official.

I risk overexplaining the politics of pension deficits. After all, many cities and states with similar electoral systems do not have serious funding problems; some have none.[91] Scholars offer several politically relevant explanations for differences in pension debt and in the capacity to fill the hole. Economist Christian Dippel shows that pension benefits rise during the terms of Democratic mayors, while payments lag.[92] Political scientists Sarah Anzia and Terry Moe show that partisan polarization around pensions rose after the 2008 recession, when Republican state officeholders felt more pressure than usual to rein in expenditures.[93] One particularly important explanation for fiscal discipline points, once again, to timelines: the prospect of lowered bond ratings, requiring greater interest payments on public debts, implies the onset of higher taxes or even the threat of default. That, in turn, risks the possibility that "population and business flee communities and states."[94] A reasonably well-functioning polity may find these countervailing incentives strong enough to contend against the desire for short-term gains at the expense of long-term budget stability. Chicago and Illinois have seldom been such polities.

Public Opinion

Unsurprisingly, surveys rarely probe views of pensions since they are almost never salient to the public at large. A question in a 2016 national poll asking for the most important problem in respondents' state yielded only an asterisk for a pension crisis.[95] Five years later, only 1 percent of New Jersey's registered voters placed public pensions or benefits among the state's most important issues despite recently severe and highly publicized problems.[96]

When induced to consider public-sector pensions, survey respondents across the country offer the same contradictory views as Chicagoans. On the one hand, majorities endorse fulfilling pension promises or reject unilateral cuts in established plans. Two 2011 surveys asked views on reducing public-sector employees' support as a way to control state expenditures; the Gallup sample responded to wording of "reducing state worker pay and benefits" with 43 percent support, while wording of "cutting pensions and benefits for retired government workers" found only 30 percent agreement among a CNN sample.[97] In a New Jersey survey a decade later, again only three in ten would "reduce state contributions to pension funds for public workers" in order to address a COVID-related state budget deficit. Following the impeccable political logic of postponement, almost twice as many would "borrow money through bonds and federal loans."[98] In a different measure of support, only two-fifths of registered voters in Los Angeles agreed in 2009 that local public-sector unions "have too much influence . . . over the city government."[99]

On the other hand, majorities also worry about the costs of public-sector pensions. In the same year (2011) that most CNN respondents rejected curtailing them, 54 percent in a different survey favored "eliminating the rights of public employees to collectively bargain over health care, pensions, and other benefits."[100] Although about half of Californians favored Governor Newsom's 2019 proposal for a one-time-only payment to state and local pension funds of $5.3 billion, 63 percent also agreed that the amount being spent on pensions was a "big" problem or "somewhat of a" problem.[101]

Fourteen percent of the Public Policy Institute of California's 2019 respondents had no view on Newsom's pension rescue proposal; that is the most appropriate answer since few Americans have enough knowledge to judge the aptness of any plan. About two-fifths of respondents in a 2011 CNN poll answered correctly ("less than 1%," or "1 to 5%") when asked what share of the federal budget goes to government workers' pensions and benefits, while over one-third chose "6 to 30%" and another fifth perceived costs to be even higher (including a few opting for "more than 50%").[102] Americans cannot be expected to know such arcane information, so the main point of these results is to reinforce scholars' description of pensions as shrouded benefits and of the issue as opaque and lacking accountability.

Class-in-Group

So far as I know, CIG is the only survey with large enough subsamples to enable consideration of the role of race and class in attitudes toward pension funding. Also so far as I know, no other nationally representative survey asks about views of a tiered pension system; possibly no other public-facing survey of any type does.

CIG asked respondents for their preferred solution if their town lacked "enough funds to pay for all the retirement benefits for city workers." Given three response options, presented in random order, 16 percent endorsed reducing benefits in employees' contracts, 29 percent supported raising taxes to cover the benefits, and fully 55 percent chose a tiered system of maintaining benefits for retirees while reducing them for current and future workers. Poorer respondents supported tiers the least (with agreement rising from 47 to 63 percent across income groups), as did Latinos, with agreement rising from 49 percent for Latino/as to 55 percent among Blacks and 61 percent among Whites. Whites and Latinos showed strong race/class intersections. Differences are greater across income within racial or ethnic groups than across race or ethnicity within income groups—class trumps race on support for tiered pension benefits.

Not surprisingly, younger CIG respondents were considerably less enthusiastic than their elders about tiered pension plans, both across all respondents and within each racial or ethnic group.[103] It is also no surprise that CIG's public-sector workers endorsed tiered benefits less than did those who did not have a public-sector job—but only slightly (52 to 56 percent). Public-sector workers were more inclined than their private-sector counterparts to raise taxes to cover retirement costs (36 to 27 percent).[104]

Regression analyses show few substantively or statistically significant differences when controlling for other possible associations with pension views. (See detailed results in appendix table D.4.) CIG respondents with a high income and those over age fifty-five were significantly more likely to endorse tiered pension plans than those who were less affluent or younger. None of the two-way (race/class) or three-way (race/class/gender) interactions show any clear pattern. As with LAUSD's charter school dispute, public opinion provides little or no grounds for arguing that foundational race/class inequality is driving the policy and politics of Chicago's pension deficit.

Race and Class

> *Citizens just want it solved. "Tax us as little as possible,*
> *fix the schools, police, crime. Don't tell me about it."*
> *[They recognize] lots of financial problems.*
> —White public official

In a late chapter of *American Slavery, American Freedom*—one of the most insightful books ever written about American racial dynamics—historian Edmund Morgan writes, "It has been possible thus far to describe Virginia's conversion to slavery [from mainly White indentured servitude] without mentioning race. It has required a little restraint to do so, but only a little because the actions that produced slavery . . . had no necessary connection with race."[105] That is a startling sentence. I cannot explore it here; instead, I use Morgan's claim that he could write about slavery's origins almost without mentioning race to frame a parallel statement: I have been able to write about Chicago's public-sector pension travail with not much mention of race. It has required only a little of Morgan's restraint to do so, because the actions that produced pension deficits and responses to them had little direct connection with group inequality or conflict. As one indicator, *none* of our thirty-eight interview subjects, unlike most New York or Atlanta interview subjects, invoked racial or ethnic categories either spontaneously or in response to a question about the nature of disagreements over pension policy. Only after the interview was at least half completed, when we explicitly asked each person to reflect on the topic, did race, class, or their intersection become part of the conversation.

Once invited, several interview subjects agreed that "race is there, yes," in the words of a Black union representative. "The Black elite is absolutely silent [regarding pension issues]. Their children are not in the public schools, don't use services, not in unions. Some are working against our interests, in hedge funds. We [unions] have reached out and tried to work with them, but they don't want to." A White union representative made a similar comment, also in response to a direct question:

> I think that often there is a latent racist subtext to a tax . . . [for] public service workers. That has not been really an element of the debate around the state-funded pensions. But I think that it's a part of the mix in an unspoken way in the city pension debate. . . . Certainly the most transparent from

where I sit is saying, you know, "Is Chicago going to be the next Detroit?" I think that's a racist dog whistle.

A White advocacy group member is even more blunt: "You say 'state employee' and people think 'Black people.' . . . And then there's this whole perception that gets sort of woven into a lot of the political arguments. . . . 'State workers are lazy,' this and that, that plays into this context without even using the word "race." . . . So there's buzzwords that I think . . . it's a very racist narrative."

That was about the extent of responses to our queries about race and racism. A few comments pointed to other dimensions of inequality. One interviewee, for example, noted an "uproar" about the new garbage tax "in kind of the lesser influence neighborhoods, where they felt like, 'Our residents are being nickeled-and-dimed and now this one more.'" This White economic actor clarified that the disgruntled were "senior citizens, you know." A White union spokesperson observed, "We like to say that 'This isn't just teacher security, this is women's [security],' and 'The people that are trying to disband K-12 education defined-benefit pensions are basically undermining the retirement security of women.'" To promote this framing, in 2014 the Chicago Teachers Union published *The Great Chicago Pension Caper*, in which it stated that "women make up three-quarters of the Chicago Teachers Pension Fund and 60% of the Municipal Fund (MEABF), and the public sector jobs that provided people of color a pathway to the middle class also provide a dignified retirement. Cuts to pensions thus disproportionately impact women and people of color." The report discussed harms likely to befall five predominantly Black communities if pensions were cut.[106] A labor coalition released the report just in time for a Springfield rally. Google shows three references to it; I have seen no other references in any published documents and no interview subject mentioned the report. (Almost no one referred to gender in any way.)

Most interview subjects, in fact, either had no response to queries about racial and class dynamics or explicitly denied their importance. Consider, first, elected officials or their spokespeople:

(*After describing anger over higher taxes or fees*) I don't think it's race considering that the Black community with their Latino alderman are happier together than the Latino aldermen with their Latino constituents. . . . I don't think it's race (Latino alderperson).

(*Response when asked how constituents were reacting to increasing property taxes*): You've really found on the property tax bill a big split between (*pause*)— the brand-new aldermen were the ones who were voting no. The aldermen that had been around were the ones who were voting yes (White union representative).

(Response when asked whether racial politics were at play with the pension issue): No. I just don't [see it]. It's, what's a good way of putting it? It sounds really cynical, but it's really about the money. It's about who brought you to the dance. . . . It also has a little bit to do with, "Where do these public employees live?" Black, white, brown—for certain aldermen, that's the constituency they need to play to. Those are the folks that elect them.[107] The ones that don't have that [constituency] dynamic? They're getting hundreds of thousands of dollars for their campaigns from the public employee unions. But no. I think trying to turn this into a racial thing . . . no, the pension thing has very little to do with race (White alderperson).

(Response when asked whether state legislative debates on pensions were "a race story, either in the state or in Chicago") No. I have never asked myself that question, "Is this a race/class story?" regarding the state government. No one else has framed it that way. Even state legislators who are hyper race-sensitive framed it as "retirees," or "middle class," never "race," not even in caucus. Also not on the Republican side. If it were a race issue, I would not have gotten involved. *(Was there any dog-whistle political speech?)* No. There *is* a class context—"rich White fat cats." That is coming from unions, not from Blacks (White public official).

We have a Black caucus in the city of Chicago, but the Black caucus has never united on *nothing* since I've been there. Nothing. . . . And the Hispanic caucus is the same way. Because what happens is, you have the administration, picks off key people in the caucus and says, "Okay, hey, we're going to get extra this, we're going to get a little extra," . . . and it's *crumbs*. It ain't even enough to amount to anything that's going to change your community, but you think you're getting more because "I'm on the inside, you know, I'm part of the team!" (Black alderperson).

Public officials may have personal, political, or ideological reasons to deny racial or class conflict in this arena, although that certainly does not obtain for other issues in Chicago. If that were the case, we might see more discussion of race/class dynamics from knowledgeable observers, whose job it is to peer below the surface and who have less incentive to frame issues in palatable ways. But the staffs or members of civic associations, research organizations, and even advocacy groups made similar comments:

You encounter people [who] will think, "Well, I don't have retirement security, so why do people in the public sector?" *(Any type of people in particular?)* I don't think I have a demographic in mind, I think more just like the general public . . . like when we give presentations, that's what I'll encounter (White civic association member).

Property taxes *were* a big issue—explaining it to people is a challenging issue. *(A bigger issue for some groups or factions?)* More just individual, "I as

[a] constituent see my taxes are too big—explain why you had to raise my taxes for no benefit!" (White economic actor).

You have to act before the point of blight. . . . And politicians have a hard time doing that. This is really not a race issue (White civic association member).

I bet you could get data from the pension systems . . . then you could show how pensions are also a racial issue. (*Is it phrased that way in public discourse?*) No, oh no, no, not at all. I mean, in the public discourse nobody . . . (*trails off*) (White civic association member).

(*Response when asked whether racial politics is associated with the pension issue*) Race doesn't pervade the pension issue all that much, more public versus private sector. (*Any dynamic of class within race?*) Might be some of that. I haven't really picked up on it much (White civic association member).

(*Response when asked about the possibility of a city income tax*) I would say there's generally not a class story there because a number of the progressive members of the city council also represent wealthier parts of the city (White public official).

It's complex. . . . Like, you will have an allegiance in one respect maybe as a fellow city employee. Another will be, just even within the firefighters . . . if you're an African American firefighter who's been there twenty years, you're maybe going to defend the Fire Department promotion policies, but you're angry too if you feel like the Irish, Italians cheat. It's like the constant changing of all these allegiances (White economic actor).

Social scientists and law faculty may have an even stronger incentive to ferret out underlying racial and class conflict. But they too "have to say that there aren't" any such conflicts around pension funding, in the words of a White professor; if there are, this interviewee added, "I've never heard of it." Instead, reported a Black professor, "the Chicago Machine still operates. Everyone agrees, including me—developers are in bed with politicians, with nonprofits, with Chicago civic committee, all are corrupt. It's not racialized, all are caught up in passing money around."

Finally, despite the Chicago Teachers Union's *Great Chicago Pension Caper*, even union representatives found little purchase in a racial, class, or gender formulation:

We say, "The public pension plans are kind of the last vestiges of a secure retirement, future, for minorities." (*How does that rhetoric play?*) It doesn't really pick up much, no. I can't say people are really responding to that well (White union representative).

I think there is definitely a racial aspect to certain Republican politicians generally when they blame public-sector employees for making too much money or being lazy or whatever they say. . . . It's been effective in Wisconsin. . . . You would think that if somebody were racist they would have more opportunity to be racist here because there are more minorities. But I don't think it's worked out that way. I think it's the opposite because you actually have real-life experience with minorities [in Chicago], and so people can see that they're the same as they are. Also, there's that voting power that they [minorities] have that prevents them [racists] from taking advantage [in Chicago] of the way they work in their smaller population [of Wisconsin] (White union representative).

Are people who live on the Gold Coast probably less in favor of making sure pensions are funded than people who live in the Bungalow Belt? Yeah, I'm sure they are. But . . . the city won't be able to borrow at reasonable rates if this isn't taken care of. So were they cheering against us at the [Illinois] Supreme Court? Sure. I bet a lot of them were. But I think they get it now. Not that we're right up their ideological alley but practically (White union representative).

All of these comments could be multiplied. It remains possible that our interview subjects, for some obscure reason, were mostly blind to race/class conflict in the pension arena, or that they refrained from speaking about it with us. But the media are similarly silent on race, class, or race/class intersections in reporting about pension funding. Two research assistants independently searched hundreds of articles published across a decade about public-sector pensions in the *Chicago Tribune* and through several news aggregators, including ProQuest Ethnic News Watch. Each found roughly a dozen items (with some but not complete overlap) that addressed race, class, or something like systemic inequality in this arena. Asked why so few, one responded, "Your topic [was] tangentially related to very hot topics for the press but they did not explicitly mention or insinuate any awareness of the issues that you were looking at."[108] The other noted simply, "I found few relevant items especially when trying to filter for race—I couldn't really find much substantive information."[109]

Finally, as I noted earlier in this chapter, information on the racial or ethnic composition of Chicago's public-sector workers in aggregations that match pension fund boundaries is unavailable. The Information Portal of the Office of Inspector General provides current salaries for men and women, separately by race or ethnicity, for thirty-seven City of Chicago departments, involving over 30,400 active employees. But the information is organized by job categories; a fairly small unit such as the Police Department, for example, reports demographic data on 94 job titles and 13 bargaining units, with no indication of which are in the Policemen's Annuity and Benefit Fund. Conversely, members of the Laborers' and Retirement Board Employees' Annuity and Benefit Fund or the Municipal Employees' Annuity and Benefit Fund work across many departments. In any case, these data refer to active, not retired, employees. Contrast this with the detailed records on the race, gender, age, and location of people stopped in New York's SQF operation; those records were crucial for mobilizing actors and demonstrating unconstitutional bias in the *Floyd* case. Relevant data might enable analyses of patterns of racially inflected wins and losses in Chicago's pension reform efforts, but whether intentionally or not, they are not available in usable form.

Denouement: The Four Questions and the Puzzle of *Race/Class Conflict and Urban Financial Threat*

America's foundation of race/class inequality has high, durable walls and has settled into bedrock over centuries. But it is not impregnable. In the case of Chicago's public-sector pension funding, even with somewhere between $35 billion and $60 billion at stake, neither laws, contractual provisions, implementation strategies, political alliances, media or scholarly analyses, expressions of public opinion, key actors' perceptions, benefits or penalties to recipients, nor policy outputs revolve around race, ethnicity, or class.[110] The driving force is instead a Timeline, encompassing both the effects of past choices on the city's current situation and plans for the future that are intended to solve it.

Once again, I turn to the four analytic questions that enable answers to *Race/Class Conflict and Urban Financial Threat*'s central puzzle: *When* is race/class inequality at the core of a policy issue? *How* is it manifested? And if race/class inequality is not at the core of a policy issue, *why* is some alternative force more important?

Is the policy intended to affect race, class, or race/class inequality? No. Neither contract or legal provisions setting pension terms nor decisions about how to fund the resulting commitments include group equality as a central or even recognized goal. Efforts to make support for pensions into a racialized, classed, or gendered political movement have fallen flat.

Is implementation intended to, or does it in fact, affect race, class, or race/class inequality? Yes, marginally. City officials and union leaders are presumably aware of the role of public-sector employment and pensions in the economic transactions of Chicagoans, and especially of the impact of public employment on the upward mobility of disadvantaged racial/ethnic groups.[111] That awareness is surely relevant to deliberations, past and present. But these considerations play no discernible role in specific policy choices. In an important instance, city administrators rely on property taxes to fill pension deficits, not because of the race, ethnicity, or even class standing of homeowners, but because property taxes are the largest available source of revenue.[112]

Are actors consensually identifiable by race and/or class, or do they consistently invoke race/class categories in their engagement with the policy or political arena? No. Mayors, budget officials, state legislators, civic association leaders, and Chicago-based union leaders have all been disproportionately White; Chicago's economic and political elite does not resemble Atlanta's Grid. (The City Council is an important exception, but by its own telling, its members follow rather than lead on this issue.) So Whites arguably have more impact on setting terms for pensions and seeking solutions for the deficit than do people of color. But disagreements are not characterized by actors' race or ethnicity, and race/ethnicity plays little or no role in the content of those disagreements.

Are policy recipients who consistently gain or lose, or policy outcomes that consistently affect the city's residents, consensually identifiable by race and/or class? No, for race; a little, for class. Each of the five unions includes, to a greater or lesser degree, Black, White, Hispanic, and Asian members; across all five, there is strong representation of all races and ethnicities. So overall, pension recipiency or risks to pensions are not racialized. Similarly, all Chicago residents are subject to the same taxes and fees, regardless of race or ethnicity.

The class dynamics of the pension funding issue are more complex. Economic inequality is salient in advocacy groups' proposals to tax the Gold Coast, or intermittent scandals about exorbitant pensions for a few favored retirees. There are periodic (so far unsuccessful) efforts to make the Illinois income tax more progressive, and countervailing efforts to avoid new taxes on business transactions or earnings. However, some members of the City Council's Progressive Caucus represent wealthy districts, and some representatives of poorer communities are among the most conservative alderpersons. The poor and those on fixed incomes get relief on property taxes, and unions are often wary of antagonizing employers that could leave the city and take jobs with them. So class politics are muted and class-oriented policy initiatives are rare.

In sum, the answers to the four evaluative questions resolve the puzzle's first layer: *When* is race/class conflict at the core of a policy issue? The answer is, not in Chicago's pension issue. That moots the puzzle's second layer: *how* race/class inequality is manifested. We are left with the third layer, *why* some alternative force supersedes. The answer is broadly the same as in LAUSD's charter school war: engagement with a financial and political threat that could be existential drives out other considerations. Like L.A. Unified's teachers and administrators, Chicago's politicians and union leaders see the danger of losing their positions, power, and institutions if they do not resolve (or at least work around) the problem

Figure 5.5   Share of Chicago's Population by Race and Ethnicity, 1940–2020

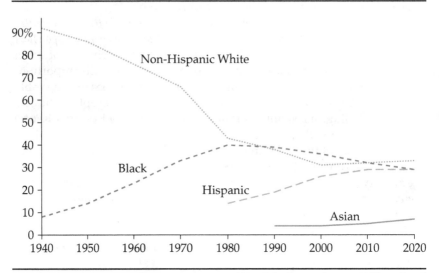

Sources: 1940: U.S. Census Bureau 1940, p. 6; 1950: U.S. Census Bureau 1950, p. 7 and *Human Relations News of Chicago* 1961, p. 1; 1960: U.S. Census Bureau 1960, p. 19 and *Human Relations News of Chicago* 1961, p. 1; 1970: U.S. Census Bureau 1970, tables P-1, P-2; 1980: U.S. Department of Housing and Urban Development n.d.; 1990: U.S. Census Bureau 1990, p. 44; 2000: Brookings Institute 2003, p. 17; 2010: U.S. Census Bureau 2010; 2020: Chicago Metropolitan Agency for Planning 2024, p. 23.
Note: Percentages do not sum to 100 percent for a given year because "other" groups are not included. The Census Bureau changed the mode of enumeration, definitions of each racial or ethnic group, and set of races and ethnicities to be enumerated between 1940 and 2020. Therefore, the data points in figure 5.5 are not precisely comparable across decades. Nonetheless, the trend lines accurately portray the changing demographic characteristics of Chicago's population over the past eighty years.

looming before them. At worst, the city could even confront the "D word"— Detroit-style bankruptcy.

The actual problems are, of course, different in the two cases. LAUSD's response to its precarity centers on a bitter fight for supremacy between two institutional actors with, so far, no mutually tolerable pathway to resolution. Chicago's actors are luckier or smarter; they have found a pathway to a significant part of the resolution by passing the problem on to powerless others through a structure of generational injustice. The Timeline replaces Open Borders, a Grid, and a Target; less fancifully, inequalities of age replace inequalities of borders, class, and race.

The Return of Race/Ethnicity

That is not quite the end of the narrative, however; the Timeline metaphor points to one more feature of the pension funding issue. Consider the changes in Chicago's demography over the past eight decades shown in figure 5.5. Workers who were hired up to roughly 1970, and who therefore retired by 2010, were almost all non-Hispanic Whites. Workers hired in the decades after 1980 have been, and seem likely to remain, evenly distributed among non-Hispanic Whites, Blacks, and Hispanics. This is a particular variant of a wider transformation: the White share of older Americans was almost 28 percent larger in 2020 than the White share of younger Americans. In the Chicago metro area, Whites' median age was forty-four in 2020; comparable median ages for Blacks and Hispanics were thirty-seven and thirty.[113] Thus, for the foreseeable future most recipients of the tiered pension system will be workers of color, who will be partly subsidizing the retirements of mostly White workers.

When I presented this material in a seminar, one of my students immediately saw the implications of tiers for race/class inequality. But none of our 2016 interview subjects noted it, and I have no reason to think that any actor in Chicago intends the linkage between tier-based injustice and changing demography. This may be a case of strong correlation with no causation (especially given the fact that other cities with tiered pension systems have a different demographic profile). Chicago's policy and political actors, perhaps rightly, are focused on current problems more than future injustices; as a White alderperson summarized, "As long as we've got this massive liability problem, the critical programs, like keeping schools open, neighborhood safety initiatives, after-school programs, jobs for youth, all suffer. Because we've got this huge black hole sucking all of our revenue into the pension disaster."

$=$ Chapter 6 $=$

Toward an Explanation
of Policies and Politics
in American Cities

The four cases in *Race/Class Conflict and Urban Financial Threat*—
policing, development, schooling, and budgeting—are core issues
in any city's governance regime. The four cities—New York, Atlanta,
Los Angeles, and Chicago—are among the most important in the United
States. Although these facts are uncontestable, my treatment of the four
cases in the four cities might well be contested on both methodological
and substantive grounds.

Methodologically, I follow an inductive strategy, now largely set aside
by political scientists,[1] of developing a broad argument out of mainly
qualitative evidence in particular circumstances. In this logic, the argument could be subjected to rigorous quantitative or textual testing, but
inductive analysis does not necessarily need to be confirmed by deductive
examination to be compelling. (As one not-altogether-complimentary
reviewer put it, the book takes a "perhaps even antiquated approach
toward its subject.") Substantively, the research yields two claims: (1) the
United States' foundational race/class inequality *still* shapes important
urban conflicts with, in some cases, little change over several hundred
years, and (2) the United States' foundational race/class inequality *does
not always* shape important urban conflicts, because some other force may
supersede the foundational inequality. The goal of the book has been to
support each claim and to explain how both can be true. This chapter aims
to complete that task.

I have framed the analysis around the puzzle of *when* and *how* race/
class conflict shapes a policy issue and *why* it sometimes does not. The
stripped-down version of its resolution is surprisingly simple. With regard
to *when*: race/class conflict is initially assumed to shape a policy issue if
*the goal, implementation, political activity, or policy outcomes of an issue can
be consensually characterized as racialized and constructed through material*

https://doi.org/10.7758/ptkg1499.5351

inequality. With regard to *how*: race/class hierarchy and race/class inter-action are two manifestations; there may well be others. With regard to *why*: some other force may supersede race/class conflict if *one or more sets of core actors perceive a threat to their economic well-being, capacity for political success, or institutional setting to be so severe that it seems existential.*

To justify acceptance of this argument or development of more quanti-tative tests of it, the cases must be appropriate starting points for possible generalization. Idiosyncrasy and uniqueness have great charms as well as the capacity to illuminate but would be misplaced in a claim to have portrayed contemporary urban America's race/class inequality. So each case must both epitomize its policy arena and have features generalizable to other locations.

The Cases Epitomize Their Issue and Generalize to Other Cities

Stop-Question-Frisk

Stop-question-frisk (SQF) is a standard and perhaps essential police tactic in many of the almost eighteen thousand U.S. law enforcement agencies. For more than a decade it was a seldom challenged cornerstone of NYPD's strategy to maintain order and prevent crime. But after fairly restrained use, SQF ballooned into the unconstitutional practice of targeting poor young Black men and Latinos. The 2013 *Floyd v. City of New York* decision drastically cut the number of stops, arguably made possible de Blasio's mayoralty, and forced NYPD to revise its policing strategy and tactics.

New York's SQF policy epitomizes not only a canonical case of race/class conflict but also three other insights promulgated by scholars of public policy or racial politics. First, as economist Albert Hirschman taught us, a policy intended to promote social justice and good order can be implemented in a way that perversely generates the opposite effects and simultaneously jeopardizes consensually held values.[2] Second, as polit-ical scientist Michael Lipsky described, street-level implementation of an apparently sensible strategy can have powerful unintended impacts on the actions of political elites, implementers themselves, and the public.[3] Third, as suggested by sociologist Orlando Patterson's concept of the "homeostatic or compensating principle of the entire system of racial domination," concerted opposition may abolish some element of race/class inequality without necessarily weakening or transforming the under-lying structure.[4]

Perhaps most American law enforcement agencies that rely on some version of stop-and-frisk have learned these and other lessons from New York's SQF. To focus on only one example, Chicago's police department has long engaged in *Terry* stops, with an almost equally long history of contention over their constitutionality. A series of lawsuits since 2003 have charged illegal and excessive stops, unwarranted violence, racial discrimination, falsification of or failure to keep records, ignoring of court orders and new rules, and all of the other challenges familiar to New Yorkers. The 2015 ACLU of Illinois report "Stop and Frisk in Chicago" asserted that "comparing stops to population, Chicagoans were stopped more than four times as often as New Yorkers at the height of New York City's stop and frisk practice." As in New York, "stop and frisk is disproportionately concentrated in the black community. Black Chicagoans were subjected to 72% of all stops, yet constitute just 32% of the city's population. And, even in majority white police districts, minorities were stopped disproportionately to the number of minority people living in those districts."[5]

After a string of investigations, local, state, and federal reports, legal challenges, and a 2021 class action suit, the city and the Chicago Police Department reached a $4.9 million settlement in 2023. The settlement specifies goals and procedural reforms in order to "protect the statutory and Constitutional rights of all members of the community" and "treat individuals with dignity and respect."[6] Chicago's history of SQF targeting and its partial reversal has distinctive characteristics, but overall it strongly resembles the dynamics of and outcomes in New York: good intentions can have perverse effects that jeopardize shared values; street-level bureaucrats can be caught up in a system that makes their work harmful; race/class conflict can be muted in some arenas but not necessarily others.

Other cities have similarly taken note of New York's experience with SQF, although their trajectories may differ. A 2023 radio news show in Philadelphia reported that "stop and frisk is being used illegally in New York City. . . . What lessons can Philly learn in this case?" One lesson is that politics matters; what radio station WHYY labeled a "contentious policing practice" is something that then–mayoral candidate Cherelle Parker "wholeheartedly embrace[d]."[7] After all, *Terry* stops are "a tool that law enforcement needs, to make the public safety of our city their number one priority. It is a legal tool."[8] Local activists, in response, scoffed at the possibility of constitutional stop-and-frisk because, without knowing a police officer's "thoughts . . . it becomes almost impossible to then actually prove the discrimination because 'How do I prove that you did this to me because I'm Black?'"[9] Parker took office in early 2024; which New York mayor's path she follows with regard to race/class targeting remains to be seen.[10]

The CIG survey enables us to compare public opinion in New York on this issue with the views of residents in other large U.S. metropolitan areas. Figure 6.1 shows the proportions agreeing with the three policing items most closely linked to SQF (previously discussed in chapter 2).

Figure 6.1   Opinions on Policing in the Seven Largest U.S. Metro Areas: Class-in-Group Survey, 2016

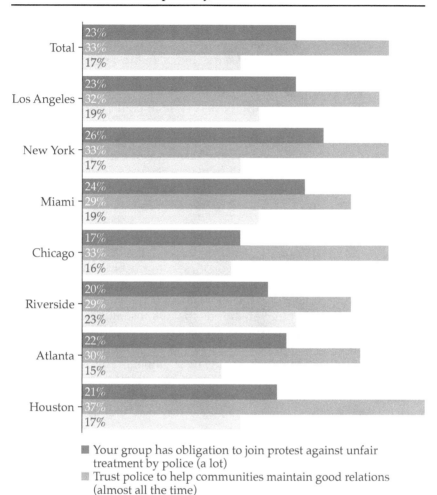

Total
23%
33%
17%

Los Angeles
23%
32%
19%

New York
26%
33%
17%

Miami
24%
29%
19%

Chicago
17%
33%
16%

Riverside
20%
29%
23%

Atlanta
22%
30%
15%

Houston
21%
37%
17%

■ Your group has obligation to join protest against unfair treatment by police (a lot)

▨ Trust police to help communities maintain good relations (almost all the time)

Police are looking to give your race a hard time (strongly agree)

Source: Author's analysis of 2016 CIG survey.
Note: Metro areas are ordered from largest (*N* = 579) to smallest (*N* = 223) sample size in CIG.

In addition to the total for the full CIG sample of twelve metro areas, the figure includes results specific to my four cases—New York, Atlanta, Los Angeles, and Chicago—and the three additional metro areas with the largest CIG sample sizes—Miami, Riverside, and Houston.

The bars show as much as nine percentage points of variation in agreement across metro areas on a few items; in the largest difference, 26 percent of New Yorkers but only 17 percent of Chicagoans agreed in 2016 that their group has an obligation to join a protest against unfair police treatment. But most differences are smaller, the metro areas do not present the same pattern across questions, and differences are not ordered by region or metro-area size (the subsamples are too small for more fine-grained analysis—for example, by race or ethnicity). The New York metro area does not stand out from the others. Overall, New York's experience of SQF resembles that of other large American cities, even if it transpired on a larger scale and earlier.

The BeltLine

Many cities are developing green spaces from the brownfields of old industrial sites or creating rail-to-trail parks from abandoned railroad beds. The BeltLine epitomizes this innovation. It was started earlier than many such projects, is more ambitious than almost all others, and has been a model for aspirants to new infrastructure transformation.

New York's High Line is 1.45 miles long. Boston's Minuteman Bikeway, a member of the national Rail-Trail Hall of Fame, is 10.1 miles long—and returns travelers to their starting point only by commuter rail.[11] The BeltLine promises 33 miles of trails when completed, and it will be circular. It is far from the longest bicycle trail; those can be several thousand miles long, conditional on the rider being "an advanced cyclist with sufficient training to complete them."[12] But overcrowded long before completion, the BeltLine has created "an astonishing journey of transformation."[13] While Ryan Gravel might be excused for exaggeration, the *New York Times* describes it similarly as "a staggeringly ambitious engine of urban revitalization" and cites one expert's opinion that the BeltLine is "'the most important rail-transit project that's been proposed in the country, possibly in the world.'"[14]

The BeltLine also epitomizes the fraught issue of rapid development in poor Black communities.[15] Paul Morris, Atlanta BeltLine Inc.'s chief executive officer from 2013 to 2017, pledged on arrival to "make sure every community is realizing tangible benefits of the program in an equitable manner."[16] But he was the CEO who resigned after the *Journal-Constitution* revealed Atlanta BeltLine Inc.'s failure with regard to affordable housing. Morris's successor repeated the pledge, as have subsequent mayors and City Council members—along with leaders in virtually all large American cities. Arguably the BeltLine is simply a recent, and spectacular, exemplar of the inherent "contradictions of sustainable development"—the "planner's triangle" of efforts to enhance the environment, promote economic development, and foster social equity among residents. According to Scott Campbell, the writer of these phrases, and as Paul Morris discovered to his cost, a three-way equilibrium "cannot be reached directly, but only approximately and indirectly, through a sustained period of confronting and resolving the triangle's conflicts."[17] When Atlanta's Grid is superimposed on the planner's triangle, we have the case as analyzed in *Race/Class Conflict and Urban Financial Threat*.

It remains possible that Atlanta can successfully manage gentrification. Most actors are striving more seriously than a decade ago to provide affordable housing; city ordinances have been multiplied and strengthened and the housing goal may yet be reached. If leaders can control market and political pressures so that low-income Black residents are not swept aside, Atlanta will be exemplary in an arena where many other cities have failed.

Other cities *are* following Atlanta's lead with regard to the BeltLine itself. Gravel's book offers a "catalog of dozens of projects" showing that "citizen activists and progressive leaders are reinventing underutilized assets in hopes of creating a better life for themselves."[18] They may be succeeding. Analyzing 619 "walkable urban places" in the thirty largest U.S. metropolitan areas as of 2016, real estate experts Christopher Leinberger and Michael Rodriguez show that walkable urban market share, in both office space and multifamily rentals, has grown in all of them. As in Atlanta, prices in New Urbanist settings are rising, yielding "substantial and growing rental rate premiums for walkable urban office (90 percent), retail (71 percent), and rental multifamily [homes] (66 percent) over drivable sub-urban products." Furthermore, Leinberger and Rodriguez find, "the most walkable urban metros are also the most socially equitable," despite rent premiums. The authors explain that surprising finding by pointing to lower transportation costs and greater access to jobs, which jointly offset higher rents for moderate-income households. Atlanta's long-lamented paucity of public transit is indeed costly; the city ranks just below the top third for increases in rental premiums and development momentum, but in the bottom third for social equity.[19] If the BeltLine can connect neighborhoods, create jobs, and facilitate access to them—all through a decent system of mass transit—its position in the social equity ranking can be predicted to rise.

Atlanta's Grid of race/class interaction is also not unique. The city's rise over the 2010s in the number of high-income African American households was matched or bettered by New York, Washington, D.C., and Houston.[20] Washington has almost as many Black-owned businesses and an equally embedded Black political establishment. Most broadly, the CIG survey shows that metro Atlantans' views of who benefits from gentrification are shared across the largest U.S. metro areas. Figure 6.2 presents the patterns.

Figure 6.2 shows a little more metro-area variation in judgments of gentrification's impact than we saw with regard to policing in figure 6.1. Fourteen percentage points separate Atlantans' agreement that gentrification will benefit the community from Los Angeles residents' less optimistic view (65 percent to 51 percent agreement). Overall, metro Atlantans are among the more optimistic respondents, but BeltLine enthusiasts have plenty of company. Like New York's SQF, the BeltLine as a case both stands on its own and offers a model for the study of similar cases of infrastructure development.

Los Angeles Charter Schools

Los Angeles has an unusually large number of independent charter schools and the most students enrolled in charters of any U.S. district. Independent charter schools teach one-quarter of L.A.'s public school students.[21] If only by sheer scale, Los Angeles charter schools exemplify the urban charter school phenomenon. They also typify these schools in a deeper way, by presenting a dramatic version of the charter school Rorschach test. Charters have been portrayed as (1) levers for challenging and ultimately strengthening traditional public schools through competition, experimentation, and demonstration; (2) safety valves that enable poor children of color to escape the stultifying and perhaps racist or xenophobic public school behemoth; (3) safety valves that allow better-off (sometimes White or Asian) children to escape the purported dangers, inadequate teaching, and resource constraints associated with inner-city schools; or (4) a move toward privatizing public school systems, whether as a gateway to liberation from stultifying state schools or as an attack on an institution essential to American democracy, depending on one's viewpoint.

These frameworks are not quite logically incompatible, but they are usually political antagonists. What is so fascinating and confusing about the case of the Los Angeles Unified School District is that all four frameworks are salient, whether at different historical moments, in different neighborhoods, or from the vantage points of different actors. Since much of the dispute's energy is expended in arguments over the appropriate framing, LAUSD's charter school war provides a template for understanding the range of charter school disputes across the U.S.

The Los Angeles charter school case is also exemplary on a different issue—the risks and benefits of operating in an institution with open borders. Extensive and excellent scholarship examines the role of geography, mobility, and boundaries in shaping structures of racialized inequality

Figure 6.2   **"Who Benefits from Gentrification?" in the Seven Largest U.S. Metro Areas: Class-in-Group Survey, 2016**

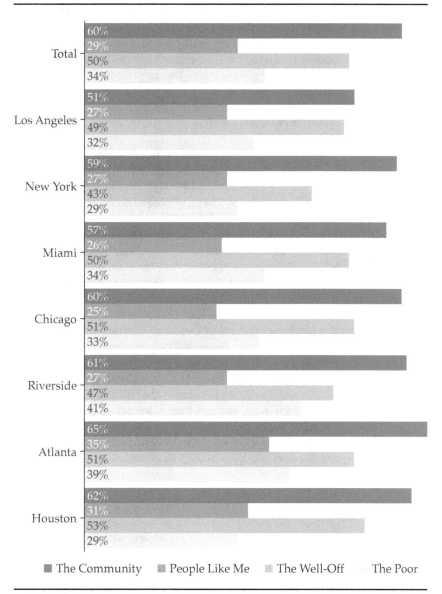

Source: Author's analysis of 2016 CIG survey.
Note: Metro areas are ordered from largest (N = 579) to smallest (N = 223) sample size in CIG.

and conflict, both in and beyond schools.[22] But arguably not enough attention has been focused on the capacity of open borders to shape an institution, whether enhancing it with new resources and actors or rendering it ineffective through loss of resources and actors. LAUSD is not unique in being threatened by outward flows; like Superintendent Carvalho, Chicago's school superintendent "has sidestepped talk of closures," emphasizing instead the need for more state funds and commitment to programs that will lure students back to the district.[23] Despite these efforts, one newspaper told its readers, "The stunning contraction in size [of Chicago Public Schools] raises important questions about the future of the public school system and the city as a whole."[24]

The case of LAUSD is also exemplary on a third issue—the ways in which a threat to what are perceived as zero-sum, diminishing, resources turns into a battle between teacher unions and charters. In 2016, the Massachusetts Teachers Association (MTA) "vowed to fight a ballot initiative to expand charter schools with everything it has." The union's president refused to work with the state legislature to pursue compromise and reform: "We will not accept any lift of the cap. That is not part of our equation."[25] An MTA caucus email asserted that "any attempt at compromise will be a total surrender to the charter school movement."[26] After a $38 million statewide campaign, the initiative to authorize a few new charters lost.[27]

Three years later, striking teachers in Oakland, California, were asked if charter schools were one of their concerns. The president of the Oakland Education Association answered, "You can't feed the minds of our students by starving their schools. . . . The OUSD [Oakland Unified School District] board has, for years, allowed charter schools to rapidly expand, and is complicit in this financial impact that is harming Oakland kids. Oakland needs an end to the unregulated growth of charter schools in our district, and the OUSD board must stop this divestment from our public schools."[28] This narrative could be repeated in other districts and states; although some charter and traditional schools work together and some charter teachers join teacher unions, "the *war* goes on."[29]

Pre-K to grade 12 enrollment is declining across the country, from 51 million in 2010 to an estimated 47 million or fewer students in 2031.[30] Open district borders are not a threat everywhere; at least before the COVID-19 pandemic, the largest southern and southwestern districts were holding their own or growing, as table 6.1 shows. But the three largest districts were already losing students, as were some smaller districts, all disproportionately poor and substantially comprised of people of color (table 6.2 gives illustrative examples). In shrinking districts, the financial, political, and institutional threat may feel dire; as one Black state representative said to us, "I've lived in Detroit. You know what happens."

Table 6.1   Changes in Enrollment in the Ten Largest U.S. Public School Districts, 2010–2019

District	2010 Enrollment	2019 Enrollment	Percent Increase (Decrease)
New York City, N.Y.	995,300	956,600	(3.9)
LAUSD, Calif.	**667,300**	**483,200**	**(27.6)**
Chicago, Ill.	405,600	347,500	(14.3)
Miami-Dade County, Fla.	347,400	347,300	0.0
Clark County, Nev.	314,100	329,000	4.8
Broward, Fla.	256,500	269,200	5.0
Houston, Tex.	204,200	210,100	2.3
Hillsborough, Fla.	194,500	223,300	14.8
Orange, Fla.	176,000	208,900	18.7
Palm Beach, Fla.	174,700	194,700	11.5

Sources: 2010: National Center for Education Statistics 2012, table 104; 2019: National Center for Education Statistics 2021, table 215.30.

Table 6.2   Declining Enrollment in Selected U.S. Public School Districts, 2010–2019

District	2010 Enrollment	2019 Enrollment	Percent Increase (Decrease)
Philadelphia, Penn.	166,200	130,600	(21.4)
San Diego, Calif.	131,800	102,300	(22.4)
Baltimore, Md.	83,800	79,200	(5.5)
Detroit, Mich.	77,800	50,600	(34.9)
San Francisco, Calif.	55,600	52,800	(5.0)
Boston, Mass.	52,800	50,500	(9.9)

Sources: 2010: National Center for Education Statistics 2012, table 104; 2019: National Center for Education Statistics 2021, table 215.30.

A final way to compare LAUSD with other districts is through comparison of public views about charter schools. Fourteen percent of CIG respondents across the twelve metro areas chose "increasing the number of charter and magnet schools" over other proffered school reforms. Chicago-area residents were the least enthusiastic, with only 6 percent support, whereas in the six other largest metro areas, between 13 and 17 percent opted for charter and magnet schools. Los Angelenos were in that mix, at 16 percent support.

In short, LAUSD epitomizes the conflict over charter schools and its underlying moral, political, and demographic structures. We can at least learn from its dismal history in pursuing the broader effort to understand when and how race/class inequality shapes urban policy arenas, and what happens when a threat that feels existential supersedes that foundation.

Chicago's Public-Sector Pensions

Both Chicago and Illinois have long been known as homes of robust machine politics, formidable labor unions, and freewheeling public finance. Chicago is the quintessential city where "we don't want nobody nobody sent."[31] Promising union pensions now to be paid for by someone else later is thoroughly in keeping with the city's traditional profile.[32]

Chicago's pension problem epitomizes that of other cities, but more so, for several reasons. Chicago pretty much invented not only public-sector pensions but also insufficiency in funding them; the two mayors Daley and Assembly Speaker Madigan lead any American list for political longevity and ruthless control; and the vacuum where actuarial discipline might have appeared was larger and emptier in Chicago than elsewhere (possibly excepting the state of Illinois itself). What is most striking, however, is that in a city known for its fierce racial conflict, race/class inequality has played little role in Chicago's political discourse and policy implementation around pensions. In a now-familiar pattern, the perception of an existential threat has superseded the more foundational conflict.

The case of Chicago, however, offers an unusual and fascinating twist. LAUSD has taken perhaps the more common route; what appears to be a zero-sum game between two entities contending over diminishing resources has generated fierce antagonism and stasis. In contrast, what Chicago's unions and public officials could have construed as a zero-sum game has been diverted into an agreement to replenish resources by extracting them from powerless future workers. The potential antagonists have united against a weaker party—thus avoiding both stasis and overt race/class conflict.

Other governments may want to take a lesson from Chicago and previously tiered systems. Although Chicago and Illinois are at the upper end of cities' and states' level of pension debt, each is on a continuum rather than being unique. As of fiscal year 2019, nine states had pension debts greater than 10 percent of residents' personal income; Illinois was second on the list.[33] Most states' pension debt grew in the decade after 2007, but three rose by more than 10 percentage points—New Jersey (13.7 percentage points), Oregon (12.7 points), and, again, Illinois (11.6 points).[34] Among cities rather than states, Truth in Accounting reported in 2022 that Chicago owed $33 billion, New York City owed $50.2 billion, and the other most-indebted cities each owed $11 billion or less. Per capita taxpayer burden is a better measure of a city's indebtedness; again according to Truth in Accounting, that burden is $71,000 for

New Yorkers, $43,000 for Chicagoans, $26,000 for Philadelphians, and $13,000 or less for residents of the other indebted cities.[35]

Illinois' tiered benefit system is also on a continuum rather than being unique. The New York State and Local Retirement System has six tiers, with tier 2 starting in 1973 and tier 6 in 2012.[36] A *New York Times* article comparing a teachers' pension fund to a legalized Ponzi scheme noted that "one study found that more than three-fourths of all American teachers hired at age 25 will end up paying more into pension plans than they ever get back."[37]

Finally, the racial and ethnic implications of Chicago's tiers are also not unique. As demographer Paul Taylor writes, "Our population is becoming majority non-white at the same time a record share is going gray. Each of these shifts would by itself be the defining demographic story of its era. The fact that both are unfolding simultaneously has generated big generation gaps that will put stress on our politics, families, pocketbooks, entitlement programs and social cohesion. . . . This is a problem of generational equity."[38]

In sum, my four cases are distinctive but not unique with regard to their respective issues. They provide the material needed to expand my argument and hopefully to develop a testable theory to explain when and how race/class conflict shapes policies and politics in American cities—and why some other force sometimes takes its place.

From Inductive Theorizing to Testable Theory

When?

How might one develop a quantitatively testable theory from my primarily qualitative argument? First, each crucial term in the four questions used to deconstruct the core puzzle will need fuller definition and operationalization. How is the policy's "goal" set and by whom? How are multiple goals arrayed, and what counts as a core goal? How should the analyst evaluate changes in goals as the policy develops? On the second question, what behaviors are encompassed in the category of "implementation"? Scholars and policy actors have long wrestled with principal-agent problems, the balancing of priorities when putting conflicting goals into practice, and changes to practice as a policy develops. Complexity is inevitable, but the theory must distinguish essential implementation practices from those that are more peripheral or uncharacteristic.

The third vexed category is "salient policy and political actors." Some, such as the mayor and leaders of the implementing organization, will always be important. But other crucial actors will vary across policy arenas. Analyzing advocacy groups and the federal court is essential for understanding New York's SQF, but real estate developers matter more for Atlanta's BeltLine. Labor unions have perhaps more impact in LAUSD's charter school dispute and Chicago's pension deficit than do any other actors. How are the behaviors of disparate actors and entities to be made comparable? Similarly, the salience of the media, public opinion, and electoral contestation varies; all three were crucial in New York's SQF but are mostly irrelevant in Chicago's pension funding travail. Determining when and how new actors (such as New York's Communities United for Police Reform) become too salient to be ignored, or old actors are moved into the background, will be important for building a testable theory.

Fourth, "policy recipients" and "policy outcomes" can perhaps be best analyzed in concentric circles. Some people, communities, and institutions will be directly affected by the policy's implementing activity—they are stopped and frisked, they live near the BeltLine, they have school-age children, or they anticipate receiving a pension. Some will be indirectly affected in more or less readily identifiable ways—they are young Black men, they live near repurposed infrastructure, or they own a home subject to property taxes. Outcomes partly track recipients in the same concentric rings, but important outcomes may not be attached to identifiable groups or entities. Researchers will need to consider broad, perhaps intangible, gains and losses from, for example, more intense policing, denser neighborhoods, school closures, or well-funded pension funds.

Finally, connections among the four questions will need to be more precisely theorized. Are they of equal importance in determining when a policy issue is shaped by race/class inequality? Are the questions truly independent of one another, as my framework implicitly posits? Conversely, if goals, implementation, actors, and outcomes are all endogenous, what strategy can be used to make distinctions and independent judgments?

How?

I began to answer *how* race/class inequality is manifested through the metaphors of targeted hierarchy and grid-like interaction, but at least three more abstract dimensions will need closer consideration.

The first is *simplicity*. It is similar to consensual identification; observers and participants concur, usually without controversy or even discussion, that actors, entities, or institutions can be described as (predominantly) Black, White, Hispanic, some other race or ethnicity, or some combination thereof. Observers and participants similarly concur at least roughly that individuals or entities are affluent, middle-class, working-class, or poor. Absent those forms of simplicity, the analyst will have much more work to do to determine how race and class intersect in a given case.

The second dimension is *linearity*, defined as a consensual understanding that races and classes line up reasonably well along a single continuum from most advantaged to most disadvantaged. Linearity is fairly straightforward, even definitional, for class, which in many usages is a relative concept organized around "more" and "less" income, wealth, education, or job status. Linearity is more complicated for race or ethnicity; as a first approximation, analysts generally agree that Blacks are overall most disadvantaged and Whites are most advantaged in the United States. In some contexts or by some measures, however, observers may not agree on judgments such as whether Latinos or Blacks are more disadvantaged, whether Asians are appropriately understood as "near-white" or people of color, or how multiracial persons or mixed communities should be categorized. Even class may not be linear since, for example, educational attainment and income do not perfectly coincide. Sorting out nonlinearities and their implications will be crucial for theorizing and testing *how* race/class inequality is manifested.

The third dimension of *how* is *parallelism*. If race and class are simple, linear, and arrayed along two parallel lines, such that the most (dis)advantaged race coincides with the most (dis)advantaged class, Whites will dominate people of color, the affluent will dominate those with few resources, well-off Whites will be in the best position and poor Blacks in the worst, and other combinations will line up somewhere in between. The result is race/class hierarchy, as in SQF Targeting.

In contrast, if race and class are not arrayed along parallel lines, such that some people or entities are racially disadvantaged but have high class status, and others are racially advantaged with low class status, the most straightforward result is an interactive Grid. But once parallelism no longer obtains, other race/class combinations and patterns are readily conceivable; one example might be a theocracy, in which a small priestly class exercises authority over and extracts resources from all of the rest of the population regardless of race or class. If simplicity or linearity of group categorizations also no longer obtain, testing for *how* becomes even more complicated.

Why Some Other Force?

Finally, the theory-builder must confront the counterfactual built into the book's title; why does some other force supersede race/class conflict in shaping a policy issue and its associated politics? My answer developed from the cases focuses on the perception of an existential threat arising from severe financial, political, and/or institutional loss or expectation of loss. To paraphrase Samuel Johnson, when a person fears literal or metaphorical bankruptcy, it concentrates the mind wonderfully.

If that formulation seems right, the analyst must determine what force is creating the purportedly existential threat. LAUSD's trajectory revolves around geography, Chicago's around time. Other policy issues might call forth different forces powerful enough to push foundational race/class inequality aside; examples include a climate catastrophe or war.

Beyond Even Race and Class?

It might be possible to extend my argument and proposed theory testing to other societal cleavages. For example, could the four questions focusing on goal, implementation, actors, and outcomes be modified to study gender inequality? Gender and societally defined gender categories differ from race and class in multiple ways, but gender inequality may be just as foundational in shaping American society and may be amenable to the same qualitative and quantitative examinations. Thus:

Goal: Is the policy intended to affect gender inequality or the relative positions of people who are transgender or gender-nonconforming?

Implementation: Is implementation intended to, or does it in fact, affect gender inequality or the relative positions of people who are transgender or gender-nonconforming? If "yes," how does it do so?

Actors and onlookers: Are actors consensually identifiable by gender or by gender nonconformity, or do they consistently invoke gendered categories in their engagement with the policy or political arena? If "yes," how are actors arrayed?

Recipients and outcomes: Are policy recipients who consistently gain or lose, or policy outcomes that consistently affect the city's residents, consensually identifiable by gender or gendered categories? If so, how are recipients and outcomes arrayed?

Answers to these questions could be deployed in the same way as in *Race/Class Conflict and Urban Financial Threat*. If the answer to at least one is "yes," the rebuttable presumption is that the relevant policy arena and its associated politics are structured through gender inequality or conflict around gender conformity; if the answers are "no" or mixed, the analyst must consider what other forces are powerful enough, or present enough of a threat, to supersede the foundational structure of gender inequality or conflict over gender conformity.

Other cleavages—age or generation, religion, nationality, or neuro-diversity—might also be amenable to a similar theoretical framework and analytic strategy. As a reader of a draft of this book put it, at its most ambitious, *Race/Class Conflict and Urban Financial Threat* is "inductively identifying the politicization of cleavages and groups in a policy landscape that generally has little structure. Isn't this the essence of politics?" I think the answer is "yes," and I dare to hope that this book succeeds in that endeavor.

Revising the Canon

I conclude by moving back from speculation about future books to the contours of the present one. Three sets of canonical but very different explorations of American politics and policy have shaped my argument, and I end by pointing out how they might be woven together. One is critical race theory.[39] Its core argument is that racial hierarchy is constitutive of American society, that laws and practices are designed to and have the effect of maintaining White supremacy, and that individual intentions and actions are much less determinative than are racialized structures and practices. The second canon, class analysis, is less distinctively American, but it too has powerful expositors.[40] It can be described in parallel terms: class differentiation is constitutive of American society, laws and practices are designed to and have the effect of maintaining wealth- or ownership-based supremacy, and individual intentions and actions are much less determinative than are economically grounded structures and practices.

The third canonical starting point seems initially not to fit with the first two. It centers on political scientist Robert Dahl's *Who Governs?* and other work on pluralist democracy in the United States.[41] This line of research is no less structural and capacious than the work of critical race theorists and class analysts, but pluralist theory portrays a different "essence of politics." Policy issues generally occupy different realms and are associated with different sets of political entities and coalitions. Although usually uninvolved in policy disputes and their associated politics, people can be aroused to action with regard to particular issues or concerns. Because electoral incentives lead political actors to compete for votes, and because of the dispersed and slack nature of potentially influential resources, the political and policy systems provide space for new activists and organizations, and for aroused laypeople to have an impact on outcomes. Race/class inequality may have been foundational and continues to play an outsize role, but the dispersion of resources, structures of democratic politics, and trajectories of different policy issues can create room for deconstruction of old foundations and creation of new ones.[42]

Race/Class Conflict and Urban Financial Threat seeks to reconcile, or at least bring into direct conversation, these very different frameworks of race and/or class immobility and pluralist maneuverability. That three-way engagement is far from showing a path toward a just liberal democracy—but it does offer more room for effective agency than does either the stasis of Afro-pessimism or class warfare, or the naivete of traditional pluralism.

= Appendix A =

https://doi.org/10.7758/ptkg1499.1572

Appendix Table A.1   Interview Subjects

		Total	Public Officials	Community or Advocacy Groups	Civic Associations	Economic Actors	Experts	Clergy
				Race or Ethnicity				
New York	Black	30	5	7	2		2	2
	White		1	1	2		2	2
	Latinx			3				
	Asian			3				
Atlanta	Black	51	8	6	3	3	3	2
	White		3	5	3	6	4	
	Latinx		2	1		1		
	Asian		1					
Los Angeles	Black	44	3		4		8	
	White		12	1			1	
	Latinx		10	2	2			
	Asian		1					
Chicago	Black	38	4	2	8		1	
	White		9	2		5	4	
	Latinx		2					
	Asian		1					

Gender

Location	Gender							
New York	Women	30	1	8	2		2	
	Men		5	5	2		2	2
	Bisexual			1				
Atlanta	Women	51	7	4	3	3	2	
	Men		7	8	3	7	5	2
Los Angeles	Women	44	12	1	3		3	
	Men		14	2	3		6	
Chicago	Women	38	4	2	2	1	2	
	Men		12	2	6	4	3	

Source: Author's analysis of interviews.

═ Appendix B ═

Appendix Table B.1   **Class-in-Group Survey of the Largest U.S. Metropolitan Areas, 2016**

Metropolitan Statistical Area	White	Black	Hispanic	Total
Los Angeles–Long Beach–Santa Ana, Calif.	104	71	404	579
New York–Newark-Edison, N.Y.-N.J.-Penn.	95	124	225	444
Miami–Fort Lauderdale–Miami Beach, Fla.	103	33	293	429
Chicago-Naperville-Joliet, Ill.-Ind.-Wisc.	102	91	59	252
Atlanta–Sandy Springs–Marietta, Ga.	101	108	17	226
Riverside–San Bernardino–Ontario, Calif.	102	25	112	239
Houston-Baytown–Sugar Land, Tex.	99	50	74	223
Washington-Arlington-Alexandria, D.C.-Va.	101	85	22	208
Dallas–Fort Worth–Arlington, Tex.	100	59	42	201
Philadelphia-Camden-Wilmington, Penn.-N.J.-Del.	102	64	21	187
Detroit-Warren-Livonia, Mich.	102	62	9	173
Baltimore-Towson, Md.	102	37	7	146
Total	**1,213**	**809**	**1,285**	**3,307**

Source: Author's analysis of 2016 CIG survey.

The fielded CIG sample included 6,867 invited participants, with 3,384 completing the survey, for a completion rate of 49.3 percent. Of them, 3,307 qualified as respondents whose views were analyzed.[1] Each respondent is weighted to be representative of his or her racial or ethnic group in the U.S. population as of 2016.

The margin of error is 2 percent for the full CIG sample, and 3 percent for each racial or ethnic group and each income category. The margin of error for each income segment within a race or ethnicity varies from 4 to 7 percent.[2]

$=$ Appendix C $=$

T he CIG survey items used in *Race/Class Conflict and Urban Financial Threat* appear here in order of presentation.

Chapter 2: New York's Stop-Question-Frisk

H01, *Index, Police Trust*: How much do you trust the police to (*randomize*)

1. help communities maintain good relations and stability among residents?
2. testify fully and accurately about a suspect when in court?
3. keep things under control in situations where public safety is threatened?

   Almost never; some of the time; almost all of the time

H02, *Police Bias*: How much do you agree that the police are looking for any reason to give a/an [*insert* "Black," "Hispanic," "immigrant," or "young" for respondents who are, respectively, Black, Hispanic, foreign-born, or White] man a hard time?
   Strongly agree; agree; neither agree nor disagree; disagree; strongly disagree

E02, *Group Obligation*: How much obligation, if any, do you feel that [Blacks/Hispanics/Americans] owe to poorer [members of their own group for Blacks and Hispanics; "Americans" for Whites] . . . to join in protests against unfair treatment by police?
   None; not much; some; a lot

H03, *Drug Sellers*: Even if neither is exactly right, which statement—the first or the second—comes closer to your views? (*randomize*)

1. We are sending too many drug sellers to prison when they should be dealt with instead through probation and treatment.
2. Sending many drug sellers to prison is the price we must pay for public safety.

H04, *Promote Safety*: People have different views about what policies their local governments should implement to promote public safety.

If your town or city government suggested these policies, which one of the following proposals do you support *most*?

1. Increasing the number of police patrolling the streets
2. Ensuring that violent criminals are punished to the full extent of the law

K01a, *Local Budget*: People have different views on how much their local government should spend on various activities. Using the numbered boxes below, please show us your views on what share of your city or town government's budget, if any, should be spent on each activity by indicating a percentage next to the activity name. Your answer in each line may range from 0 to 100, but the total number for all six lines must sum to 100. (*randomize; I analyze only number 1*)

1. Police and public safety
2. Public schools
3. Parks, museums, and recreation
4. Support for new business initiatives
5. Public housing for low-income residents
6. Programs to help immigrants

Chapter 3: Atlanta's BeltLine

L02, *Gentrification*: In many communities, developers or higher-income families buy and fix up homes or apartment buildings in working-class neighborhoods. In general, how are the following kinds of people affected by this type of redevelopment? (*randomize*)

1. Well-off residents
2. The community as a whole
3. People like me
4. Poor residents
5. Black or Latino residents

   Benefited; not affected; harmed

Chapter 4: LAUSD's Charter Schools

J02, *School Activities*: Suppose that your community's school board has enough funds in its budget to start some new activities or add to ones already in place. Which one of the following proposals do you support most? (*randomize; I analyze only number 2*)

1. Providing security guards to patrol each school
2. Providing extra educational resources to students who are struggling

3. Providing extra educational resources to students who are high-achieving
4. Developing new after-school or athletic programs

J03, *School Improvement*: People have different views about the policies most likely to improve the education of young people in the United States. Please tell us which option is most likely to improve education. (*randomize; I analyze only number 3*)

1. Increasing teachers' salaries
2. Providing public funds to support students to attend a private school
3. Increasing the number of charter and magnet schools
4. Holding students and teachers accountable through testing
5. Increasing the mix of students from different races and classes within each school
6. Shifting property tax receipts from well-funded school districts to poorly funded school districts

K01a, *Local Budget*: People have different views on how much their local government should spend on various activities. Using the numbered boxes below, please show us your views on what share of your city or town government's budget, if any, should be spent on each activity by indicating a percentage next to the activity name. Your answer in each line may range from 0 to 100, but the total number for all six lines must sum to 100. (*randomize; I analyze only number 2*)

1. Police and public safety
2. Public schools
3. Parks, museums, and recreation
4. Support for new business initiatives
5. Public housing for low-income residents
6. Programs to help immigrants

Chapter 5: Chicago's Pension Funding

K03, *Pension Funding*: If your town or city government did not have enough funds to pay for all the retirement benefits for city workers such as teachers, social workers, and firefighters, which solution would you prefer? (*randomize*)

1. Raise taxes so the benefits can be paid
2. Reduce the benefits that had been in employees' contracts
3. Maintain benefits for retired workers and reduce benefits for current workers and those hired in the future

For All Regression Analyses

L03, *Beliefs*: Please tell us if you strongly agree, agree, neither agree nor disagree, disagree, or strongly disagree with the following statements about citizenship and opportunity in the United States. (*randomize*)

> L03a, Full Citizen: I feel like a full citizen in this country with all the rights and protections that other people have.
> L03b, Equal Chance: In the United States, everyone has an equal chance to succeed.
> L03c, No Discrimination: Racial discrimination is no longer a major problem in America.

= Appendix D =

CIG Regression Analyses

For the regression tables and marginal effects plots, David Beavers used the *survey* package in R. He fit a weighted linear regression model with standard errors clustered on respondents' counties (*fips*). For the standardized coefficient plots, he used the *lm_robust* package in R and fit a weighted linear regression model with heteroskedasticity-consistent standard errors and *no clustering*. The two models are minimally different.

The standardized coefficient plots rescale the variables by subtracting their mean, dividing by their standard deviation, and refitting the model on the standardized variables. The regression coefficients can then be directly compared to each other in magnitude.

Both the standardized coefficient plots and the marginal effects plots visualize model 3, shown in the regression tables. Models 1 and 2 are available upon request.

Appendix Table D.1   Class-in-Group Regression Analyses: Stop-Question-Frisk in New York (Chapter 2)

	Index of Trust in Police		Do Police Harass Young Men in Your Group?	
Latinx	−0.105**	(0.049)	0.146*	(0.076)
Black	−0.123**	(0.053)	0.224*	(0.114)
Income: $35,000–$84,999	0.023	(0.039)	−0.027	(0.068)
Income: $85,000 and higher	0.019	(0.039)	−0.031	(0.063)
Female	−0.029	(0.044)	0.105	(0.078)
Some college	−0.003	(0.016)	0.001	(0.028)
Bachelor's degree or higher	0.010	(0.016)	−0.029	(0.029)
Ages 41–55	0.041**	(0.017)	0.005	(0.024)
Ages 56 and older	0.088***	(0.015)	−0.020	(0.026)
Moderate	−0.031*	(0.017)	0.014	(0.030)
Liberal	−0.046**	(0.018)	0.126***	(0.038)
Republican	0.034	(0.023)	−0.052	(0.039)
Undecided/independent/other	−0.065	(0.048)	−0.114*	(0.063)
Metro-area county	0.023	(0.016)	−0.002	(0.027)
Metro-area suburbs	0.033	(0.020)	0.003	(0.030)
Full citizen	0.086***	(0.015)	−0.054**	(0.023)
Equal chance	0.090***	(0.017)	−0.105***	(0.021)
No discrimination	0.035	(0.026)	0.031	(0.032)
Latinx: income, $35,000–$84,999	0.004	(0.067)	−0.109	(0.094)
Black: income, $35,000–$84,999	0.021	(0.074)	0.142	(0.137)
Latinx: income, $85,000 and higher	0.026	(0.060)	−0.074	(0.099)
Black: income, $85,000 and higher	0.018	(0.073)	−0.166	(0.120)
Latinx: female	0.059	(0.057)	−0.099	(0.099)
Black: female	0.045	(0.066)	0.013	(0.125)
Income: $35,000–$84,999, female	0.022	(0.050)	−0.112	(0.089)
Income: $85,000 and higher, female	0.025	(0.047)	−0.160*	(0.088)
Latinx: income, $35,000–$84,999, female	−0.021	(0.073)	0.215*	(0.116)
Black: income, $35,000–$84,999, female	−0.082	(0.094)	−0.029	(0.160)
Latinx: income, $85,000 and higher, female	0.019	(0.066)	0.071	(0.114)
Black: income, $85,000 and higher, female	−0.071	(0.081)	0.384***	(0.140)
Constant	0.531***	(0.045)	0.255***	(0.082)
Observations	3,126		3,121	

Source: Author's analysis of 2016 CIG survey.

Note: Excluded variables for all appendix D regression analyses are: for race, White; for income, $0 to $34,999; for gender, male; for education, high school or less; for age, eighteen to forty; for political ideology, conservative; for partisan identification, Democrat; for location, central city.

Results for each of the three variables expressing beliefs are independent measures of agreement.

*$p < 0.1$; **$p < 0.05$; ***$p < 0.01$

Appendix Table D.2   Class-in-Group Regression Analyses: The BeltLine in Atlanta (Chapter 3)

	Gentrification Benefits Community as a Whole		Gentrification Benefits People Like Me	
Latinx	−0.073	(0.087)	−0.134*	(0.076)
Black	0.109	(0.127)	0.185	(0.124)
Income: $35,000–$84,999	0.226***	(0.080)	0.053	(0.090)
Income: $85,000 and higher	0.167**	(0.080)	0.019	(0.082)
Female	0.237**	(0.091)	0.008	(0.086)
Some college	0.082**	(0.036)	0.016	(0.031)
Bachelor's degree or higher	0.138***	(0.031)	0.045	(0.031)
Ages 41–55	0.045	(0.029)	0.018	(0.032)
Ages 56 and older	0.092***	(0.027)	0.042	(0.029)
Moderate	0.016	(0.033)	0.017	(0.025)
Liberal	0.009	(0.031)	0.018	(0.028)
Republican	0.114***	(0.032)	0.037	(0.028)
Undecided/independent/other	−0.159*	(0.081)	−0.157***	(0.045)
Metro-area county	0.014	(0.025)	−0.025	(0.025)
Metro-area suburbs	−0.021	(0.029)	−0.069**	(0.031)
Full citizen	0.128***	(0.024)	0.076***	(0.028)
Equal chance	0.072***	(0.022)	0.019	(0.029)
No discrimination	−0.034	(0.034)	0.058*	(0.032)
Latinx: income, $35,000–$84,999	−0.028	(0.109)	0.149	(0.117)
Black: income, $35,000–$84,999	0.108	(0.145)	−0.144	(0.167)
Latinx: income, $85,000 and higher	−0.019	(0.091)	0.211**	(0.088)
Black: income, $85,000 and higher	−0.016	(0.156)	−0.084	(0.166)
Latinx: female	−0.174	(0.118)	0.182*	(0.109)
Black: female	−0.156	(0.196)	−0.180	(0.167)
Income: $35,000–$84,999, female	−0.294**	(0.119)	−0.042	(0.117)
Income: $85,000 and higher, female	−0.227**	(0.108)	0.035	(0.108)
Latinx: income, $35,000–$84,999, female	0.144	(0.166)	−0.197	(0.143)
Black: income, $35,000–$84,999, female	0.171	(0.192)	0.150	(0.208)
Latinx: income, $85,000 and higher, female	0.250*	(0.142)	−0.276*	(0.145)
Black: income, $85,000 and higher, female	0.194	(0.223)	0.209	(0.218)
Constant	0.200**	(0.083)	0.156*	(0.086)
Observations	3,105		3,095	

(Table continues on page 204.)

Appendix Table D.2   *Continued*

	Gentrification Benefits Well-Off Residents		Gentrification Benefits Poor Residents	
Latinx	0.059	(0.076)	−0.069	(0.078)
Black	0.052	(0.087)	0.156	(0.106)
Income: $35,000–$84,999	0.059	(0.076)	0.043	(0.083)
Income: $85,000 and higher	0.113	(0.072)	−0.047	(0.068)
Female	0.092	(0.081)	−0.044	(0.077)
Some college	0.035	(0.036)	0.024	(0.030)
Bachelor's degree or higher	0.141***	(0.036)	0.008	(0.032)
Ages 41–55	0.041	(0.037)	0.026	(0.031)
Ages 56 and older	0.018	(0.030)	0.106***	(0.033)
Moderate	−0.012	(0.031)	−0.008	(0.028)
Liberal	0.049	(0.039)	−0.028	(0.033)
Republican	−0.059**	(0.030)	0.084***	(0.028)
Undecided/independent/other	0.126	(0.101)	−0.189***	(0.060)
Metro-area county	−0.043	(0.033)	0.086***	(0.024)
Metro-area suburbs	−0.096**	(0.038)	0.049	(0.033)
Full citizen	0.053	(0.035)	0.033	(0.028)
Equal chance	0.009	(0.027)	0.105***	(0.028)
No discrimination	0.034	(0.043)	0.039	(0.039)
Latinx: income, $35,000–$84,999	−0.100	(0.100)	0.090	(0.098)
Black: income, $35,000–$84,999	−0.142	(0.112)	−0.166	(0.146)
Latinx: income, $85,000 and higher	−0.225**	(0.088)	0.020	(0.099)
Black: income, $85,000 and higher	−0.004	(0.119)	−0.016	(0.142)
Latinx: female	−0.104	(0.099)	0.063	(0.082)
Black: female	−0.154	(0.108)	−0.053	(0.131)
Income: $35,000–$84,999, female	−0.117	(0.098)	0.064	(0.101)
Income: $85,000 and higher, female	−0.047	(0.091)	0.122	(0.086)
Latinx: income $35,000–$84,999, female	0.178	(0.138)	−0.147	(0.103)
Black: income $35,000–$84,999, female	0.249*	(0.139)	0.016	(0.178)
Latinx: income, $85,000 and higher, female	0.036	(0.124)	0.026	(0.137)
Black: income, $85,000 and higher, female	0.044	(0.156)	−0.160	(0.162)
Constant	0.373***	(0.089)	0.154*	(0.089)
Observations	3,091		3,102	

Source: Author's analysis of 2016 CIG survey.
*$p < 0.1$; **$p < 0.05$; ***$p < 0.01$

Appendix Table D.3   Class-in-Group Regression Analyses: Charter Schools in Los Angeles (Chapter 4)

	Local Government Budget for Public Schools		Increased Number of Charter and Magnet Schools	
Latinx	0.053**	(0.023)	0.121***	(0.036)
Black	0.029	(0.023)	0.116**	(0.057)
Income: $35,000–$84,999	0.055***	(0.017)	0.034	(0.028)
Income: $85,000 and higher	0.092***	(0.018)	0.096***	(0.030)
Female	0.036	(0.024)	0.087*	(0.048)
Some college	0.017	(0.011)	0.015	(0.026)
Bachelor's degree or higher	0.031***	(0.011)	0.015	(0.025)
Ages 41–55	−0.008	(0.009)	0.017	(0.019)
Ages 56 and older	0.005	(0.011)	0.029	(0.021)
Moderate	−0.008	(0.010)	−0.065**	(0.025)
Liberal	0.001	(0.010)	−0.078***	(0.028)
Republican	−0.009	(0.007)	0.020	(0.021)
Undecided/independent/other	0.018	(0.020)	0.030	(0.047)
Metro-area county	0.013*	(0.008)	−0.028**	(0.012)
Metro-area suburbs	0.015	(0.010)	0.013	(0.022)
Full citizen	−0.015**	(0.007)	0.037**	(0.018)
Equal chance	−0.016*	(0.008)	0.018	(0.025)
No discrimination	−0.013	(0.009)	0.038	(0.026)
Latinx: income, $35,000–$84,999	−0.060**	(0.025)	−0.049	(0.050)
Black: income, $35,000–$84,999	−0.017	(0.031)	−0.099	(0.069)
Latinx: income, $85,000 and higher	−0.073***	(0.026)	−0.117**	(0.051)
Black: income, $85,000 and higher	−0.069**	(0.031)	0.128	(0.084)
Latinx: female	−0.070***	(0.025)	0.006	(0.064)
Black: female	−0.046	(0.035)	−0.126	(0.086)
Income: $35,000–$84,999, female	−0.047*	(0.026)	−0.029	(0.053)
Income: $85,000 and higher, female	−0.049*	(0.026)	−0.125**	(0.052)
Latinx: income, $35,000–$84,999, female	0.089***	(0.031)	−0.038	(0.097)
Black: income, $35,000–$84,999, female	0.067	(0.047)	0.116	(0.097)
Latinx: income, $85,000 and higher, female	0.098**	(0.039)	0.192**	(0.088)
Black: income, $85,000 and higher, female	0.082*	(0.044)	0.148	(0.117)
Constant	0.215***	(0.025)	0.032	(0.030)
Observations	3,136		3,128	

Source: Author's analysis of 2016 CIG survey.
*p < 0.1; **p < 0.05; ***p < 0.01

Appendix Table D.4   Class-in-Group Regression Analyses: Public Pension Funding in Chicago (Chapter 5)

	Use Tiers to Fund Pensions		Reduce Benefits to Fund Pensions		Raise Taxes to Fund Pensions	
		+Public-Sector Job		+Public-Sector Job		+Public-Sector Job
Latinx	-0.054	0.051	-0.021	-0.020	0.075	-0.031
	(0.095)	(0.148)	(0.070)	(0.103)	(0.084)	(0.159)
Black	0.077	0.224	-0.151**	-0.134	0.074	-0.091
	(0.105)	(0.158)	(0.074)	(0.100)	(0.112)	(0.170)
Income: $35,000–$84,999	0.084	0.121	-0.085	-0.075	0.001	-0.046
	(0.081)	(0.111)	(0.063)	(0.078)	(0.071)	(0.111)
Income: $85,000 and higher	0.138*	0.195*	-0.130*	-0.085	-0.009	-0.110
	(0.081)	(0.108)	(0.071)	(0.091)	(0.067)	(0.107)
Female	0.014	0.065	-0.059	-0.080	0.045	0.015
	(0.088)	(0.132)	(0.088)	(0.108)	(0.081)	(0.135)
Some college	0.001	0.027	-0.038	-0.050	0.037	0.023
	(0.028)	(0.044)	(0.027)	(0.039)	(0.029)	(0.045)
Bachelor's degree or higher	-0.026	0.003	-0.024	-0.038	0.050*	0.034
	(0.029)	(0.042)	(0.025)	(0.034)	(0.029)	(0.041)
Ages 41–55	0.019	-0.017	0.011	0.017	-0.029	0.0004
	(0.033)	(0.034)	(0.021)	(0.023)	(0.032)	(0.036)
Ages 56 and older	0.110***	0.073**	-0.037**	-0.018	-0.073***	-0.054
	(0.026)	(0.034)	(0.015)	(0.027)	(0.024)	(0.035)
Moderate	-0.004	-0.0004	-0.032	-0.008	0.036	0.009
	(0.029)	(0.042)	(0.028)	(0.033)	(0.032)	(0.050)

Liberal	0.061 (0.042)	-0.021 (0.046)	-0.024 (0.031)	-0.014 (0.045)	0.085** (0.037)	0.035 (0.052)
Republican	0.028 (0.031)	0.039 (0.039)	0.034 (0.031)	0.044 (0.040)	-0.061** (0.029)	-0.083* (0.044)
Undecided/independent/other	0.083 (0.075)	0.156 (0.106)	-0.050 (0.038)	-0.077 (0.051)	-0.033 (0.084)	-0.079 (0.110)
Metro-area county	-0.003 (0.025)	0.011 (0.044)	-0.017 (0.019)	0.001 (0.027)	0.020 (0.027)	-0.013 (0.045)
Metro-area suburbs	0.050 (0.038)	0.075 (0.048)	-0.014 (0.025)	-0.011 (0.035)	-0.036 (0.032)	-0.064 (0.042)
Public-sector job	-0.049 (0.042)	-0.049 (0.042)		-0.031 (0.032)		0.080** (0.038)
Full citizen	0.009 (0.028)	0.027 (0.034)	-0.055** (0.025)	-0.067** (0.032)	0.045* (0.026)	0.040 (0.034)
Equal chance	0.009 (0.030)	0.016 (0.040)	0.016 (0.026)	0.018 (0.032)	-0.025 (0.026)	-0.034 (0.036)
No discrimination	0.014 (0.037)	0.006 (0.049)	0.090*** (0.033)	0.102** (0.046)	-0.104*** (0.030)	-0.108*** (0.040)
Latinx: income, $35,000–$84,999	0.046 (0.110)	-0.074 (0.173)	0.072 (0.076)	0.114 (0.099)	-0.118 (0.103)	-0.040 (0.167)
Black: income, $35,000–$84,999	-0.053 (0.151)	-0.053 (0.201)	0.093 (0.083)	0.116 (0.102)	-0.040 (0.133)	-0.063 (0.199)
Latinx: income, $85,000 and higher	0.010 (0.120)	-0.112 (0.169)	0.095 (0.091)	0.106 (0.125)	-0.105 (0.092)	0.005 (0.163)
Black: income, $85,000 and higher	-0.023 (0.133)	-0.103 (0.198)	0.080 (0.080)	0.050 (0.113)	-0.058 (0.132)	0.053 (0.205)
Latinx: female	-0.031 (0.126)	-0.171 (0.187)	0.073 (0.094)	0.140 (0.139)	-0.042 (0.119)	0.032 (0.203)

(Table continues on page 208.)

Appendix Table D.4 *Continued*

	Use Tiers to Fund Pensions		Reduce Benefits to Fund Pensions		Raise Taxes to Fund Pensions	
		+Public-Sector Job		+Public-Sector Job		+Public-Sector Job
Black: female	-0.055	-0.288	0.178	0.290*	-0.123	-0.002
	(0.113)	(0.175)	(0.110)	(0.158)	(0.138)	(0.217)
Income: $35,000–$84,999, female	-0.042	-0.074	0.093	0.126	-0.050	-0.052
	(0.114)	(0.151)	(0.099)	(0.109)	(0.099)	(0.153)
Income: $85,000 and higher, female	0.021	-0.052	0.067	0.105	-0.089	-0.052
	(0.109)	(0.141)	(0.098)	(0.122)	(0.093)	(0.149)
Latinx: income: $35,000–$84,999, female	0.016	0.125	-0.174	-0.195	0.157	0.070
	(0.158)	(0.232)	(0.122)	(0.158)	(0.159)	(0.249)
Black: income: $35,000–$84,999, female	-0.027	0.034	-0.202	-0.285	0.229	0.251
	(0.174)	(0.217)	(0.125)	(0.172)	(0.163)	(0.244)
Latinx: income: $85,000 and higher, female	-0.042	0.205	-0.039	-0.116	0.081	-0.089
	(0.193)	(0.234)	(0.155)	(0.203)	(0.146)	(0.223)
Black: income: $85,000 and higher, female	-0.076	0.153	-0.091	-0.193	0.167	0.040
	(0.169)	(0.243)	(0.133)	(0.186)	(0.172)	(0.258)
Constant	0.446***	0.356***	0.297***	0.242**	0.258**	0.402***
	(0.086)	(0.106)	(0.082)	(0.114)	(0.090)	(0.135)
Observations	3,093	1,657	3,093	1,657	3,093	1,657

Source: Author's analysis of 2016 CIG survey.
*$p < 0.1$; **$p < 0.05$; ***$p < 0.01$

═ Notes ═

Chapter 1: Race, Class, Metaphors, and Cases

1. Citations not included in this section are in chapters 2 through 5, respectively.
2. Smith 2023.
3. Green 2021b.
4. On race, see Fredrickson 2002; Lee and Bean 2004; Prewitt 2013; Sen and Wasow 2016. On class, see Hout, Brooks, and Manza 1995; Jackman and Jackman 1983; Katznelson and Zolberg 1986; McNall, Levine, and Fantasia 2018; Piston 2018.
5. These terms and classification of people within them are problematic; analyses of multiracialism, racialization, racial regimes, the genetics of biogeographic ancestry, and identity fluidity deepen the problems. But I set those concerns aside in the interests of developing focused analyses of cases in urban politics and policy.
6. "White" means "non-Hispanic White" throughout *Race/Class Conflict and Urban Financial Threat.*
7. Three-fifths of Latinos identified their race as White and about 2 percent as Black in the 2020 census. Many others wrote their country of origin in the race category.
8. I first published an article with "Race and Class" in the title in 2005 (Hochschild 2005).
9. Berlin 2000; Du Bois 1935/2007; Higginbotham 1998.
10. Morgan 1975.
11. Einhorn 2006. Political scientist David Ericson (2011) makes roughly the opposite argument: that development and protection of race-based slavery increased the scope and power of the federal government in the economy, the military, and foreign relations. Regardless of whether Einhorn or Ericson has the more persuasive argument, in either case racial hierarchy was built into the structure of the new United States.
12. Frymer 2019.
13. The phrase is from Zolberg 2006; see also Gerstle 2001; Lee 2002; Ngai 2004; Tichenor 2002.
14. Foner 2020.
15. Newsome 2023; Thorn 2012.
16. Kulikoff 1992, 1.
17. Dahl 1977; de Tocqueville 1848/1966; Lind 2012.
18. Alesina, Londregon, and Rosenthal 1993; Gerstle 2022; Lindblom 1980. Examples in Google Scholar include foreign policy, foreign aid, trade

negotiations, urban economic development, skills, patent policy reform, banking, and more.

19. O'Brien 2015, back cover. For more scholarly, if less vivid, analyses, see Binder and Spindel 2017; Blinder 2022; Jacobs and King 2021.
20. Baptist 2016; Beckert 2014; Williams 1944/2022.
21. Rana 2014.
22. Deaton 2015; see also Chang 2019; Hirschman and Mogford 2009; Montejano 1987.
23. Jenkins 2021; Katznelson 2005.
24. Fortner 2023; Lassiter 2005; Sugrue 1996; Trounstine 2018.
25. Kruse 2005; Logan, Zhang, and Oakley 2017; Sugrue 1996.
26. Connolly 2014; Rothwell and Massey 2009; K.-Y. Taylor 2019.
27. Rothstein 2017, K.-Y. Taylor 2019, and Wright 2022 (on segregation); Cashin 2022, Highsmith 2020, and Trounstine 2018 (on public services).
28. De Souza Briggs 2005; O'Connor, Tilly, and Bobo 2003; Sasso, Matthews, and Newkirk 2019.
29. Brown-Nagin 2011 (on opposition); Abott and Magazinnik 2020, Ford 1994, and Komisarchik 2020 (on rules).
30. Orr and Johnson 2008; Reed 1988; Rich 1996; Arena 2012; Rodriguez 2021.
31. Dhingra, Kilborn, and Woldemikael 2022; Hacker et al. 2015; Waters and Kasinitz 2015.
32. That was 18 percent of 2021's would-be migrants; the next most popular country was Canada, with 8 percent aspiring to live there (Pugliese and Ray 2023).
33. Bobo 2011; Gerstle 2001; Hochschild, Weaver, and Burch 2012; King and Smith 2011; Smith and King 2024.
34. Ballotpedia, n.d.
35. O'Neill 2023.
36. My book coauthored with Vesla Weaver and Traci Burch (2012) offers a sustained, though tempered, analysis of grounds for optimism.
37. Although American household incomes are more equally distributed than is wealth, they too are more unequal now than at any time since 1940 (Atkinson et al. 2017).
38. Chetty et al. 2016.
39. Quote from Gary Burtless, coauthor of the study explicated in Tavernise 2016.
40. Corak 2013, 84.
41. Chetty et al. 2020, 714–15.
42. Chetty et al. 2020, 714, emphasis in original. See also Bloome 2014.
43. Chetty et al. 2020, 715, emphasis in original. Analogous gender differences hold for high school educational attainment, matriculation in college, jobs, and incarceration. In fact, "Black women have higher college attendance rates than white *men*, conditional on parental income" (716, emphasis in original).

Given the rich scholarship on race/class/gender intersectionality, the fact that Black women's economic outcomes resemble those of White women more than those of Black men is striking; it implies that the elements of the triadic intersection are not symmetrical and could usefully be disaggregated. Arguably Black women do better on average than Black men in socioeconomic achievement and mobility, but are more vulnerable to physical violence, sexual abuse, family instability, and daily insult. A book about race and class is not the place to engage with that disaggregation, but a different one should do so.

44. Collins 1990; Crenshaw 1989; Hancock 2016; Simien 2006.
45. Bird and Rieker 2008; Roberts 2022; Ross and Solinger 2017.
46. See Waters and Kasinitz 2015 (on undocumented immigration); Yemane 2020 (on religious discrimination); Carpenter, Eppink, and Gonzales 2020 (on sexual orientation and gender identity); Watson and Vehmas 2020 (on mental or physical disability).
47. Emanuel 2020, 12.
48. Muwakkil 2011.
49. Johnson 2016, 250.
50. Hochschild 2009.
51. Quotations are exact, with two exceptions. I silently corrected grammar or edited out hesitation, redundancy, and irrelevant comments. More importantly, quotes may express only part of an interviewee's views on a particular topic, since I use comments to develop or illuminate one of the book's themes rather than to fully explore the stance of particular individuals or the entities they represent.

    With due protections for confidentiality, the interview transcripts can be made available to fellow researchers.
52. Ipsos, n.d.
53. Unfortunately, CIG does not include Asian Americans or Native Americans; there were few of either group in the GfK respondent sample, and it was prohibitively expensive to create appropriate samples.
54. Tom Robinson of the London School of Economics offers a different strategy for approaching my puzzle. "You were essentially looking at three different levels: the level of contestation ('does race/class structure the policy contest itself?'), the level of perceptions ('is this an area where we think race/class matters?'), and the level of outcomes ('is this an area where one's race/ class mean you are impacted differentially?'). Of course, what makes this so hard is that those three levels (can) interact, but I think it is possible to think of them as theoretically separable." He then offers a way of constructing each of the four cases through different combinations of positive answers to his three questions. Email from Tom Robinson to author, February 23, 2024.
55. On the complexities of implementation, see Derthick 1972; Pressman and Wildavsky 1973; Wilson 1989; and Honig 2006.

Chapter 2: Race, Class, and Policing: Stop-Question-Frisk in New York

1. New York City Police Department, n.d.
2. New York City Police Department 2022.
3. New York City Police Department 2008. Blacks and Whites are non-Hispanic in these reports. The New York City population was about 24 percent Black in 2008.
4. In a broader context, public authorities have long sought to control the behavior of poor young Black men and Latinos or their communities. On men, see

Mazumder 2020; Muhammad 2011; Rios 2011. On communities, see Brown 2022; Hinton 2021; Sugrue 1996.

5. Jacobson 2001, 171–72. See also Office of the Attorney General 1999; White and Fradella 2019.

6. Quinnipiac University 1997. A 1993 *Newsday* poll had found a similar fear of crime among its respondents (Richards 1993, cited in Office of the Attorney General 1999, 52).

7. Crime control was the only arena in which Blacks approved of Giuliani's actions. No more than three in ten Blacks endorsed his handling of the budget, the economy and jobs, education, taxes, and poverty. Respondents in other groups tended to be more favorable toward Giuliani (Quinnipiac University 1997).

8. Quinnipiac University 1999.

9. White and Fradella 2019, 187.

10. New York Civil Liberties Union 2012, 7; see also Gelman, Fagan, and Kiss 2007, 816; Hood 2022. On 2011 stops, see New York Civil Liberties Union 2019.

11. New York Civil Liberties Union 2023; see also Fagan 2022; Jones-Brown and Stoudt 2013; Legewie 2016, 395.

12. The remainder were transgender females, genderqueer, or did not identify with a gender (Khan et al. 2021).

13. New York Civil Liberties Union 2022.

14. MacDonald, Fagan, and Geller 2016; see also Evans, Maragh, and Porter 2014; Levchak 2017. In a different interactive race/class dynamic, police were also likely to stop young minority men walking in disproportionately White neighborhoods and young White men in predominantly Black or Latinx neighborhoods. These were "racial incongruity" stops (Gelman, Fagan, and Kiss 2007; see also Carroll and Gonzalez 2014).

15. New York Civil Liberties Union 2022; see also Hood 2022.

16. Evans, Maragh, and Porter 2014, 141; see also Bloch, Fessenden, and Roberts 2010.

17. New York Civil Liberties Union 2022.

18. Soss and Weaver 2017; Weaver and Prowse 2020. See, for example, Baumgartner, Epp, and Shoub 2018 on other policing tactics that target by race, class, age, and gender.

19. *Terry v. Ohio*, 392 U.S. 1 (1968).

20. Harris 2013; Jones-Brown and Stoudt 2013.

21. Kelling and Wilson 1982.

22. Here & Now 2014. By 2015, Bratton and Kelling described SQF as "entirely distinct from" broken windows policing. In their view, SQF practice had disastrously evolved from an integral part of a working relationship between police and community members to maintain social order into a tense encounter to interrupt crime or confiscate drugs or guns, with the effect of increasing racial mistrust and hostility (Bratton and Kelling 2015).

23. Police Foundation 2017.

24. Rodriguez 2022; see also Glueck and Southall 2022; New York Civil Liberties Union 2023. In June 2023, the monitor, whose position was created as part of the *Floyd* ruling, reported that one-quarter of stops by newly created

"neighborhood safety teams" were unconstitutional. Further discussion appears later in this chapter.

25. Cramer and Mays 2023.
26. Office of the Attorney General 1999, 56–57, 59.
27. White and Fradella 2019, fig. 4.1.
28. White and Fradella (2019, 64, 89) suggest that police stops were considerably underreported.
29. Center for Constitutional Rights 2012.
30. *Floyd v. City of New York*, 959 F. Supp. 2d 540 (S.D.N.Y. 2013).
31. Goodman 2013.
32. Center for Constitutional Rights 2024; see also Clarence Taylor 2019; White and Fradella 2019.
33. Toobin 2013.
34. John Mollenkopf and Raphael Sonenshein (2013) provide an overview of New York's political configurations during the SQF period.
35. Quoted in Gelman 2013.
36. Quoted in Croucher 2020; see also Astor 2020; Rieger 2020.
37. Coviello and Persico 2015.
38. New York City Police Department 2013, C-1.
39. Or even, albeit with less sophisticated data analysis, as early as 1999 (Office of the Attorney General 1999).
40. Gelman, Fagan, and Kiss 2007, 813, 820–21.
41. Legewie 2016, 395.
42. Goel, Rao, and Shroff 2016, 365; see also Levchak 2017; White and Fradella 2019.
43. New York City Police Department 2013, C-1.
44. New York City Department of Health and Mental Hygiene 2013, paraphrased in Bellin 2014.
45. Quoted in Butterfield 1997.
46. New York Civil Liberties Union 2019.
47. White and Fradella 2019.
48. MacDonald, Fagan, and Geller 2016, abstract.
49. Weisburd et al. 2016, 46, 50.
50. Ibid., 32, 47.
51. MacDonald 2020. White and Fradella (2019) summarize all of this research well.
52. Fagan et al. 2010, 314.
53. I dislike the pejorative term "gentrification." I do not necessarily disagree with its implied critiques, but in my view value judgments should be explicitly developed rather than built into vocabulary choices. I use "gentrification," nonetheless, because no synonyms avoid an awkward deployment of too many syllables (such as, "movement of high-income residents into formerly poor neighborhoods as a consequence of new development").
54. Bloch et al. 2010.
55. Office of the Attorney General 1999, 79–80.
56. Both quoted in Southall and Gold 2019. This observation points to a tension in the politics of opposition to SQF. I, along with most actors in this policy arena, focus on the bull's-eye in the Target—the disproportionate stopping

of poor, young Black men or Latinos in poor minority neighborhoods. But a subsidiary theme is the breadth of *Terry* stops across all Black men: "The police don't care what kind of Black person you are," said a White attorney. "They're really bad at stopping criminals. If you're Black, that's it. That's all they see." Even if relatively few well-off Black men were stopped, these incidents had considerable impact on the politics around SQF. This attorney added that City Council member Jumaane Williams "basically came to this side of his political life after getting arrested at the West Indian Day Parade.... And then just two weeks ago we were with Michael Blake, who's an Assembly member from the Bronx, who was thrown up against a fence at a block party in his neighborhood."

57. Weaver and Prowse 2020, 1176.
58. Quoted in Lehrer 2012.
59. Rivera 2010.
60. Both quoted in Greenberg 2013.
61. Quoted in Devereaux 2012.
62. Taylor 2012b.
63. Quoted in New York Civil Liberties Union 2012.
64. City of New York 2013. About one-fifth of registered voters participated in the primary—"a middling turnout, by historical standards" (Roberts 2013).
65. Greenberg 2013.
66. Kirsten Walters collected news articles from New York's mainstream and Black-oriented newspapers from 2000 through 2020; she identified 3,062 relevant articles in the former and 644 in the latter. Keywords for all searches were: (new york *or* nyc *or* new york city) *and* (stop and frisk *or* stop, question, and frisk *or* SQF). For the Black-oriented press, we also searched on (African American / Caribbean / African). Given availability in Nexis Uni, we drew articles from the *New York Times, New York Daily News, New York Sun,* and *New York Observer* (and a smattering from the *Daily Record of Rochester*). Given what was available in ProQuest Ethnic News Watch, we drew articles from the *New York Amsterdam News, New York Beacon, New Voice of New York,* and *Tri-State Defender.*
67. The exact methods and six thematic word lists are available upon request.
68. We chose articles with the most references to our keywords or the most detail about the policy and its practice and context, spread across the two decades and all available newspapers.
69. In 2011, noted the same interview subject, "we also started to hear from police officers who were complaining that they didn't like doing this stuff.... We got contacted by some of those officers saying, 'We want to come forward. Can you help us do that?' So that was an interesting piece to throw into the mix."
70. Goodman 2013. The full proposed act would have banned racial profiling in policing, established independent oversight of the NYPD, and required NYPD officers to provide subjects of stops with information and justification for the encounter.
71. New York Civil Liberties Union's advocacy director, quoted in Taylor 2012b.
72. Our media analyses show that New York's mainstream press cited the NYCLU reports or quoted its leaders far more than they did any other organization or umbrella group.

73. Taylor 2012a.
74. Leland and Moynihan 2012.
75. Arinde 2007; Barker 2011; Shabazz 2009.
76. CBS News / *New York Times* 2011.
77. "Last year more than 800,000 [sic] New Yorkers were stopped by the police and questioned under this policy. Some people say this is excessive and innocent people are being harassed. Other people say this is acceptable to make New York City safer" (*New York Times* 2012).
78. Quinnipiac University (n.d.) is "a nationally recognized leader in public opinion research taking the pulse of American voters, on a continual basis. . . . The Poll collects data using live phone interviewers and scientific based methodology considered to be the gold standard in the industry." Samples range in size from about one thousand to about two thousand; margins of error range from 2.6 to 3.3.
79. CBS News / *New York Times* Poll 2011. Compared with their male counterparts, higher proportions of Black women and Latinas described racially disparate police stops as unjustified. Whites showed no gender difference.
80. In 2012, Black and Hispanic women, but not White women, were again more likely than their male counterparts to deem SQF "excessive." Both *New York Times* polls include too few Asians to report results.
81. The final three polls in this series are worded differently from the first seven. Note that the question was asked at irregular intervals, which is not apparent in the figure.
82. *New York Times* 2012.
83. Quinnipiac University 2012c, 2013f, 2013g, 2014a, 2014b. However, when directly asked in 2013 to choose either "reforming stop and frisk" or "keeping crime rates down," twice as many New York City voters opted for crime control. Blacks endorsed SQF reform much more than did Whites, but a majority of African Americans also were more concerned about crime than about SQF excesses (Quinnipiac University 2013g).

    Three years later, 73 percent of a representative American sample, with similar views among Blacks, Whites, and Hispanics, agreed that police should aim to prevent crime, "but not if those steps could violate your basic civil liberties," rather than agreeing that the police should do what is needed to prevent crime "even if it means some of your basic civil liberties could be violated" (Quinnipiac University 2016a). These two items are not directly contradictory, but responses certainly tend in opposite directions.
84. *New York Times* 2012.
85. Quinnipiac University 2014c, 2014d, 2014e, 2016b, 2017.
86. Quinnipiac University 2009 (New York City); Quinnipiac University 2014c, 2015a, 2015b, 2015c (New York City and "your neighborhood").
87. Bratton and Kelling 2015; see note 22.
88. CBS News / *New York Times* 2011 (on profiling); *New York Times* 2012 (on SQF).
89. *New York Times* 2012.
90. The core belief items were first published in Cohen 2010.
91. The weighted difference in means between high- and low-income White women, and between high- and low-income Latinas, is statistically significant.

92. One item in the CIG index closely tracks one rationale for SQF: "Do you trust the police . . . to help communities maintain good relations and stability among residents?" Crosstabs show clear differences by race or ethnicity, some differences by class, and consistent but smaller differences that accord with race/class interaction.

93. Immigrants were asked about "immigrant men" in CIG, but here their responses are incorporated into the relevant racial or ethnic group. About 60 percent of CIG Hispanics are immigrants; conversely, about 85 percent of immigrants are Hispanic. Six percent of White CIG respondents and 9 percent of Black CIG respondents are immigrants. Middle- and high-income immigrants are slightly more likely than middle- and high-income non-immigrants to perceive police harassment.

94. At each class position, Hispanics are between Blacks and Whites in perceptions of unfair police treatment of their group.

95. Especially the most affluent Black men.

96. Although almost twice as many poor as affluent respondents (34 to 18 percent) say the same about group obligations to poor members, intersections between race and class are weak. The question was one of five with the same stem about group obligations; items were rotated randomly.

97. See Bell 2016; Carr, Napolitano, and Keating 2007; Foreman 2017; Fortner 2020; Parker and Hurst 2021; Zoorob 2020.

98. Weighted average support for probation is 10.9 percent among Whites and 11.0 percent among Blacks.

99. Greenberg 2014.

100. New York City Police Department, n.d.

101. Note that this interview took place in 2016, before the spate of police killings and accompanying national focus on George Floyd, Breanna Taylor, and others.

102. Clarence Taylor 2019, 206.

103. New York Civil Liberties Union 2023. New York's Black and White populations were stable at about 23 and 33 percent, respectively, from 2010 through 2022.

104. Denerstein 2023, 25. Officials from NYPD and the mayor's office contest the report's methodology and conclusions (Kilgannon 2023).

105. Akinnibi 2023.

Chapter 3: Race, Class, and Development: The Atlanta BeltLine

1. Although he does not deploy the Grid metaphor, Maurice Hobson (2017) uses the same logic in depicting both the slightly racially imbalanced success of the Grid's top row and the class divide that generates its very different bottom row.

2. Atlanta BeltLine Inc., n.d.-a.

3. The data are provided at the level of 2020 census tracts. No Atlanta census tract has more than 8 percent Latinx or Asian residents; maps with data on these residents in the vicinity of the BeltLine are available from the author.

4. DePietro 2022.

5. Jackson 2022.
6. Hwang, Fitzpatrick, and Helms 1998; Wiltz 2022.
7. Atlanta BeltLine Inc., n.d.-a.
8. Nathaniel Smith, quoted in Immergluck 2022, frontispiece.
9. Ferguson 2002, 268, quoted in Hyra 2024, 199. In something of an understatement, Hyra comments, "This is still true today" (ibid., see more generally 194–99).
10. Atlanta BeltLine Inc., n.d.-b.
11. Pendergrast 2017, x.
12. Atlanta BeltLine Inc. 2023.
13. Gravel has spoken at conferences sponsored by the Congress of New Urbanism, so he presumably sees the connections that I am positing. Mark Pendergrast (2017, 138–39) describes how Atlantans linked a "New Urbanism health mantra" to the BeltLine in a way that could "forever change the face of Atlanta."
14. Jacobs 1961/2011; see also, for example, Speck 2013.
15. Congress for the New Urbanism 2001.
16. Gravel 2016, 97. On the initial goal of transit, see Pendergrast 2017, 18–26.
17. Gravel 2016, 109–25.
18. Aragon 2023.
19. Quoted in McDonald 2019.
20. JLL 2021, 4, 14.
21. Green 2021a.
22. Quoted in Pendergrast 2017, 157.
23. Finn and Douglas 2020, 20–21.
24. BeltLine leadership exemplifies the Grid's racially mixed, affluent top row. The fundraising arm, the Atlanta BeltLine Partnership, has a board of directors with roughly two dozen members, including, in 2021, C-suite executives from most of Atlanta's or Fulton County's largest private-sector employers (Home Depot, Cox Enterprises, Piedmont Healthcare, Coca-Cola, Merrill Lynch, Warner Media, Truist Financial Corporation), along with executives from six construction, architectural, and commercial real estate firms and a sprinkling of clergy and others. At least thirteen of the deep-pocketed board members, including the chair, appeared from their official photos or other information (such as websites) to be persons of color (Atlanta BeltLine Inc. 2021).
25. Pressman and Wildavsky 1973; Wegrich 2015.
26. Stone 2008, 277.
27. Pendergrast 2017, 58–62.
28. Federal Highway Administration Center for Innovative Financial Support, n.d.; Hart 2008.
29. Atlanta BeltLine Inc. 2024.
30. Atlanta BeltLine Inc. 2022.
31. Quoted in Saporta 2016.
32. In one version of the article's headline (Mariano, Conway, and Ondieki 2017).
33. Howard 2017.
34. Mariano, Conway, and Ondieki 2017.
35. Ibid. See also Mariano 2017.

36. Atlanta BeltLine Inc. 2022, 28.
37. Keenan 2022. He then adds, "But experts say it's far from enough." Political scientist Daniel Immergluck (2022, 59–94) exhaustively analyzes the city government's failure to engage with Atlanta's multi-decade loss of affordable housing; harms caused by BeltLine construction figure prominently in his analysis. He too argues that recent reforms are too little, too late (see, for example, 118–20).
38. Mock 2022; see also Immergluck 2022; Immergluck and Balen 2018.
39. City of Atlanta, GA 2020, emphasis in original.
40. Mock 2022.
41. Immergluck 2009; Immergluck and Balen 2018.
42. Malone 2017.
43. Wheatley 2017. Although left-leaning community activists and scholars are usually critical of urban redevelopment projects that can displace residents, such as the BeltLine, politicians find such projects almost irresistible. One reason is that they are not, in fact, associated with partisan polarization among the broader public (see views on gentrification in this chapter's section on public opinion.) Historian Bruce Schulman locates one "vein of neo-consensus history" in "'a national model of suburban politics and metropolitan development.' ... Politics of the neighborhood ... nourished a political consensus fueled by unexpected coalitions that cut across class, racial, regional, and party lines" (Schulman 2019, 483–85; internal quote by Bonnie Goodman, in note 7).
44. Quoted in Hurt 2021.
45. These civic association members would presumably concur with Adolph Reed's assessment of the problem they face. The issue is "not that black regimes are led by inept, uncaring, or mean-spirited elitists." Instead, the Black urban regime "forms and legitimizes itself . . . in a local political culture and system dominated hegemonically by the imperatives of the very 'growth machine' that is the engine of black marginalization" (Reed 1999, 98–99).
46. Jonsson 2021.
47. Quoted in Wilkins 2022.
48. Wilkins 2022.
49. Quoted in Wilkins 2022.
50. An article by Owens and Brown (2014) both exemplifies this anxiety and analyzes why a White candidate might win Atlanta's mayoralty and how that could affect the city's racial dynamics.
51. Brown-Nagin 2011; Sjoquist 2002; Stone 1989.
52. DeKalb, into which Atlanta extends, is the second-wealthiest predominantly Black county in the United States. Atlanta has more Black-owned businesses than all other U.S. cities except New York, which has about twice as many Black adults (Stirgus 2020).
53. Immergluck 2022, 56–57.
54. Bullard 2011; see also Bullard 2007.
55. Herskind 2023.
56. Quoted in Quirk 2016.
57. Wilkins 2022.

58. Pendergrast 2017.
59. Frankston et al. 2004; Hairston 2004; Pendered 2006b.
60. Donsky 2007.
61. Saporta 2007.
62. Saporta 2008; Kempner 2016.
63. Alex Garvin & Associates 2004; Donsky 2008; Pendered 2006a.
64. Mariano, Conway, and Ondieki 2017; see also Pendergrast 2017, 88–90, 129.
65. Atlanta's 25 Neighborhood Planning Units, which encompass the city's 240 designated neighborhoods, were established in 1974. They are "the official avenue for residents to express concern and provide input in developing plans to address the needs of each neighborhood, as well as to receive updates from City government" (City of Atlanta, GA, n.d.). Many NPUs can be thought of as the official organizational manifestation of the Grid's bottom row.
66. Most initial opposition to the BeltLine came, in fact, from largely White, upper-income neighborhoods in North and Northeast Atlanta; their views were the mirror image of the later fear of displacement in southern and western neighborhoods. Affluent neighborhood associations and NPUs successfully used the zoning process to resist a developer's early proposal to rezone a stretch along a new northeastern BeltLine park for high-rise, possibly affordable, apartments (Pendered 2006b; Olansky 2006).
67. Quoted in Rhone 2018. Recent research on the complexities of displacement includes Hwang and Sampson 2014; Leslie and Trubey 2014; Martin and Beck 2018; Zuk, Bierbaum, and Loukaitou-Sideris 2017.
68. Gravel 2016, 171.
69. Interview subjects also pointed to more generic impediments to coalitional success. One is Atlanta's small scale; advocacy groups compete for the relatively few mobilizable residents. As one person put it, "You can state what the problem is, but if you don't have a certain level of community organization or community involvement on advocating for the particular issues that are in your best interest, then it can be neutralized." This Black public official also cited competition over scarce resources as another moment when "the clash comes." Many anecdotes told by interview subjects pointed out that tactics useful for working within one geographically rooted group can get in the way of moving beyond the group's literal and metaphorical boundaries to work with similarly rooted groups. Zero-sum conflicts can readily occur. More generally, see Berry, Portney, and Thomson 1993; Han, McKenna, and Oyakawa 2021; Orr 1999; Yerena 2015.
70. Brummet and Reed 2019; Dragan, Ellen, and Glied 2020. Edward Glaeser, Michael Luca, and Erica Moszkowski (2023, emphasis added) look at the effects of neighborhood gentrification on "neighborhood retail amenities" and find "faster growth in both the number of retail establishments *and* business closure rates than their non-gentrifying counterparts."
71. Sasso, Matthews, and Newkirk 2019. Cross-class, intragroup tension over community change is not limited to African Americans. Latino communities across the United States can experience what is often pejoratively termed "gentefication" (see, for example, Dávila 2003; Delgado and Swanson 2021; Escalante 2017). The same holds for Asian American communities (Naram 2017; Sander 2023). More generally, see Hwang 2015; Rucks-Ahidiana 2021.

Of course, wealthier immigrants, sometimes of different European nationalities (or "races," in the parlance of the time), have been gentrifying poor urban White communities at least since the late nineteenth century.

72. Van Mead 2018.

73. As I write, the long tradition of dispute among elites about the best way to provide new public transit continues (Bagby 2023).

74. ProQuest Ethnic News Watch yielded only eight relevant articles in the Black-oriented Atlanta press between 2000 and 2020.

75. Maya Bharara and I examined media for the six months prior to each election. For Nexis Uni searches, the keywords were "(atlanta) AND (beltline OR belt line) AND (mayor OR election OR *Candidate's last name*)."

76. Staff of *Atlanta Journal-Constitution* 2009.

77. For example, in a forum in October 2017, candidates noted the BeltLine in their affirmations of support for affordable housing and better public transit (Klugerman 2017)

78. Wickert 2021.

79. Published results used in *Race/Class Conflict and Urban Financial Threat* are available at ARC Research 2016; Atlanta Regional Commission 2017, 2018, 2019, 2021; Ghimire 2019. Ramesh Ghimire's (2019) site is especially helpful because it provides results from all Metro Atlanta Speaks survey items from 2016 through 2019; they can be disaggregated by demography and metro-area county.

    From 2013 to 2019, Metro Atlanta Speaks used a random digit dial sample survey of residents in the region. Sample sizes ranged from 2,100 in 2013 to almost 5,500 in 2016–2019. In 2020 and 2021, the sample was generated by a random digit dialing of 2,700 targeted respondents and an online panel of another 2,100 targeted respondents (see Atlanta Regional Commission and Metro Atlanta Speaks 2021). In each iteration from 2016 through 2019, the years with the most useful items for my purposes, about 400 respondents lived in the city of Atlanta. The text distinguishes metro-area from city-only responses.

80. For the survey's thirteen counties in the Atlanta metro area, averaging across responses from several years, women, young adults, Blacks and Latinos, those with less than a BA, low- and moderate-income respondents, the unemployed, and renters—that is, the bottom row of the Grid—were especially likely to describe affordability as "poor."

81. The category of "White" includes a few whom Metro Atlanta Speaks identifies as "other." I was unable to attain parallel results for 2016.

82. Favorable views were responses of "good" and "excellent." I set aside the category of "fair."

83. For the sake of clarity of exposition, I do not include the middle-income group. CIG also includes questions about gentrification's impact on Blacks and Latinos. I do not report them here since they showed no clear patterns. Results are available on request.

84. CIG results also show differences by class. Forty-three percent of the lowest-income group, compared with 69 percent of the highest-income group, expected the community as a whole to benefit from gentrification. The other three gentrification items show the same pattern of majority gratification among the best-off and greater concern among the worst-off.

85. Immergluck 2022, 59.
86. Pendergrast 2017, x.
87. Immergluck 2022, viii–ix.
88. Tracey 2022.
89. Greer 2017, 83.
90. As former Mayor Franklin put it in our conversation, "There's more investment in hospitals because people expect a different kind of care. . . . A group of businesspeople said, 'This doesn't work, it's a trauma 1 hospital. Without it, there's a lot of pressure on the private hospitals, so we need to fix it.' . . . That would not have happened if you had not seen this kind of influx. The hospital serves—60 percent of the people are low-income. They benefit from this new interest in the vitality of the city." She even conceded that "not my favorite, but . . . the new Walmart on Howell Mill Road has 600 employees!"
91. Stone 1989. Stone's analyses have had considerable impact on research in other cities; see, for example, Henig, et al. 1999; Hyra 2008; Orr 1999; Pattillo 2007; Reed 2016; Smith 2012. Albeit with sharper critical edges, Arena (2012) and Rodriguez (2021) also analyze the impact on development of urban regimes structured by a race/class Grid. The former focuses on New Orleans and the latter on pre-BeltLine Atlanta.
92. Stone 1989, xi.

Chapter 4: Race, Class, and Schooling:
Charter Schools in Los Angeles

1. Zimmerman 2019. Zimmerman continues, schools "are supposed to teach young people how to debate their differences in a civil manner." [But] in American cities, "it's mainly a civil war among Democrats" in which "charter schools . . . remain the major (if not always acknowledged) battlefield" (37).
2. Or, in some equally authoritative documents, thirty-one adjoining political entities.
3. Los Angeles Unified School District 2023.
4. For a sense of the complexity of L.A. schools, see Whitney 2018. This is the third edition of an almost three-hundred-page description of only sixty of the hundreds of Los Angeles public schools. The then-chair of the school board, Steve Zimmer, provided a laudatory foreword.
5. Lauen, Fuller, and Dauter 2015. They are sometimes described as "boutique charters."
6. Dale 2023; see also Zinshteyn 2017.
7. For most of the data in this paragraph, see National Alliance for Public Charter Schools 2022.
8. Ibid. The next largest cohorts are in New York City, with about 138,000, and Dade County, Florida, with about 73,000.
9. Quoted in Ziebarth 2021, 14.
10. Antonucci 2020. UTLA budget information is not public, and I was unable to find more recent figures.
11. United Teachers Los Angeles, n.d.-a.
12. McGahan 2021.

13. Fuller 2022, 878–88.
14. Scholars concur with this informant's observation. As of 2013, "organized labor has now largely supplanted the business community as the main organizational force in city politics in Los Angeles." Organized labor in Los Angeles has a distinctive "social movement orientation" (Mollenkopf and Sonenshein 2013, 144).
15. *LA School Report* 2018.
16. Potter and Inouye 2021.
17. Stokes 2022.
18. Enrollment figures differ in various sources; for example, the website of the California Department of Education reports two different figures in two locations (California Department of Education, n.d., 2023a). These variations reflect differences in definition, complications in the logistics of measurement, and perhaps districts' and charters' budgetary and political incentives to report high enrollment figures.
19. Stokes 2022. John Fensterwald and Daniel Willis (2023) report the even lower enrollment figure of 388,000 in 2022–2023.
20. Sequeira 2022b; see also Gomez 2022.
21. Barnard 2018; see also Whitmire 2016.
22. Quoted in Stokes 2020.
23. The California Department of Education defines students as socioeconomically disadvantaged if their parents did not graduate from high school or their family income is below 185 percent of the federal poverty line, about $51,000 in 2023.
24. At least in affiliated charters' early years, one or both parents of two-fifths of their students held a graduate degree (Fuller 2022, 112).
25. Taylor Swaak (2019) also notes but does not explain affiliated charters' low performance.
26. The most prominent evaluation, as of this writing, is Center for Research on Education Outcomes (CREDO) 2023. Other relatively recent evaluations include Baude et al. 2020; Cohodes 2018; Fuller 2022; Swaak 2019; Zimmer et al. 2019.
27. Quoted in McGahan 2021.
28. United Teachers Los Angeles 2020.
29. Ibid.
30. Ibid.
31. Quoted in McGahan 2021; see also Potter and Inouye 2021.
32. LA Promise Fund, n.d.
33. Stokes 2019.
34. Caprice Young, founder of the California Charter Schools Association, quoted in Fuller 2022, 93. The mission statement of the charter management operation Green Dot Public Schools described its goal as "transform[ing] public education in Los Angeles. . . . Green Dot's work is directly focused on influencing LAUSD to transform its failing high schools . . . and helping the District reinvent itself" (Kerchner et al. 2008, 191).
35. Fay 2019; Ingenium Schools 2023; Chapman 2024.
36. This document, written to encourage teachers to "Join UTLA Today!," offers a similar list of dangers that "a weakened union opens the door to." Four of

the seven bullet points address potential harms facing teachers, including "attacks on pensions and healthcare," "stagnant wages," layoffs, and a "weakened political voice" in school board, state, and federal elections. Two dangers are educational: school closures and the absence of a "collective voice to . . . stand up for student learning." The final danger is most relevant here: "increasingly aggressive privatization attacks" (United Teachers Los Angeles, n.d.-b).
37. Nicole Narea (2023) analyzes the 2023 LAUSD staff strike, supported by UTLA.
38. The law includes a process for appealing to a different educational entity if the local school board rejects the proposal. The California Department of Education also provides rules or guidance with regard to administrative functions, dedicated grants, facilities, complaints and appeals, and other management questions (California Department of Education 2024a).
39. California Department of Education 2024b.
40. Fensterwald 2019.
41. Ibid.
42. Comment by Myrna Castrejón, executive director of the California Charter Schools Association, in Stokes 2019.
43. Soto 2020; see also Stokes 2020.
44. Burke 2020.
45. Jacobson 2020.
46. Quoted in Dale 2024.
47. United Teachers Los Angeles, n.d.-c.
48. Seshadri 2024.
49. For example, Anguiano et al. 2015; Izumi 2023.
50. Los Angeles Unified School District, n.d.
51. Stokes 2019.
52. Stokes 2019.
53. In the Public Interest 2016.
54. United Teachers Los Angeles and In the Public Interest 2016; see also Zoller 2016.

Traditional school proponents also argue that charter schools are less well equipped to teach students with severe disabilities, so traditional schools enroll a disproportionate share of students with expensive and urgent needs. Charter proponents dispute this claim as at least an exaggeration and at most a cynical manipulation of vulnerable families' struggles. I was not able to find systematic evidence on this point. The state subsidizes some costs of educating children with disabilities.
55. Stokes 2016b.
56. Ibid.
57. Favot 2017.
58. Attributed in Whitmire 2016 to "others."
59. On contention over school closings, see Ewing 2018; Nuamah 2022; Russo 2014. On LAUSD and school closings, see Gomez 2022; Sequeira 2022b, 2022c; Spencer 2022.
60. For a low estimate of 11 percent, see Nation 2017, 65. In 2017, the district estimated that pensions would comprise 22 percent of general fund revenue

by 2031–32 (Snell et al. 2018, figure 13). Fuller (2022, 76) reports a projection in which pension costs could eventually absorb half of district funds. The LA Unified Advisory Task Force (2018) provides a useful overview of LAUSD costs and expenditures as of 2017.

61. Pew Charitable Trusts 2019b, fig. 6.

62. By one calculation, a 2023 labor agreement brings the average teacher's salary to $106,000 by mid-2023 (Dale 2023). Like everything else in LAUSD, other calculations yield different results.

63. Blume 2020b.

64. For a detailed history of that effort in the early 2000s, see Kerchner et al. 2008, esp. 171–82.

65. Compared to school personnel, a larger share of Los Angeles residents are centrist or even conservative. In the 2022 mayoral election, Rick Caruso, a relatively conservative billionaire business developer who switched from no party affiliation to the Democratic Party in early 2022, ran against Karen Bass, an outspokenly liberal community organizer and Democratic member of Congress since 2010. Caruso received 45 percent of the vote.

    Mollenkopf and Sonenshein (2013) analyze L.A. city politics in the 2010s. For a useful analysis comparing LAUSD with New York's public school system, see Wrigley 2013.

66. Ballotpedia 2017.

67. Szymanski 2017.

68. Lopez 2020; see also Blume 2017c. Two institutional conditions contribute to the intensity of this political competition. First, LAUSD board members enjoy arguably unique power. The position is full-time, with an annual salary of $125,000—at least several times the salaries of members of most other school boards (Sequeira 2022a). Each member has a staff of five or more; the board has administrative staff and a research unit, and it controls the Office of the Inspector General. Board members receive public employee pensions and health benefits, including some on which they make policy decisions. The result is "what is in effect a parallel power structure" to LAUSD leadership, with constituency ties and sometimes competing agendas (Freedberg 2021).

    Second, and relatedly, the school board has strong but complicated links with the officially separate governance system of Los Angeles. Board members often aspire to the City Council and may have personal and professional ties to city officials. Conversely, Los Angeles mayors typically see links to the school board as their only means to exert influence over LAUSD, which is important for their political future but not subject to their control. Since many city residents care a great deal about the quality of schools, most mayors do what they can to influence the district despite their structural impotence.

69. The most lavishly funded candidates, however, do not always win. Perhaps for that reason, campaign expenditures for two school board seats in 2022 declined to a still unheard-of $8.4 million (Blume 2022). For comparison, a news article headlined "Conservative Groups Are Spending Big on School Board Races" reports on a new PAC that raised about $3 million in 2022. The 1776 Project funded 58 candidates, averaging up to $25,000 per race. "Traditionally, school board candidates spend $1000 or less" (Hughes 2022).

70. Blume 2017a, 2020a; *The Economist* 2017; Szymanski 2017. See also Anzia 2013.

71. Commitment to this effort has a race/class inflection, since the 2005 policy was aimed at achieving "educational equity" for disadvantaged Black and Latino students (see, for example, Jones 2017).

72. Caputo-Pearl 2016. Austin Beutner is an investment banker who served as deputy mayor of Los Angeles from 2010 to 2013 and later cochaired the 2020 Commission to examine and make recommendations on the city's financial management. Although he chaired a reform-oriented task force for LAUSD before becoming superintendent, he had no previous professional background in education.

73. United Teachers Los Angeles, n.d.-c.

74. On the Broad proposal and its impact, see Blume 2015; Fuller 2022, 72–74, 108–9.

75. Quoted in Blume 2017b.

76. The photo appears in Stokes (2016a), whom I thank for all his help.

77. Quoted in Medina and Goldstein 2019. The speaker was referring to board support for a ten-month "moratorium" on new charter schools.

78. Kerchner 2017.

79. In fact, we found few articles that addressed, in more than a cursory way, race, class, or race/class inequality in any aspect of schooling in Los Angeles. Two research assistants independently skimmed the headlines and first pages of the hundreds of articles in the *Los Angeles Times* from 2013 through 2021 identified through the search term "(LA OR Los Angeles) AND (LAUSD OR charter schools OR magnet schools)." Of course, race, ethnicity, and class may be the subtext of many media stories, but if my trained and well-educated research assistants did not perceive it, arguably many Angelenos do not either.

80. Jamali 2019.

81. Quoted in Blume 2020c.

82. Ibid.

83. For relevant histories and context, see Davis 1990; Kerchner et al. 2008; Saito 2022; Sonenshein 1993.

84. It is, of course, possible that interview subjects avoided talking about race, ethnicity, and class with a White Harvard professor and her students. But that was not my experience in New York or Atlanta, nor did my Black coauthor, Vesla Weaver, receive information or views withheld from me. Media reports and election results similarly differed in tone and content from those in New York and Atlanta.

85. Milkman 2006.

86. Pastor 2015, 55. Kim Voss and Irene Bloemraad (2011) and Chris Zepeda-Millán (2017) analyze the organizational capacity demonstrated by the city's 2006 immigrant rights marches.

87. Hondagneu-Sotelo and Pastor 2021.

88. Fuller 2022.

89. Wrigley 2013, 277.

90. Although they may be more extreme than in most cities, L.A.'s difficulties in education reform are not at all new. See, among others, Hochschild and Scovronick 2003; Morel 2018; Orr 1999; Payne 2008; Ryan 2011; Stone et al. 2001.

91. Barone, Laurens, and Munyan-Penney 2019; graphics accompanying Cheng et al. 2018; Collingwood, Jochim, and Oskooii 2018; GenForward 2017; Valant 2019.
92. Schaeffer 2024.
93. National Alliance for Public Charter Schools 2022; Camarena Lopez 2022. Poverty is also more concentrated in charter schools; three-tenths of charter school students, compared with one-fifth of traditional public school students, attend schools where more than three-quarters of their fellow students qualify for free or reduced-price meals.
94. Schaeffer 2024.
95. National Alliance for Public Charter Schools 2022.
96. Craig et al. 2016; Vasquez Heilig 2016; Klein 2016.
97. Klein 2019.
98. *The Economist* 2019a.
99. Baldassare et al. 2019, 17.
100. Baldassare et al. 2020, 15.
101. Baldassare et al. 2019, 2020. For both surveys, see also "Full Crosstabs— All Respondents," at ppic.org/wp-content/uploads/crosstabs-all-adults-0419.pdf (for 2019), and at ppic.org/wp-content/uploads/crosstabs-all-adults-0420.pdf (for 2020).
102. Thomas and Dorothy Leavey Center for the Study of Los Angeles (StudyLA) 2022.
103. The Angeleno Poll does not ask whether individuals live within LAUSD boundaries, but the Loyola Marymount researchers were able to use zip codes to identify district residents (email from Brianne Gilbert to the author, August 24, 2022).
104. Since LAUSD has no school buses for almost all students, some parents are motivated by the crucial non-educational fact of location: "Transportation is a huge issue. . . . Frankly," said a Black city official, "L.A. does a good job of keeping quiet on [the fact that] it's the number-one issue in the city."
105. As part of the context for understanding CIG results, note that one-third of the Latinos in the survey (404 of the 1,285) lived in the Los Angeles metropolitan area.
106. Choy and Gifford 1980; Fuller 2022; Glenn 1979; Hochschild 1984; Rogers and Morrell 2010.
107. Fensterwald and Willis 2023; Xie and Willis 2022. As I noted earlier, LAUSD enrollment figures are slippery, but all reports of data show this steep decline.
108. Quoted in Sequeira 2022c.
109. Quoted in Peele 2022.
110. Ibid.
111. There is an alternative. As education scholar Kay Merseth points out, "There is greater cooperation and sharing among traditional public schools and charters than the traditional narrative of competition suggests. Examples of common application processes (e.g. School Choice in Denver) and shared classroom practices (e.g. 'Do Now's homework policies) offer evidence of cooperation" (Kay Merseth, email to the author, August 1, 2023; see also Merseth 2009). Several school districts in Idaho are partnering with charter schools to offer classes or curricula that otherwise would not be available.

As one superintendent put it, "We want . . . to ensure every kid graduates high school. We're not catching some of those kids early enough in the process, or providing enough support to them, but Elevate could be able to do that." Charters are helping some underenrolled schools stay open (Flandro 2024). While these examples are hardly setting a trend, they are at least existence proof that charter and traditional schools need not be sworn enemies.

112. Orfield, Siegel-Hawley, and Kucsera 2011, 3.
113. Fuller 2022, 61; see also Johnson, Reed, and Hayes 2008.
114. In these data, L.A. Unified had about 548,300 students in 2021–2022, while Los Angeles County districts included about 788,200 students. See California Department of Education 2023a, 2023b.
115. Clotfelter 2001; Kruse 2005; Logan, Zhang, and Oakley 2017; Orfield and Jarvie 2020; Zhang and Ruther 2021.
116. Agius Vallejo 2013; Fuller 2022; García Bedolla 2005; Pan 2010.
117. See Newman 2019, 92–107.
118. FitchRatings 2023. Moody's and Standard & Poor's, however, did not lower LAUSD's bond rating.

Chapter 5: Race, Class, and Budgets: Public-Sector Pensions in Chicago

1. A small but robust stream of scholarship examines time as an independent variable able to "cause" important political outcomes, or as itself a political tool (for example, Bevernage 2010; Kreuzer 2023; Pierson 2004). One especially relevant examination is Joel Rast's (2012) analysis of "the role of time and temporality in explaining social and political outcomes." He emphasizes, as does Pierson and my metaphor of a Timeline, that "many social processes require extended periods of time to 'work themselves out'" (both quotes on p. 12; internal quote has no source).
2. Cherone 2023a; Civic Federation 2023b, 11. Even in this low estimate, unfunded retiree health care benefits add $2 billion more debt (Truth in Accounting 2024b).
3. Dabrowski and Klingner 2021. The Civic Federation of Chicago reported in 2023 that "the estimated amount of unfunded pension liabilities across all State and local pension funds in Illinois is over $210 billion." The deficits of the five state retirement funds (that is, not including local government pension funds) have increased by more than 150 percent over the past fifteen years (Civic Federation 2023a).
4. City of Chicago 2023, 38.
5. Her explanation of that phrase was one of the most succinct depictions that we heard of why Chicago's repeated cycle of "must, can't, try, must, won't" may not be sustainable forever: "There is no pension problem because you have to pay them [see later in this chapter for discussion of this point]. But it will take so much money out of the city coffers to pay the city pensions, the amount of money the mayor gives to education won't be there. If the schools aren't there, people will leave the city. If people leave the city, then

there's not enough people paying taxes in order to be able to afford the structure and the police and fire and all that nonsense. And if there's not police and fire, people like me who make a lot of money who don't have kids won't live in the city. So it's the circular pot."

6. Carlson 2023.
7. See Singh 2023a.
8. Bauer 2019b.
9. See Singh 2023b.
10. Cherone 2023b.
11. Anzia 2022, 8.
12. Civic Federation 2022.
13. Ibid.
14. Quoted in Madiar 2014, 5.
15. Ibid., 30.
16. Ibid., 12.
17. Quoted in ibid., 16. An additional 16 percent of the funding deficit came from stock market losses, 10 percent from mistaken actuarial assumptions (pensioners were living longer), and 9 percent from benefit increases.
18. *Chicago Tribune* 2013.
19. Civic Federation 2022.
20. Ted Dabrowski, John Klingner, and Tait Jensen (2015) offer a highly colored but informative history of how Chicago Public Schools pensions moved "from retirement security to political slush fund," and the consequences thereof. See McGee (2016) for analysis of debt service costs for Chicago Public Schools.
21. Civic Federation 2022.
22. Chicago also has other public-sector pension funds for which taxpayers are ultimately responsible but which are governed in somewhat different ways. These funds, such as for the park service, matter enormously to participants, but they are relatively small and their depiction is not necessary for this book's purposes.
23. Monahan 2017, 359, citations not included.
24. For more detail and some disagreement with that judgment, see Bauer 2019a.
25. City of Chicago 2018.
26. Truth in Accounting 2022. Note that some analysts see Truth in Accounting as excessively alarmist.
27. Civic Federation 2021.
28. Chicago Teachers' Pension Fund 2024; Civic Federation 2021. About half of the MEABF members are nonteaching employees of Chicago Public Schools. As in other cities, many Chicago Teachers' Pension Fund recipients are also not classroom teachers.
29. Illinois Report Card 2022–2023.
30. Office of Inspector General 2021.
31. SEIU Local 73, n.d.
32. SEIU Local 1, n.d.
33. Civic Federation 2023c.

34. An alderperson from a poor Black ward explained to us that property tax increases did not concern his constituents because they could not afford a house above the rebate threshold in any case ("The word alderperson became Illinois law in 2021, replacing any legal reference to alderman" [Victory 2023].)
35. Cherone 2023b.
36. Center for Municipal Finance 2021.
37. There are grounds for concern about services. Anzia finds that compared with other localities, local governments with larger pension expenditures and union-based collective bargaining respond to budgetary pressure with larger workforce reductions, which presumably imply diminished services (Anzia 2022). See also Kiewiet and McCubbins 2014.
38. Chicago Teachers' Pension Fund 2021, 7.
39. Monahan 2017, 356.
40. Schattschneider 1960.
41. Kingdon 1984.
42. Civic Federation 2023b.
43. Hawkins 2022.
44. Sharkey 2022.
45. Myers 2022.
46. Hawkins 2022; Singh 2023a.
47. Quoted in Glennon 2022; see also Bauer 2021.
48. In an exploration of "democracy and time," Schedler and Santiso (1998, 10) point out that "all constitutive elements of political timetables—duration, tempo, timing, sequencing, and rhythm—are susceptible to strategic calculation and variation. They all represent key variables in everyday struggles for power and policies." Arguably, my exploration of Chicago's pension funding issue is an operationalization of that observation. Dara Strolovitch's (2012, 387) phrase "longitudinal trajectories of political battles," although used for a different purpose, has also influenced my development of the Timeline metaphor. Scholarship on path dependency is illuminating, especially with regard to the structural features of Chicago's pensions; see Greener 2005; Kay 2005; Mahoney 2000; Pierson 2000. Klaus Goetz and Jan-Hinrik Meyer-Sahling (2009) examine how European Union institutions endeavor to control "political time"—with only occasional success. See Rast (2012) for a depiction of the rise, fall, and need for rebirth of temporally focused scholarship in urban politics.
49. The conservative Manhattan Institute estimated in 2016 that "70 to 80 cents of every taxpayer dollar contributed to public pensions will be used to pay for pension benefits that workers have already earned, rather than fund the pension benefits that workers will earn in the future" (McGee 2016, 4).
50. The Chicago Transit Authority instituted a tier 2 system in 2008.
51. Commission on Government Forecasting and Accountability 2022, 5–8.
52. Quoted in Bauer 2022.
53. Ibid.
54. Chicago Public Schools 2022, 41.
55. Civic Federation 2023a; GRS Consulting 2022, 43.

56. McGee 2016, 10–11.
57. An analysis of all Illinois teachers yields different substantive results but shows the same relative disadvantage for tier 2 teachers: "Most teachers . . . do not work long enough to benefit much from the [new] plan. . . . Sixty-six percent of teachers in the more generous, pre-reform pension plan lose financially by participating in the plan because the pensions they earn are worth less than their required plan contributions. In the plan available to teachers hired in 2011 and later, 84 percent suffer financial losses by participating" (Johnson and Southgate 2014, 3–4). Pensions for long-term tier 1 teachers can be worth $1.3 million over their lifetimes, whereas equivalent pensions for tier 2 teachers are worth $609,000 over their lifetimes. For each set of service years, twice as many tier 1 as tier 2 teachers will receive more pension benefits than they have contributed to the plan (ibid., 1–2, 12–14, 17). I have relegated this analysis to a note because it does not consider how retirement plans for Chicago teachers differ from those elsewhere in Illinois. See also Kan, Fuchs, and Aldeman 2016, 4.
58. Civic Federation 2023a.
59. GRS Consulting 2022, 23.
60. The Government Finance Officers Association staidly admonishes local governments constructing tiered systems for new workers to "keep in mind the effect of pension benefit tiers on the equitable treatment of employees, employee morale, and the jurisdiction's ability to recruit, motivate, and retain employees." Nonetheless, the Finance Officers concede that "formidable financial challenges" require governments to make "difficult decisions to ensure the continued sustainability of their pension plans" (Government Finance Officers Association 2011).
61. As Andy Rotherham of the nonprofit Bellwether Education Partners observes, "The last thing unions want to introduce into the conversation is something their younger members would be pissed off about" (quoted in *The Economist* 2019b).
62. Costrell 2020; Johnson and Southgate 2014.
63. Civic Federation 2023a.
64. Nitkin 2023.
65. Lane 2017.
66. Glennon 2023. Comedian Dave Barry's "2023 Year in Review" characterized federal negotiations over the debt ceiling as follows: Bill and Jane Johnson have run up trillions of dollars of debt, and they agree to continue to do so. Their debt "will eventually (Bill and Jane prefer not to think about this) become unsustainable. At some future point, after Bill and Jane have retired on the generous pensions that they have awarded to themselves, their children—let's call them Suzy and Bobby—will be living in appliance cartons and subsisting on off-brand dog food. This might seem unfair to Suzy and Bobby, but it's their own fault for not having been born earlier" (Barry 2023).
67. Similarly, *The Economist* (2024a) asks rhetorically, "Is the most powerful teachers union in America overreaching?"
68. Or perhaps Thomas Stafford, in the early 1700s (https://quoteinvestigator.com/2018/05/09/posterity-ever/).
69. Vallas for Mayor 2023.

70. Quoted in Weinberg 2023.
71. B. Johnson 2023.
72. Dabrowski, Klingner, and Jensen 2015, 15.
73. As a Black alderperson summarized, "You know, we are a Democratic city. In my tenure we've only had one Republican elected to the City Council. And he couldn't do much because he was his own caucus."
74. See also Monahan 2015.
75. Anzia 2019.
76. These dynamics are widespread. An EU analyst observed ruefully that "many governments have concluded the future funding needed to meet expected shifts in the dependency ratio requires public finances to be in surplus over an extensive period of time. But how can such an ambition be defended when it comes under permanent and heavy cross-fire from two different sides, the tax-cutters mainly on the right and the benefit-raisers mainly on the left?" (Tarschys 2003, 97).
77. Glaeser and Ponzetto 2014.
78. In 2010, "when a major winter storm hit New York City, Gothamites and Chicagoans alike invoked the specter of Michael Bilandic, whose 1979 loss in the Democratic mayoral primary to Jane Byrne is like a ghost story elected officials and public planners tell each other—'Plow the streets, or you'll end up just like Mayor Bilandic'" (Moser 2011).
79. A small indicator of pensions' invisibility: a fifty-year veteran of Chicago politics who held positions as an alderperson, mayoral adviser, appointed official, and respected scholar of urban politics published *Democracy's Rebirth: The View from Chicago* in 2022. The wide-ranging book's index does not include "pensions," "unions," "public employment," or any comparable term (Simpson 2022).
80. Jacobs 2016, 439, emphasis added.
81. Wilson 1980.
82. Jacobs 2016, 441, citations not included; see also DiSalvo 2015.
83. The Illinois State Board of Elections reports that Chicago's public-sector unions contributed $100,000 to 2011 mayoral candidate Gery Chico, over $530,000 to Jesús Garcia in 2015, almost $300,000 to Toni Preckwinkle in 2019, and $2,716,000 to Brandon Johnson, a Chicago Teachers Union organizer, in 2023. (Some of the contributions were in-kind.) The first three of these four lost their election; unions are not invincible (Illinois State Board of Elections, n.d.).

    The Illinois Board also reports that Chicago's public sector unions contributed over $4,900,000 in campaign contributions to Assembly Speaker Madigan from 2010 through 2020. Madigan was indeed invincible for an astonishing thirty-eight years (as Speaker from 1983 to 2021 except for two years), till brought down by federal racketeering charges.
84. Lewis quote is in Burnett 2014. Comment about Lightfoot is in Cherone 2022.
85. Pagliari 2020.
86. Meisel 2020.
87. Pew Charitable Trusts 2019a; Monahan 2013.
88. *Jones et al. v. MEABF et al.*, 2016 IL 119618; see also Franczek 2016; Madiar 2016.

89. Grotto and Dardick 2012.
90. Moody's downgrade of Chicago's credit rating "reflects the city's massive and growing unfunded pension liabilities, which threaten the city's fiscal solvency absent major revenue and other budgetary adjustments adopted in the near term and sustained for years to come" (quoted in Guarino 2014; see also Pierog 2015).

    FitchRatings, and Standard & Poor's, both referring to its pension liabilities, downgraded Chicago's credit ratings in the same period. They also downgraded the state of Illinois in 2014 to a level that *The Economist* (2014) described as "on a par with Botswana. (An incensed editorial in the *Chicago Tribune* asked what Botswana had done to be so insulted.)."
91. Munnell and Aubry 2017, 125; Munnell, Haverstock, and Aubry 2008. Furthermore, Mayors Emanuel and Lightfoot did take action to staunch the rising costs. (Perhaps causally, both subsequently left office sooner than intended).
92. Dippel 2022, 2, 4.
93. Anzia and Moe 2017, 39. Although the central point made by Erick Elder and Gary Wagner (2015) seems correct ("The political environments of state and local governments play a pivotal role in pension underfunding"), the case of Chicago appears to contradict their more specific findings.
94. Nothdurft and Weinberg 2014/2017, 268–69.
95. Henry J. Kaiser Family Foundation 2016.
96. Monmouth University Polling Institute 2021.
97. CNN 2011a; Gallup 2024; see also NBC News/*Wall Street Journal* 2011.
98. Fairleigh Dickinson University 2020.
99. *Los Angeles Times* 2009.
100. Public Religion Research Institute 2011.
101. Baldassare et al. 2019. Another survey offers many options to address public-sector pension deficits. However, with a sponsor that defines itself as "promoting libertarian principles," the survey items are slanted, in my view, toward hostility to public employees. So I report the results hesitantly. In any case, in 2015, 82 percent of respondents would require public employees to "contribute more toward their own future pensions and benefits," and 44 percent would reduce future pensions for current workers. No other option received support from more than one-quarter of respondents (Arthur N. Rupe Foundation/Reason Foundation 2015).
102. CNN 2011b. Federal employee pensions comprised less than 1 percent of the gross domestic product in 2020 (Chantrill, n.d.). Fiscal year 2021 federal spending was 30 percent of the gross domestic product (DataLab, n.d.), so pension spending was less than 5 percent of the federal budget.
103. Support rises from 49 percent of those aged forty and younger to 53 percent among those forty-one to fifty-five years old, to 63 percent of those over age fifty-five.
104. Including public-sector employment as an independent variable in regression analyses shows no effect on support for increasing taxes to pay retirement benefits, or for reducing benefits. Public-sector employees support tiered benefits significantly more than do private-sector workers when other variables are controlled. The substantive differences in views, however, are small. See appendix table D.4.

105. Morgan 1975, 313–14.
106. Chicago Teachers Union Research Department 2014.
107. Chicago's Office of Inspector General (2021) provides a map showing the proportion of public employees living in each community area and ward of the city.
108. C. J. Passarella, email correspondence with the author, July 9, 2023.
109. Jose Rivera, email correspondence with the author, May 23, 2023.
110. Except insofar as union members mostly occupy a particular job stratum and have moderate incomes. Certainly, those are economically relevant facts, but few American scholars or public actors consider them through the lens of a structural class analysis.
111. Eisinger 1986; Lewis and Frank 2002; Moss 1988.
112. As many have shown, the history of race/class inequality is crucially important in determining homeownership and housing values in urban communities. That fact is central to Chicago's overall profile, but not to the particular case of pension funding. If anything, it implies that Whites are paying more into pension funds than are taxpayers of color.
113. Frey 2023, table E.

Chapter 6: Toward an Explanation of Policies and Politics in American Cities

1. Not entirely set aside, of course; see among others, Gerring 2017, Glesne 2016, Lamont and White 2009.
2. Hirschman 1991.
3. Hupe 2019; Lipsky 2010.
4. Patterson 1989, 484.
5. American Civil Liberties Union of Illinois 2015, 3.
6. Romanucci & Blandin Law 2023; see also Skogan 2018.
7. "[C]ontentious" is in Caiola 2023b; "wholeheartedly embrace" is in Caiola 2023a.
8. Parker quoted in Caiola 2023a.
9. Community activist Rikeyah Lindsay, quoted in Caiola 2023b.
10. For other analyses of SQF, see McNeil 2020; Torres 2015. The history of police stops in Philadelphia, as in Chicago, resembles that of New York—a rising number of *Terry* stops over the early 2000s, a lawsuit (settled here by consent decree) yielding a drastic decline in the number of stops, data showing that Black men were disproportionately targeted, and continued police assertions that stops have "always been a mainstay in policing across the nation for decades. And so we use them as part of our normal work" (Police Commissioner Kevin Bethel, quoted in Dean 2024).
11. For other examples, see Gravel 2016.
12. Wright 2023.
13. Gravel 2016, xii.
14. Fausset 2016, internal quote from Christopher Leinberger.
15. As of April 2024, Google Scholar reports over 1,100 items in response to the keywords Gentrification + Atlanta + BeltLine.

16. Quoted in Pendergrast 2017, 158.
17. Campbell, 1996, 296.
18. Gravel 2016, 142.
19. Leinberger and Rodriguez 2016.
20. Sasso, Matthews, and Newkirk 2019.
21. National Alliance for Public Charter Schools 2022.
22. See, among others, Dreier, Mollenkopf, and Swanstrom 2014; Kruse 2005; Lens 2022; Oliver 2001; Rothwell and Massey 2010; Sugrue 1996; Trounstine 2018.
23. Koumpilova, Barnum, and Binkley 2022.
24. Vevea and Peña 2022.
25. Quoted in Murphy 2016.
26. Quoted in ibid.; see also Jason 2017.
27. Blum 2017; Keller 2023.
28. Strauss 2019. As in LAUSD, enrollment in the Oakland Unified School District declined by about 35 percent from 2000 to 2020. About one-third of Oakland's students are in charters. The school board proposed in 2021 to exclude charter schools from public school guides for parents and district maps. The initiating board member explained that "I understand that it is going to impact charter schools. My answer to them is, I'm on the board of OUSD and I'm trying to protect our fiscal health and enrollment." Another was blunter: "The reality is that we've lost a lot of public school students to charters. Our budget is such that as we continue to lose students, we have to continue to cut and close schools." A parent observed in response, "I feel the whole purpose for it is to divide and conquer. So they can point the finger and say 'They're the reason they don't get money, that we can't pay teachers'" (all quoted in McBride 2021). About four-fifths of Oakland parents apply to both charter and traditional schools during the annual enrollment period (ibid.).
29. Pankovits 2022.
30. National Center for Education Statistics 2022, table 203.10. Even California's charter school sector, which in some previous years had seen "staggering growth," has recently seen slight declines (Fensterwald 2022).
31. Rakove 1979.
32. Erie 1988; Finegold 1995; Grimshaw 1995; Peterson 1976; Rakove 1976.
33. New Jersey led with a debt of 20.2 percent of personal income, followed closely by Illinois (19.4 percent) and Hawaii (18 percent), and then by Alaska (16.3 percent) and New Mexico (15.7 percent) (Biernacka-Lievestro and Fleming 2022).
34. Ibid.
35. Truth in Accounting 2024a. This analysis combines pension debt, unfunded OPEB (other post-employment benefits, mainly health care), and "other bills" in calculating residents' debt. Pensions are by far the largest component.
36. New York State and Local Retirement System 2021. Detroit's tiered pension system for public-sector employees emerged from postbankruptcy financial arrangements (Walsh 2014; see also Clark 2012; Newman 2019). Katherine Newman (2019, 150) describes comparable private-sector tiered pension systems as "a case of every generation for itself." Anzia (2023) provides other details on school system pension plans.

37. Walsh 2017.
38. Taylor 2014, abstract, final section. See also Frey 2023. Changes in the dependency ratio of workers to retirees deepens the demographic stress. Andrew Biggs calculates that "in 2001, the median teacher plan had 2.3 active employees per beneficiary, falling to only 1.3 employees per retiree in 2019"— leaving plans much more vulnerable to overestimates of investment returns, political manipulations, and any other miscalculation (Biggs 2023).
39. Bell 1992; Crenshaw 1990; Delgado and Stefancic 2023.
40. Michaels and Reed 2023; Przeworski 1986; Wright 1982.
41. Dahl 1971, 2005.
42. For the best portrayal of this sort of politics in action, see Frank 2015.

Appendix B

1. Nukulkij 2016.
2. For more detail, see Ipsos, n.d.

═ References ═

Abott, Carolyn, and Asya Magazinnik. 2020. "At-Large Elections and Minority Representation in Local Government." *American Journal of Political Science* 64(3): 717–33.

Agius Vallejo, Jody. 2013. *Barrios to Burbs: The Making of the Mexican American Middle Class*. Stanford, Calif.: Stanford University Press.

Akinnibi, Fola. 2023. "NYPD Tactics Raise Concern of Return to 'Stop and Frisk.'" *Bloomberg News*, February 14. https://www.bloomberg.com/news/articles /2023-02-14/nypd-stop-and-frisk-tactics-raise-concerns.

Aladangady, Aditya, and Akila Forde. 2021. "Wealth Inequality and the Racial Wealth Gap." Board of Governors of the Federal Reserve System, October 22. https://www.federalreserve.gov/econres/notes/feds-notes/wealth-inequality -and-the-racial-wealth-gap-20211022.html.

Alesina, Alberto, John Londregon, and Howard Rosenthal. 1993. "A Model of the Political Economy of the United States." *American Political Science Review* 87(1): 12–33.

Alex Garvin & Associates, Inc. 2004. "The Beltline Emerald Necklace: Atlanta's New Public Realm." Prepared for The Trust for Public Land. https://a-us .storyblok.com/f/1020195/b0d5527807/the-beltline-emerald-necklace-study_ alex-garvin-associates-inc.pdf.

American Civil Liberties Union of Illinois. 2015. "Stop and Frisk in Chicago." March. https://www.aclu-il.org/sites/default/files/wp-content/uploads /2015/03/ACLU_StopandFrisk_6.pdf.

Anguiano, Maria, et al. 2015. "Report of the Independent Financial Review Panel." Los Angeles Unified School District, November 10. https://www .laschoolreport.com/wp-content/uploads/2015/11/LAUSD_IFRP_FINAL _REPORT-110215.pdf.

Antonucci, Mike. 2020. "Analysis: Four Years Ago, UTLA Increased Its Member Dues by 33 Percent. What Did the Union Do with the Money?" *LASchoolReport*, January 14. https://www.laschoolreport.com/analysis-four-years-ago-utla -increased-its-member-dues-by-33-percent-what-did-the-union-do-with-the -money/.

Anzia, Sarah. 2013. *Timing and Turnout: How Off-Cycle Elections Favor Organized Groups*. Chicago: University of Chicago Press.

———. 2019. "Looking for Influence in All the Wrong Places: How Studying Subnational Policy Can Revive Research on Interest Groups." *Journal of Politics* 81(1): 343–51.

———. 2022. "Pensions in the Trenches: How Pension Spending Is Affecting U.S. Local Government." *Urban Affairs Review* 58(1): 3–32.

———. 2023. "Public Schools and Their Pensions: How Is Pension Spending Affecting U.S. School Districts?" *Education Finance and Policy*. 1–26. https://doi.org/10.1162/edfp_a_00412.

Anzia, Sarah, and Terry Moe. 2017. "Polarization and Policy: The Politics of Public-Sector Pensions." *Legislative Studies Quarterly* 42(1): 33–62.

Aragon, Rachel. 2023. "Solar-Powered Bar Set to Open along Atlanta Beltline." PeachtreeTV, May 19. https://www.peachtreetv.com/2023/05/19/solar-powered-bar-set-to-open-along-atlanta-beltline/.

ARC Research (Atlanta Regional Commission). 2016. "2016 Metro Atlanta Speaks Survey Results—Regional Snapshot." https://33n.atlantaregional.com/regional-snapshot/2016-metro-atlanta-speaks-survey-results.

Arena, John. 2012. *Driven from New Orleans: How Nonprofits Betray Public Housing and Promote Privatization*. Minneapolis: University of Minnesota Press.

Arinde, Nayaba. 2007. "Frisk This!" *New York Amsterdam News*, February 8.

Arthur N. Rupe Foundation/Reason Foundation. 2015. "Arthur N. Rupe Foundation/Reason Foundation Poll, January 29–February 2." Roper Center for Public Opinion Research. https://doi.org/10.25940/ROPER-31113625 (access for members only).

Astor, Maggie. 2020. "Bloomberg's Shifting Views on Stop-and-Frisk Policing." *New York Times*, February 20.

Atkinson, Tony, Joe Hasell, Salvatore Morelli, and Max Roser. 2017. "The Chartbook of Economic Inequality." University of Oxford, Institute for New Economic Thinking. https://www.chartbookofeconomicinequality.com.

Atlanta BeltLine Inc. 2021. "Atlanta Beltline Partnership Welcomes New Board Chair and Board Members." January 27. https://beltline.org/2021/01/27/atlanta-beltline-partnership-welcomes-new-board-chair-and-board-members/.

———. 2022. "Building Today, Shaping Tomorrow: Annual Report 2022." https://beltline.org/2022-annual-report/.

———. 2023. "Atlanta Beltline Design and Construction Updates: April 2023." April 30. https://beltline.org/2023/04/30/atlanta-beltline-design-and-construction-updates-april-2023/.

———. 2024. "Securing Economic Resources to Get the Project Done." https://beltline.org/organizer/atlanta-beltline-inc/.

———. n.d.-a. "About Us: Where Atlanta Comes Together." https://beltline.org/about-us/.

———. n.d.-b. "Project Goals." https://beltline.org/the-project/project-goals/?highlight=project%20goals.

Atlanta Regional Commission. 2017. "Review of 2017 Results with Data from Prior Years (Where Available)." October. https://cdn.atlantaregional.org/wp-content/uploads/mas-regionalslides-oct2017-v1-full-presentation.pdf.

———. 2018. "2018 Metro Atlanta Speaks Survey Results." September. https://cdn.atlantaregional.org/wp-content/uploads/mas-2018-full-report-ksu.pdf.

———. 2019. "Metro Atlanta Speaks: Perceptions of Life in Metro Atlanta." November. https://33n.atlantaregional.com/wp-content/uploads/2019/11/RS_MAS-2019_ToPost_FINALBLOG_LB.pdf.

———. 2021. "2021 'Metro Atlanta Speaks' Survey Results." September. https://cdn.atlantaregional.org/wp-content/uploads/2021-metro-atlanta-speaks-report-final-for-arc.pdf.

Atlanta Regional Commission and Metro Atlanta Speaks. 2021. *"Full Slide Deck*: 2021 MAS Results Review." https://cdn.atlantaregional.org/wp-content/uploads/mas-full-summarydeck-2021-nov.pdf.

Bagby, Dyana. 2023. "Beltline Rail Project Challenged by New Group of Business, Community Leaders." *RoughDraft Atlanta*, October 20. https://roughdraftatlanta.com/2023/10/20/beltline-rail-project-challenged-by-new-group-of-business-community-leaders/.

Baldassare, Mark, Dean Bonner, Alyssa Dykman, and Rachel Ward. 2019. "Californians and Education: PPIC Statewide Survey." Public Policy Institute of California, April. https://www.ppic.org/wp-content/uploads/ppic-statewide-survey-californians-and-education-april-2019.pdf.

Baldassare, Mark, Dean Bonner, Alyssa Dykman, and Rachel Lawler. 2020. "Californians and Education: PPIC Statewide Survey." Public Policy Institute of California, April. https://www.ppic.org/wp-content/uploads/ppic-statewide-survey-californians-and-education-april-2020.pdf.

Ballotpedia. 2017. "Los Angeles Unified School District Elections (2017)." https://ballotpedia.org/Los_Angeles_Unified_School_District_elections_(2017).

———. n.d. "Proportion of Each Party's National U.S. House Vote and Share of Seats Won in U.S. House of Representatives Elections." https://ballotpedia.org/Proportion_of_each_party%27s_national_U.S._House_vote_and_share_of_seats_won_in_U.S._House_of_Representatives_elections.

Baptist, Edward. 2016. *The Half That Has Never Been Told: Slavery and the Making of American Capitalism*. New York: Basic Books.

Barker, Cyril. 2011. "Black Officials Beat Down by Police." *New York Amsterdam News*, September 8.

Barnard, Christian. 2018. "The Teachers Union's Demands Would Drive LAUSD to Bankruptcy." *Los Angeles Daily News*, September 5.

Barone, Charles, Dana Laurens, and Nicholas Munyan-Penney. 2019. "A Democratic Guide to Public Charter Schools: Public Opinion." Democrats for Education Reform, May. http://dfer.org/wp-content/uploads/2019/06/A-Democratic-Guide-to-Public-Charter-Schools-2nd-Edition.pdf.

Barry, Dave. 2023. "Dave Barry's 2023 Year in Review." *Boston Globe*, December 31.

Baude, Patrick, Marcus Casey, Eric Hanushek, Gregory Phellan, and Steven Rivkin. 2020. "The Evolution of Charter School Equality." *Economica* 87(345): 158–89.

Bauer, Elizabeth. 2019a. "Chicago Fire, Chicago Police, Chicago Pensions: Why a COLA Change Isn't a Cure-All." *Forbes*, September 6.

———. 2019b. "Is Your City Safe from Pension Debt?" *Forbes*, January 29.

———. 2021. "The Story behind Illinois' Latest Public Pension Liability Boost, and Why It's So Very Illinois." *Forbes*, January 13.

———. 2022. "'We Don't Have Actuarial Numbers Relative to This Amendment': Illinois' Tier 2 Pension in Their Own Words." *Forbes*, February 22.

Baumgartner, Frank, Derek Epp, and Kelsey Shoub. 2018. *Suspect Citizens: What 20 Million Traffic Stops Tell Us about Policing and Race*. Cambridge: Cambridge University Press.

Beckert, Sven. 2014. *Empire of Cotton: A Global History*. New York: Alfred A. Knopf.

Bell, Derrick. 1992. *Race, Racism, and American Law*, 3rd ed. Boston: Little, Brown and Co.

Bell, Monica. 2016. "Situational Trust: How Disadvantaged Mothers Reconceive Legal Cynicism." *Law and Society Review* 50(2): 314–47.

Bellin, Jeffrey. 2014. "The Inverse Relationship between the Constitutionality and Effectiveness of New York City Stop and Frisk." *Boston University Law Review* 94: 1495–1550.

Berlin, Ira. 2000. *Many Thousands Gone: The First Two Centuries of Slavery in North America*. Cambridge, Mass.: Harvard University Press.

Berry, Jeffrey, Kent Portney, and Ken Thomson. 1993. *The Rebirth of Urban Democracy*. Washington, D.C.: Brookings Institution Press.

Best Neighborhood. n.d. "Where Racial Segregation and Income Disparity Align: Atlanta." https://bestneighborhood.org/where-racial-segregation-and -income-disparity-align-atlanta/ (accessed January 22, 2024).

Bevernage, Berber. 2010. "Writing the Past Out of the Present: History and the Politics of Time in Transitional Justice." *History Workshop Journal* 69(1, Spring): 111–31.

Biernacka-Lievestro, Joanna, and Joe Fleming. 2022. "States' Unfunded Pension Liabilities Persist as Major Long-Term Challenge." Pew Research Center, July 7. https://www.pewtrusts.org/en/research-and-analysis/articles/2022/07/07 /states-unfunded-pension-liabilities-persist-as-major-long-term-challenge #:~:text=After%20New%20Jersey%20(20.2%25%20of,value%20of%20what %20they%20owed.

Biggs, Andrew. 2023. "The Long-Term Solvency of Teacher Pension Plans: How We Got to Now and Prospects for Recovery." *Educational Researcher* 52(2).

Binder, Amy, and Mark Spindel. 2017. *The Myth of Independence: How Congress Governs the Federal Reserve*. Princeton, N.J.: Princeton University Press.

Bird, Chloe, and Patricia Rieker. 2008. *Gender and Health: The Effects of Constrained Choices and Social Policies*. Cambridge: Cambridge University Press.

Blinder, Alan. 2022. *A Monetary and Fiscal History of the United States, 1961–2021*. Princeton, N.J.: Princeton University Press.

Bloch, Matthew, Ford Fessenden, and Janet Roberts. 2010. "Stop, Question, and Frisk in New York Neighborhoods." *New York Times*, July 11.

Bloome, Deirdre. 2014. "Racial Inequality Trends and the Intergenerational Persistence of Income and Family Structure." *American Sociological Review* 79(6): 1196–1225.

Blum, Lawrence. 2017. "What We Can Learn from the Massachusetts Ballot Question Campaign on Charter School Expansion." National Education Policy Center, March. https://nepc.colorado.edu/sites/default/files/publications /PM%20Blum%20MA%20charters.pdf.

Blume, Howard. 2015. "Backers Want Half of LAUSD Students in Charter Schools in Eight Years, Report Says." *Los Angeles Times*, September 23.

———. 2017a. "The L.A. School Board Race: Brutal, Expensive and Important." *Los Angeles Times*, May 13.

———. 2017b. "Could the L.A. School Board's Balance of Power Shift Pro-Charter?" *Los Angeles Times*, March 5.

———. 2017c. "School Board Member or . . . Killer? Hard to Tell." *Los Angeles Times*, February 3.

———. 2020a. "L.A. School Board Races Show Split between Union- and Charter-Backed Candidates." *Los Angeles Times*, November 4.

———. 2020b. "L.A. Schools Are in COVID-19 Crisis Mode. What Do School Board Candidates Have to Say?" *Los Angeles Times*, October 20.

———. 2020c. "LAUSD Board Members Elect Young President." *Los Angeles Times*, December 16.

———. 2022. "In Two Tight Races for L.A. Unified Board, President Kelly Gonez and Maria Brenes Lead." *Los Angeles Times*, November 9.

Bobo, Lawrence. 2011. "Somewhere between Jim Crow and Post-Racialism: Reflections on the Racial Divide in America Today." *Daedalus* 140(2, Spring): 11–36.

Bratton, William, and George Kelling. 2015. "Why We Need Broken Windows Policing." *City Journal* (Winter): 1–14.

Brookings Institute. 2003. "Chicago in Focus: A Profile from 2000." https://www.brookings.edu/wp-content/uploads/2016/07/chicago.pdf.

Brown, Lawrence. 2022. *The Black Butterfly: The Harmful Politics of Race and Space in America*. Baltimore: Johns Hopkins University Press.

Brown-Nagin, Tomiko. 2011. *Courage to Dissent: Atlanta and the Long History of the Civil Rights Movement*. New York: Oxford University Press.

Brummet, Quentin, and Davin Reed. 2019. "The Effects of Gentrification on the Well-being and Opportunity of Original Resident Adults and Children." Working paper. Federal Reserve Board of Philadelphia, July. https://www.philadelphiafed.org/-/media/frbp/assets/working-papers/2019/wp19-30.pdf.

Bullard, Robert, ed. 2007. *The Black Metropolis in the Twenty-First Century: Race, Power, and the Politics of Place*. Lanham, Md.: Rowman and Littlefield.

———. 2011. "Twenty Point Plan to Depopulate Black Atlanta." *Autumn Awakening* 18(2). https://www.reimaginerpe.org/18-2/bullard.

Burke, Michael. 2020. "Los Angeles Is Ground Zero for the Interpretation of California's New Charter Schools Law." EdSource, August 10. https://edsource.org/2020/los-angeles-is-ground-zero-for-the-interpretation-of-californias-new-charter-schools-law/637898.

Burnett, Sara. 2014. "Pensions Pose Latest Challenge for Chicago Mayor." *AP News*, April 7. https://apnews.com/45bd25896a8e46188fe7f3e105bd4cd0.

Butterfield, Fox. 1997. "Scared Straight; The Wisdom of Children Who Have Known Too Much." *New York Times*, June 8.

Caiola, Sammy. 2023a. "Democratic Mayoral Nominee Cherelle Parker Wants to Strengthen Police, Lean on Stops and Searches to Tackle Gun Violence" *WHYY News*, May 30. https://whyy.org/articles/philadelphia-cherelle-parker-policing-mayor-election-stop-and-frisk-gun-violence/.

———. 2023b. "Stop and Frisk Is Being Used Illegally in New York City, a New Report Shows. What Lessons Can Philly Learn?" *WHYY News*, June 8. https://whyy.org/articles/new-york-police-department-stop-and-frisk-data-philadelphia-lessons/.

California Department of Education. 2018–2019. "Certificated Staff by Ethnicity for 2018–19, Staff Type: Teachers." https://dq.cde.ca.gov/dataquest/Staff/StaffByEth.aspx?cSelect=1964733—Los%20Angeles%20Unified&cYear=2018-19&cChoice=DstTeach&cType=T&cGender=B&cLevel=District&cTopic=Paif&myTimeFrame=S.

———. 2022. "Data Quest: 2021–22 Four-Year Adjusted Cohort Graduation Rate." Los Angeles Unified District Report (19-64733). Data Reporting Office. https://dq.cde.ca.gov/dataquest/dqcensus/CohRate.aspx?agglevel=district&year=2021-22&cds=1964733.

———. 2023a. "Data Quest: 2022–23 Enrollment by Ethnicity for Charter and Non-Charter Schools." Los Angeles Unified Report (19-64733). Data Reporting Office. https://dq.cde.ca.gov/dataquest/dqcensus/EnrCharterEth.aspx?cds=1964733&agglevel=district&year=2022-23.

———. 2023b. "Data Quest: 2022–23 Enrollment by Subgroup for Charter and Non-Charter Schools." Los Angeles Unified Report (19-64733). Data Reporting Office. https://dq.cde.ca.gov/dataquest/dqcensus/EnrCharterSub.aspx?cds=1964733&agglevel=district&year=2022-23&ro=y.

———. 2024a. "Charter Schools." Updated June 17, 2024. https://www.cde.ca.gov/sp/ch/index.asp.

———. 2024b. "Charter Schools—*CalEdFacts*." Updated May 13, 2024. https://www.cde.ca.gov/sp/ch/cefcharterschools.asp.

———. n.d. "District Profile: Los Angeles Unified." https://www.cde.ca.gov/sdprofile/details.aspx?cds=19647330000000.

Camarena Lopez, Natalie. 2022. "Who Attends Charter Schools?" *Charter School Data Digest*, December 19. https://data.publiccharters.org/digest/charter-school-data-digest/who-attends-charter-schools/.

Campbell, Scott. 1996. "Green Cities, Growing Cities, Just Cities? Urban Planning and the Contradictions of Sustainable Development." *Journal of the American Planning Association* 62(3): 296–312.

Caputo-Pearl, Alex. 2016. "Why Los Angeles Teachers May Have to Strike" (op-ed). *Los Angeles Times*, January 6.

Carlson, Justin. 2023. "Chicago Has More Pension Debt than 44 States." Illinois Policy Institute, March 28. https://www.illinoispolicy.org/chicago-has-more-pension-debt-than-44-states/.

Carpenter, Christopher, Samuel Eppink, and Gilbert Gonzales. 2020. "Transgender Status, Gender Identity, and Socioeconomic Outcomes in the United States." *ILR Review* 73(3): 573—99.

Carr, Patrick, Laura Napolitano, and Jessica Keating. 2007. "We Never Call the Cops and Here Is Why: A Qualitative Examination of Legal Cynicism in Three Philadelphia Neighborhoods." *Criminology* 45(2): 445–80.

Carroll, Leo, and M. Lilliana Gonzalez. 2014. "Out of Place: Racial Stereotypes and the Ecology of Frisks and Searches Following Traffic Stops." *Journal of Research in Crime and Delinquency* 51(5): 559–84.

Cashin, Sheryll. 2022. *White Space, Black Hood: Opportunity Hoarding and Segregation in the Age of Inequality.* Boston: Beacon Press.

CBS News/*New York Times*. 2011. "CBS News/*New York Times* Poll, August 19–23." Roper Center for Public Opinion Research. https://doi.org/10.25940/ROPER-31112508 (access for members only).

Center for Constitutional Rights. 2012. "Daniels, et al. v. The City of New York." October 1. https://ccrjustice.org/home/what-we-do/our-cases/daniels-et-al-v-city-new-york#files.

———. 2024. "Floyd, et al. v. City of New York, et al." May 21. https://ccrjustice.org/home/what-we-do/our-cases/floyd-et-al-v-city-new-york-et-al.

Center for Municipal Finance. 2021. "Property Tax Fairness: Interactive Reports: Chicago." University of Chicago, Harris School of Public Policy. https://fiftycities.s3.us-east-2.amazonaws.com/WebsiteCitiesReports/CHICAGO.html.

Center for Research on Education Outcomes (CREDO). 2023. "As a Matter of Fact: The National Charter School Study III 2023." Stanford University, updated

June 19, 2023. https://ncss3.stanford.edu/wp-content/uploads/2023/06/Credo-NCSS3-Report.pdf.

Chang, Gordon. 2019. *Ghosts of Gold Mountain: The Epic Story of the Chinese Who Built the Transcontinental Railroad.* Boston: Mariner Books.

Chantrill, Christopher. n.d. "U.S. Pensions Spending History from 1900." https://www.usgovernmentspending.com/pensions_spending.

Chapman, Ben. 2024. "LA's Charter School Wars Are Headed to Court. Here's What's at Stake." *LA School Report,* May 8.

Cheng, Albert, Michael Henderson, Paul Peterson, and Martin West. 2018. "Public Support Climbs for Teacher Pay, School Expenditures, Charter Schools, and Universal Vouchers: Results from the 2018 EdNext Poll." *Education Next* 19(1, August 2). https://www.educationnext.org/public-support-climbs-teacher-pay-school-expenditures-charter-schools-universal-vouchers-2018-ednext-poll/.

Cherone, Heather. 2022. "Mayor Lori Lightfoot Touts Glow at End of Chicago's Pension Debt Tunnel." *WTTW News,* August 16. https://news.wttw.com/2022/08/16/mayor-lori-lightfoot-touts-glow-end-chicago-s-pension-debt-tunnel.

———. 2023a. "Chicago's Pension Debt Continues to Rise, Increasing $1.74 Billion in 2022 to $35.4 Billion: City Analysis." *WTTW News,* July 5. https://news.wttw.com/2023/07/05/chicago-s-pension-debt-continues-rise-increasing-174-billion-2022-354-billion-city.

———. 2023b. "Johnson Set to Start Tackling Chicago's Pension Woes, Hemmed in by Vow Not to Raise Property Taxes." *WTTW News,* June 19. https://news.wttw.com/2023/06/19/johnson-set-start-tackling-chicago-s-pension-woes-hemmed-vow-not-raise-property-taxes.

Chetty, Raj, Michael Stepner, Sarah Abraham, Shelby Lin, Benjamin Scuderi, Nicholas Turner, Augustin Bergeron, and David Cutler. 2016. "The Association between Income and Life Expectancy in the United States, 2001–2014." *Journal of the American Medical Association* 315(6): 1750–66.

Chetty, Raj, Nathaniel Hendren, Maggie R. Jones, and Sonya R. Porter. 2020. "Race and Economic Opportunity in the United States: An Intergenerational Perspective." *Quarterly Journal of Economics* 135(2, May): 711–83. https://doi.org/10.1093/qje/qjz042.

Chicago Metropolitan Agency for Planning. 2024. "Community Data Snapshot: Chicago Community Area Series." July. https://www.cmap.illinois.gov/wp-content/uploads/dlm_uploads/Logan-Square.pdf.

Chicago Public Schools. 2022. *Budget 2022–2023.* https://www.cps.edu/globalassets/cps-pages/about-cps/finance/budget/budget-2023/docs/fy23-budget-book.pdf.

Chicago Teachers' Pension Fund. 2021. "126th Popular Annual Financial Report." https://ctpf.org/sites/files/2022-07/2021_PAFR_Draft_vk4_FINAL.pdf.

———. 2024. "Fund Facts." https://ctpf.org/sites/files/2023-07/Fund%20Facts_CTPF%20Website_6302023_vk1.pdf.

Chicago Teachers Union Research Department. 2014. "'The Great Chicago Pension Caper': Neighborhood Destabilization in an Age of Austerity." February 17. https://www.ctulocal1.org/wp-content/uploads/2018/10/ChicagoPensionCaper021714.2.pdf.

Chicago Tribune. 2013. "They Failed You." *Chicago Tribune,* March 21.

Choy, Ronald, and Bernard Gifford. 1980. "Resource Allocation in a Segregated School System: The Case of Los Angeles." *Journal of Education Finance* 6(1): 34–50.

City of Atlanta, GA. 2020. "Housing Affordability Action Plan." December. https://www.atlantaga.gov/home/showpublisheddocument/50144.

———. n.d. "Neighborhood Planning Units." https://www.atlantaga.gov/government/departments/city-planning/neighborhood-planning-units.

City of Chicago. 2018. "Strengthening Chicago' Pensions." https://www.chicago.gov/content/dam/city/depts/mayor/Press%20Room/Press%20Releases/2018/December/PensionBooklet.pdf.

———. 2022. *2022 Budget Overview.* https://www.chicago.gov/content/dam/city/depts/obm/supp_info/2022Budget/2022OverviewFINAL.pdf.

———. 2023. *2023 Budget Overview.* https://www.chicago.gov/content/dam/city/depts/obm/supp_info/2023Budget/2023-OVERVIEW.pdf.

City of New York. 2013. "Mayor Bloomberg Details Progress on Resiliency Projects Outlined in the City's Long-Term Plan to Protect City against the Effects of Climate Change on Hurricane Sandy Anniversary." October 29. http://www1.nyc.gov/office-of-the-mayor/news/348-13/mayor-bloomberg-details-progress-resiliency-projects-outlined-the-city-s-long-term-plan-to/#/0.

Civic Federation. 2021. "City of Chicago FY2022 Proposed Budget: Pension Funds." October 15. https://www.civicfed.org/civic-federation/blog/city-chicago-fy2022-proposed-budget-pension-funds.

———. 2022. "Funding Status of the Chicago Teachers' Pension Fund." July 29. https://www.civicfed.org/civic-federation/blog/funding-status-chicago-teachers%E2%80%99-pension-fund.

———. 2023a. "Before Enhancing Tier 2 Benefits, Evaluate the Financial Impact of Illinois Pension Proposals." April 28. https://www.civicfed.org/civic-federation/blog/enhancing-tier-2-benefits-evaluate-financial-impact-illinois-pension-proposals.

———. 2023b. "Financial Challenges Facing the Chicago Mayor and City Council: Options and Recommendations." June 14. https://www.civicfed.org/sites/default/files/chicagofinancialchallenges2023.pdf.

———. 2023c. "How Should the City of Chicago Evaluate Property Tax Increases?" June 21. https://www.civicfed.org/civic-federation/blog/how-should-city-chicago-evaluate-property-tax-increases.

Clark, Robert. 2012. "Evolution of Public-Sector Retirement Plans: Crisis, Challenges, and Change." *The Labor Lawyer* 27(2): 257–73.

Clotfelter, Charles. 2001. "Are Whites Still Fleeing? Racial Patterns and Enrollment Shifts in Urban Public Schools, 1987–1996." *Journal of Policy Analysis and Management* 20(2): 199–221.

CNN (Cable News Network). 2011a. "CNN/ORC Poll: Politics/Federal Debt Ceiling/Space Program/Elections, July 18–20." Roper Center for Public Opinion Research. https://doi.org/10.25940/ROPER-31095491 (access for members only).

CNN. 2011b. "CNN/ORC Poll: Economy/Federal Budget/Libya, March 11–13." Roper Center for Public Opinion Research. https://doi.org/10.25940/ROPER-31095484 (access for members only).

Cohen, Cathy. 2010. *Democracy Remixed: Black Youth and the Future of American Politics.* New York: Oxford University Press.

Cohodes, Sarah. 2018. "Policy Issue: Charter Schools and the Achievement Gap." *The Future of Children* (Winter): 1–16.

Collingwood, Loren, Ashley Jochim, and Kassra Oskooii. 2018. "The Politics of Choice Reconsidered: Partisanship, Ideology, and Minority Politics in Washington's Charter School Initiative." *State Politics and Policy Quarterly* 18(1): 61–92.

Collins, Patricia. 1990. *Black Feminist Thought: Knowledge, Consciousness, and the Politics of Empowerment*. New York: Routledge.

Commission on Government Forecasting and Accountability. 2022. "Illinois State Retirement Systems: Financial Condition as of June 30, 2021." September. https://cgfa.ilga.gov/Upload/FinConditionILStateRetirementSysSept2022.pdf.

Congress for the New Urbanism. 2001. "The Charter of the New Urbanism." https://www.cnu.org/sites/default/files/Charter_TwoPager.pdf.

Connolly, Nathan. 2014. *A World More Concrete: Real Estate and the Remaking of Jim Crow South Florida*. Chicago: University of Chicago Press.

Corak, Miles. 2013. "Income Inequality, Equality of Opportunity, and Inter-generational Mobility." *Journal of Economic Perspectives* 27(3): 79–102.

Costrell, Robert. 2020. "Cross-Subsidization of Teacher Pension Benefits: The Impact of the Discount Rate." *Journal of Pension Economics and Finance* 19(2): 147–62.

Coviello, Decio, and Nicola Persico. 2015. "An Economic Analysis of Black-White Disparities in the New York Police Department's Stop-and-Frisk Program." *Journal of Legal Studies* 44(2): 315–60.

Craig, Rev. David, et al. 2016. "Letter to NAACP Board Members." September 21. https://masscharterschools.org/wp-content/uploads/legacy/docs/news/naacpresponse_final_9212016.pdf.

Cramer, Maria, and Jeffery Mays. 2023. "New York Mayor Accused of Breaking His Promise for a New Kind of Policing." *New York Times*, November 11.

Crenshaw, Kimberlé. 1989. "Demarginalizing the Intersection of Race and Sex: A Black Feminist Critique of Antidiscrimination Doctrine, Feminist Theory, and Antiracist Politics." *University of Chicago Legal Forum* 140: 139–67.

———. 1990. "A Black Feminist Critique of Antidiscrimination Law and Politics." In *The Politics of Law*, 2nd ed., edited by David Kairys. New York: Pantheon.

Croucher, Shane. 2020. "Bloomberg Stop and Frisk Comments Resurface, Said He Put 'All the Cops' in Minority Neighborhoods 'Where All the Crime Is.'" *Newsweek*, February 11.

Dabrowski, Ted, and John Klingner. 2021. "Wirepoints Special Report: Illinois Pension Shortfall Surpasses $500 Billion, Average Debt Burden Now $110,000 per Household." Wirepoints, November 17. https://wirepoints.org/illinois-pension-shortfall-surpasses-500-billion-average-debt-burden-now-110000-per-household-wirepoints-special-report/.

Dabrowski, Ted, John Klingner, and Tait Jensen. 2015. "CPS Pensions: From Retirement Security to Political Slush Fund." Illinois Policy Institute, August. https://files.illinoispolicy.org/wp-content/uploads/2015/10/CPS_Paper-1.pdf.

Dahl, Robert. 1971. *Polyarchy: Participation and Opposition*. New Haven, Conn.: Yale University Press.

———. 1977. "On Removing Certain Impediments to Democracy in the United States." *Political Science Quarterly* 92(1): 1–20.

————. 2005. *Who Governs? Democracy and Power in an American City*, 2nd ed. New Haven, Conn.: Yale University Press.

Dale, Mariana. 2024. "How Charter Schools Are Steered Away from LAUSD's 'Most Fragile' Campuses." *LAist*, February 12. https://laist.com/news/education/lausd-charter-school-co-location-proposition-39-vote-february-2024.

————. 2023. "LAUSD Ratifies Contract with Teachers, Bringing Higher Wages and Smaller Classes." *LAist*, May 11.

DataLab. n.d. "In 2021, the Government Spent $6.82 Trillion." https://datalab.usaspending.gov/americas-finance-guide/spending/.

Dávila, Arlene. 2003. "Dreams of Place: Housing, Gentrification, and the Marketing of Space in El Barrio." *Centro Journal* 15(1): 112–37.

Davis, Mike. 1990. *City of Quartz: Excavating the Future in Los Angeles*. London: Verso.

Dean, Mensah. 2024. "Philly Has a Fraught History with Stop-and-Frisk Policing. Will Mayor Parker Expand Its Use?" *The Trace*, April 3. https://www.thetrace.org/2024/04/philadelphia-stop-and-frisk-policing/#:~:text=Cherelle%20Parker%20capped%20her%20campaign,someone%20down%20for%20investigative%20purposes.

Deaton, Angus. 2015. *The Great Escape: Health, Wealth, and the Origins of Inequality*. Princeton, N.J.: Princeton University Press.

Deere, Stephen. 2019. "Atlanta Beltline Demonstrators: 'We Pay the tax, Now Lay the Tracks.'" *Atlanta Journal-Constitution*, October 6.

Delgado, Emanuel, and Kate Swanson. 2021. "Gentefication in the Barrio: Displacement and Urban Change in Southern California." *Journal of Urban Affairs* 43(7): 925–40.

Delgado, Richard, and Jean Stefancic. 2023. *Critical Race Theory: An Introduction*, 4th ed. New York: New York University Press.

Denerstein, Mylan. 2023. "Nineteenth Report of the Independent Monitor: Monitor's Audit of the Neighborhood Safety Teams." NYPD Monitor, June 5. https://www.nypdmonitor.org/wp-content/uploads/2023/06/NST-Report.pdf.

DePietro, Andrew. 2022. "20 Cities with the Worst Income Inequality in America in 2022." *Forbes*, March 31.

Derthick, Martha. 1972. *New Towns in Town: Why a Federal Program Failed*. Washington, D.C.: Urban Institute.

De Souza Briggs, Xavier, ed. 2005. *The Geography of Opportunity: Race and Housing Choice in Metropolitan America*. Washington, D.C.: Brookings Institution Press.

De Tocqueville, Alexis. 1966. *Democracy in America*, translated by George Lawrence, edited by J. P. Mayer and Max Lerner. New York: Harper & Row. (Originally published in 1848.)

Devereaux, Ryan. 2012. "NYPD Facing Court Challenge over Controversial Stop-and-Frisk Tactics." *Guardian*, May 4.

Dhingra, Reva, Mitchell Kilborn, and Olivia Woldemikael. 2022. "Immigration Policies and Access to the Justice System: The Effect of Enforcement Escalations on Undocumented Immigrants and Their Communities." *Political Behavior* 44(3): 1359–87.

Dippel, Christian. 2022. "Political Parties Do Matter in U.S. Cities . . . for Their Unfunded Pensions." *American Economic Journal: Economic Policy* 14(3): 33–54.

DiSalvo, Daniel. 2015. *Government against Itself: Public Union Power and Its Consequences*. New York: Oxford University Press.

Donsky, Paul. 2007. "Beltline Work Begins; Volunteers to Start Blazing Trail in Southwest Atlanta." *Atlanta Journal-Constitution*, October 20.

———. 2008. "Advisers Criticize Beltline Outreach Efforts." *Atlanta Journal-Constitution*, April 13.

Dragan, Kacie, Ingrid Ellen, and Sherry Glied. 2020. "Does Gentrification Displace Poor Children and Their Families? New Evidence from Medicaid Data in New York City." *Regional Science and Urban Economics* 83: 103481.

Dreier, Peter, John Mollenkopf, and Todd Swanstrom. 2014. *Place Matters: Metropolitics for the Twenty-First Century*, 3rd ed. Lawrence: University Press of Kansas.

Du Bois, W.E.B. 2007. *Black Reconstruction in America 1860–1880.* New York: Oxford University Press. (Originally published in 1935.)

Economist, The. 2014. "America's Greece?" *The Economist*, December 20.

———. 2017. "Boardroom Battles." *The Economist*, November 11.

———. 2019a. "Class Struggle." *The Economist*, May 18.

———. 2019b. "Civics 101." *The Economist*, March 2.

———. 2024a. "Is the Most Powerful Teachers Union in America Overreaching?" *The Economist*, March 23.

———. 2024b. "Emptying and Fuming." *The Economist*. April 20.

Einhorn, Robin. 2006. *American Taxation, American Slavery.* Chicago: University of Chicago Press.

Eisinger, Peter. 1986. "Local Civil Service Employment and Black Socioeconomic Mobility." *Social Science Quarterly* 67(1): 169–75.

Elder, Erick, and Gary Wagner. 2015. "Political Effects on Pension Underfunding." *Economics and Politics* 27(1, March): 1–27.

Emanuel, Rahm. 2020. *The Nation City: Why Mayors Are Now Running the World.* New York: Vintage.

Ericson, David. 2011. *Slavery in the American Republic: Developing the Federal Government, 1791–1861.* Lawrence: University Press of Kansas.

Erie, Steven. 1988. *Rainbow's End: Irish-Americans and the Dilemmas of Urban Machine Politics, 1840–1985.* Berkeley: University of California Press.

Escalante, Ubaldo. 2017. "There Goes the Barrio: Measuring Gentefication in Boyle Heights, Los Angeles." Master's thesis, Columbia University.

Evans, Douglas, Cynthia-Lee Maragh, and Jeremy Porter. 2014. "What Do We Know about NYC's Stop and Frisk Program? A Spatial and Statistical Analysis." *Advances in Social Sciences Research Journal* 1(2): 130–44.

Ewing, Eve. 2018. *Ghosts in the Schoolyard: Racism and School Closings on Chicago's South Side.* Chicago: University of Chicago Press.

Fagan, Jeffrey. 2022. "No Runs, Few Hits, and Many Errors: Street Stops, Bias, and Proactive Policing." *UCLA Law Review* 68: 1584–1676.

Fagan, Jeffrey, Amanda Geller, Gareth Davies, and Valeria West. 2010. "Street Stops and Broken Windows Revisited: The Demography and Logic of Proactive Policing in a Safe and Changing City." In *Race, Ethnicity, and Policing: New and Essential Readings*, edited by Stephen Rice and Michael White. New York: New York University Press.

Fairleigh Dickinson University. 2020. "New Jersey Poll, June 18–30." Roper Center for Public Opinion Research. https://doi./org/10.25940/ROPER-31117564 (access for members only).

Fausset, Richard. 2016. "A Glorified Sidewalk, and the Path to Transform Atlanta." *New York Times*, September 11.

Favot, Sarah. 2017. "Ballooning Pension Costs Mean LAUSD and Other California School Districts Are Headed for Cuts, Stanford Study Says." *LA School Report*, October 12. https://www.laschoolreport.com/ballooning-pension-costs-mean -lausd-and-other-california-school-districts-are-headed-for-cuts-stanford -study-says/.

Fay, Laura. 2019. "Seen and Heard: Thousands of Pro–Charter School Parents Turn Out to Rally Ahead of Controversial Moratorium Vote at L.A. Board Meeting." *The 74*, January 29. https://www.the74million.org/seen-and -heard-thousands-of-pro-charter-school-parents-turn-out-to-rally-ahead-of -controversial-moratorium-vote-at-l-a-board-meeting/.

Federal Highway Administration Center for Innovative Financial Support. n.d. "Atlanta Beltline Tax Allocation District." U.S. Department of Transportation.

Federal Reserve Bank of St. Louis. n.d. "Income Gini Ratio for Households by Race of Householder." https://fred.stlouisfed.org/series/GINIALLRH.

Fensterwald, John. 2019. "New Era for Charter Schools: Newsom Signs Bill after Intensive Negotiations." EdSource, October 3. https://edsource.org/2019/new -era-for-charter-schools-newsom-signs-bill-with-compromises-he-negotiated /618099.

———. 2022. "A New Chapter for Charter Schools in California as Enrollment Drops for First Time in 3 Decades." EdSource, April 25. https://edsource.org /2022/a-new-chapter-for-charter-schools-in-california-as-enrollment-drops -for-first-time-in-3-decades/670868.

Fensterwald, John, and Daniel Willis. 2023. "California's TK-12 Enrollment Fails to Rebound in a Return to 'Normalcy.'" EdSource, April 4. https://edsource .org/2023/californias-tk-12-enrollment-fails-to-rebound-in-a-return-to -normalcy/688123.

Ferguson, Karen. 2002. *Black Politics in New Deal Atlanta*. Chapel Hill: University of North Carolina Press.

Finegold, Kenneth. 1995. *Experts and Politicians: Reform Challenges to Machine Politics in New York, Cleveland, and Chicago*. Princeton, N.J.: Princeton University Press.

Finn, Donovan, and Gordon Douglas. 2020. "DIY Urbanism." In *A Research Agenda for New Urbanism*, edited by Emily Talen. Cheltenham, U.K.: Edward Elgar Publishing.

FitchRatings. 2023. "Fitch Rates Los Angeles USD, CA's $384.26 Million Series 2023a Cops 'A–'; Outlook Stable." August 9. https://www.fitchratings.com /research/us-public-finance/fitch-rates-los-angeles-usd-ca-384-26-million -series-2023a-cops-a-outlook-stable-09-08-2023.

Flandro, Carly. 2024. "Some Districts, Charters Are Bucking History and Creating Partnerships." *Idaho Ed News*. July 29.

Foner, Eric. 2020. *The Second Founding: How the Civil War and Reconstruction Remade the Constitution*. New York: W. W. Norton.

Ford, Richard Thompson. 1994. "The Boundaries of Race: Political Geography in Legal Analysis." *Harvard Law Review* 107(8): 1841–1921.

Foreman, James, Jr. 2017. *Locking Up Our Own: Crime and Punishment in Black America*. New York: Farrar, Straus and Giroux.

Fortner, Michael Javen. 2020. "Hearing What Black Voices Really Say about Police." *City Journal*, July 5. https://www.city-journal.org/article/hearing-what-black -voices-really-say-about-police.

———. 2023. "Racial Capitalism and City Politics: Toward a Theoretical Synthesis." *Urban Affairs Review* 59(2): 630–53.

Franczek, P. C. 2016. "Illinois Supreme Court Strikes Down City of Chicago Pension Reform Legislation." JD Supra, March 29. https://www.jdsupra.com /legalnews/illinois-supreme-court-strikes-down-41912.

Frank, Barney. 2015. *Frank: A Life in Politics from the Great Society to Same-Sex Marriage.* New York: Farrar, Straus and Giroux.

Frankston, Janet, et al. 2004. "Ahead of the Curve." *Atlanta Journal-Constitution*, August 16.

Fredrickson, George. 2002. *Racism: A Short History.* Princeton, N.J.: Princeton University Press.

Freedberg, Louis. 2021. "Does Los Angeles Unified's Powerful School Board Contribute to Leadership Turnover?" EdSource, November 17. https://edsource .org/2021/los-angeles-unifieds-powerful-school-board-does-it-contribute-to -leadership-turnover-many-think-it-does/663757.

Frey, William. 2023. "New 2020 Census Data Shows an Aging America and Wide Racial Gaps between Generations." Brookings Institution, August 1. https:// www.brookings.edu/articles/new-2020-census-data-shows-an-aging-america -and-wide-racial-gaps-between-generations/.

Frymer, Paul. 2019. *Building an American Empire: The Era of Territorial and Political Expansion.* Princeton, N.J.: Princeton University Press.

Fuller, Bruce. 2022. *When Schools Work: Pluralist Politics and Educational Reform in Los Angeles.* Baltimore: Johns Hopkins University Press.

Gallup. 2024. "Labor Unions." https://news.gallup.com/poll/12751/labor -unions.aspx#:~:text=Trend%20in%20Americans'%20approval%20and,and %2020%25%20said%20they%20disapproved.

García Bedolla, Lisa. 2005. *Fluid Borders: Latino Power, Identity, and Politics in Los Angeles.* Berkeley: University of California Press.

Gelman, Andrew. 2013. "'Stop and Frisk' Statistics." Statistical Modeling, Causal Inference, and Social Science, July 17. https://statmodeling.stat.columbia .edu/2013/07/17/stop-and-frisk-statistics/.

Gelman, Andrew, Jeffrey Fagan, and Alex Kiss. 2007. "An Analysis of the New York City Police Department's 'Stop-and-Frisk' Policy in the Context of Claims of Racial Bias." *Journal of the American Statistical Association* 102(479): 813–23.

GenForward. 2017. "2017—July—Toplines—Millennial's Views on Education." https://genforwardsurvey.com/download/did=104.

Gerring, John. 2017. *Case Study Research: Principles and Practices,* 2nd ed. New York: Cambridge University Press.

Gerstle, Gary. 2001. *American Crucible: Race and Nation in the Twentieth Century.* Princeton, N.J.: Princeton University Press.

———. 2022. *The Rise and Fall of the Neoliberal Order: America and the World in the Free Market Era.* New York: Oxford University Press.

Ghimire, Ramesh. 2019. "Metro Atlanta Speaks Survey Dashboard." November 6. https://public.tableau.com/app/profile/ramesh.ghimire/viz/mas_all_year _viz/Introduction.

Glaeser, Edward, Michael Luca, and Erica Moszkowski. 2023. "Gentrification and Retail Churn: Theory and Evidence." *Regional Science and Urban Economics* 100(May): 103879.

Glaeser, Edward, and Giacomo Ponzetto. 2014. "Shrouded Costs of Government: The Political Economy of State and Local Public Pensions." *Journal of Public Economics* 116: 89–105.

Glenn, Albert. 1979. "State Court Desegregation Orders: Multi-District Busing, Supreme Court Review, and the Los Angeles School Case." *UCLA Law Review* 26(5): 1183–1230.

Glennon, Mark. 2022. "Senator Martwick at It Again, Leading Move to Increase Chicago Pension Liability by Billions." Wirepoints, January 28. https://wire points.org/senator-robert-martwick-at-it-again-leading-move-to-increase -chicago-pension-liability-by-billions-wirepoints/.

———. 2023. "Pension Reform, Illinois Style: Legislation to 'Fix' the Tier 2 Problem." Wirepoints, April 17. https://madisonrecord.com/stories/641691721-pension -reform-illinois-style-legislation-to-fix-the-tier-2-problem.

Glesne, Corinne. 2016. *Becoming Qualitative Researchers: An Introduction*, 5th ed. Boston: Pearson.

Glueck, Katie, and Ashley Southall. 2022. "Can Adams Fix 'Broken Windows'?" *New York Times*, March 26.

Goel, Sharad, Justin Rao, and Ravi Shroff. 2016. "Precinct or Prejudice? Under-standing Racial Disparities in New York City's Stop-and-Frisk Policy." *Annals of Applied Statistics* 10(1): 365–94.

Goetz, Klaus, and Jan-Hinrik Meyer-Sahling. 2009. "Political Time in the EU: Dimensions, Perspectives, Theories." *Journal of European Public Policy* 16(2): 180–201.

Gomez, Melissa. 2022. "Some L.A. Schools Face Uncertain Futures as Student Enrollment Declines Dramatically." *Los Angeles Times*, March 8.

Goodman, J. David. 2013. "Council Reverses Bloomberg Veto of Policing Bills." *New York Times*, August 22.

Government Finance Officers Association. 2011. "Sustainable Pension Benefit Tiers." Approved May 31, 2011. https://www.gfoa.org/materials/sustainable -pension-benefit-tiers.

Gravel, Ryan. 2016. *Where We Want to Live: Reclaiming Infrastructure for a New Generation of Cities*. New York: St. Martin's Press.

Green, Josh. 2021a. "Report: Atlanta Is 3rd Fastest Growing Metro, but (Relative) Affordability Remains." *Urbanize Atlanta*, October 19. https://atlanta.urbanize .city/post/report-atlanta-3rd-fastest-growing-metro-relative-affordability -remains.

———. 2021b. "Timeline: Evolution of the Atlanta BeltLine." *Atlanta*, April 21.

Greenberg, Michael. 2013. "How Different Is de Blasio?" *New York Review of Books*, September 23.

———. 2014. "'Broken Windows' and the New York Police." *New York Review of Books*, November 6.

Greener, Ian. 2005. "The Potential of Path Dependence in Political Studies." *Politics* 25(1): 62–72.

Greer, Tammy. 2017. "Cooperative Growth: The Political Economy Impacts on the Recipient Communities in Metropolitan Atlanta, Ga." PhD diss., Clark Atlanta University.

Grimshaw, William. 1995. *Bitter Fruit: Black Politics and the Chicago Machine, 1931–1991*. Chicago: University of Chicago Press.

Grotto, Jason, and Hal Dardick. 2012. "Generous Rules Govern Aldermen's Pensions." *Chicago Tribune*, May 1.

GRS Consulting. 2022. "Public School Teachers' Pension and Retirement Fund of Chicago: Actuarial Valuation Report as of June 30, 2022." October 19. https://publicplansdata.org/reports/IL_CHICAGOCITY-CTPF_AV_2022_11.pdf.

Guarino, Mark. 2014. "Chicago's Credit Rating Downgraded." *Christian Science Monitor*, March 5.

Hacker, Karen, Maria Anies, Barbara Folb, and Leah Zallman. 2015. "Barriers to Health Care for Undocumented Immigrants: A Literature Review." *Risk Management and Healthcare Policy* 8(October 30): 175–83.

Hairston, Julie. 2004. "Belt Line Plan Gathers Support." *Atlanta Journal-Constitution*, April 12.

Han, Hahrie, Elizabeth McKenna, and Michelle Oyakawa. 2021. *Prisms of the People: Power and Organizing in Twenty-First-Century America*. Chicago: University of Chicago Press.

Hancock, Ange-Marie. 2016. *Intersectionality: An Intellectual History*. New York: Oxford University Press.

Harris, David. 2013. "Across the Hudson: Taking the Stop and Frisk Debate beyond New York City." *New York University Journal of Legislation and Public Policy* 16: 853–82. https://scholarship.law.pitt.edu/fac_articles/116.

Hart, Ariel. 2008. "MARTA Loan Fills Gap in Beltline Study Funds." *Atlanta Journal-Constitution*, May 13.

Hawkins, Mackenzie. 2022. "Chicago's High Property Taxes Pay for Squeezed Retiree Benefits." Bloomberg, September 20.

Henig, Jeffrey, Richard Hula, Marion Orr, and Desiree Pedescleaux. 1999. *The Color of School Reform: Race, Politics, and the Challenge of Urban Education*. Princeton, N.J.: Princeton University Press.

Henry J. Kaiser Family Foundation. 2016. "Kaiser Family Foundation Poll: Kaiser Health Tracking Poll, March 7–14." Roper Center for Public Opinion Research. https://doi.org/10.25940/ROPER-31092737 (access for members only).

Here & Now. 2014. "Bill Bratton: You Can't Police without Stop-and-Frisk." WBUR, February 25. https://www.wbur.org/hereandnow/2014/02/25/bill-bratton-nypd.

Herskind, Micah. 2023. "This Is the Atlanta Way: A Primer on Cop City." *Black Agenda Report*, May 10. https://blackagendareport.com/atlanta-way-primer-cop-city.

Higginbotham, A. Leon. 1998. *Shades of Freedom: Racial Politics and Presumptions of the American Legal Process*. New York: Oxford University Press.

Highsmith, Brian. 2020. "The Structural Violence of Municipal Hoarding." *American Prospect*, July 6.

Hinton, Elizabeth. 2021. *America on Fire: The Untold History of Police Violence and Black Rebellion since the 60's*. New York: Liveright.

Hirschman, Albert. 1991. *The Rhetoric of Reaction: Perversity, Futility, Jeopardy*. Cambridge, Mass.: Harvard University Press.

Hirschman, Charles, and Elizabeth Mogford. 2009. "Immigration and the American Industrial Revolution from 1880 to 1920." *Social Science Research* 38(4): 897–920.

Hobson, Maurice. 2017. *The Legend of the Black Mecca: Politics and Class in the Making of Modern Atlanta*. Chapel Hill: University of North Carolina Press.

Hochschild, Jennifer. 1984. *The New American Dilemma: Liberal Democracy and School Desegregation*. New Haven, Conn.: Yale University Press.

———. 2005. "Race and Class in Political Science." *Michigan Journal of Race and Law* 11(1): 99–114.

———. 2009. "Conducting Intensive Interviews and Elite Interviews." In *Workshop on Interdisciplinary Standards for Systematic Qualitative Research*, edited by Michèle Lamont and Patricia White. Washington, D.C.: National Science Foundation.

Hochschild, Jennifer, and Nathan Scovronick. 2003. *The American Dream and the Public Schools*. New York: Oxford University Press.

Hochschild, Jennifer, Vesla Weaver, and Traci Burch. 2012. *Creating a New Racial Order: How Immigration, Multiracialism, Genomics, and the Young Can Remake Race in America*. Princeton, N.J.: Princeton University Press.

Hondagneu-Sotelo, Pierette, and Manuel Pastor. 2021. *South Central Dreams: Finding Home and Building Community in South L.A.* New York: New York Universitiy Press.

Honig, Meredith, ed. 2006. *New Directions in Education Policy Implementation: Confronting Complexity*. Albany: State University of New York Press.

Hood, Quinn. 2022. "Civic Advocate Data Journalism: Stop, Question, and Frisk Visualized." NYC OpenData. https://opendata.cityofnewyork.us/projects/stop-question-and-frisk-visualized/.

Hout, Michael, Clem Brooks, and Jeff Manza. 1995. "The Democratic Class Struggle in the United States: 1948–1992." *American Sociological Review* 60(6): 805–28.

Howard, Alex. 2017. "Here's How a Journalist in Atlanta Mapped Closed Data for Accountability." Sunlight Foundation, July 19. https://sunlightfoundation.com/2017/07/19/heres-how-a-journalist-in-atlanta-mapped-closed-data-for-accountability/.

Hughes, Stephanie. 2022. "Conservative Groups Are Spending Big on School Board Races." *Marketplace*, November 7. https://www.marketplace.org/2022/11/07/conservative-groups-are-spending-big-on-school-board-races/.

Human Relations News of Chicago. 1961. "Non-White Population Changes, 1950–1960." *Human Relations News of Chicago* 3(3; July). https://www.nlm.nih.gov/exhibition/forallthepeople/img/1234.pdf.

Hupe, Peter, ed. 2019. *Research Handbook on Street-Level Bureaucracy: The Ground Floor of Government in Context*. Northampton, Mass.: Edward Elgar.

Hurt, Emma. 2021. "Former Atlanta Mayor Kasim Reed Takes Steps toward 3rd Bid for City Hall." WABE, June 9. https://www.wabe.org/former-atlanta-mayor-kasim-reed-takes-steps-toward-3rd-bid-for-city-hall/.

Hwang, Jackelyn. 2015. "Gentrification in Changing Cities: Immigration, New Diversity, and Racial Inequality in Neighborhood Renewal." *Annals of the American Academy of Political and Social Science* 660(1): 319–40.

Hwang, Jackelyn, and Robert Sampson. 2014. "Divergent Pathways of Gentrification: Racial Inequality and the Social Order of Renewal in Chicago Neighborhoods." *American Sociological Review* 79(4): 726–51.

Hwang, Sean-Shong, Kevin Fitzpatrick, and David Helms. 1998. "Class Differences in Racial Attitudes: A Divided Black America?" *Sociological Perspectives* 41(2): 367–80.

Hyra, Derek. 2008. *The New Urban Renewal: The Economic Transformation of Harlem and Bronzeville*. Chicago: University of Chicago Press.

———. 2024. *Slow and Sudden Violence: Why and When Uprisings Occur*. Oakland: University of California Press.

Illinois Report Card. 2022–2023. "Chicago Public Schools District 299: Demographics." Illinois State Board of Education. https://www.illinoisreportcard.com/district.aspx?districtid=15016299025&source=teachers&source2=teacher demographics.

Illinois State Board of Elections. n.d. "Campaign Disclosure Menu." https://www.elections.il.gov/CampaignDisclosure.aspx?MID=rfZ%2buidMSDY%3d.

Immergluck, Dan. 2009. "Large Redevelopment Initiatives, Housing Values, and Gentrification: The Case of the Atlanta Beltline." *Urban Studies* 46(8): 1723–45.

———. 2022. *Red Hot City: Housing, Race, and Exclusion in Twenty-First Century Atlanta*. Oakland: University of California Press.

Immergluck, Dan, and Tharunya Balen. 2018. "Sustainable for Whom? Green Urban Development, Environmental Gentrification, and the Atlanta Beltline." *Urban Geography* 39(4): 546–62.

Ingenium Schools. 2023. "Defending Proposition 39: Ingenium Schools And Other Charters Unite Against LAUSD Resolution." September 19. https://ingeniumschools.org/news/ingenium/defending-proposition-39-ingenium-schools-and-other-charters-unite-against-lausd-resolution/.

In the Public Interest. 2016. "Policy Brief: The Cost of Charter Schools for Los Angeles Unified School District (LAUSD)." May. https://inthepublicinterest.org/wp-content/uploads/ITPI_LAUSDCharters_PolicyBrief_May2016.pdf.

Ipsos. n.d. "Public Affairs KnowledgePanel." https://www.ipsos.com/en-us/solutions/public-affairs/knowledgepanel.

Izumi, Lance. 2023. "The LAUSD Strike and the State Budget Deficit: Train Wreck Ahead." Pacific Research Institute, April 10. https://www.pacificresearch.org/the-lausd-strike-and-the-state-budget-deficit-train-wreck-ahead/.

Jackman, Mary, and Robert Jackman. 1983. *Class Awareness in the United States*. Berkeley: University of California Press.

Jackson, Dylan. 2022. "Atlanta Has the Highest Income Inequality in the Nation, Census Data Shows." *Atlanta Journal-Constitution*, November 28.

Jacobs, Alan. 2016. "Policy Making for the Long Term in Advanced Democracies." *Annual Review of Political Science* 19: 433–54.

Jacobs, Jane. 2011. *The Death and Life of Great American Cities*, 50th anniversary edition. New York: Modern Library. (Originally published in 1961.)

Jacobs, Lawrence, and Desmond King. 2021. *Fed Power: How Finance Wins*, 2nd ed. New York: Oxford University Press.

Jacobson, Linda. 2020. "As California's New Charter Law Takes Effect, Schools Bracing for Shutdowns Could Win Reprieve from Pandemic." *LA School Report*, November 24.

Jacobson, Michael. 2001. "From the 'Back' to the 'Front': The Changing Character of Punishment in New York City." In *Rethinking the Urban Agenda: Reinvigorating the*

Liberal Tradition in New York City and Urban America, edited by John Mollenkopf and Ken Emerson. New York: Century Foundation.

Jamali, Lily. 2019. "Why Race Matters in Today's LAUSD School Board Election." *KQED*, May 14. https://www.kqed.org/news/11747007/why-race-matters-in-todays-lausd-school-board-election.

Jason, Zachary. 2017. "The Battle over Charter Schools." *Education*, May 20. https://www.gse.harvard.edu/ideas/ed-magazine/17/05/battle-over-charter-schools.

Jenkins, Destin. 2021. *The Bonds of Inequality: Debt and the Making of the American City*. Chicago: University of Chicago Press.

JLL. 2021. "Why Atlanta?" https://indd.adobe.com/view/7a758c3f-efca-4048-8146-ca0fce72299f.

Johnson, Brandon. 2023. "Chicago for the People." https://www.brandonfor chicago.com/ (website expired).

Johnson, Cedric. 2016. "The Half-Life of the Black Urban Regime: Adolph Reed, Jr. on Race, Capitalism, and Urban Governance." *Labor Studies Journal* 41(3): 248–55.

Johnson, Hans, Deborah Reed, and Joseph Hayes. 2008. "The Inland Empire in 2015." Public Policy Institute of California. https://core.ac.uk/reader/71352280.

Johnson, Richard, and Benjamin Southgate. 2014. "Evaluating Retirement Income Security for Illinois Public School Teachers." Urban Institute, July. https://files .eric.ed.gov/fulltext/ED559321.pdf.

Jones, Barbara. 2017. "In Controversial Move, LAUSD's Deasy Wants to Raise High-School Graduation Requirements." *Los Angeles Daily News*, August 28.

Jones-Brown, Delores, and Brett Stoudt, eds. 2013. *Stop, Question, and Frisk Policing Practices in New York City: A Primer*, rev. ed. New York: John Jay College of Criminal Justice, Center on Race, Crime, and Justice.

Jonsson, Patrik. 2021. "An Atlanta Neighborhood Tries to Preserve 'a Sense of Place.'" *Christian Science Monitor*, March 4.

Kan, Leslie, Daniel Fuchs, and Chad Aldeman. 2016. "Pennies on the Dollar: How Illinois Shortchanges Its Teachers' Retirement." Bellwether Education Partners and TeachersPensions.org, February. https://www.teacherpensions.org /sites/default/files/Bellwether_TP_Illinois_Final.pdf.

Katznelson, Ira. 2005. *When Affirmative Action Was White: An Untold History of Racial Inequality in Twentieth-Century America*. New York: W. W. Norton.

Katznelson, Ira, and Aristide Zolberg, eds. 1986. *Working-Class Formation: Nineteenth-Century Patterns in Western Europe and the United States*. Princeton, N.J.: Princeton University Press.

Kay, Adrian. 2005. "A Critique of the Use of Path Dependency in Policy Studies." *Public Administration* 83(3): 553–71.

Keenan, Sean. 2022. "How to Make Housing Affordable in Atlanta." *Atlanta*, September 26.

Keller, Jon. 2023. "Are Teachers Unions Allowing Students to Fail?" *Boston*, September 6, 92–97, 167–69. https://www.bostonmagazine.com/news/2023 /09/06/teachers-unions-massachusetts/.

Kelling, George, and James Q. Wilson. 1982. "Broken Windows: The Police and Neighborhood Safety." *Atlantic*, March.

Kempner, Matt. 2016. "House Hunting along the Beltline's Frontier." *Atlanta Journal-Constitution*, November 27.

Kerchner, Charles. 2017. "Stop Charter School War; Build a New Learning System." *EducationWeek*, June 5.

Kerchner, Charles, David Menefee-Libey, Laura Mulfinger, and Stephanie Clayton. 2008. *Learning from L.A.: Institutional Change in American Public Education.* Cambridge, Mass.: Harvard Education Press.

Khan, Maria, Farzana Kapadia, Amanda Geller, Medha Mazumdar, Joy Scheidell, Kristen Krause, Richard Martino, Charles Cleland, Typhanye Dyer, Danielle Ompad, and Perry Halkitis. 2021. "Racial and Ethnic Disparities in 'Stop-and-Frisk' Experience among Young Sexual Minority Men in New York City." *PLoS One* 16(8): e0256201.

Kiewiet, D. Roderick, and Mathew McCubbins. 2014. "State and Local Government Finance: The New Fiscal Ice Age." *Annual Review of Political Science* 17: 105–22.

Kilgannon, Corey. 2023. "NYPD Anti-Crime Units Still Stopping People Illegally, Report Shows." *New York Times*, June 6.

King, Desmond, and Rogers Smith. 2011. *Still a House Divided: Race and Politics in Obama's America.* Princeton, N.J.: Princeton University Press.

Kingdon, John. 1984. *Agendas, Alternatives, and Public Policies.* Glenview, Ill.: Scott, Foresman, and Co.

Klein, Rebecca. 2016. "The NAACP Takes a Major Stand against the Growth of Charter Schools." *HuffPost*, October 16.

———. 2019. "Inside the NAACP's Civil War over Charter Schools." *HuffPost*, August 6.

Klugerman, Alex. 2017. "Atlanta Mayoral Candidates Discuss Annexation, Affordable Housing at Forum." *Emory Wheel: Emory University.* October 3.

Komisarchik, Mayya. 2020. "Electoral Protectionism: How Southern Counties Eliminated Elected Offices in Response to the Voting Rights Act." Unpublished paper. University of Rochester.

Koumpilova, Mila, Matt Barnum, and Collin Binkley. 2022. "As Fewer Kids Enroll, Big Cities Face a Small Schools Crisis." *Chalkbeat*, August 1.

Kreuzer, Marcus. 2023. *The Grammar of Time: A Toolbox for Comparative Historical Analysis.* Cambridge: Cambridge University Press.

Kruse, Kevin. 2005. *White Flight: Atlanta and the Making of Modern Conservatism.* Princeton, N.J.: Princeton University Press.

Kulikoff, Alan. 1992. *The Agrarian Origins of American Capitalism.* Charlottesville: University Press of Virginia.

LA Promise Fund. n.d. "Who We Are." https://www.lapromisefund.org/who -we-are/#mission-vision.

LA School Report. 2018. "Even as UTLA Looks to Bolster Declining Union Membership with Push into Charters, One School's Teachers Voted to Decertify after Just Two Years." *LA School Report*, February 12. https://www.laschool report.com/even-as-utla-looks-to-bolster-declining-union-membership-with -push-into-charters-one-schools-teachers-voted-to-decertify-after-just-two-years/.

LA Unified Advisory Task Force. 2018. *Hard Choices.* Los Angeles, June. https:// aala.us/docs/2018/07/LAUSD-Task-Force-Hard-Choices-report-FINAL.pdf.

Laborers' and Retirement Board Employees' Annuity and Benefit Fund of Chicago. n.d. "Membership." https://www.labfchicago.org/members/membership -and-benefits/membership/.

Lamont, Michèle, and Patricia White, eds. 2009. *Workshop on Interdisciplinary Standards for Systematic Qualitative Research.* Washington D.C.: National Science Foundation, http://www.nsf.gov/sbe/ses/soc/ISSQR_workshop_rpt.pdf.

Lane, Charles. 2017. "Rahm Emanuel Gears Up for a Modern-Day *Brown v. Board.*" *Washington Post,* April 5.

Lassiter, Matthew. 2005. *The Silent Majority: Suburban Politics in the Sunbelt South.* Princeton, N.J.: Princeton University Press.

Lauen, Douglas, Bruce Fuller, and Luke Dauter. 2015. "Positioning Charter Schools in Los Angeles: Diversity of Form and Homogeneity of Effects." *American Journal of Education* 121(2): 213–39.

LAUSD Unified. 2023. "School Directories: Charter Schools Directory 2023–2024." https://www.lausd.org/Page/1827.

Lee, Erika. 2002. "The Chinese Exclusion Example: Race, Immigration, and American Gatekeeping, 1882–1924." *Journal of American Ethnic History* 21(3): 36–62.

Lee, Jennifer, and Frank Bean. 2004. "America's Changing Color Lines: Immigration, Race/Ethnicity, and Multiracial Identification." *Annual Review of Sociology* 30(August): 221–42.

Legewie, Joscha. 2016. "Racial Profiling and Use of Force in Police Stops: How Local Events Trigger Periods of Increased Discrimination." *American Journal of Sociology* 122(3): 379–424.

Lehrer, Brian. 2012. "Reverend Flake on Stop and Frisk." *The Brian Lehrer Show,* WNYC, June 14. https://www.wnycstudios.org/podcasts/bl/segments/216235-reverend-flake-stop-and-frisk.

Leinberger, Christopher, and Michael Rodriguez. 2016. "Foot Traffic Ahead: Ranking Walkable Urbanism in America's Largest Metros." George Washington University School of Business.

Leland, John, and Colin Moynihan. 2012. "Thousands March Silently to Protest Stop-and-Frisk Policies." *New York Times,* June 17.

Lens, Michael. 2022. "Zoning, Land Use, and the Reproduction of Urban Inequality." *Annual Review of Sociology* 48: 421–39. https://doi.org/10.1146/annurev-soc-030420-122027.

Leslie, Katie, and J. Scott Trubey. 2014. "Western Leg of Beltline Begins." *Atlanta Journal-Constitution,* November 12.

Levchak, Philip. 2017. "Do Precinct Characteristics Influence Stop-and-Frisk in New York City? A Multi-Level Analysis of Post-Stop Outcomes." *Justice Quarterly* 34(3): 377–406.

Lewis, Gregory, and Sue Frank. 2002. "Who Wants to Work for the Government?" *Public Administration Review* 62(4): 395–404.

Lind, Michael. 2012. *Land of Promise: An Economic History of the United States.* New York: HarperCollins.

Lindblom, Charles. 1980. *Politics and Markets: The World's Political-Economic Systems.* New York: Basic Books.

Lipsky, Michael. 2010. *Street-Level Bureaucracy: Dilemmas of the Individual in Public Service,* 30th anniversary edition. New York: Russell Sage Foundation.

Logan, John, Weiwei Zhang, and Deirdre Oakley. 2017. "Court Orders, White Flight, and School District Segregation, 1970–2010." *Social Forces* 95(3): 1049–75.

Lopez, Steve. 2020. "Column: You'll Need a Shower after Reading about This School Board Race That's Descended into the Gutter." *Los Angeles Times*, February 22.

Los Angeles Times. 2009. "Frequency Questionnaire: June 10–16, 2009." In *Los Angeles Times* Poll Archive, edited by *Los Angeles Times*. Greenberg Quinlan Rosner Research, June. https://ca-times.brightspotcdn.com/00/3a/da9b864246d7bb7ac2173b61ad37/june-10-16-2009-demprimary-la-times-fq1-converted.pdf.

Los Angeles Unified School District (LAUSD). 2023. "Fingertip Facts 2022–2023." In "FAQ Notebook: K-12 Classroom Teachers and Certificated Administrators, 2022–2023." Human Resources Division. https://www.lausd.org/cms/lib/CA01000043/Centricity/Domain/468/2022-2023%20TDemo.pdf.

———. n.d. "A Closer Look at Los Angeles Unified's Budget." https://achieve.lausd.net/cms/lib/CA01000043/Centricity/ModuleInstance/45663/Closer%20Look%20at%20the%20Budget%20and%20Class%20Size%2001-02-19.pdf.

MacDonald, John. 2020. "Does Stop-and-Frisk Reduce Crime?" Unpublished paper. University of Pennsylvania. https://crim.sas.upenn.edu/fact-check/does-stop-and-frisk-reduce-crime.

MacDonald, John, Jeffrey Fagan, and Amanda Geller. 2016. "The Effects of Local Police Surges on Crime and Arrests in New York City." *PLoS One* 11(6): e0157223.

Madiar, Eric. 2014. "Illinois Public Pension Reform: What's Past Is Prologue." *Illinois Public Employee Relations Report* 31.

———. 2016. "Illinois Public Pensions: Where to from Here?" *Illinois Public Employee Relations Report* 33.

Mahoney, James. 2000. "Path Dependence in Historical Sociology." *Theory and Society* 29(4): 507–48.

Malone, Tess. 2017. "Slow. Down. A Guide to Good Beltline Manners." *Atlanta*, November 14.

Mariano, Willoughby. 2017. "Beltline CEO: I Put Affordable Housing First, but Deserve a 'C' for Effort." *Atlanta Journal-Constitution*, August 9.

Mariano, Willoughby, Lindsey Conway, and Anastaciah Ondieki. 2017. "How the Atlanta Beltline Broke Its Promise on Affordable Housing." *Atlanta Journal-Constitution*, July 13.

Martin, Isaac, and Kevin Beck. 2018. "Gentrification, Property Tax Limitation, and Displacement." *Urban Affairs Review* 54(1): 33–73.

Mazumder, Soumyajit. 2020. "A Brief Moment in the Sun: The Racialized (Re)Construction of Punishment in the American South." Unpublished paper. Harvard University.

McBride, Ashley. 2021. "OUSD Could Remove Mention of Charters from Enrollment Materials." *The Oaklandside*, January 25.

McCarthy, Jesse. 2015. "Love's Austere and Lonely Offices." *The Nation*, December 7.

McDonald, Lauren. 2019. "Atlanta Beltline Visionary Shares Story of Community Revitalization." *Brunswick News*, March 22.

McGahan, Jason. 2021. "Exclusive: Cecily Myart-Cruz's Hostile Takeover of L.A.'s Public Schools." *Los Angeles*, August 26.

McGee, Josh. 2016. "Chicago Crowd-Out: How Rising Pension Costs Harm Current Teachers—and Students." Issue Brief 52. Manhattan Institute, May. https://media4.manhattan-institute.org/sites/default/files/IB-JM-0516.pdf.

McNall, Scott, Rhonda Levine, and Rick Fantasia, eds. 2018. *Bringing Class Back In: Contemporary and Historical Perspectives.* New York: Routledge.

McNeil, Brian. 2020. "Stop-and-Frisk in New York, Philadelphia, and Chicago: Slowly Approaching an Uneasy Synthesis or Running Out of Time to Justify Its Freight." *Widener Commonwealth Law Review* 29: 69–104.

Medina, Jennifer, and Dana Goldstein. 2019. "Success of Los Angeles Teachers Strike Rocks Charter Schools, and a Rich Supporter." *New York Times*, January 28.

Meisel, Hannah. 2020. "Graduated Income Tax Referendum Fails, Dealing Major Blow to Pritzker." *NPR Illinois*, November 4. https://www.nprillinois.org /statehouse/2020-11-04/graduated-income-tax-referendum-fails-dealing-major -blow-to-pritzker.

Merseth, Katherine. 2009. *Inside Urban Charter Schools: Promising Practices and Strategies in Five High-Performing Schools.* Cambridge, Mass.: Harvard Educational Review.

Michaels, Walter Benn, and Adolph Reed Jr. 2023. *No Politics but Class Politics.* London: Eris.

Milkman, Ruth. 2006. *L.A. Story: Immigrant Workers and the Future of the U.S. Labor Movement.* New York: Russell Sage Foundation.

Mock, Brentin. 2022. "Why Metro Atlanta Is the Poster Child for the U.S. Housing Crisis." *Bloomberg CityLab*, December 8.

Mollenkopf, John, and Raphael Sonenshein. 2013. "New York City and Los Angeles: Government and Political Influence." In *New York and Los Angeles: The Uncertain Future*, edited by David Halle and Andrew Beveridge. New York: Oxford University Press.

Monahan, Amy. 2013. "Understanding the Legal Limits on Public Pension Reform." American Enterprise Institute, May. https://www.aei.org/research-products /report/understanding-the-legal-limits-on-public-pension-reform/.

———. 2015. "State Fiscal Constitutions and the Law and Politics of Public Pensions." *University of Illinois Law Review* 2015(1): 117–74.

———. 2017. "When a Promise Is Not a Promise: Chicago-Style Pensions." *UCLA Law Review* 64(2): 356–413.

Monmouth University Polling Institute. 2021. "Monmouth University New Jersey Poll, August 11–16." Roper Center for Public Opinion Research. https://doi.org /10.25940/ROPER-31118609 (access for members only).

Montejano, David. 1987. *Anglos and Mexicans in the Making of Texas, 1836–1986.* Austin: University of Texas Press.

Morel, Domingo. 2018. *Takeover: Race, Education, and American Democracy.* New York: Oxford University Press.

Morgan, Edmund. 1975. *American Slavery, American Freedom: The Ordeal of Colonial Virginia.* New York: W. W. Norton.

Moser, Whet. 2011. "Snowpocalypse Then: How the Blizzard of 1979 Cost the Election for Michael Bilandic." *Chicago*, February 2.

Moss, Philip. 1988. "Employment Gains by Minorities, Women in Large City Government, 1976–83." *Monthly Labor Review* 111(11): 18–24.

Muhammad, Khalil. 2011. *The Condemnation of Blackness: Race, Crime, and the Making of Modern Urban America.* Cambridge, Mass.: Harvard University Press.

Munnell, Alicia, and Jean-Pierre Aubry. 2017. "An Overview of the State and Local Government Pension/OPEB Landscape." *Journal of Retirement* 5(1): 117–37.

Munnell, Alicia, Kelly Haverstock, and Jean-Pierre Aubry. 2008. "Why Does Funding Status Vary among State and Local Plans?" Boston College, Center for Retirement Research, May 6. https://crr.bc.edu/why-does-funding-status-vary-among-state-and-local-plans/.

Murphy, Matt. 2016. "Charter Battle Exposes Rift in Teachers Union." *Common-Wealth*, February 3.

Muwakkil, Salim. 2011. "Black Chicago Divided: Class and Generational Conflicts Intensify as African Americans Cope with the Great Recession." *In These Times* 35(8): 20.

Myers, Quinn. 2022. "City Council Passes $16.4 Billion 2023 Budget That Avoids Property Tax Increase." *Block Club Chicago*, November 7. https://blockclub chicago.org/2022/11/07/city-council-passes-16-4-billion-2023-budget-that-avoids-property-tax-increase/.

Naram, Kartik. 2017. "No Place Like Home: Racial Capitalism, Gentrification, and the Identity of Chinatown." *Asian American Policy Review* 27: 1–26.

Narea, Nicole. 2023. "The Massive Los Angeles Public School Worker Strike, Explained." *Vox*, March 21. https://www.vox.com/2023/3/21/23650526/lausd-strike-los-angeles-teacher-salary-wages.

Nation, Joe. 2017. "Pension Math: Public Pension Spending and Service Crowd Out in California, 2003–2030." Stanford, Calif.: Stanford University, Institute for Economic Policy Research.

National Alliance for Public Charter Schools. 2022. "Knowledge Base: Charter School Data Dashboard." https://data.publiccharters.org/digest/charter-school-data-digest/.

National Center for Education Statistics. 2012. *Digest of Education Statistics*. U.S. Department of Education. https://nces.ed.gov/pubsearch/pubsinfo.asp?pubid=2014015.

———. 2021. *Digest of Education Statistics*. U.S. Department of Education. https://nces.ed.gov/pubsearch/pubsinfo.asp?pubid=2023009.

———. 2022. *Digest of Education Statistics*. U.S. Department of Education. https://nces.ed.gov/programs/digest/2022menu_tables.asp.

NBC News/*Wall Street Journal*. 2011. "NBC News/*Wall Street Journal* Poll: Government/2010 Presidential Election/Budget Deficits, February 24–28." Roper Center for Public Opinion Research. https://doi.org/10.25940/ROPER-31094897 (access for members only).

Newman, Katherine. 2019. *Downhill from Here: Retirement Insecurity in the Age of Inequality.* New York: Metropolitan Books.

Newsome, Melba. 2023. "Islands of Illness." *Scientific American* (October): S26–S27.

New York City Department of Health and Mental Hygiene. 2013. "Firearm Deaths and Injuries in New York City." *Epi Search Report*, April. www.nyc.gov/html/om/pdf/2013/firearms_report.pdf.

New York Police Department. 2008. "Crime and Enforcement Activity in New York City (January 1–December 31, 2008)." https://www.nyc.gov/assets/nypd/downloads/pdf/analysis_and_planning/YearEnd2008EnforcementReport.pdf.

———. 2013. "Crime and Enforcement Activity in New York City (January 1–December 31, 2012)." https://www.nyc.gov/assets/nypd/downloads/pdf/analysis_and_planning/2012_year_end_enforcement_report.pdf.

———. 2022. "Seven Major Felony Offenses." www.nyc.gov/assets/nypd/downloads/pdf/analysis_and_planning/historical-crime-data/seven-major-felony-offenses-2000-2022.pdf.

———. n.d. "Historical New York City Crime Data." https://www1.nyc.gov/site/nypd/stats/crime-statistics/historical.page.

New York Civil Liberties Union. 2012. "NYCLU Analysis Reveals NYPD Street Stops Soar 600% over Course of Bloomberg Administration." February 14. https://www.nyclu.org/press-release/nyclu-analysis-reveals-nypd-street-stops-soar-600-over-course-bloomberg.

———. 2019. "Stop-and-Frisk Data." March 14. https://www.nyclu.org/data/stop-and-frisk-data.

———. 2022. "A Closer Look at Stop-and-Frisk in NYC." December 12. https://www.nyclu.org/en/closer-look-stop-and-frisk-nyc.

———. 2023. "Stop-and-Frisk Data" (through 2023). https://www.nyclu.org/en/stop-and-frisk-data.

New York State and Local Retirement System. 2021. "What Tier Are You In?" Office of the New York State Comptroller, updated January 2021. https://www.osc.ny.gov/retirement/members/what-tier-are-you.

New York Times. 2012. "New York City Poll." August 10–15. Roper Center for Public Opinion Research (access for members only).

Ngai, Mae. 2004. *Impossible Subjects: Illegal Aliens and the Making of Modern America.* Princeton, N.J.: Princeton University Press.

Nitkin, Alex. 2023. "A Pension 'Fix' Could Blow a Hole in City Budgets. Here's Why Supporters Say It's Worth It." *Illinois Answers Project,* May 10. https://illinoisanswers.org/2023/05/10/a-pension-fix-could-blow-a-hole-in-city-budgets-heres-why-supporters-say-its-worth-it/.

Nothdurft, John, and Sheila Weinberg. 2017. "The Municipal Government Debt Crisis." In *Twenty-First Century Chicago,* 2nd, rev. ed., edited by Dick Simpson, Constance Mixon, and Melissa Mouritsen. San Diego: Cognella Academic Publishing. (Originally published in 2014.)

Nuamah, Sally. 2022. *Closed for Democracy: How Mass School Closure Undermines the Citizenship of Black Americans.* New York: Cambridge University Press.

Nukulkij, Poom (GfK Project Director). 2016. "The GfK Group Project Report for 'They Treat Us Like a Different Race': A Multi-City Project on Class-in-Race Inequality." GfK, September 7.

O'Brien, Brian. 2015. *The Tyranny of the Federal Reserve.* Scotts Valley, Calif.: CreateSpace Independent Publishing Platform.

O'Connor, Alice, Chris Tilly, and Lawrence Bobo, eds. 2003. *Urban Inequality: Evidence from Four Cities.* New York: Russell Sage Foundation.

O'Neill, Aaron. 2023. "Share of Popular Votes for the Democratic and Republican Parties in Presidential Elections from 1860 to 2020." Statista, May 23. https://www.statista.com/statistics/1035521/popular-votes-republican-democratic-parties-since-1828/.

Office of the Attorney General. 1999. *New York City Police Department's "Stop & Frisk" Practices: Report to the People of the State of New York from the Office of the Attorney General.* https://ur.ag.ny.gov/sites/default/files/reports/stp_frsk.pdf.

Office of Inspector General. 2021. "City of Chicago Active Employees: Demographics." https://informationportal.igchicago.org/city-of-chicago-active-employees/.

Olansky, Dianne. 2006. "City Shouldn't Compromise on Plans for Beltline." *Atlanta Journal-Constitution*, September 14.

Oliver, J. Eric. 2001. *Democracy in Suburbia*. Princeton, N.J.: Princeton University Press.

Orfield, Gary, and Danielle Jarvie. 2020. "Black Segregation Matters: School Resegregation and Black Educational Opportunity." UCLA, Civil Rights Project, December 17. https://civilrightsproject.ucla.edu/research/k-12-education/integration-and-diversity/black-segregation-matters-school-resegregation-and-black-educational-opportunity.

Orfield, Gary, Genevieve Siegel-Hawley, and John Kucsera. 2011. "Divided We Fail: Segregated and Unequal Schools in the Southland." UCLA, Civil Rights Project, March 18. https://civilrightsproject.ucla.edu/research/metro-and-regional-inequalities/lasanti-project-los-angeles-san-diego-tijuana/divided-we-fail-segregated-and-unequal-schools-in-the-southfield.

Orr, Marion. 1999. *Black Social Capital: The Politics of School Reform in Baltimore, 1986–1998.* Lawrence: University Press of Kansas.

Orr, Marion, and Valerie Johnson, eds. 2008. *Power in the City; Clarence Stone and the Politics of Inequality.* Lawrence: University Press of Kansas.

Owens, Michael Leo, and Jacob Brown. 2014. "Weakening Strong Black Political Empowerment: Implications from Atlanta's 2009 Mayoral Election." *Journal of Urban Affairs* 36(4): 663–81.

Pagliari, Joseph L., Jr. 2020. "Thoughts on the Looming Pension Problems Facing Chicago, Cook County, and Illinois." University of Chicago Booth School of Business. http://dx.doi.org/10.2139/ssrn.3564725.

Pan, Ying. 2010. "Does Latino Population Induce White Flight? Evidence from Los Angeles County." Working paper 2011-06. Louisiana State University, May. https://lsu.edu/business/economics/files/workingpapers/pap11_06.pdf.

Pankovits, Tressa. 2022. "Charter Schools Win a Washington Battle." *Wall Street Journal*, July 17.

Parker, Kim, and Kiley Hurst. 2021. "Growing Share of Americans Say They Want More Spending on Police in Their Area." Pew Research Center, October 26. https://www.pewresearch.org/short-reads/2021/10/26/growing-share-of-americans-say-they-want-more-spending-on-police-in-their-area/.

Pastor, Manuel. 2015. "How Immigrant Activists Changed L.A." *Dissent* (Winter): 55–63.

Patterson, Orlando. 1989. "Toward a Study of Black America." *Dissent* (Fall): 476–86.

Pattillo, Mary. 2007. *Black on the Block: The Politics of Race and Class in the City.* Chicago: University of Chicago Press.

Payne, Charles. 2008. *So Much Reform, So Little Change.* Cambridge, Mass.: Harvard Education Press.

Peele, Thomas. 2022. "Enrollment Decline: LAUSD's Carvalho Says Families Leaving the State or Choosing to Home-School." EdSource, July 24. https://edsource.org/2022/enrollment-decline-lausds-carvalho-says-families-leaving-the-state-or-choosing-to-home-school/675830.

Pendered, David. 2006a. "Beltline Broken? How a Key Piece of One of the Most Promising Development Deals in Recent Atlanta History Fell Apart." *Atlanta Journal-Constitution*, September 23.

———. 2006b. "Beltline: Ring of Renewal a Costly Jewel: Assessments Soar, Questions Raised." *Atlanta Journal-Constitution*, March 18.

Pendergrast, Mark. 2017. *City on the Verge: Atlanta and the Fight for America's Urban Future*. New York: Basic Books.

Peterson, Paul. 1976. *School Politics, Chicago Style*. Chicago: University of Chicago Press.

Pew Charitable Trusts. 2019a. "Legal Protections for State Pension and Retiree Health Benefits." May 30. https://www.pewtrusts.org/en/research-and-analysis/issue-briefs/2019/05/legal-protections-for-state-pension-and-retiree-health-benefits.

———. 2019b. "The School District of Philadelphia's Pension Costs." November 15. https://www.pewtrusts.org/-/media/assets/2019/11/pri_the_school_district_of_philadelphias_pension_costs_final-v1.pdf.

Pierog, Karen. 2015. "Moody's Drops Chicago's Credit Rating to 'Junk.'" *Reuters*, May 12.

Pierson, Paul. 2000. "Increasing Returns, Path Dependence, and the Study of Politics." *American Political Science Review* 94(2): 251–67.

———. 2004. *Politics in Time: History, Institutions, and Social Analysis*. Princeton, N.J.: Princeton University Press.

Piston, Spencer. 2018. *Class Attitudes in America: Sympathy for the Poor, Resentment of the Rich, and Political Implications*. New York: Cambridge University Press.

Police Foundation. 2017. "5 Things You Need to Know about Stop, Question, and Frisk," March. https://www.policinginstitute.org/wp-content/uploads/2018/07/5-THINGS-Stop_Question_Frisk.pdf.

Potter, Jackson, and Arlene Inouye. 2021. "The Resurgence of Teachers Unions." *The Forge*, March 4. forgeorganizing.org/article/resurgence-teachers-unions.

Pressman, Jeffrey, and Aaron Wildavsky. 1973. *Implementation*. Berkeley: University of California Press.

Prewitt, Kenneth. 2013. *What Is "Your" Race? The Census and Our Flawed Efforts to Classify Americans*. Princeton, N.J.: Princeton University Press.

Przeworski, Adam. 1986. *Capitalism and Social Democracy*. New York: Cambridge University Press.

Public Religion Research Institute. 2011. "PRRI Poll: American Values Survey, September 22–October 2." Roper Center for Public Opinion Research, September 22. https://doi./org/10.25940/ROPER-31096426 (access for members only).

Pugliese, Anita, and Julie Ray. 2023. "Nearly 900 Million Worldwide Wanted to Migrate in 2021." Gallup, January 24. https://news.gallup.com/poll/468218/nearly-900-million-worldwide-wanted-migrate-2021.aspx#:~:text=This%20was%20true%20in%202021,as%20their%20desired%20future%20residence.

Quinnipiac University. 1997. "Poll: Giuliani Polishes up Likability as Approval Tops 2–1, Quinnipiac College Poll Finds; Mayor Tops Messinger by 18 Points." August 5. https://poll.qu.edu/Poll-Release-Legacy?releaseid=803.

———. 1999. "Poll: Despite Crime Approval, Mayor's Job Rating Is Negative, Quinnipiac College Poll Finds; New Yorkers Concerned with Race Relations, Police." April 8. https://poll.qu.edu/Poll-Release-Legacy?releaseid=731.

———. 2009. "New Yorkers Split on New Tax for Subways, Quinnipiac University Poll Finds; Voters Want Mayor to Keep Control of Public Schools." January 29. https://poll.qu.edu/Poll-Release-Legacy?releaseid=1253.

———. 2012a. "New Yorkers Say 2–1 Cops Treat Muslims Fairly, Quinnipiac University Poll Finds; Strong Approval for NYPD, Kelly, Bloomberg on Crime." March 13. https://poll.qu.edu/Poll-Release-Legacy?releaseid=1716.

———. 2012b. "Fire School Workers Who Touch Kids, 92% of New Yorkers Tell Quinnipiac University Poll; Big Racial Gap as Voters Oppose Stop & Frisk." June 14. https://poll.qu.edu/Poll-Release-Legacy?releaseid=1764.

———. 2012c. "Cutting Stop and Frisk Won't Increase Crime, More New Yorkers Tell Quinnipiac University Poll; Voters Oppose Soda Limits, Back Liquor Crack-down." August 16. https://poll.qu.edu/Poll-Release-Legacy?releaseid=1788.

———. 2013a. "Support for Kelly, Cops at New High, Quinnipiac University New York City Poll Finds; Voters Give Mayor a 'B' as in Bloomberg." January 17. https://poll.qu.edu/Poll-Release-Legacy?releaseid=1832.

———. 2013b. "New Yorkers Back Ban on Take-Out Foam More than 2–1, Quinnipiac University Poll Finds; Giuliani Ranked Best Mayor, with Koch, Bloomberg Tied." February 28. https://poll.qu.edu/Poll-Release-Legacy?releaseid=1856.

———. 2013c. "New York City Voters Back NYPD Monitor More than 2–1, Quinnipiac University Poll Finds; Hide the Cigarettes, Voters Say 2–1." April 11. https://poll.qu.edu/Poll-Release-Legacy?releaseid=1880.

———. 2013d. "New York City Voters Smile for the Security Cameras, Quinnipiac University Poll Finds; Worried about Terrorism, but Won't Change Their Life." May 23. https://poll.qu.edu/Poll-Release-Legacy?releaseid=1897.

———. 2013e. "Big Racial Gap in de Blasio Blowout in New York City, Quinnipiac University Poll Finds; Dem Ties Lhota on Taxes and Leads Every Other Measure." September 19. https://poll.qu.edu/Poll-Release-Legacy?releaseid=1955.

———. 2013f. "De Blasio Landslide Buries Lhota in New York City, Quinnipiac University Poll Finds; Voters Want Insider for Next Police Commissioner." October 3. https://poll.qu.edu/Poll-Release-Legacy?releaseid=1960.

———. 2013g. "De Blasio Up 3–1 in New York City Mayoral Race, Quinnipiac University Poll Finds; Low Crime Tops Fixing Stop and Frisk, Voters Say 2–1." October 21. https://poll.qu.edu/Poll-Release-Legacy?releaseid=1967.

———. 2014a. "New York Voters Optimistic 3–1 about Mayor de Blasio, Quinnipiac University Poll Finds; Education, Jobs, Not Income Inequality, Are Priorities." January 16. https://poll.qu.edu/Poll-Release-Legacy?releaseid=1996.

———. 2014b. "Put Police Back in Projects, New York City Voters Say 2–1, Quinnipiac University Poll Finds; Police Approval Drops as Voters Want More Cops." June 12. https://poll.qu.edu/Poll-Release-Legacy?releaseid=2051.

———. 2014c. "New York City Voters Want Their Broken Windows Fixed, Quinnipiac University Poll Finds; 'No Excuse' for Garner Death, Voters Say Almost 3–1." August 27. https://poll.qu.edu/Poll-Release-Legacy?releaseid=2075.

———. 2014d. "Crime, Police Brutality Still Serious Problems, New York City Voters Tell Quinnipiac University Poll; Voters Want Smaller Role for First Lady." November 19. https://poll.qu.edu/Poll-Release-Legacy?releaseid=2113.

———. 2014e. "New York City Voters Say Keep Protestors Off Streets, Quinnipiac University Poll Finds; Attorney General Should Probe Police, Voters Say 2–1." December 17. https://poll.qu.edu/Poll-Release-Legacy?releaseid=2119.

———. 2015a. "New Yorkers Back 'Broken Windows' Policing, Quinnipiac University Poll Finds; Bratton, Cops Outscore Mayor de Blasio." May 13. https://poll.qu.edu/Poll-Release-Legacy?releaseid=2226.

———. 2015b. "Worries about Crime, Homeless Grow in New York City, Quinnipiac University Poll Finds; Voters Will Pay More for $15 Fast-Food Wage." August 6. https://poll.qu.edu/Poll-Release-Legacy?releaseid=2267.

———. 2015c. "Mayor Gets Negative 2–1 Marks on Poverty, Quinnipiac University Poll Finds; 53 Percent Say Quality of Life Is Worse." October 30. https://poll.qu.edu/Poll-Release-Legacy?releaseid=2297.

———. 2016a. "Big Racial Gap as Americans Say No to Anthem Protests, Quinnipiac University National Poll Finds; Blacks Disapprove of Cops, but Like Cops They Know." October 11. https://poll.qu.edu/Poll-Release-Legacy?releaseid=2387.

———. 2016b. "Homelessness, Crime, Corruption Are Serious, New York City Voters Tell Quinnipiac University Poll; Voters Disapprove 2–1 of Mayor's Job on Poverty." November 17. https://poll.qu.edu/Poll-Release-Legacy?releaseid=2403.

———. 2017. "New Yorkers Divided on Mayor Fighting Trump, Quinnipiac University Poll Finds; Cuomo Would Better Protect City, Voters Say 3–1." January 19. https://poll.qu.edu/Poll-Release-Legacy?releaseid=2419.

———. n.d. "Quinnipiac University Poll: About." https://poll.qu.edu/about.

Quirk, Vanessa. 2016. "Citing Equity Issues, Founder of Atlanta BeltLine Leaves Board." *Metropolis*, September 27. https://metropolismag.com/viewpoints/citing-equity-issues-founder-of-atlanta-beltline-leaves-board/.

Rakove, Milton. 1976. *Don't Make No Waves . . . Don't Back No Losers: An Insiders' Analysis of the Daley Machine*. Bloomington: Indiana University Press.

———. 1979. *We Don't Want Nobody Nobody Sent: An Oral History of the Daley Years*. Bloomington: Indiana University Press.

Rana, Aziz. 2014. *The Two Faces of American Freedom*. Cambridge, Mass.: Harvard University Press.

Randazzo, Anthony, and Jonathan Moody. 2024. "State of Pensions 2024: Equable Institute's Annual Report, 5th Edition." Equable Institute. https://equable.org/wp-content/uploads/2024/07/Equable-Institute_State-of-Pensions-2024_FINAL.pdf.

Rast, Joel. 2012. "Why History (Still) Matters: Time and Temporality in Urban Political Analysis." *Urban Affairs Review* 48(1): 3–36.

Reed, Adolph, Jr. 1988. "The Black Urban Regime: Structural Origins and Constraints." *Comparative Urban Research* 12: 140–87.

———. 1999. *Stirrings in the Jug: Black Politics in the Post-segregation Era*. Minneapolis: University of Minnesota Press.

———. 2016. "The Post-1965 Trajectory of Race, Class, and Urban Politics in the United States Reconsidered." *Labor Studies Journal* 41(3): 260–91.

Rhone, Nedra. 2018. "Can Beltline Solve Its Image Problem?" *Atlanta Journal-Constitution*, May 1.

Rich, Wilbur. 1996. *Black Mayors and School Politics: The Failure of Reform in Detroit, Gary, and Newark*. New York: Garland.

Richards, C. F. 1993. "Fears about Crime Jump." *Newsday*, December 16.

Rieger, JM. 2020. "It 'Saved Countless Lives': How Mike Bloomberg Defended Stop-and-Frisk for Years before Running for President." *Washington Post*, February 21.

Rios, Victor. 2011. *Punished: Policing the Lives of Black and Latino Boys*. New York: New York University Press.

Rivera, Ray. 2010. "At Council Hearing on Stop-and-Frisk Policy, the Police Stay Silent." *New York Times*, September 29.

Roberts, Dorothy. 2022. *Torn Apart: How the Child Welfare System Destroys Black Families—and How Abolition Can Build a Safer World*. New York: Basic Books.

Roberts, Sam. 2013. "20% Turnout in New York Primaries." *New York Times*, September 12.

Rodriguez, Akira Drake. 2021. *Diverging Space for Deviants: The Politics of Atlanta's Public Housing*. Athens: University of Georgia Press.

Rodriguez, Isidoro. 2022. "New York City Police Have Stopped and Questioned More People This Year than Last, as Mayor Adams Cracks Down on Crime." *Gothamist*, December 31. https://gothamist.com/news/new-york-city-police-have-stopped-and-questioned-more-people-this-year-than-last-as-mayor-adams-cracks-down-on-crime.

Rogers, John, and Ernest Morrell. 2010. "'A Force to Be Reckoned With': The Campaign for College Access in Los Angeles." In *Public Engagement for Public Education: Joining Forces to Revitalize Democracy and Equalize Schools*, edited by John Rogers and Marion Orr. Stanford, Calif.: Stanford University Press.

Romanucci & Blandin Law. 2023. "Romanucci & Blandin and Hart McLaughlin & Eldridge Joint Statement with City of Chicago and Chicago Police Department on Settlement of Investigatory Stop Class Action Cases." July 19. https://www.rblaw.net/pressrelease-statement-chicago-settlement-stop-frisk-class-action.

Ross, Loretta, and Rickie Solinger. 2017. *Reproductive Justice: An Introduction*. Oakland: University of California Press.

Rothstein, Richard. 2017. *The Color of Law: A Forgotten History of How Our Government Segregated America*. New York: Liveright.

Rothwell, Jonathan, and Douglas Massey. 2009. "The Effect of Density Zoning on Racial Segregation in U.S. Urban Areas." *Urban Affairs Review* 44(6): 779–806.

———. 2010. "Density Zoning and Class Segregation in U.S. Metropolitan Areas." *Social Science Quarterly* 91(5): 1123–43.

Rucks-Ahidiana, Zawadi. 2021. "Racial Composition and Trajectories of Gentrification in the United States." *Urban Studies* 58(13): 2721–41.

Russo, Alexander. 2014. "Mayoral Control in the Windy City: Rahm Emanuel Battles to Improve Chicago Schools." *Education Next* 14(2): 36–45.

Ryan, James. 2011. *Five Miles Away, a World Apart: One City, Two Schools, and the Story of Educational Opportunity in Modern America*. New York: Oxford University Press.

Saito, Leland. 2022. *Building Downtown Los Angeles: The Politics of Race and Place in Urban America*. Stanford, Calif.: Stanford University Press.

Sander, Hilary. 2023. "The Specter of Gentrification in a Pan-Asian Immigrant Neighborhood: Community Development and Resistance to Displacement in Portland's Jade District." *Society* 60(5): 694–707.

Saporta, Maria. 2007. "Business, Civic Heavyweights Line Up for Beltline." *Atlanta Journal-Constitution*, January 11.

———. 2008. "Beltline Donors Unfazed by Ruling on Financing." *Atlanta Journal-Constitution*, February 14.

———. 2016. "Ryan Gravel and Nathaniel Smith Resign from Beltline Partnership Board over Equity Concerns." *Saporta Report*, September 26. https://saporta report.com/ryan-gravel-nathaniel-smith-resign-beltline-partnership-board -equity-concerns/sections/reports/maria_saporta/.

Sasso, Michael, Steve Matthews, and Margaret Newkirk. 2019. "The Gathering Spot: Atlanta Attracts Wealthy Black Transplants." Bloomberg Businessweek, February 1. https://thegatheringspot.club/atlanta-attracts-wealthy-black -transplants/.

Schaeffer, Katherine. 2024. "U.S. Public, Private and Charter Schools in 5 Charts." Washington D.C.: Pew Research Center. https://www.pewresearch.org/short -reads/2024/06/06/us-public-private-and-charter-schools-in-5-charts/?utm _source=Pew+Research+Center&utm_campaign=1d9b23d526-Weekly_6-8-24 &utm_medium=email&utm_term=0_-1d9b23d526-%5BLIST_EMAIL_ID%5D #where-is-enrollment-growing-and-shrinking.

Schattschneider, E. E. 1960. *The Semi-Sovereign People: A Realist's View of Democracy in America.* New York: Holt, Rinehart and Winston.

Schedler, Andreas, and Javier Santiso. 1998. "Democracy and Time: An Invitation." *International Political Science Review* 19(1): 5–18.

Schulman, Bruce. 2019. "Post-1968 U.S. History: Neo-Consensus History for the Age of Polarization." *Reviews in American History* 47: 479-499.

SEIU Local 1. n.d. "About SEIU Local 1." https://www.seiu1.org/about.

SEIU Local 73. n.d. "About Us." https://seiu73.org/about/.

Sen, Maya, and Omar Wasow. 2016. "Race as a Bundle of Sticks: Designs That Estimate Effects of Seemingly Immutable Characteristics." *Annual Review of Political Science* 19(May): 499–522.

Sequeira, Kate. 2022a. "LAUSD's Hefty School Board Salaries Spared by Senate Bill." EdSource, August 30. https://edsource.org/2022/senate-bill-would -modify-state-law-to-allow-higher-school-board-salaries-but-only-for-lausd /677464.

———. 2022b. "New LAUSD Superintendent on Enrollment Declines, School Choice and COVID: Q&A." EdSource, March 2. https://edsource.org/2022 /new-lausd-superintendent-outlines-challenges-priorities-for-the-district /668234.

———. 2022c. "Schools Adapt in a Shrinking Los Angeles Unified." EdSource, May 27. https://www.mtsac.edu/president/cabinet-notes/2021-22/06-june /1e_Schools_adapt_in_a_shrinking_Los_Angeles_Unified.pdf.

Seshadri, Mallika. 2024. "Charter Schools Association Sues LAUSD over Charter Co-location Policy." *EdSource*, April 2. https://edsource.org/2024/charter -schools-association-sues-lausd-over-charter-co-location-policy/708951# :~:text=The%20California%20Charter%20Schools%20Association,Achievement %20Plan%20schools%20and%20community.

Shabazz, Saeed. 2009. "Al Sharpton Calls upon Feds to Tackle Police Misconduct." *New York Beacon*, January 15.

Sharkey, Dylan. 2022. "Lightfoot Policy Change Could Quadruple Chicago Property Tax in 2023." Illinois Policy Institute, July 19. https://www.illinois policy.org/lightfoot-policy-change-could-quadruple-chicago-property-tax -hike-in-2023/.

Simien, Evelyn. 2006. *Black Feminist Voices in Politics*. Albany: State University of New York Press.

Simpson, Dick. 2022. *Democracy's Rebirth: The View from Chicago*. Urbana: University of Illinois Press.

Singh, Shruti. 2023a. "Chicago's Next Mayor Must Have a Plan to Tackle the City's $34 Billion in Pension Debt." *Bloomberg CityLab*, March 2. https://www .bloomberg.com/news/articles/2023-03-02/chicago-s-next-mayor-vallas-or -johnson-will-face-financial-challenges.

———. 2023b. "Worst American City for Pensions Confronts a $35 Billion Crisis." *Bloomberg CityLab*, July 14. https://www.bloomberg.com/news/articles /2023-07-14/worst-american-city-for-pensions-confronts-a-35-billion-crisis.

Sjoquist, David, ed. 2002. *The Atlanta Paradox*. New York: Russell Sage Foundation.

Skogan, Wesley. 2018. *Stop and Frisk and the Politics of Crime in Chicago*. New York: Oxford University Press.

Smith, Greg. 2023. "Number of Black Patrol Cops Falls as NYPD Upper Ranks Remain Majority White." *The City*, October 12. https://www.thecity.nyc /2020/06/24/number-of-black-cops-falls-as-nypd-upper-ranks-remain-white/.

Smith, Preston. 2012. *Racial Democracy and the Black Metropolis: Housing Policy in Postwar Chicago*. Minneapolis: University of Minnesota Press.

Smith, Rogers, and Desmond King. 2024. *America's New Racial Battle Lines: Protect versus Repair*. Chicago: University of Chicago Press.

Snell, Lisa, Aaron Garth Smith, Tyler Koteskey, Marc Joffe, and Truong Bui. 2018. *A 2018 Evaluation of LAUSD's Fiscal Outlook: Revisiting the Findings of the 2015 Independent Financial Review Panel*. Reason Foundation. https://reason.org /wp-content/uploads/2018/06/2018-evaluation-of-lausd-fiscal-outlook.pdf.

Sonenshein, Raphael. 1993. *Politics in Black and White: Race and Power in Los Angeles*. Princeton, N.J.: Princeton University Press.

Soss, Joe, and Vesla Weaver. 2017. "Police Are Our Government: Politics, Political Science, and the Policing of Race-Class Subjugated Communities." *Annual Review of Political Science* 20(May): 565–91.

Soto, Ricardo (Chief Advocacy Officer and General Counsel, California Charter Schools Association). 2020. "LAUSD Policy and Procedures for Charter Schools," letter to David Holmquist, Office of the General Counsel, Los Angeles Unified School District. July 27. https://s3.documentcloud.org/documents /7031289/Calif-Charter-Schools-Assn-Letter-To-LAUSD-New.pdf.

Southall, Ashley, and Michael Gold. 2019. "Why 'Stop-and-Frisk' Inflamed Black and Hispanic Neighborhoods." *New York Times*, November 17.

Speck, Jeff. 2013. *Walkable City: How Downtown Can Save America, One Step at a Time*. New York: North Point Press.

Spencer, Cari. 2022. "Leaving Los Angeles: These 10 LAUSD Schools Lost the Most Students during COVID." *LA School Report*, October 6. https://www .laschoolreport.com/leaving-los-angeles-these-10-lausd-schools-lost-the-most -students-during-covid/.

Staff of *Atlanta Journal-Constitution*. 2009. "Where Candidates Stand." *Atlanta Journal-Constitution*, November 1.

Stirgus, Eric. 2020. "Atlanta and Black Wealth: Success for Many, but Not for All." *Atlanta Journal-Constitution*, February 22.

Stokes, Kyle. 2016a. "After Teachers Union Protest, Tensions Rise on Shared LAUSD-Charter Campus." KPCC, May 6. https://laist.com/news/kpcc-archive/after-teachers-union-protest-tensions-rise-on-shar.

———. 2016b. "How Much Do Charter Schools Cost L.A. Unified? Fact-Checking the Teachers Union's Estimate." *LAist*, May 23 (originally published on KPCC .org). https://www.kpcc.org/news/2016/05/23/60893/how-much-do-charter-schools-cost-la-unified-fact-c/.

———. 2019. "What Is a Charter School, Exactly? A Field Guide." *LAist*, May 28. https://laist.com/news/education/charter-school-field-guide-la.

———. 2020. "Huge Changes to California's Charter School Law Just Took Effect. Already, LAUSD Charters Are Worried." *LAist*, August 1. https://laist.com/news/lausd-charter-schools-ab1505-school-board-shut-down-renewal.

———. 2022. "LAUSD Enrollment Shrank Again This Year—but Not as Much as Predicted." *LAist*, October 18. https://laist.com/news/education/lausd-enrollment-decline-slowing-pandemic-distance-learning-kindergarten-preschool.

Stone, Clarence. 1989. *Regime Politics: Governing Atlanta, 1948–1988.* Lawrence: University Press of Kansas.

———. 2008. "Urban Politics Then and Now." In *Power in the City: Clarence Stone and the Politics of Inequality*, edited by Marion Orr and Valerie Johnson. Lawrence: University Press of Kansas.

Stone, Clarence, Jeffrey Henig, Bryan Jones, and Carol Pierannunzi. 2001. *Building Civic Capacity: The Politics of Reforming Urban Schools.* Lawrence: University Press of Kansas.

Strauss, Valerie. 2019. "Why Oakland Teachers Are Striking: 'You Can't Feed the Minds of Our Students by Starving Their Schools.'" *Washington Post*, February 21.

Strolovitch, Dara. 2012. "Intersectionality in Time: Sexuality and the Shifting Boundaries of Intersectional Marginalization." *Politics and Gender* 8(3): 386–96.

Sugrue, Thomas. 1996. *The Origins of the Urban Crisis: Race and Inequality in Postwar Detroit.* Princeton, N.J.: Princeton University Press.

Sun-Times Media Wire. 2022. "Chicago's Budget Forecast Includes $42.7m Increase in Property Taxes." *5Chicago*, August 10. https://www.nbcchicago.com/news/local/chicago-politics/chicagos-budget-forecast-includes-42-7m-increase-in-property-taxes/2911588/.

Swaak, Taylor. 2019. "86% of L.A. Charter School Graduates Are Eligible for State Universities—Two Dozen Points Higher than LAUSD Grads." *Los Angeles Daily News*, May 1.

Szymanski, Mike. 2017. "More Voters Turned Out for School Board than City Elections." *LA School Report*, May 30. https://www.laschoolreport.com/more-voters-turned-out-for-school-board-than-city-elections/.

Tarschys, Daniel. 2003. "Time Horizons in Budgeting." *OECD Journal on Budgeting* 2(2): 77–103.

Tavernise, Sabrina. 2016. "Life Spans of the Rich Leave the Poor Behind." *New York Times*, February 13.

Taylor, Clarence. 2019. *Fight the Power: African Americans and the Long History of Police Brutality in New York City*. New York: New York University Press.

Taylor, Kate. 2012a. "Black Leaders, Gay Advocates, March in Step." *New York Times*, June 10.

———. 2012b. "Stop-and-Frisk Opponents Set Sights on Mayoral Race." *New York Times*, February 21.

Taylor, Keeanga-Yamahtta. 2019. *Race for Profit: How Banks and the Real Estate Industry Undermined Black Homeownership*. Chapel Hill: University of North Carolina Press.

Taylor, Paul. 2014. *The Next America*. Pew Research Center, April 10. https://www.pewresearch.org/next-america/.

Thomas and Dorothy Leavey Center for the Study of Los Angeles (StudyLA). 2022. "30 Years Later—Angeleno Opinions on Race Relations Data Brief: 2022 Los Angeles Public Opinion Survey." Loyola Marymount University, Spring. https://lmu.app.box.com/s/xdygo5u048h8pw4s4sx193aiyzhlv7m9.

Thorn, John. 2012. "Did African American Slaves Play Baseball?" *Our Game* (Major League Baseball blog), December 26. https://ourgame.mlblogs.com/did-african-american-slaves-play-baseball-1b63bed0fd26.

Tichenor, Daniel. 2002. *Dividing Lines: The Politics of Immigration Control in America*. Princeton, N.J.: Princeton University Press.

Toobin, Jeffrey. 2013. "Bratton's Endorsement of Stop-and-Frisk." *The New Yorker*, December 5.

Torres, Jose. 2015. "Race/Ethnicity and Stop-and-Frisk: Past, Present, Future." *Sociology Compass* 9(11): 931–39.

Tracey, Melissa. 2022. "10 Housing Markets Expected to Lead the Nation in 2023." *Realtor*, December 13.

Trounstine, Jessica. 2018. *Segregation by Design: Local Politics and Inequality in American Cities*. New York: Cambridge University Press.

Truth in Accounting. 2022. "City Combined Taxpayer Burden™ Report: Taxpayers on the Hook for Much More than They Think." May. https://www.truthinaccounting.org/library/doclib/city-combined-taxpayer-burden-report-2022.pdf.

———. 2024a. "Data-Z: Chicago IL." Truth in Accounting, January 15. https://www.data-z.org/state_data_and_comparisons/city/chicago.

———. 2024b. "Data-Z: Pension Database; IL City/County 2022." https://www.data-z.org/pension_database/.

United Teachers Los Angeles. 2020. "The Same Storm, but Different Boats: The Safe and Equitable Conditions for Starting LAUSD in 2020–21." July. https://hoystory.com/wp-content/uploads/2021/02/samestormdiffboats_final.pdf.

———. n.d.-a. "History of UTLA." https://www.utla.net/about-us/history-utla.

———. n.d.-b. "Join UTLA." https://www.utla.net/join-utla.

———. n.d.-c. "Co-Location and Prop 39." https://utla.net/resources/co-location-prop-39/#:~:text=In%20Los%20Angeles%2C%20there%20are,destructive%20tactic%20of%20co%2Dlocation.

United Teachers Los Angeles and In the Public Interest. 2016. "LAUSD Loses More than Half a Billion Dollars to Charter School Growth." http://thecostof charterschools.org/ccs/wp-content/uploads/2016/05/ITPI_Release_Final.pdf.

U.S. Census Bureau. 1940. "Sixteenth Census of the United States: 1940—Population Housing: Statistics for Census Tract and Community Areas, Chicago, Ill." Hathitrust. https://babel.hathitrust.org/cgi/pt?id=pst.000073640455&seq=14.

———. 1950. "1950 United States Census of Population: Chicago, Ill—Census Tracts." Bulletin P-D10. Hathitrust. https://babel.hathitrust.org/cgi/pt?id=umn.31951d030002184&seq=1.

———. 1960. "Census Tracts: Chicago, IL: Standard Metropolitan Statistical Area." https://www2.census.gov/library/publications/decennial/1960/population-and-housing-phc-1/41953654v2ch02.pdf.

———. 1970. "Census Tracts: Chicago, IL: Standard Metropolitan Statistical Area." https://www2.census.gov/library/publications/decennial/1970/phc-1/39204513p4ch04.pdf.

———. 1990. "General Population Characteristics: Illinois, 1990." https://www2.census.gov/library/publications/decennial/1990/cp-1/cp-1-15.pdf.

———. 2010. "B01003 Total Population." https://data.census.gov/table/ACSDT5YSPT2010.B01003?t=-0C:004&g=160XX00US1714000&y=2010.

U.S. Department of Housing and Urban Development. n.d. "SOCDS Census Data: Output for Chicago City, IL." https://socds.huduser.gov/Census/race.odb?msacitylist=1600.017000140001.0&=msa.

Valant, Jon. 2019. "Democrats' Views on Charters Diverge by Race as 2020 Elections Loom." Brookings Institution, May 21. https://www.brookings.edu/articles/democrats-views-on-charters-diverge-by-race-as-2020-elections-loom/?utm_campaign=Brookings%20Brief&utm_source=hs_email&utm_medium=email&utm_content=72912031.

Vallas for Mayor. 2023. "Paul's Plan to Solve the City's Pension Crisis." https://www.paulvallas2023.com/pensions (website expired).

Van Mead, Nick. 2018. "A City Cursed by Sprawl: Can the Beltline Save Atlanta?" *Guardian*, October 25.

Vasquez Heilig, Julian. 2016. "Breaking News: @NAACP Calls for National Moratorium on Charters." Cloaking Inequity, July 29. https://cloakinginequity.com/2016/07/29/breaking-news-naacp-calls-for-national-moratorium-on-charters/.

Vevea, Becky, and Mauricio Peña. 2022. "Chicago Public Schools No Longer Nation's Third Largest District." *Chalkbeat Chicago*, September 28. https://chicago.chalkbeat.org/2022/9/28/23377565/chicago-school-enrollment-miami-dade-third-largest.

Victory, Lauren. 2023. "Alderman, Alderperson, Alderwoman? The Great City Council Debate Continues." *CBS News Chicago*, May 11. https://www.cbsnews.com/chicago/news/alderman-alderperson-alderwoman-debate/.

Voss, Kim, and Irene Bloemraad, eds. 2011. *Rallying for Immigrant Rights: The Fight for Inclusion in 21st Century America*. Berkeley: University of California Press.

Walsh, Mary Williams. 2014. "Detroit Rolls Out New Model: A Hybrid Pension Plan." *New York Times*, June 18.

———. 2017. "In Puerto Rico, Teachers Pension Fund Works Like a Ponzi Scheme." *New York Times*, March 8.

Waters, Mary, and Philip Kasinitz. 2015. "The War on Crime and the War on Immigrants: Racial and Legal Exclusion in the Twenty-First-Century United States." In *Fear, Anxiety, and National Identity: Immigration and Belonging in North*

America and Western Europe, edited by Nancy Foner and Patrick Simon. New York: Russell Sage Foundation.

Watson, Nick, and Simo Vehmas, eds. 2020. *Routledge Handbook of Disability Studies*, 2nd ed. London: Routledge.

Weaver, Vesla, and Gwen Prowse. 2020. "Racial Authoritarianism in U.S. Democracy." *Science* 369(6508): 1176–78.

Wegrich, Kai. 2015. "Jeffrey L. Pressman and Aaron B. Wildavsky, 'Implementation.'" In *Oxford Handbook of Classics in Public Policy and Administration*, edited by Martin Lodge, Edward Page, and Steven Balla. Oxford: Oxford University Press.

Weinberg, Tessa. 2023. "Runoff Campaign: Vallas' and Johnson's Pension, Property Tax Plans Underwhelm Fiscal Experts." *Chicago Sun-Times*, March 13.

Weisburd, David, Alese Wooditch, Sarit Weisburd, and Sue-Ming Yang. 2016. "Do Stop, Question, and Frisk Practices Deter Crime?" *Criminology and Public Policy* 15(1): 31–56.

Wheatley, Thomas. 2017. "Can the Atlanta Beltline Find Its Way?" *Atlanta*, November 14.

White, Michael, and Henry Fradella. 2019. *Stop and Frisk: The Use and Abuse of a Controversial Policing Tactic*. New York: New York University Press.

Whitmire, Richard. 2016. "Battle in Los Angeles." *Education Next* (Fall): 16–25.

Whitney, Fiona. 2018. *The Whitney Guide: The Los Angeles Public School Guide*, 3rd ed. Los Angeles: Tree House Press.

Wickert, David. 2021. "Mayoral Candidates Discuss Top Transit Issues." *Atlanta Journal-Constitution*, September 13.

Wilkins, Tyler. 2022. "T. Dallas Smith: Atlanta Brokers Should Rethink 'Wrong Side of the Tracks.'" *Atlanta Business Chronicle*, December 8, https://www.bizjournals.com/atlanta/news/2022/12/08/t-dallas-smith-acbr-brokers-southside-westside.html.

Williams, Eric. 2022. *Capitalism and Slavery*. New York: Penguin Classics. (Originally published in 1944.)

Wilson, James Q. 1980. *The Politics of Regulation*. New York: Basic Books.

———. 1989. *Bureaucracy: What Government Agencies Do and Why They Do It*. New York: Basic Books.

Wiltz, Teresa. 2022. "How Atlanta Became a City I Barely Recognize." *Politico*, September 16. https://www.politico.com/news/magazine/2022/09/16/atlanta-black-mecca-inequality-00055390.

Wright, Eric Olin. 1982. "The American Class Structure." *American Sociological Review* 47(6): 709–26.

Wright, Jeremiah. 2023. "The Longest Biking Trails in the United States." AZ Animals, June 29. https://a-z-animals.com/blog/the-longest-biking-trails-in-the-united-states/.

Wright, Lawrence. 2022. *The Black Butterfly: The Harmful Politics of Race and Space in America*. Baltimore: Johns Hopkins University Press.

Wrigley, Julia. 2013. "Los Angeles and New York City Schools." In *New York and Los Angeles: The Uncertain Future*, edited by David Halle and Andrew Beveridge. New York: Oxford University Press.

Xie, Yuxuan, and Daniel Willis. 2022. "Updated with 2021–22 Data: Pandemic Drop in K-12 California Enrollment Caps Two Decades of Swings." EdSource,

April 11. https://edsource.org/2022/california-school-enrollment-over-two-decades-gains-and-losses-by-region-with-pandemic-year-drops/669058.

Yemane, Ruta. 2020. "Cumulative Disadvantage? The Role of Race Compared to Ethnicity, Religion, and Non-White Phenotype in Explaining Hiring Discrimination in the U.S. Labour Market." *Research in Social Stratification and Mobility* 69 (October): 100552.

Yerena, Anaid. 2015. "The Impact of Advocacy Organizations on Low-Income Housing Policy in U.S. Cities." *Urban Affairs Review* 51(6): 843–70.

Zepeda-Millán, Chris. 2017. *Latino Mass Mobilization: Immigration, Racialization, and Activism*. New York: Cambridge University Press.

Zhang, Charlie, and Matt Ruther. 2021. "Contemporary Patterns and Issues of School Segregation and White Flight in U.S. Metropolitan Areas: Towards Spatial Inquiries." *GeoJournal* 86(3): 1511–26.

Ziebarth, Todd. 2021. "Measuring Up to the Model: A Ranking of State Public Charter School Laws," 12th ed. National Alliance for Public School Charters, February. https://files.eric.ed.gov/fulltext/ED612980.pdf.

Zimmer, Ron, Richard Buddin, Sarah Smith, and Danielle Duffy. 2019. "Nearly Three Decades into the Charter School Movement, What Has Research Told Us about Charter Schools?" Brown University, Annenberg Institute.

Zimmerman, Jonathan. 2019. "The Uncivil War over Schools." *New York Review of Books*, March 21, 37–39.

Zinshteyn, Mikhail. 2017. "In a City of Charters, the L.A. School District Runs Many of Them." EdSource, June 13. https://edsource.org/2017/in-a-city-of-charters-the-la-school-district-runs-many-of-them/582671.

Zolberg, Aristide. 2006. *A Nation by Design: Immigration Policy in the Fashioning of America*. New York and Cambridge, Mass.: Russell Sage Foundation and Harvard University Press.

Zoller, Suan. 2016. *Review: Fiscal Impact of Charter Schools on LAUSD*. Tallahassee: MGT of America Consulting.

Zoorob, Michael. 2020. "Do Police Brutality Stories Reduce 911 Calls? Reassessing an Important Criminological Finding." *American Sociological Review* 85(1): 178–83.

Zuk, Miriam, Ariel Bierbaum, Karen Chapple, Karolina Gorska, and Anastasia Loukaitou-Sideris. 2018. "Gentrification, Displacement, and the Role of Public Investment." *Journal of Planning Literature* 33(1): 31–44.

═ Index ═

Tables and figures are listed in **boldface**.

White Americans: charter schools, support for, 126–27; colonization and slavery, benefits for, 9–11, 209n11; economic inequality and, 13–15, **14–15**; intergenerational mobility, 16–17; post–World War II success of, 11; residential segregation and access to employment, 11. *See also* race and ethnicity
White flight, 120, 135
White supremacy, 189
Who Governs? (Dahl), 189

Williams, Jumaane, 214n56
Williams, Samantha, 132
Wilson, James Q., 31
Winthrop, John, 12
Woolard, Cathy, 75
Wrigley, Julia, 125

Young, Caprice, 222n34
Youth Policy Institute, 125

Zimmer, Steve, 221n4
Zimmerman, Jonathan, 100, 131, 221n1